Stalin's Last War

Stalin's Last War

Korea and the Approach to World War III

ALAN J. LEVINE

McFarland & Company, Inc., Publishers
Jefferson, North Carolina, and London

LIBRARY OF CONGRESS CATALOGUING-IN-PUBLICATION DATA

Levine, Alan J.
   Stalin's last war : Korea and the approach to World War III /
Alan J. Levine.
      p.   cm.
   Includes bibliographical references and index.

   ISBN 0-7864-2088-X (softcover : 50# alkaline paper) ∞

   1. Korean War, 1950–1953.   2. Korean War, 1950–1953 —
Soviet Union.   3. Soviet Union — Relations — Korea (North)
4. Korea (North) — Relations — Soviet Union.   5. World
politics — 1945–1989.   6. Communism — Korea — History.
I. Title.
DS918.L425   2005
951.904'2347 — dc22   2005009186

British Library cataloguing data are available

©2005 Alan J. Levine. All rights reserved

*No part of this book may be reproduced or transmitted in any form
or by any means, electronic or mechanical, including photocopying
or recording, or by any information storage and retrieval system,
without permission in writing from the publisher.*

Cover photograph ©2005 Pictures Now

Manufactured in the United States of America

McFarland & Company, Inc., Publishers
   Box 611, Jefferson, North Carolina 28640
      www.mcfarlandpub.com

To the memory of my uncle, Israel Levine

Table of Contents

Preface   1
Introduction: Forgotten War?   3

1. The Cold War to 1950   7
2. The World Situation in 1950: Prelude to the Korean War   23
3. The War Begins: ROK Defeat and UN Intervention   46
4. The Defense of South Korea   60
5. Victory in South Korea   80
6. Chinese and Soviet Intervention   96
7. The Immediate Consequences of the Korean War   115
8. Disaster in North Korea   124
9. The War Scare of 1950–1951   139
10. Nadir and Recovery   152
11. Stalin's Decision for World War III   170
12. The Chinese Are Defeated: February to June 1951   184
13. The Truman-MacArthur Conflict Continues   204

14. Armistice Talks Begin	212
15. The Cold War Outside Korea, 1951–1952	227
16. Panmunjom: Negotiations to Deadlock	244
17. Stalin's Last Year	266
18. The End of the War	276
Notes	287
Bibliography	305
Index	311

Preface

This book was inspired by my belief that the Korean War was one of the most critical episodes of the Cold War. In many ways, it was more important and more interesting than the Second Indochina War (the Vietnam War), about which far more has been written. It has been almost as badly understood, although for different reasons, as that later tragic conflict. As will become apparent, I have tried to put events in Korea into the larger context of the Cold War in the early 1950s, without which what happened in Korea does not make much sense. That context has, if anything, been even more neglected than the Korean War itself.

I hope that I have been better than most recent writers at conveying the odd atmosphere of that era. I hope, too, that I have conveyed a different interpretation of the war than has been fashionable. I have, of course, been greatly assisted by many revelations from the Communist side provided by the Cold War International History Project. In a sense, this book is revisionist, although not in the manner of the once influential Cold War revisionist school. The historiography of the Korean War is a remarkably tangled affair. Writing in the 1960s, Robert Leckie and David Rees, despite their lack of access to information from the Communist side, American documents, or American official histories, produced works that stand up far better than most books on the Korean War written in the 1970s and 1980s. (The chief exception is Burton Kaufman's excellent *The Korean War*.) This is not to say I have not been helped by later writers, notably Clay Blair and Bevin Alexander. Yet their books, while full of valuable details on the ground war, neglect other aspects of the conflict. On political matters they often reflect almost comical misunderstandings and the projection of common false ideas of the 1970s and 1980s back onto the very different world of the early 1950s. Since the end of the Cold War, things have become a bit better, and I have derived a great deal of value from the works of William Stueck, Conrad Crane and others. Still, I was not satisfied with the overall standard picture of the war. This book is the result.

I would like to thank Eduard Mark of the Center of Air Force History for some advice that cured me of a serious misunderstanding, as well as my friend Paul Gottfried, and the librarians of Queens College and the Queens Public Library. I would like to dedicate this book to the memory of my uncle, Israel Levine. This was the last book I wrote that benefited from his advice and editing. All responsibility for mistakes is mine.

Introduction:
Forgotten War?

It has become common, in the last decade or two to describe the Korean War as "the Forgotten War." I am not quite sure that that description is accurate. To the extent that the war has slipped from American national memory, it might be truer to call it the war that has been shoved under the rug. It is a comment on the writing of what passes for the history of the United States in that period that the early 1950s is often referred to as the "McCarthy era" rather than the "Korean War era." Quite apart from the overestimation of the importance of Senator Joe McCarthy, that suggests a rather bizarre scale of values. Even worse, perhaps, have been the attempts of Cold War revisionists in the 1970s and 1980s to "reinterpret" the war and make Korea into "the war before Vietnam," assimilating it to the fashionable image (not necessarily a realistic one) of the later war. On the whole, however, these attempts do not seem to have been very successful or had much impact. Time and revelations from the Communist side have not dealt kindly with them.

Whether the war has been really forgotten or deliberately pushed aside, its disappearance from memory would be very strange indeed. For the Korean War was the *only* major war following World War II. It was the only war between major powers—the United States and China—of the post–World War II era. It was the biggest military conflict of the Cold War, was almost as bloody as the Indochina war, and had a greater impact on the world; it was one of the most important events of the early part of the Cold War. This book is an attempt to give a new account of the Korean War, using newly available sources from the Communist side, and understand it within the larger framework of the early Cold War. I have tried to supply a broader account of the military side of the war than other historians have been able to do, giving more attention to its "grand strategy"; to what is now known of the Communist side in Korea; to the problems and achievements of the South Korean forces; and to the war in the air, whose importance has often been underestimated.

It will become apparent, I think, that my analysis of the political history of this war is considerably different from recent conventional wisdom. Indeed, as will become apparent in Chapter 11, my interpretation of Stalin's policies in the last two years of his life puts the war in a radically different light. It was a departure — and almost a fatal departure — from what might be called, for lack of a better term, the "normal course" of the Cold War. Begun as a significant but limited move in the Cold War struggle, the Korean War became, for Stalin, something else — a preliminary phase of World War III. This is one of the reasons I have given a considerable amount of space to matters in Europe and elsewhere that might at first sight seem rather far removed from Korea, such as German rearmament and the Japanese peace treaty; but it is not the only reason. Even if the theory presented in Chapter 11 is erroneous, it is nevertheless true that the Korean War was deeply affected by the perceived necessities of a worldwide mobilization by the Western powers to head off a Soviet attack, which, they feared, might be imminent. (They nevertheless did not understand Stalin's plans.) It is impossible to understand how the United States fought the Korean War without grasping this point. Korea was subordinated to the defense of Western Europe and Japan. Moreover, it is impossible to understand the war without realizing that, contrary to the usual assumption, the issue of whether the war would be "expanded" outside Korea was not seen as purely a matter for the Americans, or the UN, to decide. At crucial moments, there was considerable fear in the West that it was the Communists who would extend the war beyond the confines of Korea.

The latter's aims turn out to be a good deal more complicated than has generally been assumed. The Communist partners differed among themselves, and their aims changed over time. The war was started for one set of reasons but continued for others. Apart from Stalin's switch to more radical policies in 1951 and his probable double-dealing with Mao, the Chinese turn out to have been considerably more aggressive than has usually been supposed. Mao, at least, did not, as was usually assumed up to the 1990s, enter the war reluctantly to save the North Korean regime; there was a considerable component of aggression in his decision. Contrary to what has been generally supposed, it seems that the Chinese might well have entered the Korean War even had the UN forces not crossed the 38th

Parallel in October 1950, and they fought not to save North Korea but to conquer the whole of the country. Nor did Mao, when he entered the armistice negotiations in 1951, necessarily want peace in the Western sense, or, perhaps, in any sense. For some time difficult to determine, he thought of the armistice merely as a truce that would last for just a few years, after which the Communists would resume the war.

Americans ought to be able to understand their own country's policies and attitudes in the Korean War a bit better than the rather alien mentality of the Communist rulers, but they have had a surprisingly hard time doing so. Not merely a half a century but several obscuring layers of ideology lie between us and the people who fought the Korean War. Perhaps the first and most understandable confusion originated in the first few years after the war, when Americans and other Westerners first tried to understand the novelty of a "limited war" and draw lessons from the Korean experience. Faced with the grim prospect of more conflicts with the Communist countries, Westerners in the 1950s and early 1960s developed theories of how to fight future local wars successfully, while avoiding their escalation into a dreadful nuclear exchange. No one who recalls that period will criticize this. But many scholars of the Korean War fell into the error of projecting the real or supposed lessons of the war back onto the war itself. They often assumed that decisionmakers of the early 1950s had chosen to limit the war for the same reasons and in the same way that the limited war theorists prescribed. This was not always true.

Others, with less excuse, fell into the dogma that American policymakers of the earlier era had been confused by the idea that Communism was "monolithic," and that there was no serious disagreement or potential conflict between the Soviets and Chinese. As we shall see, the American leaders in the 1940s and 1950s held no such assumption. In fact, one reason they underestimated the danger of China's intervening in the war was that they supposed the Chinese leaders would want to avoid the dependence on the Soviets that would result.

Biases for and against — since the 1950s largely against — General MacArthur in his conflict with the Truman administration have been a potent element in confusing the history of the war. It is very common to encounter the false notion that only MacArthur ever favored expanding the war to China. Alternatively, many have bought the notion (fostered by MacArthur, among others) that the Chinese intervened only because they somehow "knew" the Americans would not retaliate against them (a neat trick since the Americans in fact expected to do just that and changed their minds only after the Chinese moved). Yet other errors apparent in many accounts of the Korean War stem from ideological confusion over what the Cold War as a whole was about and the political alignment within the Western countries early in the Cold War.

Among these errors is the conception of the Cold War as a conflict between "the superpowers" (a term little used in the 1940s and 1950s), as some sort of Soviet-American duel, rather than a struggle between the Soviets and the West as a whole, in which Britain, not the United States, was initially the chief Western protagonist. Yet another idea with little basis in the reality of the era is the assumption — true in the last stages of the Cold War but not at all in the 1940s and early 1950s — that the "right" in Western countries was anti–Communist while the "left" was, if not pro–Soviet, at least "soft" on the issue. But many American conservatives in this period remained isolationists, while liberal supporters of the Truman administration were strongly anti–Communist; indeed, as we shall see, some liberals even favored implementing at least part of MacArthur's program. The Korean War, indeed the early Cold War as a whole, shows how projecting today's (or even yesterday's) politics onto the past imperils our understanding of history.

A few words about terminology are necessary. There is no good term for the anti–Soviet side in the Cold War. Because of both the propaganda manipulation of the term "free world" to cover some decidedly unfree countries, and the exaggerated backlash to it, I have avoided it and generally refer to the Western powers or the democracies. The former term was, if anything, more used than "free world" in the early 1950s. If it is inexact, it is nevertheless true that most of the opposition to the Soviets was by the Western countries. Nor do I think it unreasonable to identify the anti–Communist side as the democratic one. Whatever unsavory allies may have been forced on them, the democratic countries were the core of the opposition to Communist totalitarianism. To save space, and spare my readers propaganda, I have generally avoided the official terms "People's Republic of China" and "People's Liberation Army" or the contemporary American terms "Communist China" and "Chinese Communist forces." References to China and the Chinese Army after 1949 are to the Communist government, its subjects, and its military forces, except where otherwise specified. Chinese names are given in pinyin form, with the traditional Western transliteration given in parentheses when first used. Korean names are given in the most familiar Western form, with, in one or two cases, the proper Korean form given in parentheses.

1

The Cold War to 1950

It was the insoluble problem of the Nazis that the Allies agreed on destroying them. It was the insoluble problem of the Allies that they agreed on nothing else.

The Cold War between the Soviet Union and the Western powers had begun even before the end of World War II. The Red Army's advance into East-Central Europe enabled the Soviets to resume the efforts at expansion interrupted by the Nazi attack in 1941. As the Axis powers went down to defeat, it became apparent, to those in the West who cared to see, (though in 1945 they were not many), that the struggle between the Soviets and the democracies would be the central fact of world politics for the foreseeable future. It would be an ugly and sometimes very bloody struggle, less violent than total war but very far from peace as traditionally defined, overhung by the threat of nuclear war.

In Europe, the boundary between the Western powers and the Soviets would be stabilized at about where it had been at the end of World War II, but not without a great deal of turmoil. In East and Southeast Asia, where Soviet ambitions interacted with genuine, domestically based revolutionary movements, there was a vast expansion of Communist totalitarianism, although not of the area under Soviet rule. The recovery and development of the advanced countries and the post-colonial development of Southeast Asia were all powerfully affected by the Cold War. In that struggle, Britain, not the United States, was at first the leading opponent of the Soviets, and remained so until well into 1946. Only during the Berlin crisis of 1948–1949 did the United States begin to take a "harder" line than its transatlantic ally.

Cold Revolution and Failed Negotiations

The division of Europe had begun during 1944. In that year, the ultimate border between the Soviets and the Western powers in Europe — the boundary of the occupation zones in Germany — was agreed on, although few then realized that the line between the Soviet and the British and American zones would become a permanent frontier. The ruthless subjugation of Poland, Romania and Bulgaria was well underway, using a more sophisticated version of the pattern of "cold revolution" employed earlier in Mongolia and extended to the rest of Soviet-occupied Europe and North Korea, and, briefly, northern Iran. In Yugoslavia and Albania, the Communist guerillas had smashed their rivals and took power with only slight Soviet help. In Western Europe, the Communist-controlled elements of the resistance, confronted with superior force, were largely disarmed. In France and Italy, however, the Communist parties remained strong and for some years their taking power, even without a Soviet invasion, seemed possible. In Greece, outright war between the British, supporting the Greek government-in-exile, and the Greek Communists ended in the latter's defeat and partial disarmament, but the Communists would resume their efforts in 1946.

While democratic governments were restored in Western Europe and less successfully in Greece, the Western powers found that the Yalta and other agreements were little better than wastepaper in restraining the Soviets. Soviet actions in Poland and Romania sparked the first, hesitant resistance by the British and Americans to the Soviet takeover of East-Central Europe. They had tacitly accepted that the regimes there would be under heavy Soviet influence, but not that the Soviets would impose outright puppet governments. But their opposition soon ebbed. In July 1945, the Western powers recognized a slightly altered version of the Soviet-installed Polish government. As World War II ended, they were still far from ready to give up hope of negotiating their differences with the Soviets.

Stalin, for his part, did not want a sharp and open break that would ensure that the Western powers, still vastly stronger than the USSR, would resolutely oppose him. He expected another world war, but in 15 to 20 years. It would require careful preparation and would be something for his successors to undertake. It was for him to make the aggressive moves, under the cover of continuing the wartime alliance, and "united fronts" between Communists and other groups. Let the Western powers decide what they *really* meant. His ambitions ran far beyond the line held by the Red Army at the end of the war in Europe. His main goals in 1945 were not just to complete the conquest of East-Central Europe, but to control all of Germany and, in the east, Manchuria. The last was his primary aim in entering at the last minute the war against Japan. Achieving the first goal would almost certainly guarantee Communist takeovers in France and Italy, which might take place anyway. The conquest of Manchuria, the only industrialized part of China, would likely lead to the eventual control of the rest of the country, although Stalin probably did not care much about that in 1945.

At the Potsdam Conference in July–August 1945, the focus of contention began to shift to Germany, overshadowing the weakening effort to preserve some independence for the countries further east. In a few cases, Stalin would make minor and ultimately meaningless concessions, such as right after Hiroshima when the appearance of the atomic bomb made him exceptionally cautious for a time, at the Moscow conference of December 1945 and during the Iranian crisis in the spring of 1946. But on maintaining control over East-Central Europe, he seemed fundamentally inflexible. By the end of the war, both the Western powers and the Soviets had abandoned deliberately breaking up Germany into small states or "de-industrializing" it. The British and Americans envisaged a unified democratic Germany, disarmed and neutralized. While its economy would be allowed to recover, it would not be completely restored. Stalin, of course, wanted a very different Germany, under his control and not necessarily disarmed. The division of Germany developed not as a matter of agreement or by the decision of either side, but was the product of their diametrically opposed wills. Each side had to settle for transforming its own part of Germany.

Attempts to agree on policies toward Germany, Japan, and the "liberated" countries of Austria and Korea, the negotiation of peace treaties with the minor Axis powers and Western attempts to secure international control of nuclear energy became the primary subjects of negotiations for the next year and a half. In a parallel development, the United States tried to arrange a settlement in China between the Nationalist government and the Communists.

But the efforts at negotiations produced only peace treaties with Italy, Hungary, Romania and Bulgaria, which did not affect Soviet control of the latter. The Cold War developed with increasing violence on several fronts. As Soviet-occupied Europe was brought under Stalin's puppets, his agents tried to bring Yugoslavia under direct control. The French and Italian Communists maneuvered to gain control of their countries by political means, while the Greek Communists, supported from bases in the Communist-ruled countries to the north, renewed the war against the Greek government. On the Middle Eastern front, the Soviets brought pressure to bear on Turkey to force that country to agree to arrangements that would reduce it to a satellite. In Iran, the Soviets, keeping their forces in the area they had occupied in 1941, tried to break off Azerbaijan and Kurdistan, while tentatively moving toward control of the rest of the country. In East Asia, North Korea became a standard Soviet satellite. The Soviets tried to retain control of Manchuria and bolster the Communist position in China, although Stalin did not expect the Chinese Communists to conquer all of China at an early date.

All of this took place amid unparalleled devastation, with much of Europe and Japan on the brink of famine. Germany and Japan especially lay in ruins. Notwithstanding their desire to do as little as possible to help Germany, the Western powers were forced in 1945–46 to take steps to increase food and fuel production there. The British, in particular, found that their army in Germany had one more battle to win, the "Battle of the Winter," and were forced to the heroic expedient of imposing bread rationing on their own people, avoided during the whole of the war, to keep the Germans alive. Only massive food shipments from North America prevented famine in Germany, Japan and several other countries. Despite this, the response to the world economic collapse remained inadequate until 1947.

The destruction and disruption caused by World War II and the West's irresolution and ignorance of Soviet reality made the postwar situation far more fluid than simple calculations of the ratio of economic and military strength between the Western powers and the Soviets would imply. Psychologically, the West was on the defensive. In the middle and late 1940s the Soviet Union and the world Communist movement were at the height of their popularity and prestige, and had succeeded, to a remarkable extent, in impressing even many non–Communists with the belief that Communism was "progressive" and that Communists had been the toughest opponents of Nazism. (Though weakened, these absurd ideas were still widespread in the Korean War era and are by no means completely dead even today.)

The elementary facts about the Soviet regime had been shoved under the rug, and it was widely believed that while the Soviets might not be properly democratic, the West had much to learn from them. There were widespread optimistic theories that the Soviets had dropped "world revolution" and that their foreign policies were aimed at assuring their security from a revived German threat, and securing reparations and/or aid. These ideas proved exceeding difficult to reconcile with their actual rejection of American offers to permanently disarm both Germany and Japan, and the Soviets disinterest in international control of nuclear energy. Conversely, the prestige of private enterprise and the market economy, outside the United States, was at a low ebb; "nationalization" and "planning," were the economic nostrum of the period, not free markets.

Continental Europeans, as opposed to the English-speaking peoples, were deeply demoralized, while the Germans were feared and hated by everyone. There was little faith that a decent order could be created in Germany. The West might have a monopoly on the atomic bomb, but few had been built. The effort to manufacture more was not pushed, nor was any way ever found to make political capital out of it. Indeed, in 1945 and after Americans seemed almost apologetic about having the bomb.

Had any country other than the United States developed nuclear weapons first, it probably would have used them to take over the planet, or, at least, have secured a permanent nuclear monopoly and set up a world order favorable to itself. But, thanks to various peculiarities of the American national character, such a course was not rejected, but was hardly even considered. The failure of the attempt to arrange international control of nuclear energy was accepted with remarkable placidity.

After a few nervous weeks right after Hiroshima, Stalin realized that he did not have to worry too much about the American nuclear monopoly, though he resolved to break it as soon as possible. His policies had ruled out a major war anyway. After August 1945, he did not seem to worry too much about what the Americans might do as long as he refrained from any direct provocation, and he assumed the situation was still developing to his advantage. He hoped there would be a major conflict between the British and the Americans, that the latter would soon pull out of Europe, and that the whole capitalist world might soon be paralyzed by a depression. Revolutionary situations existed, or would soon develop, in many countries. Nor was there much of a local counterweight to Soviet power. Although, like the Western powers, the Soviets demobilized much of their armed forces, the Red Army retained a higher proportion of its wartime strength, and, unlike the disorganized American forces, was reduced to a hard core of combat-ready divisions that could occupy continental Europe and much of the Middle East and East Asia in the first stages of a war, giving the Soviets a psychological ascendancy over the Europeans, Turks and Iranians. But it was hard for Stalin to gauge the risks involved. After the Americans failed to make use of the atomic bomb to take a stronger position once World War II ended, and continued their demobilization, he seems to have been confident he could subjugate East-Central Europe without much interference from them. Meaningless concessions over Romania and Bulgaria in late 1945, which reproduced the Yalta conference agreement on Poland (already broken) in an even weaker form in return for minor U.S. concessions over Japan, proved Stalin's last gesture at moderation in East-Central Europe.

Nevertheless, the Western powers were becoming warier.

American Policy, 1945–1946

For their part, the British and Americans did not "sellout" East-Central Europe, nor did they ever embark on all out resistance to Soviet conquest there. As Walt Rostow later pointed out, American policy in East-Central Europe was similar to that toward the Japanese conquest of Manchuria in the 1930s; the Americans were ready to protest against Stalin's actions, but did not consider it worth risking American blood to prevent the outcome.

President Franklin Roosevelt, trailing well behind Churchill, had begun to worry seriously about the Soviets by the fall of 1944 and had been completely disillusioned by the Soviet violations of the Yalta agreements. His death caused the learning process to almost begin over again. When his initial protests over some Soviet actions had no effect, President Truman, ill-supported by his weak and poorly informed Secretary of State James Byrnes, essentially reverted to the ideas Roosevelt had abandoned before his death. Trying to placate the Soviets and distance themselves from the British, they only slowly based American policy on the assessment that the Soviets aimed at world domination (much more slowly than either later admitted). Truman and Byrnes did try to bargain somewhat harder on some issues, notably the German economy. The Americans excluded the Soviets from an occupation zone in Japan, insisted that Soviet as well as American forces evacuate Czechoslovakia, and occupied South Korea when Japan surrendered to ensure that the Soviets would not seize the whole of Korea. They encouraged Jiang Jieshi (Chiang Kai-shek) to resist Soviet demands for even greater concessions than the Americans had agreed on at the Yalta Conference, but Jiang gave in anyway.

But these limited actions did not reflect recognition that a long grim struggle lay ahead, and represented something less than total opposition to Soviet plans. The American government barely reacted to Stalin's initial moves against Turkey and Iran, and ignored the Soviet effort to make their zone of Germany communist, well-described by the German Communist leader Walter Ulbricht's immortal line: "It must look democratic, but all power must be in our hands." Truman saw Stalin as just another politician, not a very nice one but a man with whom it would be possible to make a deal. It was characteristic that, in 1945 and 1946, Truman often compared Stalin to Tom Pendergast, the crooked political boss who had promoted his rise in politics, a man who resembled Stalin the way a mouse resembles a king cobra.

Iranian Crisis and Containment

The Soviet refusal to evacuate Iran on schedule in March 1946, as they had pledged, proved the first big crisis of the Cold War. Under strong American pressure, the Soviets finally left. Stalin found it prudent to belatedly keep his pledge to evacuate Manchuria as well.

The Soviet moves in Iran and against Turkey not merely failed but backfired. The Iranian crisis, along with Churchill's "Iron Curtain" speech of March 5, 1946 with its hostile and accurate depiction of Soviet policy, greatly influenced public opinion. Although the initial reception of that famous speech was actually quite hostile, the phrase "Iron Curtain" and the clarity of its analysis guaranteed his remarks would stick in the minds even of those who could not yet accept that he was right. All this played an important role in galvanizing the United States into adopting a policy of "containing" further Soviet expansion — in effect, putting its weight behind a policy that the British were already trying to carry out, a policy that became the chief external preoccupation of the United States for the next 40 years. Containment, most skillfully elaborated by the diplomat George Kennan, aimed to stop the Soviets from expanding beyond the area they had already grabbed and supporting the reconstruction of Western Europe and Japan. The American leaders hardly even considered a "preventive war" against the Soviets. Rather, they aimed to build what Dean Acheson later described as "situations of strength" around the Soviet orbit. Beginning in Western Europe, they would eliminate the political and economic weaknesses exploited by the Soviets and the local Communists, and, coupled with the maintenance of adequate military strength, would head off any Soviet decision to resort to war (which was not regarded as a near-term danger in the late 1940s).

American policies, for a time, remained inconsistent, and were heavily influenced by legalistic and psychological quirks. They accounted for the strange, if little-discussed fact, that the Western powers rescued the Iranians but not East-Central Europe, although the latter area was more important and was inhabited by peoples for whom they would normally be expected to feel more sympathy. In Iran, the Soviets happened to break a clear-cut agreement to leave by a certain date, while Iran still had a government that could complain about it. In East-Central Europe, the Western powers were inhibited by the belief that the Soviets had some kind of legitimate security interest there (no one thought that Soviet actions in

Iran or Turkey were so motivated), and were a legal occupying power in Germany and the Axis satellites. Even in Poland, the government the Soviets had installed claimed to be the legitimate offspring of Yalta and later agreements, and had been recognized by the Western powers. The fact that they had a legal pretext for their presence and some of their actions was confusing enough to help smother counteractions. The Truman administration was also hindered by the president's unpopularity and its perception (probably inaccurate) that the American people were not yet ready for a major effort.

For these and other reasons, containment did not develop abruptly or overnight. There was a lengthy period of transition. Just as there was no one point at which the Western powers "wrote off" East-Central Europe, there was no one point at which they, or even the United States, finally resolved to resist further Soviet advances at all costs. Instead, during 1946 and 1947, there was a whole series of decisions, in a process taking at least a year to make containment effective. Nor was it a total, abrupt break with the past, but the last stages of a gradual disillusionment with the Soviets and hardening of American policy that had begun in September 1944 and had gone on in fits and starts ever since. There was never any time after September 1944 when there was no resistance at all to Soviet actions. No matter how unhappy the American leaders were about the fact, American interests, principles and aims usually wound up cutting across Soviet policies. A state of unplanned conflict was gradually transformed into a firm, consistent policy of opposing Soviet conquest.

During the lengthy period of transition, in fact, simple practical steps aimed at protecting the immediate interests of the Western powers, or even humanitarian aims, sometimes had more effect on the developing Cold War than means deliberately aimed at the USSR. Nor was the development of containment neatly separated chronologically from the feeble diplomatic effort to preserve a degree of freedom in East-Central Europe and negotiate with the Soviets about other matters. Indeed, attempts to negotiate with the Soviets never really ended. They were simply overshadowed, after a time, by other things, and most people ceased to expect they would accomplish much. It even became generally recognized for a while that, for the Soviets, negotiations were just another weapon in the Cold War.

During 1946 and early 1947, illusions among the public were shattered by the subjugation of East-Central Europe, Soviet attempts to expand elsewhere, and the dismal results of negotiations. The vague hopes for a better future were replaced by growing anger, bitterness and fear. President Truman and others in 1946 had still hoped — although they did not really expect — that the Soviets might come around, although only if their aggressive actions were frustrated. Truman refrained from trying to actively arouse the public or formulating an overall program or strategy. Secretary Byrnes remained addicted to disconnected reactions and improvisations, and tenaciously pursued diplomatic agreements until General George Marshall replaced him early in 1947. He did, however, make clear, contrary to Stalin's hopes, that American forces would stay in Germany as long as the other occupying powers.

Economic Collapse and Open Cold War

It took another, bigger crisis, or a convergence of several crises, to force the U.S. government to draw up a real program and call on the resources to carry it out. Western Europe's recovery from the war had been far slower than expected, and, as 1946 came to an end, Italy in particular was already on the verge of economic collapse. With the dreadful winter of 1946–1947, it seemed that what little recovery had taken place in Europe was endangered. On top of this, the overstretched British warned the Americans that they would have to withdraw their forces from Greece. They warned that the Greek government was already in desperate straits and that Turkey could not hold out against Soviet pressure without aid that the British could no longer supply. The Truman administration now launched a major effort to arouse public opinion, first to the need to aid Greece and Turkey, and generally oppose Soviet expansion, and second, to support a reconstruction program for Western Europe. In March 1947, Truman addressed a joint session of Congress, explaining the situation in Greece and Turkey, and declaring that it should be American policy to support free people resisting subjugation by armed minorities and foreign powers. This was promptly dubbed the Truman Doctrine. Truman won overwhelming support, and a Greek-Turkish aid bill was signed on May 22.

This was followed by the development of the European Recovery Program, better known as the Marshall Plan, which began in 1948. The Economic Cooperation Administration, which administered the plan, was a government investment bank that steered both American aid and European "counterpart funds" into useful capital investments on the basis of plans actually formulated by the European countries and coordinated by the international Organization for Economic Cooperation. A concomitant feature of the Marshall Plan was the shift to full-scale reconstruction in western Germany and tentative moves toward forming a West German government.

The plan triumphed in spite of bitter Soviet hostility. The Soviets reacted to the Marshall Plan by dropping any pretense that the wartime alliance still existed, and their followers turned openly against the democratic socialists they had tried to court as coalition partners. The Soviets declared that the Marshall Plan was a scheme to subjugate Europe and prevent an American depression. Stressing that the capitalist and colonial systems were in a desperate crisis, they bluntly likened the United States to Nazi Germany, claiming it planned an alliance with a restored Germany and a world war, although this could be prevented by vigorous action.

Stalin resolved to smash the Marshall Plan. He appears to have calculated that the local Communists could disrupt the French, Belgian and Italian economies and that, at least in the case of Italy, this would lead to a Communist seizure of power. But political strikes and sabotage, especially by the French and Italian Communists, failed to disrupt the plan and even backfired. The Italian Communists failed to achieve the hoped-for success in the elections of 1948. In a related move, the Communist parties in Southeast Asia, apart from the Vietnamese who had taken over their country in 1945 and had been resisting French reconquest since, were encouraged to try to seize power. These parties had attained considerable strength during and after World War II. A coup against the Indonesian Nationalist government failed, while guerilla wars started in Malaya, the Philippines and Burma. They lasted for many years and, at least until 1950–1951, the Communists seemed to be winning.

The Soviets were more successful at finishing the subjugation of East-Central Europe. The Czech Communists, already the dominant element in the government, seized power in a coup that further alarmed the West and ignited the first war scare of the Cold War. Stalin had been ready to send in the Soviet Army if need be, but that had not been necessary.

There was no war. Instead, in June 1948, the Soviets, hoping to disrupt the Western program in Germany and retard or reverse the move toward a West German government, clamped a blockade on the western sectors of Berlin, isolated deep in the Soviet Zone of Germany. But, in a success few expected even in the West, the Western powers flew in enough food and fuel to keep the city going, while a "counter-blockade" hurt the economy of the Soviet Zone. In 1949, Stalin quietly backed down and lifted the blockade. Like the Soviet move in Iran, the Berlin Blockade actually backfired, improving relations between the Western occupiers and the Germans, and furthering the development of the North Atlantic Alliance. In the same year, the Greek Communists were finally beaten, while a secret Western counterblow aimed at liberating Albania misfired. The Cold War boundaries in Europe solidified along the lines they would take until 1989.

During 1948, Stalin's effort to undermine Tito and make Yugoslavia an out-and-out puppet state misfired, producing the first open break between Communist countries. This seemed to indicate what might happen between the Soviets and the victorious Chinese Communists. Exploiting the possibility of what was called "Chinese Titoism"—the so-called "wedge strategy"—was a growing interest for the Western leaders, while avoiding it was an anxious concern for the Soviets.

The Communist Victory in China

In East Asia, the Soviets were shut out of the only advanced country and for a long time insisted that the Japanese Communists exercise caution in view of the American occupation, although they seem to have entertained highly exaggerated ideas of the potential of the Japanese Party throughout the post–World War II era. In China, however, an unexpected early victory by the Chinese Communists, despite Stalin's misgivings about Mao Zedong, proved some recompense for frustrations elsewhere.

World War II had gravely weakened the Chinese Nationalists. Never very popular, they were riven by factions. The reformist elements of the Guomindang (Kuomintang), the Political Study Group and the Guangsi (Kwangsi) Clique, had lost ground to the reactionary factions and Jiang Jieshi's associates. The regime was really a loose coalition; Jiang directly controlled only part of China's territory and army. Staggering hyperinflation, corruption (at least partly a response to inflation), an oppressive tax system, lack of land reform, and the exploitation of the areas reoccupied by government troops at the end of the war made the Nationalists even more unpopular. Jiang's severe limitations as a leader, his bitter hostility to non–Communist rivals (an often underestimated factor), his consistent favoring of the incompetent generals of his own clique, and his contempt for American advice further undermined the Nationalists' military chances. The Communists had since the late 1930s built a strong base of power in the areas nominally occupied, but not actually controlled by the Japanese, which they ably administered. They rode to power on their record of resistance to the invaders and their appeals, however deceptive in the long run, to the peasantry. Although perhaps not really popular outside the former Japanese-occupied areas, they at least had the appeal of the new, and they neutralized much of China's small middle class. The Nationalists took the line that "everyone who is not with us is against us," and, lacking any popular appeal or positive program, proceeded to alienate almost everyone.

When the war ended, both sides raced to overrun the Japanese-held areas. The Communist base areas were actually closer to the more critical points. The Americans insisted that the Japanese and their Chinese puppet troops surrender only to the Nationalists as the legitimate government of China, and Nationalist emissaries persuaded most of the puppet forces to obey this order. Only that, along with the American air and sealift of Nationalist troops from the far west and south, and the landing of two U.S. Marine divisions on the coast, saved the Nationalists from immediate defeat.

The Communists swallowed their rage at this and went along with the American effort, begun in 1944, to prevent a civil war by mediating the Nationalist-Communist conflict and uniting the two sides in a coalition government — not a very practical aim. In Manchuria, the Soviets turned most of the country and all of the arms surrendered by the Japanese over to the Communists, while the Nationalists were fobbed off with a few cities. Stalin, however, underestimated the strength of the Chinese Communists and probably overestimated American readiness to intervene to block a Communist victory. He did not regard the latter as possible, important or perhaps even desirable in the near future.

He favored a nominal coalition government that would mask the reality of a divided China. The Nationalists would continue to hold much of the country, while the Chinese Communists controlled the north. Manchuria, if possible, would remain under Soviet occupation. Help to the Communists would improve their position in the area south of the Great Wall and ensure they could at least hold Manchuria if the Soviets had to leave. The Soviet plans broke down for several reasons. Mao, realizing that he was stronger than Stalin supposed, took a harder line than Stalin wanted. He did not really expect a coalition, but hoped to manipulate the American mediation effort for his own ends The Nationalists did not really want a coalition, assuming that it would be suicidal for them. The American stand in Iran led Stalin to decide that prudence required evacuating Manchuria as well. The Nationalists, much against American warnings that their forces would become hopelessly overextended, had insisted on trying to reoccupy Manchuria. Fighting in Manchuria would lead to the collapse of the truce that General Marshall had negotiated, all-out civil war and the destruction of the best Nationalist armies.

Marshall's mission, starting in December 1945, aimed to secure a truce to stop the ongoing fighting, an agreement on integrating the Nationalist and Communist armies, and a political agreement. He achieved the first two items surprisingly quickly in early 1946, including an integration agreement favorable to the Nationalists. But the Nationalists balked at the political agreement. The integration agreement was not carried out, and both sides repeatedly broke the truce. At least at first, Marshall seems to have considered the Nationalists somewhat more blameworthy than the Communists, and the Americans imposed an embargo on further arms shipments to the Nationalists. This failed to placate the Communists, who now were openly hostile to the Americans although the latter were hardly helping the Nationalists at all. In 1947, the Soviets renewed aid to the Communists. Jiang, encouraged by early tactical successes in Manchuria and insanely overconfident in general — he told Marshall, just before the latter left China in December 1946, that he would smash the Communists in another eight to ten months — continued to overextend his forces, plunging far into Manchuria although his position in the North China plain was anything but secure. He further dissipated his strength in various strategically eccentric operations. While his overall strategy was recklessly offensive, the incompetent commanders he favored remained addicted to static defensive tactics. They were defeated in detail. When his armies were beaten, Jiang forbade retreat. During 1947 and 1948, the Communists crushed the corridor the Nationalists held in the northern plain and Manchuria and destroyed their forces piecemeal. Having eliminated the best remaining Nationalist forces in early 1949, they easily crossed the Chang Jiang (Yangtze) and swept over the rest of China without much difficulty. Jiang's government and remaining forces fled to Taiwan where the Communists planned to follow him.

The Americans and China

Following the failure of the Marshall mission, American policy in China lapsed into confusion. During 1947–1948, the Americans provided half-hearted help to the Nationalists without conviction that they would make intelligent use of it. The poorly administered China Aid Act of 1948 was largely a sop to the China bloc in American politics, which clung to the unrealistic heroic image of Jiang Jieshi and the Nationalists popularized during World War II. Its attitude toward the Nationalist government oddly resembled that of later liberals toward the UN: it might be completely ineffective and a reeking mass of corruption, but it was the only hope. The China bloc, led by some prominent Republicans and the influential Luce publications, maintained that Jiang was a capable leader who with adequate material support could defeat the Communists. Later it insisted that his defeat was due to Soviet intervention, the "betrayal" of the Yalta agreements and the search for a coalition government. It should be noted that this was a purely American notion. Practically no one outside the United States, however anti–Communist, believed this. Just how widely

Americans believed it is unclear, but it would seem that too many Americans had been in China during and after the war for these notions to be really popular, although the China bloc was strong enough to prevent any move to cut loose from the Nationalist government at an early date. In any case, the Truman administration necessarily focused its attention on Europe. Further, important figures in the administration simply held a low opinion of China's importance. It was not only underdeveloped, but, apart from population pressure, lacked the resources to be a serious menace in the future or add much weight to the Soviet side. It was also expected that, while the Communists would win the civil war, it would take them a long time to do so and still longer to rebuild China.

During 1948, it became clear that the Communists would win much sooner than had been expected. The Americans now based their Asia-Pacific policy on defending the offshore island perimeter, centering on a rebuilt Japan and the Philippines. Unfortunately, the place of South Korea in this picture was unresolved. It was regarded as important, but not vital, and the Americans were anxious to remove their military forces from Korea as soon as possible. The position of mainland Southeast Asia was even vaguer. But, as in the case of Europe and the Middle East, the need to defend the far southern flank of the advanced countries that were America's allies and assure their access to vital resources would help draw the United States into an originally unwanted involvement there. There was growing interest in fostering "Chinese Titoism," an idea that did not recede in importance until the Chinese intervened in the Korean War. (Nor, contrary to what is widely assumed, was it absent from public discussion, where interest in a split between the Soviets and Chinese did not disappear until the same period.)

During 1949, the hostility of the Chinese Communists became more and more obvious, and the American leaders became less hopeful about "Chinese Titoism" in the near future, deciding a break between the Soviets and Chinese would take several years. In 1949 the Truman administration even considered radical steps to try to help anti-Communists — not closely associated with the Nationalist government — to hold some part of the mainland, notably by aiding Muslim forces in the northwest and forming a new version of the Flying Tigers. But the Communists moved too fast, and no action was taken to grasp at these straws. Some aid continued to the Nationalists on Taiwan. It was generally expected, in early 1950, that the Communists would take Taiwan that year, and, in due course, the United States would join Britain in recognizing Mao's government — something Mao cared about very little. Although there was a growing interest in and outside the Truman administration in denying Taiwan to the Communists by one means or another, nothing was done about this by the outbreak of the Korean War.¹

The Soviet-Chinese Alliance

Unfortunately, disenchantment with the hope for an early break between the Soviets and Chinese was well founded. Stalin probably distrusted Mao—although he also distrusted everyone else—and was well aware and worried by American interest in "Chinese Titoism." But he had no desire to repeat the mistakes made with Yugoslavia and trigger an open break with the Chinese. Mao, for his part, was a hard-line revolutionary, had always been consistently hostile to the Western countries and had only feigned any other view for tactical purposes. He was completely comfortable on the Soviet side in the Cold War. On a few important occasions he may have disobeyed Stalin, but he had no desire for an open dispute with the senior Communist ruler. With victory in sight, he tried hard to win Stalin over. And, while Stalin may have distrusted Mao, given the Communist conquest of China a low priority and given Mao less help than the latter would have liked, he had in fact provided considerable aid at crucial points. And, contrary to what has sometimes been claimed, there is no evidence that he deliberately obstructed a Chinese Communist victory. In the summer of 1949, he was downright apologetic to a Chinese delegation for mistakes he had made earlier. Underneath his apparently friendly policy, he may still have envisaged replacing Mao with the more pro–Soviet Gao Gang (Kao Kang), the effective viceroy of Manchuria, but this intrigue seems to have had remarkably little effect on other aspects of Soviet-Chinese relations. Mao may have calculated that he need merely hold off Gao Gang for a few years; since he would outlive the much older Soviet leader. On matters of immediate interest, Stalin and Mao proved in substantial agreement, surprisingly so for two notoriously sneaky, touchy and quarrelsome tyrants.

When Mao journeyed to Moscow in December 1949 for an extended visit, the two sides were cautious and slow to get down to business. Language was also a problem for the Communist allies. Apart from the sheer tedium of translation, interpreting some of Mao's idiomatic expressions in his talks with Stalin proved difficult. (Later, some of the translations from Chinese into Russian in their correspondence during the Korean War seem to have been downright bad. Perhaps the Soviets and Chinese should have copied the former Axis powers and settled on English as a common language.) But in the end, Mao seems to have been satisfied with the results. He got a wholly new alliance with the USSR, not just the revision of the old 1945 treaty between the Soviets and the Nationalists (which was all Stalin had originally wanted) and a loan and aid arrangements on the terms he desired. They remained in accord on revolutionary strategy in Asia, where Mao was conceded the lead, outside Korea. Stalin may have given Mao the ultimate accolade in January 1950 by betraying Gao Gang and giving up the plan to replace Mao. (Khrushchev maintained, however, that this step was not taken until 1952.) To be sure, this was not an unambiguous alliance of equals. Stalin tried to make sure that Chinese relations with the West would remain minimal and bad. One of his purposes in entering the Korean War may have been to provoke the Americans into reversing their policy toward Taiwan and protecting the place, which should ensure that Chinese relations with the United States would remain hostile. Indeed, he may have gone further and envisaged, at least as a possibility, pushing China into an out-and-out war with the United States, whether to guarantee that the Chinese would remain subordinate to the USSR or as part of some larger purpose.

These speculations aside, Stalin seems to have found it fairly easy to manipulate Mao during the Korean War. Mao's belligerency, his cruder version of Leninism, lesser knowledge of the world outside China, and his tendency, which lasted right into the 1960s, to envisage a future all-out war with the West as a sort of repetition of the Sino-Japanese War made Stalin look like a sophisticated thinker by comparison.[2] To be sure, Stalin's view of the world was not realistic either. His mind ran to more complex delusions about manipulating differences between his enemies and victims and replicating the strategy that had led to the Nazi-Soviet Pact and World War II in a "bigger and better" way. He indulged in fantasies, most clearly developed in his last published work, *Economic Problems of Socialism* (1952), that the Germans and Japanese would turn against the Western occupying powers, (Ironically, the only revolt in any of the occupied ex–Axis states would be the East German uprising of June 1953.) Stalin never really adjusted to the peculiarities of the Cold War world in which two fairly solid alliances were jammed up tight against each other without much room for maneuver, in which the remaining neutrals were not very important and a split in the "capitalist" ranks was not likely.[3]

2

The World Situation in 1950: Prelude to the Korean War

The gloomy world of 1950 was a very different place from the one that the Western peoples had dreamed of during World War II. They faced a continual threat from the most brutal and tyrannical regimes that had ever existed, and chaotic political situations seemingly made to order for them. The advanced Western countries had grouped themselves around the United States, and, more or less, stabilized themselves; but that achievement was not yet fully complete. Economic recovery was at least in sight, typified by the shift in Marshall Plan aid from items like food to capital goods. A government had been formed for western Germany, and while the occupation of West Germany and Japan continued for several more years, the Allied authorities rarely intervened in their internal affairs after 1949. The formation of the European Coal and Steel Community, foreshadowing the Common Market, and the first step in European integration had been taken. But whether the process would go on no one could be sure. That West Germany and Japan would successfully be integrated into a Western democratic system was not yet obvious in 1950. There were still widespread unfounded fears that those countries would once again become dangerous. In Europe, the Cold War front had frozen into a lasting stalemate, although Yugoslavia was seriously threatened by the Soviets and Berlin, quasi-isolated behind Soviet lines, was always a sore point. A "little blockade" had been imposed on the city early in 1950.

Outside Europe, the democracies faced something approaching chaos. The impact of modernization, rising nationalist sentiment, and the end, or approaching end, of European and Japanese rule, exacerbated in some cases by the after-effects of Japanese occupation during World War II, were throwing Asia, Africa and Latin America into continual crisis. This opened a vast field of maneuver for Soviet and Chinese manipulation, the local Communists and a variety of more obscure sorts of unpleasant fanaticism.

The Asian colonial countries had mostly completed their transition to independence by the end of 1949. The process had been more or less peaceful in countries under British and American rule, although its sequel was sometimes very bloody. But the independence struggle was very violent in French and Dutch colonies. The newly independent states formed a vast disputed zone between the Soviet-Chinese alliance and the Western powers. Southeast Asia was an outright battlefield; the Viet Minh Communists in Indochina were now receiving direct support from the Chinese. Indonesia remained unstable, while guerrilla wars raged in Malaya, the Philippines and Burma, complicated in the last case by uprisings by minority nationalities. The struggle would not turn clearly in favor of the anti–Communist side until 1951. The Americans and British were moving, slowly, to extend the line of containment in East and Southeast Asia. But the process remained incomplete at the time of the Korean War, which was, in fact, a major cause of that war. Korea was divided into Communist and non–Communist halves, but South Korea was not clearly stable or inside the Western defense zone, while Taiwan seemed doomed to Communist conquest. The relatively stable South Asian countries, although already bitterly at odds with each other, followed "neutralist" policies. The Indian government hoped to draw China away from the USSR into an Indian-led "neutralist" bloc, but such hopes would be disappointed just as much as Western hopes for early "Chinese Titoism." In practice, the "neutralists" would not become a major independent force, but would veer and tack individually between the two sides. In a process only starting around 1950, they sorted themselves into three classes with shifting memberships: "neutralists" that were really neutral, "neutralists" that were pro–Soviet and "neutralists" that were pro–Western.

In the Middle East and North Africa, it was not yet absolutely clear that the Arab-Israeli conflict, then stalemated, would be more or less permanent. There were, however, plenty of other serious conflicts in the region, mainly between the British and French and the Arab countries. North Africa, under French rule, was restive, while alliances with Britain and British bases were violently unpopular in Egypt and Iraq. The British dominated Iran's oil production (still the main oil source in the Middle East) on which Western Europe and Japan were becoming dependent. Iranians bitterly hated the British. Iran, badly run by a corrupt elite with a discontented populace and the British as handy scapegoats, seemed particularly threatened by the Soviets. The Iranian Communists were strong and getting stronger. Throughout the early 1950s, the West feared that either purely internal events or a clash between the British and the Iranians would allow a Communist seizure of power and/or Soviet intervention in Iran.[1] Iran would be an important distraction during the Korean War, along with Berlin, Yugoslavia and Southeast Asia.

During 1949 there were growing fears that the Cold War was moving to the disadvantage of the Western powers. The stabilization of Western Europe allowed a breathing space to see how bad things were elsewhere. The unexpectedly early victory of the Communists in China, and growing disillusionment with hopes for an early split between them and the Soviets, was coupled with a growing Soviet military threat. In August 1949, the Soviets tested an atomic bomb two years before the most pessimistic official estimates had predicted. The next step in the arms race, the hydrogen or H-bomb, was a growing preoccupation. After painful deliberations, President Truman in January 1950 authorized development of the thermonuclear bomb, a step the Soviets had already taken without much brooding. However, until 1952–1953, their project aimed at a type of bomb, the "Alarm Clock" or "layer cake," which the Americans had rejected as having limited potential. On March 10, Truman made it a "crash program." The race for an effective H-bomb would continue during the Korean War.[2]

The discussions leading to the H-bomb decision led to a major reappraisal of American policy and strategy. Most people in the U.S. government (George Kennan was an exception) agreed there had been a major turn to the disadvantage of the West and that the Soviets were becoming increasingly bold. The danger of war, if only by miscalculation, was growing. Earlier, almost all had assumed that a third World War, while not unlikely, was a long way off. The American public was even more concerned about war in the near future: Gallup polls in March and June 1950 showed that a majority of Americans thought the Soviets were winning the Cold War, and 57 percent of those questioned expected a world war within five years. (Curiously, this idea seems to also have been common in China.) Interestingly, despite polls showing interest in Senator Joe McCarthy's wild charges, only one percent of Americans polled favored an intensified campaign against domestic Communists. This is one of many indications that, despite what is often said, most Americans regarded the struggle against Communism as a foreign policy issue and that the influence of, and support for, "McCarthyism" is often vastly exaggerated.

In April 1950, Paul Nitze, head of the State Department's Policy Planning Staff, and a special committee of State and Defense Department officials produced NSC-68, a review of American objectives and national security programs. Recounting the present crisis, it reaffirmed containment and carefully analyzed and rejected both deliberate isolation and a "preventive war" against the Soviets before they acquired a large nuclear stockpile. Negotiations were not a prospect, and any substantial increase in the area under Soviet domination would be extremely dangerous. Non-Communist Asia was particularly vulnerable, and Nitze implicitly agreed with the State Department's appraisal that any break between the Soviets and Chinese was at least three years away. The Soviets were developing their strength at such a rate that by mid–1954 they could seriously damage the United States. By then, American military superiority could be eliminated, and war would be a real possibility. The current American military effort was inadequate. But it could easily be greatly increased, along with economic assistance to other countries, and any Soviet decision for war could be headed off. Realizing that NSC-68 would require an enormous increase in the defense budget, Truman was unwilling to implement it. He did not approve NSC-68 until September 30, 1950, three months after the start of the Korean War.

American policy in Asia was a particularly difficult and controversial issue. Recriminations over the Communist victory in China almost drowned out rational discussion of policy toward the rest of Asia. Secretary of State Dean Acheson, a particular target of attack, made a major speech on January 12, 1950, defending the record of the Truman administration and enunciating policy toward Asia. Asia, he stressed, was diverse; there could be no simple, uniform policy toward it. There were, however, two common factors operating over the whole region: disgust with poverty and opposition to foreign domination. Acheson noted that the two were linked because many Asians believed that foreign imperialism caused poverty—an idea, which, he bluntly pointed out, was false. He argued that the Chinese Nationalists had lost because of their own incompetence, not anything the Americans had done or not done. The United States had no clash of interests with the peoples of Asia, but the Soviets did. Communism was just a new weapon of Russian imperialism. At first sight this seemed to imply that the Chinese Communists were just Soviet puppets, but Acheson went on to explain that the Soviets were detaching China's northern regions—Manchuria, Mongolia and Xinjiang. This was the most important fact, and nothing Americans might do should obscure this. He implicitly rejected intervening to protect Taiwan from the expected Communist invasion. Acheson implied that at some point the Chinese Communist leaders must oppose the Soviets or be discredited with their own people. The United States was committed to defend Japan, and a defense perimeter running through the Ryukyus and the Philippines. It could not formally guarantee other areas. In the event of an armed attack, "the initial reliance must be on the people attacked to resist it and then upon the commitments of the entire civilized world under the Charter of the United Nations, which so far has not proved a weak reed to lean on...." This was a reading of history that might have puzzled people in East-Central Europe. Acheson deprecated the importance of military problems in Asia, but this comparatively minor part of his speech drew more attention and criticism than anything else he said. He would be bitterly criticized for leaving Korea, as well as Taiwan, outside the declared American defense perimeter. Many people blamed the whole Korean War on this one speech.[3] Although that is almost certainly exaggerated, and Acheson was merely referring to a well-known policy revealed by MacArthur in March 1949, the speech probably influenced Stalin's decision to launch the war.

Korea — Prelude to War

The Korean people became the greatest victims of the Cold War. The seeds of disaster were already well planted in 1945–1946. The Soviets efficiently built a typical satellite regime in North Korea, although their brute-force methods alienated people not originally ill disposed toward either Communism or Russians. The American occupation of South Korea was one of the less glorious episodes of the immediate postwar period; since efforts to build a democratic government were bumbling and not too effective. As in Germany, a fundamental clash of political systems led to the division of the country. But the situation in the South let the Communists play a larger role there than in western Germany.

The Soviets treated North Korea almost as if it were a detached part of East-Central Europe. Their policies were particularly similar to those used in East Germany, but, in Korea, unlike Germany, they shut the border between the Soviet and Western occupation zones completely, evidently concluding that commercial dealings with the South had little to offer. The Communist takeover was rapid; its main peculiarity was the extreme factionalism and disorganization of the Communists. Those who had stayed in Korea were largely shoved aside by Kim Il Sung, a previously little-known Soviet protégé, and a group of Soviet Koreans who were, Russified members of the Korean minority in Siberia. Inside Korea, the "native" Communists had been concentrated in the South, not the Soviet-occupied North. Their party, long since destroyed by the Japanese, was only reestablished in August 1945.

Shortly after Japan surrendered, Korean nationalist and Communist leaders in Seoul formed a "Preparatory Committee for Korean Independence." On September 6, the group proclaimed a "Korean People's Republic" as the government of Korea. This was a united front including center and rightist elements. Although not originally Communist-controlled, it gradually fell under their domination. When American forces arrived in the South, they ignored the Republic, rejecting its claims just as they ignored the conservative Korean government-in-exile in China.[4]

The Soviets had invaded Korea on August 8. One of the odder lapses in Allied planning and negotiations was a near-total failure to make arrangements for Korea before the Soviets entered the Pacific War. Such arrangements now had to be hastily formulated. (The Allies had vaguely agreed to establish a trusteeship for Korea as a prelude to full independence, but not anything else.) It should be noted that, had the Pacific War lasted longer as was generally expected, the Soviets would probably have taken all of Korea. The American occupation of South Korea and the creation of a non–Communist Korean state was a byproduct of the early end of the war and perhaps of the atomic bomb. The division of the country into Soviet and American zones was the result of a hasty, last-minute American proposal, and was one of the first steps taken to block Soviet expansion. The American Ambassador to the Soviet Union, Averell Harriman, and some others had been urging Washington for some time to counter the growth of Soviet power in East Asia by landing U.S. forces in Korea and at Dairen in Manchuria if the war ended at an early date. President Truman and General Marshall were receptive to such ideas. On August 10, after Japan first offered to surrender, American military planners working on General Order Number One, the post-surrender order to Japan, sought to establish a Soviet-American boundary as far north as possible. They noticed that the 38th Parallel cut Korea approximately in half, just north of Seoul and a nearby prisoner of war camp. Some planners suggested fixing the zonal boundary at the 39th Parallel, but it was decided the Soviets would not accept it. It was resolved to land troops at Pusan even if the Soviets refused to accept the 38th Parallel.

On August 11, Truman ordered that American troops land at both Dairen and a "port in Korea (Seoul)" if the Soviets did not get there first. They moved fast enough to prevent the landing at Dairen, but they readily accepted the American suggestion to divide Korea into occupation zones at the 38th Parallel, although they might have overrun most of the peninsula before the Americans could have gotten there. Stalin showed a similar caution and a desire not to provoke the Americans in several other areas at the same time, apparently prompted by an initial fearful reaction to the atomic bomb. He may also have hoped that moderation in this matter might help him get American consent to his occupying part of Japan. But this calculation proved mistaken.[5]

He had, however, acquired the more valuable part of Korea. North Korea had more industry than the South, or for that matter the Balkan satellites, and valuable minerals. (The overwhelmingly agrarian South caught up with and overtook the North only long after the Korean War.) Unlike the Americans, the Soviets never formed a military government in Korea. While carefully sealing off the North, they nominally recognized the authority of the People's Republic. They were not, however, popular. The misbehavior of Soviet troops, their appropriation of food and their looting of Korean industry somewhat neutralized Koreans' initial gratitude toward their liberators. Cho Man-sik, the Republic's leader in the North, was more conservative than his counterparts in the South. From the start, however, the Soviets forced him to follow the lead of the Communists. In late August, even before the Republic was formed, the Soviets insisted that the local branch of the Preparatory Committee for Independence be reorganized as a "People's Political Committee" with an equal number of Communist and non–Communist members. Cho was told to cooperate or else. With Soviet help, the Communists soon gained control of the People's Political Committees that exercised local government functions. In October, a "Five Provinces Administrative Bureau" was formed to run the whole of North Korea.

The headquarters of the reformed Korean Communist Party remained in the South. Authority over the Communists in the North fell to Kim Il Sung's "Kapsan" group and the Soviet Koreans. Kim had long been associated with the Chinese Communists in Manchuria, who had been only loosely connected with the Party headquarters south of the Great Wall. He had led Korean guerillas in Manchuria in the 1930s before he had to flee into Soviet territory. Still a young man, this bloodthirsty megalomaniac would be the longest-lived of Stalin's satraps and ultimately became quite independent of the Soviets, surviving the downfall of the USSR and establishing the first Communist hereditary monarchy. Kim was an even more repellent figure than the other "little Stalins" the Soviets imposed on East-Central Europe. (Men like Ulbricht and Rakosi were not attractive figures, but it is hard to imagine them dotting a countryside suffering famine with giant statues of themselves.) Korean Communists returning from the Chinese Communist capital at Ya'anan (Yenan) formed their own faction, which later became a separate party, the Sinmindang, in both halves of Korea. Their arrival was not too welcome to the Soviets, who disarmed their armed force when it arrived in November 1945 and later sent it to Manchuria. But the "Chinese" faction formed an alliance with Kim against the "home" Communists, led by Pak Hon-yong, who stayed in the South. Late in 1945 the Soviets started organizing police and security forces in North Korea. Some Koreans went to the Soviet Union for military training.

In October, the Soviets banned all political groups suspected of being anti–Communist and started arresting political opponents. In December, they deposed Cho Man-sik, who was never seen again. In February 1946, the Five Provinces Bureau was replaced by the North Korean Interim People's Committee, with Kim Il Sung as chairman. Non-Communists were rapidly purged, although two tightly controlled satellite parties remained in the Communists' North Korean United Front. By August 1946 the various Communist groups were welded into one North Korean Workers' Party. Industry (almost all Japanese-owned) was promptly nationalized, but small business was left alone. The peasantry was placated with a drastic land reform, but collectivization was put off. North Korea became a reliable Soviet satellite, exploited through the usual joint-stock companies. In September, organization of a Korean People's army began. The main initial preoccupation of that organization was not uniting Korea, but supporting the Chinese Communist war effort in Manchuria. Over 100,000 Koreans were serving with the Chinese Communist forces there, although it is still unclear to what extent they were drawn from the Korean minority in Manchuria rather than North Korea.

The Soviets soon withdrew most of their occupation troops. [6] The Soviet technical advisers who stayed seem to have been competent and had good relations with the Koreans. On the whole, the North Korean regime, while not really liked, was probably less unpopular than its European counterparts. The Koreans had been in a somewhat more malleable mental state than the peoples of East-Central Europe when they fell into Soviet clutches, and the initial effects of Communist rule were not all bad. Education and health facilities were improved, and urban workers were better off than they had been. Nevertheless, at least half a million people fled south, an enormous number for a small country.

As in East Germany, the Communists did not call their regime a government or admit that their armed forces existed until the non–Communist zone got its own government and army — thus trying to throw the blame for the division of the country onto the non–Communists and the West. But in Korea, as in Germany, the West actually trailed behind the Soviets in both political and military organization.

In contrast with the Soviets, the Americans arrived without set plans, policies or chosen political allies in a country they did not know much about. They had assumed during the war that Korea would be put under

Allied trusteeship before attaining full independence. General John Hodge, the military governor, was a competent combat commander but not well suited for his job. His State Department advisers were mediocre. The Americans lacked personnel with experience in Korea and depended on unreliable Korean interpreters. They promptly antagonized the Koreans by retaining Japanese administrators and police as temporary measure. This caused such a violent reaction that they then had to get rid not just of the administrators and police but even technicians whose early removal was economically disastrous. There were few trained Koreans to replace the departing Japanese. Conditions in South Korea were bad. Chemical fertilizer and food were in short supply, and there was severe inflation, and a shortage of housing as the South was flooded with refugees from the North and Manchuria. Price controls were lifted at an ill-chosen moment. The military government never got a grip on things. It was an unpopular, cumbersome bureaucracy with low morale. Korea became the U.S. Army's equivalent of Siberia.[7]

General Hodge warned Washington that trusteeship would be very unpopular in Korea. But Secretary of State Byrnes characteristically ignored this unpleasant advice and at the Moscow conference in December 1945 secured an agreement to administer Korea as a UN trusteeship for five years. It was also agreed to form a Joint Commission to arrange economic unity in Korea and form a provisional national government. A preliminary meeting of representatives of the Soviet and American commands took place in Seoul on January 15, 1946. The Americans proposed joint operation of power, rail and communications systems, free movement between zones, and establishing uniform policies for banking and commerce throughout Korea, But the Soviets would discuss only a few specific issues: the supply of electric power to the South from the North, some aspects of transportation and commerce, and removing Japanese troops and civilians from North Korea. Because the South could not then supply the North with rice as it did in normal times, commercial exchange was ruled out. There was a very limited agreement on communications and liaison between the two commands. The Soviets flatly refused to allow free circulation of newspapers and information.[8]

As Hodge predicted, the trusteeship agreement enraged the Koreans. It was a dismally familiar pattern of nationalist hysteria: a people who had not had the slightest prospect of freedom a short time before were now furious at the idea of even a brief subordination to the Allies. The trusteeship issue became an instrument of Soviet policy, and, to a lesser extent, it worked in favor of the right in southern politics. In a fantastic development, the Soviets used the very unpopularity of trusteeship to try to gain

Communist control of all of Korea. The prospects of the Communists in the South, for a time, seemed promising. Koreans were in a frenzy over independence, unity and land reform. Political life was a maze of personal factions with little real party organization. The military government's rice-collection policy, its use of Koreans who had worked with the Japanese and an initial bias toward the right wing and its half-hearted policy toward land reform irritated most Koreans. The Americans were happy to divide up the large amount of farmland owned by Japanese, but on legalistic grounds maintained that only a Korean government could redistribute Korean-owned land. This had the odd result that the peasants of Japan, an occupied enemy country, received a better deal than those of a liberated friendly nation.

Moderates and independent leftists had left the Korean People's Republic, which became a simple Communist front during late 1945. The Communists tried to build a broad united front under their control. They won control of the labor movement. They tried to cultivate non–Communist leaders, even Syngman Rhee, the elderly conservative who had returned from exile in America and later became the President of South Korea and their leading foe. The position of some intermediate elements was problematic. Yo Un-hyong, a popular leader of the moderate left, formed a new party, the Inmindang or People's Party. Yo's attitude toward the Communists was ambiguous. Sometimes he worked with them, sometimes he opposed them. (For a time the Americans wrongly believed Yo was a Communist.) His ambiguity reflected the opinions of his party, which was infiltrated by the Communists. During 1946 there was an important struggle between the military government and the Communists for Yo's friendship, which the Americans finally won.

The Communists in the South at first opposed trusteeship, like everyone else. But on Soviet orders they reversed themselves. The People's Party and a few other non–Communists reluctantly joined with the Communists to back a trusteeship that for most political groups in the South was unacceptable. The Communists and the People's Party formed a tentative united front, the Korean People's Democratic Front, in February 1946. The Front boycotted American efforts to develop local representative institutions in the South. This left the "Representative Democratic Council of South Korea," convened in February, in rightist hands. At the State Department's insistence, the Americans tried to persuade Yo and others to join in a broad-based coalition, although Hodge now thought that Yo was a Communist. The military government was in a very difficult position. The right supported it, but not trusteeship, while the left supported, or at least tolerated, trusteeship, but not its current activities.[9]

Hodge and other observers like George Kennan rightly thought that the Soviets would never allow a united Korea except under Communist rule. The results of the Joint Commission meetings from March 20 to May 9, 1946 bore out their suspicions. The commission soon deadlocked. The Soviets refused to consult with any Korean group opposed to the Moscow conference agreement on trusteeship. That meant excluding all South Koreans except the Communists and their weak allies from any all–Korean government. With the North already under Communist control, acceding to the Soviet demand would mean that the whole country would become Communist. The Americans refused to accept the exclusion of anti-trusteeship groups. Neither side backed down and the Commission adjourned. The Soviet press violently attacked the Americans for allegedly backing the right and trying to revise the Moscow agreement. Although further attempts to negotiate over Korea were made, the deadlock proved permanent.[10]

The Americans learned as early as March 1946 that the Soviets were subsidizing the Communists in the South and sending agents over the zonal border. But the southern Communists' united front effort began to falter. In April, Yo Un-hyong started to move away from the Communists. Hodge tried to encourage non–Communist elements to break with the People's Democratic Front. A socialist group left it in May, and Yo resigned from his party. It split, part joining the Communists while part joined Yo's new Socialist Labor Party.

In July, Communist policy swerved sharply to the left, apparently reflecting a general hardening of Soviet policy in East Asia that was visible in China and Japan at the same time, a shift probably linked to Stalin's renewed effort against Turkey and uncompromising attitude toward the American plan for the international control of atomic energy. Growing hostility toward the Americans ended in an outburst of violence in October 1946 that may have gone further than the authorities in the North wanted. Communist-led strikes turned into serious disorders aimed at disrupting elections for an interim legislature. (Half the membership was to be elected, the rest appointed.) Fortunately, friendly leftists warned the Americans of the outbreaks in advance. The violence further alienated the moderate left from the Communists, many of whom were arrested. The Communists then prudently retreated, adopting a more moderate pose for a time.[11] It became clear that their support in the South and ability to maneuver politically there was limited.

The right won the elections. There had been many irregularities directed against the left so the Americans tried to compensate for this by favoring the moderate left in their appointments to the legislature. But 1947 saw growing political polarization in South Korea, the growth of the right and the rise of Syngman Rhee. He had many prominent friends in the United States, but the State Department and the military government viewed him without enthusiasm. They much preferred Rhee's more moderate ally, Kim Kiu-sik, or even Yo Un-hyong. Hodges detested Rhee as an arrogant troublemaker. But the Americans failed to maintain the moderate coalition they wanted. Yo was murdered by rightist terrorists in July 1947. The Americans grew increasingly eager to placate Korean demands for the turnover of more authority and get out of Korea as soon as possible. In May 1947, the Korean component of the military government was redesignated the "South Korean Interim Government." At the same time a new attempt to negotiate Korean unity with the Soviets failed. The Joint Commission deadlocked on the same issue as in 1946. The Americans then proposed a conference of the major powers on Korea, and holding early elections in both zones for legislatures that would choose representatives for a national provisional legislature to meet in Seoul. The Soviets refused, merely suggesting that all foreign troops leave Korea. The Soviet refusal to negotiate seriously left Korea divided.[12]

During 1947, despite the adoption of the containment policy, the Americans had become increasingly anxious to leave Korea. Financial constraints on the defense budget, a desire to reduce military and economic commitments elsewhere while concentrating on Western Europe, and doubt that a separate South Korea could ever be economically viable contributed to this tendency. In May 1947, the Secretary of War urged withdrawing American forces from the country. The State Department managed to delay, but not prevent withdrawal. It had misgivings about such a move, as did some generals such as Dwight Eisenhower. But in August the State-War-Navy Coordinating Committee resolved to liquidate the American commitment in Korea as soon as possible, a policy ratified by the National Security Council in NSC-8 in April 1948. It was resolved to try to withdraw from Korea by the end of 1948. But Korea was not written off. The long-term objective of creating a united independent Korea remained, and aid to a South Korean government would continue. It had already been decided that the Constabulary formed in early 1946 would be expanded and receive military weapons. In February 1948, MacArthur, against Hodge's advice, had recommended against forming an army. He felt the South Koreans were not ready for it. (The North Korean regime announced the official foundation of a "Korean People's Army" on February 8.) Hodge had long held that a North Korean attack was likely. So did General Albert Wedemeyer, an important planner who had carried out a survey mission in Korea and China in 1947. The Joint Chiefs of Staff's

Joint Strategic Survey Committee warned in January 1948 that withdrawal could lead to the Communist conquest of the peninsula.

Dealing directly with the Soviets having failed, the Americans had appealed to the UN, which was rapidly becoming the last stop for hopeless causes. In November 1947 the General Assembly voted 43–0 (with six abstentions) to accept an American proposal for all–Korean elections observed by a UN Temporary Commission on Korea (UNTCOK). The Soviets refused to let it enter Korea, so elections went ahead in the South only. Many South Koreans, even on the right, opposed the elections as did some members of UNTCOK, as spelling the permanent division of Korea. As in Germany, up to the establishment of a "separate" West German government, many disliked the course being taken as "dividing" the country (as though the Soviets had not already done this) but they had no plausible alternative to offer. Rhee's old allies, Kim Koo and Kim Kiusik, who opposed the elections, proposed an "All-Korean Conference on unity" that the North Koreans took up. The two men visited Pyongyang, but were soon disillusioned with the possibility of dealing with the Communists.

The elections for the National Assembly took place on May 10, 1948. The right undoubtedly pressured voters in some areas, but UNTCOK's limited staff of observers deemed the elections a free expression of opinion. It was a triumph for Rhee and the right. The Soviets responded by ending the transmission of electric power to the South. On August 15, an independent Republic of Korea (ROK) was declared; the Communists "replied" by proclaiming a "People's Democratic Republic of Korea" on September 9. Both regimes claimed to be the rightful government of all of Korea. The ROK Constabulary became an army.

On September 20, the Soviets announced that their forces would leave Korea by the end of 1948. They then began attacking the Americans for not leaving the South. The UN deemed the ROK the legitimate government of South Korea (not the North) and urged both occupying powers to evacuate the peninsula. A permanent UN Commission on Korea replaced UNTCOK to report on Korean affairs.

In October, the Communists in the South launched a full-scale revolt against the ROK government; some military units mutinied and joined them. For a time, large areas were under Communist control. But the ROK Army and police put down the uprising by January 1949, using very brutal methods. Guerrillas, whose numbers peaked at about 3,000, fought on with decreasing effectiveness, despite reinforcements infiltrating from North Korea. Two last infiltration attempts were smashed in April 1950. The South Koreans were not passive; their agents in the North sabotaged the oil refinery at Wonsan. There were sporadic raids and artillery duels along the frontier throughout the period up to the Korean War.

Despite the fighting, conditions in South Korea improved in 1949 and early 1950. The South regained self-sufficiency in food production. The Americans had not implanted a stable democratic government. But, despite a widespread myth to the contrary, South Korea was not a dictatorship *before* the Korean War.

Despite Rhee's authoritarian inclinations and high-handed actions—such as arresting opposition National Assemblymen on trumped-up charges just before election day—civil liberties survived and the judiciary maintained its independence. In elections in the spring of 1950, Rhee's opponents made important gains. Over Rhee's opposition, the Assembly forced through a second land reform to redistribute Korean-owned land. Its implementation was interrupted by the North Korean attack. Despite the Communists, or Rhee for that matter, South Korea seemed on a stable course of development.[13]

In March 1949, the Americans decided to remove their last forces from Korea. The last troops, except for the Military Advisory Group (KMAG) attached to the ROK Army—left on June 30. The withdrawal did not command universal approval, as many people feared the results. The South Koreans were unhappy, as were some British and Australian officials and American Congressmen. The American Federation of Labor urged leaving a token force of 5,000 men as a "trip wire" to deter a North Korean attack. The Filipino representative on UNCOK publicly criticized the withdrawal. The Americans were reluctant to give South Korea a defense guarantee. Their defense policy in the Pacific remained holding an offshore island perimeter, and it was feared that a guarantee might embolden Rhee to attack North Korea. Rhee recklessly blustered about liberating the North although he obviously lacked the means to do so. The fear that he might start a war was one reason why military aid to the ROK remained limited, but many officials doubted they could absorb modern equipment or successfully defend themselves.

MacArthur was a notable adherent of this view. Since 1945 he had not shown much interest in Korea (he had direct responsibility for it for just a short time) and had little faith in the ROK ability to survive and attack. He feared that the Communists would use an attempt to build a large army as an excuse for an attack, and opposed forming a ROK air force and navy. The Americans hesitantly helped establish those services just before the war began. Rhee's undependability and the obsession with keeping him on a short leash proved costly. The U.S. Air Force units leaving Korea for Japan in 1949 were about to convert from propeller-driven fighters to jets, so they left their old planes behind. They junked 150 still useful P-38 Lightnings instead of turning them over to the Koreans.[14]

Many people on the anti–Communist side had foreseen the Korean War; unfortunately, many more contributed to the situation that made it possible.

Decision for War

The Korean War had a long prehistory. The North Korean Communists, and probably the Soviets, had long kept the possibility of war in view. As far back as mid–1946, the American Military Government had received reports and documents from several sources about a Communist "master plan" for Korea. The plan called for the southern Communists to build up their strength and develop a network of front organizations. The latter, with the Communist Party, which would profess moderation, would form a united front in which the openly Communist element would look small and innocuous. The Soviets would arrange a withdrawal of their own and American forces from Korea. After that, the southern Communists would start civil disorders, and, helped by the northern army, would seize power. The plan could not be carried out. The southern Communists were not strong or skilled enough, nor were Americans and non–Communist Koreans as gullible as the Soviets and the Korean Communists may have hoped. But, together with the formation of a Soviet-trained army in North Korea—which long preceded the build-up of the forces of the other Soviet satellites—these reports suggest that as early as 1946 the Soviets initiated long-range preparations to unite Korea under Communist rule, *if* political maneuvers and small-scale violence failed to achieve that and a suitable opportunity appeared.

Whatever the Soviets' role in the "master plan" it was soon outdated. Whatever long-term possibilities they had in mind, Korea was on the back-burner for them in the late 1940s. Those who they had installed in power, however, strongly agitated for war to unite Korea. But the Soviets, while not opposed in principle, rejected invading South Korea as impractical. They even seem to have worried in 1949 that the South might attack the North.

In March 1949, Kim Il Sung visited Stalin in Moscow to secure help. Stalin closely questioned him about the Korean situation. The tone of his questions suggests he had not paid much attention to Korea for a considerable time, although he may have been feigning ignorance to test the Korean. He once again rejected a North Korean request to attack, but there was an agreement to support a considerable buildup of the North Korean forces. In September, Kim again asked for permission to attack the South. This time, however, the request received more careful consideration. Stalin had clearly warmed to the idea of conquering South Korea. The Soviet Embassy in Pyongyang did not think much of Kim's plan of campaign and warned that the North Koreans were just not strong enough to assure a victory. Moreover, the West might intervene in a long drawn out war. Stalin again rejected the operation. The Politburo's official reply directed Ambassador Shtykov to explain that "it is not allowed" because the North Koreans were militarily and politically unprepared.

Kim may have sensed greater interest on the part of his patrons, however, and the North Koreans initiated an economic mobilization program to support a war, providing the light weapons, ammunition and food for an expanded army.[15]

On January 17, 1950, while Stalin was negotiating with Mao, Kim once again approached the Soviets about an invasion and asked to go to Moscow. Shtykov transmitted this to Stalin on January 19.

Stalin had closely studied Acheson's speech of January 12, while Soviet intelligence assured him that the Americans would not defend either Korea or Taiwan. There seemed to be plenty of evidence to support that conclusion and little to contradict it. Acheson's remarks were merely the latest and most authoritative expression of a policy based on holding an offshore island perimeter and a refusal to guarantee the defense of South Korea, from which the Americans had removed their own forces. They had left a convenient gap in their defenses, which it seemed safe to exploit, perhaps with major consequences. The Communist side was riding a wave of victory in the east: the early Communist victory in the Chinese Civil War, although it also introduced an element of intra–Communist competition, and the Soviet acquisition of the atomic bomb encouraged bolder action, just as Paul Nitze foresaw in NSC-68.

On January 30, Stalin replied that "such a large matter in regard to South Korea such as he wants to undertake needs large preparation. The matter must be organized so that there would not be too great a risk." He was willing to see Kim. Shtykov was to tell him that "I am ready to help him in this matter." In the same message he "requested" a yearly shipment of at least 25,000 tons of lead from the Koreans. Kim and Shtykov interpreted this as a clear go-ahead, and from then on Stalin paid close attention to the preparations for the war. Arms shipments to Korea were apparently increased even before he met Kim in April.

Mao was not told of this decision for some time. He and Stalin may have discussed a war in Korea (Chinese sources differ on this point), but Mao was noncommittal about whether the Americans would intervene.

He was mainly interested in his own attack on Taiwan and supporting the Viet Minh in Indochina, in itself a major effort. Stalin had previously been cool to the Taiwan invasion as possibly leading to a direct clash with the Americans, but he now offered all-out support for it. He even suggested that Mao attack Hong Kong, but the Chinese demurred — he had already perceived that the continued existence of that horrendous imperialist enclave was in his interest. Mao may have guessed what was up in Korea, for he readily acceded to Kim's request for the return of the Korean units serving with the Chinese Communists.

In April 1950, Kim met Stalin. Unfortunately there are no good records of their meeting, but it is known that Stalin expressed worry that the Americans would intervene. Kim, along with the Soviet officials present, deemed this unlikely. Kim assured Stalin that a decisive surprise attack would win the war within three days, and a Communist uprising in South Korea would support the attack. The Americans would not have time to intervene even if inclined to do so. Stalin was convinced, and the plan went ahead.

The Soviets had sent a new group of military advisers under Lt. General Vasilev. They tore up Kim's original plan and devised a new one, which was translated into Korean early in May.

The "Ya'anan faction" among the North Koreans had been kept out of the planning, and Mao was belatedly given the courtesy of being told about the war in May. Stalin had told Kim to meet Mao to inform him of the plan. While Chinese sources again conflict, Mao seems to have professed enthusiasm, although he was not told details of the military planning. He expressed even more confidence than Stalin that the Americans would not intervene. On May 14, Stalin offered to postpone the attack if Mao wished. In this message, Stalin explained his backing for the invasion as a result of the "changed international situation," and with that not exactly crystalline elaboration Mao (and for that matter, later historians) had to remain content. Either because he was not thinking too clearly or because he was afraid to anger Stalin, Mao did not ask that the invasion be postponed, although he probably would have liked to get in his attack on Taiwan first. It is interesting to note that he did accelerate preparations for the invasion of Taiwan and initiated troop movements to strengthen the rather small Chinese forces in Manchuria. (It was fortunate that this redeployment was not greater.) If Mao hoped to beat the North Korean attack with his own, however, it became clear that the idea was impractical. In early June, the Chinese leadership postponed the Taiwan invasion until 1951. Meanwhile, at the end of May, the Soviet advisers and the North Korean General Staff concurred that the North Korean forces were ready to strike. The Soviets left setting the exact date of the attack up to Kim. They had been inclined to wait until July, but Kim argued that that would mean fighting in the rainy season. He also may have wanted to achieve Korean unification by August 15, the fifth anniversary of Japan's surrender.[16]

Why Stalin decided on the Korean War is still not clear. It is unlikely he did so to please Kim Il Sung. The likeliest explanation is that he estimated that the conquest of South Korea would scare Japan away from the West by demonstrating the strength of the Soviet-Chinese alliance and the weakness, and even cowardice, of the Americans. Even if the Japanese were inclined to stand fast and the Americans reacted by strengthening their position in Japan, the conquest of Korea would improve the Soviet strategic position, putting Japan in the jaws of a nutcracker between Soviet Sakhalin and a Communist Korea. It was likely to transform the political situation in the rest of Asia in favor of the Soviets. The defeat of yet another anti–Communist regime — and one that was an offspring of the United States that had failed to protect it — might shatter the morale of the enemy, and perhaps neutralists as well, in the rest of Asia. (The reaction of many countries between June 25, 1950 and the American decision to intervene shows that such a calculation would have been well-founded.)

The Korean move was probably also aimed, although to a lesser extent, at China, with which Stalin was now in an at least implicitly competitive cooperation. The Chinese Communists had recently outshone the Soviets in furthering the world revolution in Asia. It was desirable for the Soviets, or Communists associated with them, to advance the Communist cause as well. Uniting Korea now under a Soviet puppet would also shut out Chinese influence, while a pro–Soviet Korea would partly outflank China and perhaps intimidate the Chinese leaders. Open war in East Asia would also envenom China's relations with the Western powers, which Stalin certainly considered desirable, reflected in his suggestion that Mao attack Hong Kong. Soviet actions in the UN strongly suggested to many observers that despite their professions the Soviets did *not* want the Chinese Communists seated in the UN.

It has sometimes been suggested that Stalin attacked in Korea believing that while the Americans would not intervene there, they would react by taking Taiwan under their protection, further curbing the Chinese. This is not impossible; Stalin's love for complex intrigues, and his evasive and deceptive behavior toward the Chinese before the Korean War suggests he may have hoped for this, and further that Mao at some point realized it. But it is doubtful that he counted on this or that it was ever his main aim. The same intelligence that indicated it was safe to strike in

Korea also suggested that the Americans would not defend Taiwan either. His offering Mao, albeit belatedly and probably insincerely, a veto on the Korean attack suggests that if he wanted such an American reaction he had no more than an outside hope that things would develop that way. On an emotional level, Stalin may have felt that easy success in Korea would be a recompense for recent reverses in Europe and would eliminate the last ugly anti–Communist beachhead on the mainland of Northeast Asia.[17]

During late 1949 and early 1950, at about the same time he was deciding on the Korean War, Stalin decided on several other military moves. He expanded the Soviet fleet, increased Soviet forces in Germany and began a further buildup of the Bereitschaften, the "alert units" of the East German "police" that were actually the nucleus of the East German army. Although he probably still regarded World War III as a long way off, he may now have regarded an unwanted outbreak of war as a growing possibility, or even may have begun contemplating deliberately initiating a war in the mid–1950s. He was intensely interested in developing bombers capable of reaching the United States. Fortunately for the West, the Soviets' ability to develop intercontinental delivery systems for nuclear weapons lagged far behind nuclear bomb development, and this remained the case into the 1960s.[18]

Preparations for the Korean War seem to have been connected to a major change in Communist policy in Japan. Even after 1947, the Japanese Communists had continued an unusually cautious policy. On January 6, 1950, the journal of the Communist Information Bureau (Cominform) violently criticized Japanese Communist leaders for having admitted that the American occupation played a "progressive" role, suggesting that a peaceful transition to socialism might be possible, and for submissiveness to the occupation and "helping imperialism." Stalin had directly ordered the attack. The shocked Japanese Communist leaders were at first refractory and may have appealed to the Chinese for help. But when the Chinese endorsed the Soviet view they submitted. They repudiated their old ideas and emphasized the struggle against "international monopoly capitalism" (i.e., the Americans) rather than "domestic reaction." The Japanese government was now merely a puppet of imperialism. The party spoke of a "democratic united front from below." It dropped the vain hope of an alliance with the Socialist leaders and attacked them instead. The new line, adopted in May 1950, aimed at openly disrupting the occupation and an eventual armed "people's democratic revolution." The Japanese Communists knew of the coming North Korean attack. They had always had a strong interest in Korean affairs; in 1949 the Communist leader Nozaka wrote, "if all Korea should follow the example of China, the influence on Japan would be extremely great. The island of Japan, instead of being surrounded on three sides by capitalism and reaction, would instead be surrounded by People's Democracies and socialism."

An ultraleft "International Faction," which had long opposed the "Mainstream" Nozaka-Tokuda leadership, launched open violence against the Americans in May. That was against the wishes of the leaders who wanted to attract as little attention as possible until the party apparatus was underground. The angry occupation authorities then "purged" the members of the Communist Central Committee and the editors of the chief Communist newspaper. (The "purge" in occupied Japan was basically a super-blacklist, corresponding to "de-Nazification" in Germany.) The Central Committee vanished, and an "Interim Central Directorate" assumed the function of an overt party headquarters. Although never legally banned, the Communists stayed underground until 1955. Despite their weakness and ineffectiveness, they still had a major role in Soviet planning.[19]

The North Korean attack was not originally intended to be an isolated incident. Sometime after mid-1949, Stalin had decided to deal with the Yugoslavs. The rearmament of Hungary and the Balkan satellites was keyed to the plan for war with Yugoslavia. The Hungarian General Bela Kiraly later wrote that "during 1949 and early 1950 the Hungarian army was built up with dazzling speed." It was slated to attack between the Danube and Tisza rivers, and across the Danube to seize a bridgehead for the Soviet Army. When the Korean War broke out, the East-Central European armies were poised to strike against Yugoslavia.[20] The Korean War always had a larger dimension than was apparent at first sight.

Military Preparations

By June 1950 the North Korean Army had been built up to a strength of 180,000 or more of which some 40,000 were veterans who had served with the Chinese Communists. They formed three full divisions and were an important element in two others. The additional tanks, trucks and artillery needed for an invasion had arrived in April and May. The North Korean Army had eight complete combat-ready infantry divisions and two more at half-strength, and some smaller units. It had an armored brigade with 150 T-34 tanks, raised to the status of a division soon after the war started. In addition to the tanks of the armored brigade, each infantry division had a dozen SU-76 assault guns, almost as dangerous against infantry unsupported by tanks or effective antitank weapons. The North

Korean troops were well-trained and equipped with newly-built Soviet equipment on the scale of World War II Soviet infantry divisions, but did not have the heaviest or latest model weapons. The small North Korean Air Force was equipped with 180 propeller-driven aircraft, largely Yak fighters and IL-10 Stormovik ground-attack planes. The North Korean fleet consisted of a few motor torpedo boats and small craft. The Soviets had not bothered to give the North Koreans heavy tanks, heavy artillery or heavy antitank guns, rocket launchers, jets, multi-engine bombers, or much in the way of antiaircraft weapons—oversights the Americans had reason to be grateful for. The Soviets apparently reasoned correctly that such things were hardly needed to deal with the ROK Army.

The ROK Army, numbering 98,000 men, was a lightly armed infantry force that like the U.S. Army, but with less reason and unlike its opponent, had a very large administrative and supply "tail." There were many venal, unfit or simply uninterested officers. A fair number of ROK soldiers—like some North Koreans—were veterans of the Japanese Army, but given Korean feelings about the Japanese this was not a recommendation. The American advisers of KMAG—a very undesirable assignment—had faced many difficulties, especially of language. Fortunately, a few Korean officers had been sent to the United States for training, where they did well when removed from their usual background, Against American advice, the South Koreans had insisted on forming eight infantry divisions instead of the six the Americans had programmed, that had already stretched the number of fit officers and support. The ROK division was only a sort of shadow of an American World War II infantry division—with, at best, one-fourth the artillery support of the latter.

All but one of these divisions was understrength. Three divisions, partly equipped with old Japanese equipment, and detachments from the others were off hunting guerrillas in the southern mountains. The infantry were supported by just six battalions of light howitzers, one of which one was still forming. These units were equipped with old "short" 105 mm howitzers of the type used in World War II by the "cannon companies" of American infantry regiments rather than artillery units, and they were far outranged by the vastly more numerous enemy guns. The ROK Army had 27 armored cars and some half-tracks, but no tanks, mines, adequate antitank weapons or large stocks of ammunition. Thinking that Korea was not good "tank country" and that the North had few tanks, the Americans gave the ROKs only obsolete 37 mm and 57 mm antitank guns and 2.36-inch bazookas, all of which had been inadequate in World War II. The old bazooka ammunition frequently failed. Many vehicles were inoperable for lack of spare parts. The air force, formed only in October 1949, had just a few trainers and liaison planes. Only the navy, with a few recently arrived patrol craft, compared favorably with its Communist counterpart.

Otherwise, the picture of unreadiness was perfect. On June 25, the South Koreans were not on alert. Many men serving in units along the border were on weekend leave. General Lynn Roberts, KMAG's commander, had boasted that the ROK Army was the "best doggoned shooting army outside the United States." But the ROKs and at least some of Roberts' subordinates knew better. Both ROK and KMAG officers expected war in Korea, but not soon. They tended to overestimate the numbers and importance of the Communist air force, but underestimated the number and effectiveness of the enemy's tanks.

Although the North Koreans enjoyed considerable superiority in numbers, it was their superior training, experience and firepower, especially in artillery and tanks, that was critical. The Communists were sure they would achieve surprise. The South Koreans would rise against Rhee's government, the ROK Army would be quickly defeated, and once Seoul fell—which was expected to take three to four days—the ROKs would give up, long before any help could reach them, even if the Americans were inclined to act.[21] The Communists would achieve surprise, and defeat the ROK Army, but they would not be able to destroy it. It proved a far tougher opponent than they had imagined, and every other aspect of their appreciation would blow up in their faces.

The Military Geography of Korea

The Korean War would be shaped by the rugged terrain and poor transportation system of the country. A peninsula 575 miles long separated from China and Siberia by the Yalu and Tumen rivers, roughly three-quarters of Korea was mountainous. At its narrowest point in the North, Korea was just 95 miles wide. It was generally 180 miles across elsewhere. The high Taebaek range ran along the eastern side of Korea, almost shutting off the coastal rim of the Sea of Japan from the rest of the country. Running inland in the north, it became the Nangnim range that split northern Korea into two halves. Only the western side of Korea was relatively flat, and even it was cut up by spurs running from the Taebaeks. Korea had an extreme climate, with very hot, rainy summers (although drought would make the summer of 1950 hotter than usual) and contrasting cold in winter, although extreme cold was characteristic only of the far northeast. The northeast was very rugged and thinly populated. But it contained a high proportion of Korea's industry, including the Hungnam chemical complex, the biggest in East Asia, and the country's second biggest port,

Wonsan, which contained the Korea's largest oil refinery and was a major rail center. Most of the population was concentrated in the west. Korea's communications ran mainly north and south; few lateral routes crossed the peninsula. The main railroad and north-south highway ran from Andong (Antung), now Dandong, across the Yalu in Manchuria to Sinuiju in Korea, and south through Sinanju, Pyongyang to Kaesong in South Korea, and thence through Seoul, Suwon, Taejon and Taegu to Pusan at the south end of the peninsula — Korea's biggest and only really good port. Inchon served as the port of Seoul, and, while strategically located, it was small and hard to use because of high tides. Korea had a fairly good though rundown railroad system. But its roads were few and all were narrow, rough, and apt to break up in bad weather and under heavy traffic.

An east-west route crossed North Korea from Wonsan to Pyongyang. Another ran southwest from just below Wonsan through Uijongbu to Seoul, providing the best avenue of attack on the ROK capital, which was exposed on the north bank of the Han river. While the western route from Sinuiju through Seoul to Pusan would be the main theater of war, there was an important secondary route south. A central corridor, roughly 30 miles wide, ran below the "Iron Triangle" of North Korea where railroads connecting the towns of Pyonggang (not to be confused with the Northern capital of Pyongyang), Kumwha, and Chorwon provided a good base for a supporting attack. Though mountainous and less well-supplied with roads than the area farther west, the central corridor contained railroads and roads serving Seoul and, well to the south at Taegu, actually cut into the main north-south route. East of the corridor the mass of mountains presented formidable obstacles, but the shelf along the east coast, although very narrow, proved to be a route for surprisingly dramatic advances by both sides. Korea did not have many airfields. The only really large fields suitable for jet fighters were at Kimpo, just south of Seoul, and, a bit farther south at Suwon. This, along with the American shortage of aviation engineers, made it tough to base jets in Korea unless the allied side securely held the Seoul region.

In 1950, the Korean countryside still had the aspect of a poor, underdeveloped country. Badly deforested, the hills were unpleasant to look at and worse to climb. The land was covered with muddy rice paddies. The whole country stank horribly. Bob Hope, on his first visit to Korea, visibly recoiled on stepping out of his plane. When an escorting officer explained that the Koreans used human excrement as fertilizer, Hope glumly replied, "I knew that. But *what did they do to it?*" For a Westerner to eat native food or use water that had not been boiled was an invitation to dysentery.

3

The War Begins: ROK Defeat and UN Intervention

At 4:00 A.M., Korean time on Sunday, June 25 (3:00 P.M. on June 24 in Washington), the Communist artillery opened fire. Just four of the eight South Korean divisions were nominally stationed on the 38th Parallel, and just four regiments and a battalion were actually on the line.

The main North Korean blow was in the west where roads through relatively open country led right to Seoul. Here the North Koreans had committed four divisions and 120 tanks in a pincer attack on the capital. The main effort was southwest down the Uijongbu corridor where the 3rd and 4th North Korean divisions and most of the tanks hit the ROK 7th Division. Farther west, the North Korean 1st and 6th Divisions struck southeast toward Kaesong held by the ROK 1st Division, which was badly placed.

The attack there began in a novel way. Part of the North Korean 6th Division rode into Kaesong on a train; the Communists had relaid the torn-up tracks across the zonal frontier overnight. The North Koreans were right in the middle of a South Korean regiment before the latter realized what was going on. Still farther west, the North Koreans sent a Border Constabulary brigade and an infantry regiment against the isolated ROK position on the Ongjin peninsula, which was not connected with the rest of South Korea by land. The ROK regiment there lost one battalion but managed to get out by sea.

Meanwhile, in the central corridor, a secondary attack by the 2nd and 7th North Korean Divisions hit the ROK 6th Division, the first driving from Chunchon without armor while the 7th Division, supported by 30 tanks, headed southwest from Hongchon. On the east coast, the North Korean 5th Division and the 766th Independent Unit (which consisted of men raised to infiltrate the South and join the guerrillas there but never committed) hit the ROK 8th Division. Here the Communists had no tanks. Part of the 766th Independent Unit and Communist marines landed from junks and sampans behind the ROKs. Another amphibious move, a daring attempt to seize the vital port of Pusan, took place on the night of June 25–26. An armed steamer carrying 600 men tried to reach Pusan. Had it succeeded, this move might have ensured an early and complete Communist victory in Korea. But the ROK patrol craft PC-701 sank the ship.

That was the only bright spot. The ROKs stood up well under air attack, but found their antitank weapons worthless. They were reduced to attacking the Communist tanks with satchel and pole charges, or jumped aboard to drop grenades down their hatches. Few succeeded in these practically suicidal endeavors, and the ROKs were forced back, although fighting hard.

Against the advice of its commander and U.S. advisers, General Chae, the ROK Chief of Staff, insisted on launching a counterattack in the Uijongbu corridor on June 26. The 2nd ROK Division had been committed to this area to support the 7th Division. This was a disastrous mistake. The 7th Division's attack made surprising progress at first, but the Communist tanks rammed right through the 2nd Division, and the 7th Division had to retreat as well. The North Koreans took Uijongbu. The Communist success in the Uijongbu corridor forced the 1st ROK Division, which had fought well and proved the best ROK division throughout the war, to fall back, though the 5th and Capitol Divisions joined the fighting north of the Han. On June 27, panic began to spread as the Communists reached the outskirts of Seoul. The government fled to Taejon, but ROK soldiers at Seoul were still fighting stubbornly. In the early hours of June 28, the main ROK force was still north of the Han when, in an incredible blunder, panicky officers and officials ordered the road and rail bridges over the Han blown up. Between 500 and 800 civilian refugees were killed by the blasts, while three divisions, still largely intact, were stranded on the north bank. The exact responsibility for this insane action was never fixed (it was generally attributed to General Chae, but some Americans blamed the Vice Minister of Defense). It completed the ruin of the army, which might otherwise have had at least six to eight hours for an orderly retreat. As it was, it lost practically all of its heavy weapons and vehicles. Ironically, some of the Han bridges had not been completely demolished, and the Communists found they were in good enough condition to be repaired, although this took time. The Communists took Seoul that day.

On the central front, the ROK 6th Division, whose commander had suspected that something was up and did not allow any men to go on leave, fought well. The North Korean 2nd Division's attack was halted by a regiment fighting from concrete pillboxes on a ridge north of Chunchon. The North Koreans suffered heavy losses until their 7th Division and its supporting tanks turned around to support the 2nd Division. Then the ROKs had to fall back. On the east coast, the 8th ROK Division had one regiment on the frontier and part of another at Samchok — the rest of the division was fighting guerrillas in the south. Its antitank guns sank some of the enemy craft landing at Samchok, and despite the outflanking move, it successfully withdrew on June 27–28.

Only the 6th and 8th ROK Divisions retreated relatively intact. The defeat in the west had been decisive. Although many ROK soldiers had escaped across the Han and put up a brave defense of the river line, they were discouraged and heavily outgunned. On July 1, the South Korean Army officially numbered only about 40,000 men, although many stragglers later rejoined. Only the influence of the American Embassy and General Church, who headed the U.S. survey group sent by General MacArthur, prevented a complete collapse of the ROK government and high command. Without prompt help, the South Koreans were finished. The Communists had been superior in many respects, but their tanks had been decisive. Yet, the Communists had already gone awry in critical respects. They had defeated the ROK Army and won the war — *if* there was no American intervention — but had not won the crushing victory they had expected and needed. The ROKs had fought, and were continuing to fight, much better than the Communists had expected.[1] The ROKs had delayed the North Koreans and inflicted enough losses to give the Americans time to intervene effectively.

The Decision to Intervene

The Korean War had been preceded by the usual intelligence failure, although some observers had shown astonishing foresight. As we have already seen, many people had recognized the possibility of a war in Korea.

The CIA warned in February 1949 that there was a good chance of war after the American withdrawal. In early 1949, General Bradley had been troubled about the withdrawal, and had a study prepared on how to respond to a North Korean attack. Rejecting unilateral American intervention, the study suggested that the United States might take part in a "police action" under UN sanction. But Bradley never sent this report to the National Security Council. Just before the outbreak of war, the Army prepared a contingency plan for a war in Korea that envisaged a campaign astonishingly like the one that developed. After leaving his position as commander of the American naval forces in the Western Pacific in August 1949, Admiral Oscar Badger suggested that the Communists would soon attack South Korea as well as Taiwan. Early in 1950, Alexander Sachs, a brilliant economist who had acted as a go-between for the nuclear scientists and President Roosevelt in 1939 and helped promote the development of the atomic bomb, predicted that the Soviets would exploit their nuclear test and the Chinese Communist victory by moving further, probably in Korea.

In late May and early June 1950, some of the State Department's Soviet specialists sensed that the Soviets were about to send some satellite force into action somewhere. Reviewing the possibilities, they pointed to Korea, only to be put off with claims from military sources that a Communist attack there was unlikely as the ROK forces were stronger than the Communists, as General Roberts of KMAG claimed, although the intelligence agencies did not share his view. The CIA and the armed services rated the North Korean forces as superior to the South Koreans, although they believed that it was not certain that the North Koreans could overrun the South without open Soviet or Chinese intervention. The military buildup in the North was detected, although its extent was underestimated, and an attack was generally recognized as a possibility in Seoul, Tokyo and Washington. Some reports from Korea provided strong indications there would be an attack in 1950, and some military advisers in Korea and G-2 officers in Tokyo thought an attack probable. But General Charles Willoughby, MacArthur's erratic intelligence chief, did not. Despite its views in 1949, neither did the CIA or the military intelligence agencies in Washington. It was widely thought that the North Koreans had not exhausted the possibilities of guerrilla warfare and propaganda. There appears to have been a tendency to rate South Korea as *politically* weaker than it really was, perhaps because a number of spectacular defections to the North — including two whole Army battalions and a steamship — had occurred during 1949. Apart from the expected invasion of Taiwan, some regarded Southeast Asia as the likeliest target for aggressive action.[2]

In hindsight at least, this was a strange evaluation. Things still seemed to be going well for the Communists in Southeast Asia without the dangers of a Chinese military intervention, which from Stalin's point of view might have been undesirable even if safe and was anyway unlikely until Taiwan fell. Military moves against Iran, Greece and Turkey risked collision with the West. Although Iran was in a state of crisis, any action there would have to be taken by the Soviets alone, without a satellite screen. Bulgaria could not tackle Greece or Turkey unaided. Given the premise that the Soviets were unready for a world war but contemplating local aggression, those targets all offered much danger for little gain. A process of elimination would have left Yugoslavia and South Korea the likeliest victims. They were of strategic importance. Stalin might reasonably think that the West would not fight in their defense, and satellite forces could attack them without immediate and open Soviet involvement.

The North Korean attack faced Truman with what he saw as the toughest decision of his presidency. He was at his home in Independence, Missouri, when the news of the attack reached him late on June 24. At first, it was not clear that a major invasion was underway rather than a bigger clash of the sort that had been common in the last year.

During June 25 it became clear that a full-scale war had started. There was remarkable unanimity of reaction among American officials at all levels. It was universally assumed that the Soviets were behind the North Korean attack (although there was no hard evidence for this) and that it must be resisted. The embassy in Moscow warned the invasion was a "clear-cut Soviet challenge" and a direct threat to American leadership of the free world. The Republic of Korea was a creation of American policy; and its destruction would have "calculably grave repercussions" for the United States in Japan and elsewhere.

The Soviets, however, were still not prepared to risk all-out war with the West. The State Department's Office of Intelligence Research quickly prepared an estimate that warned the South Koreans could not survive without American help. North Korea was under complete Soviet control and could not have acted without prior instruction, and the attack was not of merely local importance. It was a test of American resolution, and if successful might be followed by Chinese moves in support of Indochina, Burma, or Malaya, a satellite attack on Yugoslavia, or Soviet moves in Germany or Iran. More immediately, a severe blow would be dealt to American prestige in Asia and the feeling would grow, especially in Southeast Asia, that the Soviets were invincible. Control of Korea would help the Soviets intimidate the Japanese, discredit the United States and strengthen desires in Japan for neutrality. The Chinese would become bolder and might discount the likelihood of American intervention in Southeast Asia. American prestige in Western Europe would be significantly damaged. The estimate soon circulated through the State Department. It commanded wide agreement, though Soviet experts had reservations about the idea that the Soviets viewed the attack as a "test." A meeting of State and Defense officials on the morning of June 25 agreed that MacArthur should send aid to the ROKs and the Americans should intervene if necessary to prevent their defeat.

Already in the early hours of June 25, the Americans requested an emergency session of the UN Security Council in the slight hope that it might cause the other side to call off the invasion. The UN had long been involved in Korean affairs, and the Americans could not easily have avoided invoking it even had they wanted to. The Council met that afternoon, without the Soviets who continued boycotting it over the failure to seat the Chinese Communists in the UN. Secretary-General Trygve Lie declared that the UN Commission in Korea had confirmed other reports that the North Koreans had begun the war. Even most neutrals implicitly rejected the idea that it was a civil war. Communist claims that the North Koreans were merely counterattacking after a ROK invasion received universal contempt from non–Communists. An American resolution calling on the North Koreans to cease hostilities and withdraw was passed unanimously except for Yugoslavia. Another Security Council meeting was scheduled for June 27.

As the seriousness of the situation sank in during June 25, Truman flew back to Washington. His reactions were quite similar to those of other government officials, and, indeed, the public at large. He regarded the attack as analogous to the actions of Hitler, Mussolini and the Japanese leaders before World War II. He later wrote that if South Korea were allowed to fall the Communist leaders would be emboldened to move against other nations, and "no small nation would have the courage to resist threats and aggression by stronger Communist neighbors. If this was allowed to go unchallenged it would mean a third world war, just as similar incidents had brought on the second world war. It was also clear to me that the foundations of the principles of the United Nations were at stake unless this unprovoked attack in Korea could be stopped." Right after he reached Washington he made clear to his subordinates that he was determined to act.[3]

Truman, Secretary Acheson and the Joint Chiefs of Staff met at Blair House (the presidential residence while the White House was repaired) on the evening on June 25. All agreed the attack must be defeated. Acheson recommended supplying air cover to protect the evacuation of Americans from Korea, more supplies for the South Koreans, more aid for the French in Indochina and sending the Seventh Fleet to prevent an invasion of Taiwan, without allying the United States to Jiang. Everyone there thought the hands-off policy on Taiwan should be reversed. General Bradley and Admiral Sherman, the Chief of Naval Operations, doubted the Soviets wanted a world war; and suggested this was even a valuable opportunity to "draw the line." Sherman stressed that a Communist Korea would be a strategic threat to Japan. Bradley, the Secretary of Defense and the Secretary of the Army all disliked the idea of sending ground troops to Korea, but it was generally assumed — or at least hoped — at this point that the ROKs could stop the attack with just American air and naval support. The possibility of Soviet intervention was considered. General Hoyt Vandenberg, the Air Force Chief of Staff, assured the president that Soviet bases in the Far East could be knocked out "if we used A-bombs." Truman authorized sending supplies to the Koreans and ordered MacArthur to send a survey group to Korea. American air and naval forces would protect the evacuation of American civilians. He ordered the Air Force to prepare plans to smash all Soviet air bases in the Far East, and "careful calculation" should be made of the next probable site for Soviet action. Most officials, however, did not expect all-out war, or Soviet or Chinese intervention in Korea. Many, however, believed the Korean attack to be a test or probe that might be the first of a series of local aggressions. Truman ordered the fleet from the Philippines to Japan, but delayed a final decision about whether to defend Taiwan. There seems to be no reason to assume, as has sometimes been claimed, that Truman and Acheson felt compelled to buy off domestic critics who would argue that it was inconsistent to defend Korea and not Taiwan, nor did the military insist on it as a "price" for its support of intervention in Korea. Rather, all assumed without much discussion that the strategic situation had changed and that the Chinese were at least silent partners in the Korean attack.

During June 26 it became clear that the situation was worsening. Ambassador Muccio, at first overly optimistic, now reported a "rapid deterioration." MacArthur reported that South Korean casualties had not shown adequate resistance capabilities or the will to fight, and estimated that complete collapse was imminent. There was, however, a growing consensus in Washington that the war was a local one and not the first blow in, or a diversionary prelude, to a world war. Truman in particular had feared that Korea might be a feint or a diversion before a Soviet move into Iran, which in turn might be a prelude to world war. He believed the Soviets were short of oil and would have to take Iran to get it before they could start a larger conflict.

Another conference met at Blair House on the evening of June 26. General Vandenberg reported that planes protecting the evacuation had downed a North Korean fighter. The President approved Acheson's suggestions for all-out air and naval support for the South Koreans (below the 38th Parallel), an increase in American forces in the Philippines, more aid to the Philippines and Indochina, and the defense of Taiwan by the Seventh Fleet, though he indicated that he still did not want to get involved with the Nationalists.

No one disagreed with these moves, which constituted a decision to intervene in the Korean War. There was little doubt that if air and sea forces proved insufficient ground troops would be sent as well. The military authorities warned the President that if ground forces were committed some sort of mobilization would be needed. The Army already suspected that air and naval forces alone would not stop the enemy. Acheson had prepared a new resolution for the June 27 meeting of the Security Council, calling for active assistance to the South Koreans. But there was no assumption that if the UN failed to act the Americans would turn back. Nobody expected the Communists to respond to the UN resolution of June 25.

On the morning of June 27, Truman met the leaders of Congress who supported his actions. He made the decisions of the previous evening public. "The attack upon Korea makes it plain beyond all doubt that Communism has passed beyond the use of subversion to conquer independent nations and will now use armed invasion and war," he told them. (Truman had originally intended to refer to "centrally directed Communist imperialism" But when the British were consulted they suggested altering the wording to permit the Soviets to beat a retreat.) "In the circumstances the occupation of Formosa by Communist forces would be a direct threat to the security of the Pacific area and to United States forces performing their lawful and necessary functions in that area." Therefore, the Seventh Fleet would prevent attacks on or from Taiwan.

"The determination of the future status of Formosa must await the restoration of security in the Pacific, a peace settlement with Japan, or consideration by the United Nations," Truman further stated. Thus the Communists had to drop their invasion of Taiwan, but the Nationalists would have to stop their air attacks on the mainland, which Soviet jets were already discouraging, and lift their blockade of the coast.

That evening, the Security Council recommended that UN members "furnish such assistance to the Republic of Korea as may be necessary to repel the armed attack." Only Yugoslavia opposed the resolution, while Egypt and India abstained. The Soviets, apparently from sheer inertia, had failed to end their boycott. The Americans asked the Soviets to disavow responsibility for the attack and use their influence to obtain a withdrawal. No one expected this to do any good.

The American decision to intervene was welcomed throughout the Western world and non–Communist Asia. Even the Indian government privately made clear it was pleased. The British promptly offered the use of their naval units in East Asian waters. Thinking in the British government paralleled that in the U.S. government, although the British may have been slightly more afraid that the Korean invasion was a diversion, either as a prelude to a general war or more probably some other local but more important move, such as into Iran. But the British welcomed both U.S. intervention in Korea and the decision to protect Taiwan, even though they did not wish to be involved or associated with the last move.

At home, the decision to intervene in Korea was overwhelmingly popular, although it would not always remain so. It is important to remember the bitter hatred for the Communists common in America in 1950. The atmosphere was quite different from that of 10, much less 15 or 20 years later. The enemy was often referred to as "Reds" or "Commies," terms many would regard as indescribably vulgar by the 1960s. Attitudes ranged from a matter of fact acceptance of the idea that the Western powers were in a grim struggle with an evil, implacable enemy to some nasty fanaticism (which, however, in the form of "McCarthyism" was often turned inwards.) By the time of the major American intervention in the Second Indochina War in 1965 things had changed considerably. Matter of fact acceptance of the Cold War was the toughest attitude at all common, while "soft" or even pro–Communist attitudes had begun to reemerge. By then quite a few members of the upper class and the opinion-forming media seems to have become *bored* with the Cold War. The last attitude did not yet exist in 1950.

The well-known reporter Joseph C. Harsch had worked in Washington for 20 years: "Never before in that time have I felt such a sense of relief pass through this city." Relief was not unmixed with surprise. In a strange misreading of the character of Truman and his advisers, many in the United States and abroad (including General MacArthur) had expected inaction and dreaded the consequences. Some Republican politicians, while supporting Truman's actions, were more than grudging. Senator Taft favored entering the war, but grumbled that Truman had usurped the authority of Congress. Blaming Acheson in particular for tempting the Communists to attack, he insisted that the Secretary of State was discredited and should resign. The more irresponsible elements went further. On June 26, Senator Malone muttered that "it is fairly clear that what happened in China and what is now happening in Korea were brought about deliberately by the advisers of the President at Yalta and by the advisers of the State Department since then."

McCarthy, after a short hiatus, said even nastier things. This sort of sniping and insinuation plagued the Truman administration until 1953. By contrast, the pro–Soviet left in the United States, already small and weakening, virtually collapsed. Its most prominent figure, ex–Vice President Henry Wallace, finally disgusted with the Communists, broke with them and strongly backed Truman. Wallace remained bitterly anti–Communist thereafter. Not all pro–Soviet elements had been converted, by any means. But they could no longer say anything that sounded convincing even to themselves, and, for some years, lapsed into a sullen silence.[4]

It has been well said that the American decision to intervene in Korea must have been one of the biggest shocks of Stalin's life. He instantly became more cautious, canceling the attack on Yugoslavia. According to Khrushchev, he removed the Soviet advisers from the North Korean forces. (If they left, however, they soon returned). The Soviet press did not mention events in Korea until June 26, and then merely quoted North Korean reports. On June 28, Pravda condemned Truman's actions as "overt acts of aggression" and maintained that the Security Council's actions were unjustified. Why Stalin let the Soviet boycott go on is unclear. His advisers begged him to change policy, but he did not act. He may just have been unable to make up his mind. But he may have calculated that the Americans would go forward whatever happened in the UN, while a UN framework might inhibit them from taking drastic actions and discourage the Americans from declaring war. If so, it is likely that his decision was well-taken.

By June 29, Stalin evidently decided on a characteristic course of cautious aggression. Presumably he concluded that the North Koreans still had a chance to win, and the war could be safely continued. He would even encourage Kim when the Korean Communists showed signs of losing their nerve. But there would be no Soviet intervention or major moves elsewhere. Early that day, the Soviets answered the note the Americans had sent on June 27. The Soviet reply set the basic Communist "line" on the war. It flatly blamed the South Koreans and "those who stand behind their backs" for the war, and described it as a civil war, grumbling that "the Soviet Government adheres to the impermissibility of interference by foreign powers in the internal affairs of Korea." It asserted that the UN's actions lacked legal force because the Soviets had not been present in the Security Council. While hostile enough, the note contained no specific threats or warnings. Until July 3, the Soviet press gave little coverage to the Korean War. Then the Soviets began a violent propaganda attack on the Americans and Secretary-General Lie. Beyond keeping the North Koreans supplied, the Soviets took no active part in the war. Stalin rejected Khrushchev's advice that Marshal Rodion Malinovsky take command of the Communists and even reinforce them with a Soviet corps if necessary. The first idea was a good one, while the latter move would have ended the

Korean War — and started World War III. Stalin treated the attempts made by the British and Indians to arrange a peace move with contempt. He was already thinking, however, about what might happen if things went badly wrong. On July 5, he sent a message to the Chinese encouraging them to intervene if that became necessary. He approved their plans to transfer troops to Manchuria to back up the North Koreans and promised to try to supply air cover if they intervened.

Chinese newspapers, with one exception, did not mention the war until June 27. They treated events in Korea along the same lines as the Soviets, but reacted far more violently to Truman's announcement on June 27. The neutralization of Taiwan was "armed aggression against China," and the Americans had allegedly ordered Rhee to attack to provide a pretext for this action and further aggressions aimed at seizing all of Asia. The Chinese leaders were enraged at seeing Taiwan put beyond their reach. At first they followed the same basic policy as Stalin: support for the North Koreans, but no open intervention in the war-yet.

As early as July 2, Zhou Enlai, Mao's chief lieutenant, told Soviet Ambassador Roschin that he thought the "North Koreans" had underestimated the danger of American intervention, politely and prudently ascribing Stalin and Mao's misjudgments to others. He warned of the danger that the Americans would land at Inchon, behind the Communist front, and said that if American forces crossed the 38th Parallel China would intervene albeit disguising its troops as Koreans. It is important to note that the Chinese leaders from the start seem to have consistently assumed that if the war turned in their favor, the UN forces would try to overrun North Korea. The Chinese "postponed" the attack on Taiwan, already delayed to 1951, on June 30. On July 10 it was formally put off until 1952. On July 7, a conference chaired by Zhou recommended creating a Northeast Border Defense Army for possible intervention in Korea. The 13th Army Group of the 4th Field Army, the best part of the Chinese Army, would be redeployed to Manchuria to form the core of the new command, which would absorb the 42nd Army that was already there. A new headquarters would replace the Army Group's existing one. Mao formally approved these steps on July 13. Sometime in July or August, the Chinese ordered their antiaircraft units at Dandong in Manchuria to move to Sinuiju, just across the Yalu in Korea, to defend the most critical crossings of the river.[5]

The Soviet note of June 29 was evidence for the growing belief of American officials that the Soviets would stay out of the war and probably would not strike elsewhere. Consultants to the National Security Council, meeting that day, generally agreed that the greatest dangers were of

Soviet attacks on Yugoslavia, Iran or West Germany. But George Kennan argued cogently that the Soviets would not move in Germany or Iran unless they were ready for general war. He was not impressed by the danger to Yugoslavia either. The meeting agreed that the United States should not intervene if the Soviets attacked Yugoslavia. This last opinion would be generally held throughout the U.S. government during the Korean War era. Concealing that tentative decision from the Soviets so as not to encourage Stalin to overrun Yugoslavia would cause a lot of anxiety during the war.

General Eisenhower, while visiting Washington, warned that if ground forces were used in Korea mobilization would be needed. He held that the use of atomic bombs should be considered if suitable targets could be found, and advised against putting MacArthur, whom he had long disliked, in command (so did John Foster Dulles). During June 29, the military concluded that more was needed to save South Korea. The Secretary of Defense called for a new meeting of the National Security Council. At the quickly arranged meeting, Truman approved air and naval operations against North Korea, and sending an infantry regimental combat team as well as service forces to protect the Pusan area, still far from the battle line. That evening, Jiang Jieshi offered 33,000 Nationalist Chinese troops for service n Korea. Truman was tempted to accept, but Acheson warned that it was incongruous to take troops from Taiwan while the United States was defending it. He also suspected that the force would have to be re-equipped and would be more trouble than it was worth, anticipating the judgment of the Joint Chiefs of Staff.

On June 28–29, General MacArthur visited Korea. Enroute there he ordered the Air Force to attack North Korean airfields even before Washington authorized this action. Visiting the battle area on June 29, he concluded that only American ground forces could stop the enemy. He flatly, and unfairly, insisted that the South Koreans had not "seriously fought;" more accurately, he indicted their leadership, pointing out that they had made no preparations for defense in depth or a supply system. They had lost their heavy weapons, although the soldiers had mostly retained their personal weapons, and the people were anti–Communist. The effective ROK strength was no more than 25,000 men. It was problematical whether a Han river line could be held. He wanted to immediately send an American regimental combat team to hold the important airfield at Suwon and provide for a buildup to a force of two American divisions for an early counteroffensive. No one questioned these recommendations. On June 30, the President agreed to commit ground forces to Korea on a large scale — just in time — and to a naval blockade of North Korea. He declined the offer of Nationalist Chinese troops since Acheson warned that it might provoke or tempt the Chinese Communists to intervene. The Joint Chiefs doubted their effectiveness and thought that the transportation they would require would be better used by American forces. (MacArthur did not want them either, though he would change his mind in November.)

Truman justified his actions as the use of his inherent powers as commander-in-chief in order to support the UN. He did not seek a declaration of war against North Korea. The administration pondered asking Congress for a joint resolution to support its actions, but finally drew back. The Democratic leaders in Congress were unenthusiastic, and it was thought that a message to Congress would worsen a wave of panic buying. It has sometimes been suggested that the failure to declare war or secure a joint resolution was a bad mistake, but it is hard to see that it made any difference. Although Taft and others later revived charges that Truman's actions were unconstitutional, the public was unimpressed. It never became a major issue.[6] In contrast to the situation during the Second Indochina War, the main topic of debate during the Korean War was not whether it was illegal or immoral, but how it should be fought.

Nor was Truman's decision to enter the war truly a radical departure from previous policies, as some have suggested. While almost a reversal of policy toward Korea itself—although it should be emphasized that the United States had never made a clear-cut decision to write that country off—to Truman it was a part of the pattern of containment. The United States was filling a gap in the line left by its own blunders. The reality of the North Korean attack had instantly shocked not just the administration but practically everyone else into realizing that Korea was not just a symbol but of strategic importance, even if it was not absolutely and immediately vital. It was also evident that to let the attack go unchallenged would discredit the UN, this was important to the president and others, although probably not to Acheson, and that it was desirable to cover the American action in a UN mantle. Only in the long run did it become apparent that the UN role was something of a two-edged sword. Its involvement in the Korean War was certainly a propaganda and morale boon to the democracies. Yet, it was also an historical fluke, the result of a Soviet blunder that would never recur, and it invested the UN with an aura of credibility and effectiveness that it did not deserve. At certain points, the need to maintain a consensus in the UN would help restrain the Americans from militarily desirable actions— such as a blockade of China — that they might otherwise have taken as a matter of course. The overwhelming burden of the war fell on the South Koreans and Americans. Only the British Commonwealth contributed a really substantial force — ultimately constituting a reinforced infantry division, as well as air and naval forces, to the UN Command. However, the small forces—only battalion-sized—provided by the French and Dutch would along with the Commonwealth units on some occasions in early 1951 play a role in the fighting out of proportion to their size. Better trained than most U.S. units, they provided reinforcements at a crucial time.

4

The Defense of South Korea

The Americans entered the Korean War with a priceless asset; a base in Japan right next to Korea, and the support of Japan's people and industry. Most Japanese fully supported the United States and the UN, and regarded the defeat of the Communists as in Japan's national interests. Although defending Japan from outside attack would be a major worry for the Americans, MacArthur could safely remove almost all his forces from what nominally was still an occupied country without much anxiety about internal troubles there.

That was a good thing since in other respects the American position was a weak one. Despite the intensification of the Cold War, the armed services, recently "unified" under the new Department of Defense, had limped along with very low budgets. "Unification" and quarrels over the budget had left much bitterness between the generals and admirals. Although the Air Force was the centerpiece of American defense, even it was not all that strong; neither it nor the other services were ready to fight a conventional war. The Air Force had necessarily concentrated on getting the Strategic Air Command ready for all-out war with the USSR, but it had only recently been whipped into shape by General LeMay. The rest of the Air Force's resources were devoted largely to "counter-air" missions— air defense and gaining air superiority. There was little left for tactical air support of ground forces. Only the new F-86—and no other Western fighter at all—would be a match for the Soviet MIG-15 the Americans would meet in Korea.

The U.S. Navy had its own problems. Its carrier air arm was still largely propeller-driven. Its relatively few under-powered, straight-wing jet fighters were inferior to the MIG, and operating jets off World War II-style straight-deck carriers was difficult and dangerous. However, the pilots of the Navy and Marine propeller-driven Skyraider and Corsair attack planes were better-trained than their USAF counterparts in attacking ground targets. The Skyraider had the unique ability to deliver 2,000-pound bombs with some precision, which would be invaluable against bridges and some other targets. The Navy also was seriously short of minesweepers, which would be a problem in Korea.

The U.S. Army was in bad shape. It had suffered more from tight budgets than the other services. It was small, poorly trained and had little new equipment. A GI who had left the Army in 1945 would have seen that its weapons had changed very little, except that recoilless rifles had replaced antitank guns and the howitzers of the former cannon companies. Most of its tanks were still Shermans, obsolescent even in 1944. New model tanks, radios and self-propelled artillery were scarce. Since 1945 procurement had been limited to food, clothing and medical supplies. Many details of the infantry division's organization had changed, but they were often nominal since the divisions were understrength. Most infantry regiments had been reduced to two instead of the normal three battalions; artillery units had been similarly trimmed. The Army suffered from an odd weakness that could easily have been avoided. A small force that should have had plenty of young field-grade officers with combat experience was largely commanded at divisional and regimental level by men who had held training commands or staff positions in World War II, or who were old and in poor health. Yet another weakness was also self-inflicted. Unlike the Air Force and Navy, the Army had dragged its feet about executing Truman's 1948 order desegregating the armed forces. Black soldiers were still segregated, with the same malign effects as in World War II. Black units were often overstrength and suffered from low morale while neighboring white units needed men. As a result, they were unreliable. This would seriously impair the Army's effectiveness in the first year of the Korean War.

Big improvements had taken place in one field, however—care for the wounded. Helicopter evacuation, pushing forward surgery in the new Mobile Army Surgical Hospitals (MASH) and new antibiotics—only penicillin had been available in World War II—drastically reduced the number of deaths among wounded men in Korea.

MacArthur had four of the Army's 10 active divisions—the 7th, 24th and 25th Infantry Divisions and the 1st Cavalry Division (an infantry unit retaining the "cavalry" designation out of tradition), in the Eighth Army under General Walton Walker. It was considerably weaker than the five full-strength divisions MacArthur deemed a minimum force. In 1949, he had fought fiercely to prevent his command from being cut further. Despite a training program begun in 1949, they were still poorly trained as well as ill-equipped. The few medium tanks in Japan had been mothballed; each division had just a single company of light tanks. Things would have been even worse except for the use of Japanese civilians to perform functions usually carried out by soldiers and an immense salvage project MacArthur had launched in 1947, using Japanese industry to rebuild equipment salvaged from Pacific battlefields. The Eighth Army owed most of its equipment to this program. Yet MacArthur, preoccupied with occupation matters, does not seem to have realized how badly trained the Army was.

MacArthur was not an unmixed blessing. He has been well-described by Samuel B. Griffith as "an imaginative, bold and decisive general," but also as "arrogant, ambitious, vain and stubborn." His besetting fault as a commander was that he was apt to become fixated on the development of his own plans and was prone, as Napoleon put it, to "make a picture" of what would happen, assuming that things would go just as he planned and expected. This had contributed to defeat in the Philippines in 1941–1942 and would lead him to disaster later in 1950. He had a deserved reputation as a "political general" and for being occasionally slippery. He nursed hopes, never soundly based, of being elected president, although there was ample evidence that even people who liked him would not vote for him. His politics though have often been confused with that of the right-wing Republicans who, not always honestly, professed to admire and support him. As his conduct of the occupation of Japan should have shown, he was not, as is widely supposed, a conservative, but an old-fashioned Progressive Republican, temperamentally at odds with the New Dealers but perhaps not all that different from them.

His views on foreign affairs were "interventionist," but unlike most interventionists he was a Pacific-firster. These things, along with his genuinely hard-line attitude in the Cold War and his recognition that, contrary to China bloc dogma, the Chinese Communists were not just Soviet puppets, put him at odds with his real and nominal Republican supporters, some of whom were diehard isolationists.

Attitudes to MacArthur varied, then and later, from worship to violent hostility. He could be an eloquent speaker, but could also come across as pompous, humorless and boastful. In 1950, his prestige was enormous. Apart from his considerable genuine achievements during World War II and the occupation of Japan, most ordinary Americans tended to suppose that he had played an even bigger role in these things than he actually had. The truth was that his theater had been secondary compared to that of the Navy; it was Admiral Nimitz's drive across the Central Pacific that had been the prime factor in the defeat of Japan, and in the Occupation he had been executing, not making, policy. While still popular at home, and with

Australians, Filipinos, and Japanese, he was, however widely disliked by rank and file American servicemen (and Truman.) Most senior officers who had worked with or under him admired him, although there were significant exceptions, the most notable being General Eisenhower. MacArthur himself lacked faith in his chief subordinate, Walton Walker — unfairly since Walker, one of Patton's best corps commanders in World War II, was a very capable man.

The Far East Air Force, under General George Stratemeyer — its core was the Fifth Air Force based in Japan — was somewhat better off than the Army. But its mission was to defend Japan, and it was not in good shape to support a land campaign in Korea. Only 553 of its 1,172 planes were actually operational. Most were short-ranged F-80 Shooting Star interceptors that could use only four airfields in Japan and none in Korea. There was also a light bomber wing and a few squadrons of propeller-driven F-82 Twin Mustang all-weather fighters. Production of large auxiliary fuel tanks to extend the F-80's range had just begun, and the pilots had little training in navigation or ground attack. Some air units would be tied down in defense of Japan and Okinawa, although in practice priority was given to the Korean campaign — which badly needed support since the Eighth Army remained short of artillery for many months. The Navy in the Far East amounted to a single carrier task force, which the Chief of Naval Operations had maintained at the expense of shore establishments. It and the Far East Air Force had suffered sharp cuts just before the war, and the Pacific commands were due for further cuts during the coming fiscal year. The Pacific naval commander, Admiral Arthur Radford, later wrote that had the North Koreans waited until June 1951 to strike, American forces in the region would have been too weak to intervene. The British Commonwealth Occupation Force had already left Japan, except for an Australian fighter squadron that was about to depart when the war started. The British Far Eastern fleet was undermanned, and its sole carrier was small and in bad shape with obsolete, short-ranged planes. But the Americans would welcome the Royal Navy. They needed all the help they could get.[1]

Underestimating the North Koreans, MacArthur hoped that the ROKs and an American regimental combat team could delay them near Suwon while he brought in two full American divisions. They would launch a counteroffensive while a third division landed at Inchon to cut off the enemy's supplies and retreat. He did not yet realize that it would be a feat to hold any line in Korea at all. It would take several days for American ground forces to reach the battlefront. In late June and the first part of July, everything depended on the ROKs, the USAF, the U.S. carrier *Valley Forge* and the British carrier *Triumph*.

Delaying Action

The North Koreans crossed the Han in force only on June 30. Their difficulty in getting their tanks and guns over the river probably cost them their best chance to overrun all of Korea. Fighting without tanks, they met tough resistance in Seoul's industrial suburb of Yongdungpo, south of the Han, and their best units suffered heavy losses. Repairing a railroad bridge and decking it over so tanks could use it was delayed by air attacks. Vehicles and equipment jammed around the bridges were hit hard. Yongdungpo was finally taken on July 3 when T-34s finally clanked over the repaired railroad bridge. The next day the North Koreans finally started south for Suwon. Kim Il Sung is known to have been extremely perturbed by delays on the central front as well. Ambassador Shtykov reported to Stalin as early as July 1 that North Korean morale had been shaken by America's intervention and the bombing (which had just started) of the North. Over the next week, Stalin acceded to Kim's request for more Soviet advisers and material for the equivalent of two more divisions. The Soviets made clear that they thought that the newly equipped troops should be used to replace losses in existing units. But Kim insisted on forming more and more new divisions instead, a folly which he pursued until 1951. Simultaneously, Stalin was endorsing Chinese preparations and promising air cover for a Chinese intervention in Korea.

The Fifth Air Force was operating at extreme range from its Japanese bases. Its jets could spend little time at the front, and operations were badly coordinated, too often hitting South Korean forces by mistake. But in late June and early July, it inflicted considerable losses and delays on the Communists. As yet not well equipped with antiaircraft weapons, they recklessly bunched together and tried to keep moving during the day. The Americans quickly won control of the air. The North Koreans' planes were shot down or smashed on the ground; they were soon reduced to small hit and run attacks they tried to time to coincide with the absence of U.S. jets. Even though the opposition in the air was feeble, the Americans had some serious problems. By July 7, enemy fire made low-level attacks by light bombers too costly, although this tactic was used once or twice later against especially profitable targets. The F-82 all-weather fighters, which were scarce and precious, were withdrawn from combat the same day. Also on July 7, realizing that Korean targets were just too far for jets based in Japan, the Americans began converting six jet fighter squadrons back to propeller-driven F-51 Mustangs, which had a longer range and could fly from Taegu in Korea. The enemy advance, however, would make using Taegu difficult. Control of the sea around Korea was never an issue. On July 2, the PT boats of the tiny North Korean Navy were sunk when an attempt to run a supply convoy down the east coast ran into an Anglo-American force of cruisers and destroyers.[2]

MacArthur fed in the U.S. 24th Division piecemeal to delay the enemy as far north as possible. Although rated the least combat-ready division in Japan, it had been selected simply because it was stationed closest to Korea. The result was a costly series of delaying actions in which the outnumbered Americans did not perform well and perhaps were lucky to escape complete destruction. Some critics have held that MacArthur and Walker should not have tried to fight forward of the Kum river, or even a line farther south and east. But meeting the enemy advance on the Seoul-Taejon-Taegu axis did help save the ROKs and imposed important delays on the enemy.

Task Force Smith, comprised of two rifle companies of the 1st Battalion, 21st Infantry Regiment totaling 540 men, took up a position at Osan on the main north-south route. They were equipped with some heavy weapons and a battery of 105-mm howitzers, with a few antitank shells that were the only available effective antitank weapons. On July 5, the enemy spearhead met Task Force Smith. A column of 33 tanks, dashing far ahead of the enemy infantry, drove right into the American position. The Americans found that their old, small bazookas were worthless. One officer fired 22 rockets at a T-34 with no effect. One howitzer, sited as an antitank gun with the only antitank shells, stopped two tanks before it was knocked out. Regular high-explosive shells broke the tracks of two more T-34s and stopped them; others appeared to have been damaged and limped away. The rest drove on through to the south, having killed 20 Americans and destroyed many vehicles. The shaken Americans pulled themselves together.

An hour later, the main North Korean force arrived: two regiments of the 4th Division led by three more tanks and a truck convoy. Apparently the first column had not bothered to tell them the Americans were there. They were taken by surprise, and American mortars and .50-caliber machineguns destroyed the leading enemy trucks. But, supported by the tanks, the enemy infantry quickly attacked, outflanking the Americans on both sides. The Americans were soon forced to withdraw in disorder, abandoning all their heavy weapons. Around 150 men were killed, wounded or missing, although a few of the missing avoided capture and trickled into the American lines over the next few days.

General William Dean, the 24th Division's commander, was still bent on trying to hold well forward. He hoped to hold a line at Pyongtaek where there was a bottleneck between mountains and the sea, just before the peninsula broadened to the west. This hope proved in vain. There was a series of grim, costly delaying actions in which the American infantrymen were supported only by a few M-24 light tanks that were in poor condition and no match for the T-34s. The Americans were badly trained and in poor physical shape, facing an expert enemy. Five out of six were youngsters, the rest World War II veterans. They were unprepared for long marches over bad roads and climbing steep hills in a hot, filthy and rugged countryside. The summer of 1950 was even hotter than usual and the men staggered through 100 degree plus days. On July 9 and 10, however, the Air Force wreaked particularly heavy destruction on enemy tanks and vehicles, especially where they had jammed up in front of a bridge blown by the retreating 34th Infantry Regiment. Finally the Americans fell back behind the Kum river. They had delayed two of the best North Korean divisions for just a few days at a high price, and had protected the flank of the ROK I Corps that was falling back to the east. The ROKS were sideslipping east into mountainous areas where they were less vulnerable to enemy tanks. They still faced the bulk of the enemy army.

By the end of the first week in July, MacArthur lost any illusions that beating the North Koreans would be easy. On July 7, he warned Washington that the enemy was well led and equipped. He declared that his command would have to be raised to four or four and a half full-strength divisions with supporting units. This required sending 30,000 men from the United States at once. On July 9, he *doubled* this estimate, asking for a whole new army of four more divisions. The following day he submitted a long list of requirements for supporting units, which he must have known would be impossible to fulfill. But every kind of reinforcement was rushed to his command. When the Air Force and Army Chiefs of Staff visited Tokyo on July 13, MacArthur praised the enemy's toughness, ability to march, maneuver and attack at night, and rated their use of tanks as effective as that of the Soviet Army. He had to discard his early hopes of mounting an early landing at Inchon with the 1st Cavalry Division. It would have to follow the 24th and 25th Divisions to the front in southern Korea. But he still intended to mount an amphibious operation against the enemy rear.[3]

After the shattering air attacks of early July, the North Koreans were now moving at night and in bad weather, preferably over back roads and trails rather than main roads, and hiding by day. Their tanks operated in small groups, and they hid their gear and supplies in railroad tunnels.

The 24th Division had already been badly battered before the Communists' 3rd and 4th Divisions hit the Kum river line on July 14. The 4th Division broke through the 34th Infantry Regiment on the left, overrunning a whole artillery battalion. The Communists had a surprising amount of difficulty dealing with the 19th Infantry on the right, even though it was holding an extraordinarily wide front of 30 miles and its flank was exposed. The North Korean 3rd Division got around its flank to block the American regiment's main supply route while also breaking through its center. A counterattack had some success against the Communists' frontal assault, but the Americans could not dislodge the roadblock behind them, although many men got out around it.

Taejon, a major road and rail center where five highways met, was now the next target. Dean, whose division now had little more than the effective strength of a regiment and whose communications were poor, did not want to defend Taejon. But on July 19 Walker urged him to try to hold it for two days to give him more time to bring up the 1st Cavalry Division, which had reached Korea the previous day. Dean's division was at least getting the new 3.5-inch bazooka, which could deal with the T-34s. It was being flown across the Pacific. The result was a desperate battle, which would have been even worse had the Communists' 2nd Division reached the battlefield in time to participate as it was supposed to. Dean's 21st Regiment held on the right while the 34th Infantry held the left. The 2nd Battalion, 19th Infantry Regiment was in reserve in the city. The American southern flank was wide open.

As the 3rd North Korean Division approached from the north along the main highway from Seoul to Pusan, the 4th Division came from the north and west. Two of its regiments and most of the supporting tanks swung south on a wide outflanking sweep. Most of this force drove up the Nonsan road that entered Taejon from the southwest, while part cut the road running from Taejon southeast toward Kumsan. The Americans discovered the force attacking up the Nonsan road and moved to stop it, but did not realize that the Kumsan road had been cut. The frontal attack by the rest of the 4th Division and the 3rd Division on July 20 scattered two battalions west of Taejon and penetrated into the city. Dean and his regimental commanders were unable to communicate with their units and had little control over what was happening. In fighting inside Taejon, bazooka men — Dean himself led one bazooka team — knocked out quite a few T-34s, but the pressure was too great. Moreover, the Communists had cut the road east to Okchon, the main U.S. supply route and line of withdrawal. The Americans did not know this and found the block on the Kumsan road only as they tried to leave. Again the enemy roadblock could not be eliminated. Many men got out on foot, mostly in small groups. Dean, trying to leave via the Kumsan road, was separated from other Americans. He wandered through the countryside for 36 days before being captured. He spent the rest of the war as a prisoner. In all 1,150 men had been lost of just under 4,000 defending Taejon. The 24th Division was no longer fit to fight.[4]

The North Koreans continued their main attack down the Taejon-Taegu road, strongly supported by converging attacks down the central corridor from Wonju. The latter and the North Korean 5th Division's attacks down the east coast were opposed by the ROKs. The 5th Division might have advanced faster and farther, and even reached Pusan, but sent one of its regiments on an aimless, circuitous move through the inland mountains that simply wasted time and effort. At the other end of the front, the Communists' 6th Division on July 11 set out on a wide outflanking movement, driving almost unopposed though southwest Korea to attack Pusan from the west. Whether this was a clever maneuver that nearly succeeded — it certainly caused the Eighth Army a great deal of trouble — or a decisive blunder that deprived the main thrust down the Taejon-Taegu axis of the strength to break through is still argued. Fortunately, the 6th Division wasted time occupying all the small ports of southwestern Korea.

The ROKs were now consolidated into five divisions under two corps headquarters, numbering perhaps 60,000 men. MacArthur on July 17 estimated that they really had only the means to support four divisions, although he became more optimistic over the next three weeks. The South Koreans hastily refilled their ranks using a system that resembled a press gang rather than a conventional draft. They grabbed men right off the street and gave them *ten days of training*— sometimes less— before sending them into combat. In the fall of 1950, they succeeded in increasing the training cycle to 16 days. Western observers were often acidly critical of the performance of most ROK units (the 1st Division under the much-admired and extremely able Paik Sun Yup was universally admitted to be an exception) especially against the Chinese, but the real surprise was that the South Koreans fought as well as they did in 1950 and 1951. It was not generally realized, even by most American officers, that not only were ROK soldiers hardly trained, but that a ROK division in terms of actual fighting strength (and certainly of heavy weapons) was really the equivalent not of an American division but of a regimental combat team.

Despite the Communists' mistakes, the advance on the east coast was extremely dangerous, threatening the port of Pohang, the nearby Yonil airfield where American Mustangs were based, and the east-west lateral communications behind the ROK front. MacArthur had to cancel the plan to land the 1st Cavalry Division at Inchon, but it nevertheless went ashore in an amphibious assault at Pohang in case the North Koreans had reached it first. They did not, so the landing was unopposed. But the American division had to bolster the ROK coastal sector instead of heading for the central front as planned.

On July 23, American planes finally spotted the 6th Division's move on Pusan. Walker had the Air Force launch a major air effort against it. At his wit's end to find troops to stop it, he sent the still recuperating 24th Division and the independent 29th Regiment, recently arrived from Okinawa and hastily filled out with 400 raw recruits to the southwest. The 29th Regiment advanced to block the coastal route to Pusan, only to run into a terrible ambush at Hadong on July 26. It suffered tremendous losses.

On July 31, Walker made the long-expected decision to fall back across the Naktong river into the Pusan perimeter for a final stand. This move was completed on August 4. The Perimeter formed a rough rectangle in southeast Korea. Its northern face, about 50 miles long, ran through mountains and was held by ROKs. The longer western front, about 100 miles long, ran through more open terrain from the Taegu area south, and was held mostly by American units. The Naktong river covered most of the western front except near the coast. It was wide — 1,300 to 2,500 feet — but shallow; and there were many places where it could be waded. It is often said that the UN force now enjoyed a "continuous front," but this is not entirely true. The front was a very long one for the forces available; American divisions on the Naktong normally held stretches of line 20 or even 40 miles wide. The American units manned a thin screen of hilltop strong points overlooking the Naktong, which acted as observation posts from which to call down artillery and mortar fire and air strikes on enemy troops trying to cross. Most of the troops were kept well back to counterattack any penetration. Still, the American units were now at least in rough alignment. They knew where they were and that they had some support somewhere on each flank, which was more than they had known before. As successive threats appeared, Walker would race about by cub plane and jeep from crisis to crisis. If the Pusan Perimeter was cracked, MacArthur intended to have Eighth Army fall back to the "Davidson Line," a small beachhead around Pusan. There, he was sure naval gunfire and air support would enable the UN force to withstand anything the Communists could throw at them. He did not believe that the Americans in the last resort could be forced to evacuate. Others were not so sure, and fighting out of such a narrow toehold was not an enticing prospect.[5]

The retirement across the Naktong was the occasion for a major tragedy at Waegwan on August 3. As the 1st Cavalry Division pulled back, it prepared to demolish railroad and highway bridges there. But the huge crowds of refugees fleeing the Communists could not be stopped. Twice the Americans halted the demolition to shoo them away, but when the soldiers fell back the refugees came on again. Finally the last bridge was blown with many people still on it, and hundreds were killed. This was only the most spectacular instance of one of the most horrible features of the early part of the Korean War: the havoc wrought on refugees and those civilians who stayed behind Communist lines. Already, by mid-July, 380,000 refugees had passed through the shaky UN lines, and 25,000 more followed each day. Communist troops often used the cover of refugee movements to infiltrate the allied line, sometimes donning civilian clothes and sneaking through, sometimes using the refugees as a human shield and herding them at gunpoint across minefields, posing nightmarish dilemmas to the defending soldiers. The North Koreans, with their road and rail transportation coming under heavy attack, made increasing use of impressed South Korean porters. They could carry 44 pounds of supplies and march 12 to 20 miles a day. Sometimes teams of ten carried a half ton of supplies slung in nets on shoulder-supported poles. This, and the Communist habit of hiding tanks and men in villages during the day, led to the deaths of many civilians enroute to and near the battlefront as U.S. planes bombed and strafed villages and supply columns. Walter Karig's semi-official contemporary account described Navy and Marine pilots coming "back to their ships stinking of the vomit twisted from their vitals by the shock of what they had to do."

By early August the UN position was better than it seemed. The Army's 2nd Division and the 1st Marine Brigade (built around the 5th Marine Regimental Combat Team), which were in far better shape than the occupation units had been, arrived from America along with enough men and weapons to bring Walker's older divisions up to strength. The Marines became Walker's fire brigade. Only one U.S. division, the 7th, depleted by transfers to other units, remained in Japan. MacArthur kept it as a final reserve, which he hoped to use in his planned amphibious counterstrike. The reinforcements and heavy losses the North Koreans had suffered—far higher than anyone on the UN side yet realized, since the ROKs had fought much harder than was generally credited—had tipped the balance of forces. The UN side now numbered 92,000 ground combat troops against only about 70,000 North Koreans. There were now plenty of medium Pershing and Patton tanks to deal with the T-34s. Walker also was assisted by the reading of low-level enemy codes.

An effort that was to last for the whole of the war, the air "interdiction" of enemy supply lines chiefly aimed at railroad marshalling yards and bridges far to the rear was becoming effective. The Americans concentrated on cutting traffic south of a line running across Korea north of and including Seoul. Far East Air Force Bomber Command, reinforced from one to five B-29 wings, concentrated on marshalling yards and important bridges, while Fifth Air Force fighter-bombers and Navy planes went after other bridges. Fighters relentlessly hunted trains and trucks, which soon moved only at night. During August, the enemy suffered from a growing shortage of supplies, although they could not be choked off completely. Bridges, as in World War II, were difficult targets. Long and narrow, they were hard to hit at all. Many bombs did not hit the supports and cause major damage, but merely tore holes in the decking that were easily repaired. The main railroad bridge over the Han at Seoul was a particularly difficult target. The air commanders celebrated when combined B-29 and naval attacks finally caused it to collapse on the night of August 19–20. The North Koreans showed great ingenuity and determination at keeping supplies moving. They were remarkably good at repairing bridges and building "underwater" bridges (artificial fords) across shallow streams and sometimes laid tracks on log caissons as substitutes for destroyed bridges. They threw a special "night-only" pontoon bridge over the Han. It was assembled after dusk and taken apart before each dawn, its parts carefully concealed. Trains were hidden by day and shuttled over very short stretches of open track. Railroad tracks were camouflaged. The Communists managed to get trains as far south as Chonui. From there trucks and porters took supplies forward.

Simultaneously, the Americans waged a strategic bombing campaign against North Korea. Some B-29 wings went after enemy industrial and transportation targets (which sometimes were identical with the "interdiction" targets) deep in the North. The B-29s, facing little air opposition or antiaircraft fire at this stage, bombed accurately from relatively low altitudes. They largely eliminated North Korea's war-supporting industries in a short time at little cost in life to either side. Washington had insisted that attacks on these targets be made carefully, using only high-explosive bombs by day, overruling suggestions that it would be quicker and cheaper to permit fire-bomb attacks via radar at night or in bad weather, like those against Japan in World War II. Ironically, the Americans received a lot of abuse for these attacks in Asia and even in Europe, while the toll of life taken by "tactical" bombing in South Korea went largely unnoticed. In a further irony that the Air Force did not appreciate, the most effective "strategic" attack of all was an almost impromptu attack by Navy carrier planes. On July 18, after finding that the Pohang landing did not need close air support, *Valley Forge* launched a strike against the oil refinery at Wonsan. A remarkably effective attack by a small force of Skyraiders and Corsairs completely destroyed the plant and thousands of tons of petroleum products, producing a grave fuel shortage.[6]

The First Battle of the Pusan Perimeter

Even as the UN forces contracted into the Pusan Perimeter, Walker discerned an opportunity for a counteroffensive in the southwest. There the units assembled to stop the 6th North Korean Division, now backed by the 83rd Motorized Regiment, could be reinforced to quickly crush the relatively isolated enemy force in that area, eliminating the most immediate threat to Pusan. Relatively strong forces were assembled under "Task Force Kean," named after the commander of the 25th Division. The Task Force included Kean's own division (minus the excellent 27th Infantry Regimental Combat Team, which Walker had removed to serve as a roving reserve for the Eighth Army), the Army's 5th Regimental Combat Team, the Marine brigade and a ROK regiment. The first UN offensive operation of the war began August 7. Three American regiments set out west, on three different roads. Two regiments would converge to seize Chinju Pass, then secure the line of the Nam river. The American attack coincided with the start of the North Korean August offensive in this sector. At first, the Americans made progress, but the (Army) 5th Regimental Combat Team made a turn onto the wrong road. The Marines, attacking along the coastal road, inflicted a heavy defeat on the 83rd Motorized Regiment with the help of their supporting Corsairs, but had to halt when things went awry elsewhere and they had to rescue a battalion of the 5th RCT. The North Koreans had succeeded in infiltrating between the 5th RCT and the regiment to its north. They overran two artillery battalions supporting the advance at a place that earned the name "Bloody Gulch." The Americans could not dislodge the North Koreans from high ground overlooking their main supply route. There was exceptionally bitter fighting. The black 24th Regiment, which had been supposed to mop up behind the advancing regiments, failed to do so. It was often poorly led, but the main problem was that black soldiers would generally not fight well when treated as segregated outcasts. Its repeated failures led Kean, on September 9, to urge Walker to disband the unit and use its men to fill up his "white" regiments.

Kean, the best divisional commander in Korea, did not make such a recommendation lightly. It is evident that Kean, who was backed by the capable commanders of his other regiments, had no misgivings about how black soldiers would fight when treated like everyone else. But his correct solution would not be adopted until 1951.

The counteroffensive had been a bad mistake, leaving the Americans off balance when the enemy began its major August offensive. This was a widely dispersed effort on no less than four fronts along the Perimeter, with the most important attacks coming on the Naktong front. The Communists failed to properly concentrate their forces, or more probably, could not because of American air attacks. The greatest threat developed in the "Naktong Bulge," where the Naktong swung a loop to the west. Here a relatively short advance to Miryang would cut the road and railroad between Taegu and Pusan. The Bulge was held by the still weak 24th Division, with the most crucial area a nine-mile stretch held by one battalion of the 34th Infantry Regiment. On the night of August 5–6, the Communist 4th Division began crossing at Ohang on the northern face of the Bulge. Another force, crossing seven miles farther north, was thrown back. But in the Bulge, the enemy succeeded in establishing a bridgehead. A counterattack by a reserve battalion had some success, but the enemy reinforced the bridgehead during the following two nights and took much of the critical high ground — Cloverleaf Hill and Obong-ni ridge — dominating the main east-west road in the Bulge. "Underwater bridges" were laid across the river. A regiment of the still fresh 2nd Division was brought in, and the Americans recaptured part of the ridge. Then they were thrown off it again. More enemy troops crossed and blocked the main supply road until dislodged by the 27th Infantry Regimental Combat Team. Continued fighting for the Cloverleaf and Obong-ni ridge exhausted both sides. Walker now sent in the Marines. On August 17, they attacked Obong-ni ridge, while the 2nd Division's 9th Infantry Regiment went for the Cloverleaf. The first Marine attack was stopped, as was a counterattack by North Korean tanks. On August 18, renewed attack took the ridge, and a push to the Naktong, eliminating the enemy bridgehead, proved relatively easy. The North Korean 4th Division had been wrecked.

Almost as threatening was the enemy attack on Taegu. It appears this was the Communists' *intended* main effort, though Walker deemed the Naktong Bulge attack more dangerous. Here five North Korean divisions had been assembled on a too widespread front of 40 miles (with most of the rest of the available tanks not committed in the Bulge) against the 1st Cavalry Division and two ROK divisions, the 1st and 6th. All three cavalry regiments were in line holding an exceptionally long front. The attack began against the ROKs north of Waegwan on the night of August 4–5. The ROKs were forced steadily back, but there was no enemy breakthrough. Early on August 9, the North Korean 3rd Division began crossing in the area held by the 5th Cavalry Regiment south of Waegwan. Although thrown back in some places, the enemy established a bridgehead and captured critical high ground, "Triangulation Hill" (Hill 268). A counterattack in terrible heat was repulsed, but on August 10 a renewed attack gained the hill. Artillery had inflicted enormous losses on the North Koreans. But the Cavalry Division's troubles were not over. On August 11–12, the North Korean 10th Division crossed the Naktong to the south, overrunning a company of the 7th Cavalry Regiment before being finally stopped. On August 14 there were two more crossings, one above and one below Waegwan. Very heavy artillery fire and air strikes helped the 7th Cavalry hurl back one attack, but the other secured a bridgehead above Waegwan, and a long hill mass, Hill 303, which gave the enemy observation of a long stretch of the Naktong valley. The American company holding Hill 303, was surrounded and could not be relieved, but managed to break out at night. After heavy artillery preparations and air strikes, Hill 303 was recaptured on August 17. Twenty-six Americans were found who had their hands tied and had then been shot. In the desperate fighting, the Americans had resorted to an expedient tried with occasional success in World War II — "carpet-bombing" — bringing in the heavy bombers usually devoted to attacks deep in the enemy rear to saturate enemy positions in the field with bombs. (In World War II this had been done to help break through enemy defenses rather than break up attacking concentrations.) On August 16, 98 B-29s (now technically rated "medium" bombers rather than super-heavies as in 1945) hit an area near Waegwan. The strike failed, though North Korean soldiers observing the colossal blasting from a safe distance found it depressing. In the Tabu-dong area, east of the Naktong, two North Korean divisions threatened to push through the ROKs down the road into Taegu. Fortunately, in an odd blunder, the enemy diverted one division to support the advance through the mountains on Pohang, while Walker ordered the 27th Regimental Combat Team to bolster the ROKs. While the excellent ROK 1st Division held the hills on either side, it took up a position astride the Sangju-Taegu road. Not far away, the road forked where Communist tanks could hide during the day. On the night of August 18–19, North Korean tanks, assault guns and infantry, strongly supported by artillery and mortars, began the first of seven night attacks down what became known as the "Bowling Alley." The Americans discovered that the North Koreans here used green flares to signal "attack," and they fired their own green flares to steer the enemy right into their main defensive position. Attack after attack was defeated, piling up 13 T-34s, seven assault guns, other vehicles and thousands of dead in front of the UN positions.

At the extreme ends of the front, the U.S. 25th Division held off a North Korean attack in the southwest. The ROKs had a hard fight in the northeast against three North Korean divisions that tried to break through in the coastal corridor and the mountains. Here the ROKs enjoyed the support of naval gunfire and American Mustangs based nearby on Yonil airfield. (Although the air units had to leave on August 13, they continued to use it to refuel.) The North Korean 5th Division managed to outflank and isolate the 3rd ROK Division in the coastal corridor. It was hemmed in a beachhead, but was successfully evacuated by American landing craft and disembarked farther down the coast, southeast of Pohang. The North Koreans were simply unable to keep their forces in the region supplied with food and ammunition, and withdrew. The North Korean August offensive had failed. Now they built up for one last heave. Stalin tried to cheer up Kim Il Sung. The Soviets, he suggested, had been in worse situations. He believed, or professed to believe, that the North Koreans would still win.

The September Offensive

By the beginning of September, the Communists had built up to a strength of 98,000 troops, but their combat effectiveness was a good deal less. A third of these men were new recruits, mostly drafted South Koreans. They had swollen the number of infantry divisions to 13, and had a nominal armored division and two new armored brigades, the latter actually equal in strength to weak tank battalions with about 40 new T-34s apiece. The Communists had managed to bring up a minimum of replacement tanks, artillery pieces and mortars, ammunition and gasoline, but were short of small arms and food. New trucks and clothing were unobtainable. The Communists rather desperately hoped that concentrating on night fighting and close-in infantry combat would neutralize the UN advantage in all types of firepower. The UN Command now had 122,000 combat troops and 500 tanks. The first non–American UN unit, the British 27th Brigade, had arrived. The Americans tried a rather unpromising expedient to fill up their still understrength units, incorporating South Korean soldiers known as, "KATUSAs" into American units. With rare exceptions, this did not work well. At best, the South Koreans were of some use at digging and hauling.

The North Korean "Great Naktong Offensive" began raggedly the night of August 31–September 1, with attacks in the southwest and the Naktong Bulge. Intercepted messages gave Walker part but not all of the enemy plan, while the Communists benefited from bad weather that hampered American air support. In desperate fighting the 25th Division, backed up by the return of its roving 27th Regiment, fought off the 6th and 7th North Korean Divisions. Just north, three North Korean divisions struck again at the 2nd Division in the Naktong Bulge. This unexpected move was the Communists' main effort and the scene of the worst crisis of the September battle. The weather, the surprise the enemy attained at the Naktong Bulge, the exhaustion of many defenders, and the Communists' stress on night and close combat made the early September fighting even bloodier than the August offensive. At times the Americans and ROKs were very worried.

The 9th Infantry Regiment, holding the most critical part of the front, was caught ill disposed. One of its companies was launching a probe across the Naktong. The Communists quickly took Obong-ni and the Cloverleaf, and split the 2nd Division in two. Only a scratch force of engineers, tanks, antiaircraft weapons and a reconnaissance company prevented them from reaching Miryang. The situation was desperate. Walker had to insist on using the 1st Marine Brigade, slated to join the 1st Marine Division for the Inchon landing, to restore things at the Naktong Bulge. The Marines counterattacked on September 4 and 5, and the enemy was quickly shoved back over the Naktong. The enemy did not strike at other sectors until the night of September 2–3 (in some places it was delayed still more). Three divisions struck the 1st Cavalry Division stretched on a 35-mile front before Taegu in an attack only less serious than that in the Naktong Bulge. The 7th Cavalry had attacked to try to divert the enemy from the south, and this and other mistakes left the division poorly deployed. The diversionary attack went badly, while the 8th Cavalry Regiment, holding the old "Bowling Alley," was hit hard on September 3. One of its battalions was overrun, and the Communists took both Tabu-dong and the important Hill 902 or Ka-san, crowned by the ruins of an old fortress the Americans misnamed "the Walled City." It overlooked much of the Naktong valley and things would have been worse if the enemy had possessed the artillery ammunition to take advantage of this. Desperate fighting followed. Provisional battalions of headquarters and technical personnel were formed to hold Taegu. Things were so bad that Walker considered pulling back to the Davidson Line, as terrified Koreans fled from Pusan to the island of Tsushima. An engineer company and E Company, 8th Cavalry tried to retake Ka-san, wrongly thought to be held by just 75 men but actually occupied by a whole enemy battalion. The engineers managed to slip up on the enemy and took up a position just below the crest. After two days of fierce fighting, the engineers were forced off the mountain, losing half their numbers. The whole 1st Cavalry Division was forced into a general withdrawal. The enemy now occupied Ka-san and a whole series of important hills and prepared to drive on Taegu. The Cavalry Division, its right flank protected by the ROK 1st Division against a North Korean attempt to outflank it, regrouped and counterattacked. A difficult battle ensued to retake enemy-occupied high ground. The ROK 1st Division gained Ka-san on September 15. On the northern front, the North Korean II Corps attacked the ROKs with four divisions. As in August, the Communists seem to have concentrated forces there that would have been better used in the Taegu sector, although they were actually harder to supply in the mountains than they would have been around Taegu. Local attacks in the north had already had some success in late August. The Communists struck on the morning of September 3, and the next night the whole northern front collapsed. The enemy penetrated at Kyongju and turned east, taking Pohang on the night of September 5–6. The U.S. 24th Division was rushed north to support the ROKs, who, as they would frequently do throughout the war, bounced back quickly. With American air support and naval gunfire, they continued to do most of the ground fighting in the north. The North Korean 8th and 12th Divisions were practically destroyed. Although hard fighting still raged in the Taegu sector on September 15, the North Koreans were beaten and exhausted as MacArthur's long-planned amphibious counterstroke fell on their rear.

The price of defending South Korea had been great. By September 15, American casualties alone totaled 19,165 — 4,280 killed, 12,377 wounded, of whom 319 later died, 401 were known captured, and no less than 2,107 missing. Many of the missing were still alive as prisoners, but would not return from the horrible Communist prisoner of war camps. ROK casualties are not accurately known but were far greater.[7]

The Politics of the War

While the battle for South Korea was fought out, feeble attempts had been made to arrange a political settlement of the war. On July 1, the British Ambassador in Moscow sounded out the Soviets about arranging a withdrawal of the North Korean forces, linking this to a change in American policy on Taiwan. Truman and Acheson refused to agree to what amounted to a trade of Taiwan for a withdrawal from South Korea, thinking that this would whet the Communist powers' appetites. In any case, Stalin regarded the proposal with contempt, scrawling the comment "impertinent" on the paper conveying the idea. India advanced a similar but vaguer proposal to China at the same time, sending a slightly different version of it to the Western powers. The Indians proposed that Beijing receive China's seat in the UN. Then the Soviet delegate, still engaged in a boycott, could return to the Security Council, and informal contacts between the Americans, Soviets and Chinese would explore the Korean problem. The Indians envisaged the solution as an immediate cease-fire followed by a Communist withdrawal to the 38th Parallel. Prime Minister Nehru sent the proposal in letters to Stalin and Acheson on July 13. Stalin accepted it; Acheson rejected it. The Americans objected to the whole idea of transferring the focus of attention from Korea to China and making a major concession just for the sake of opening discussions.

On August 1 the rotating chairmanship of the Security Council passed to the Soviets. They abruptly ended the boycott and returned to the Council. On August 4, the Soviet representative, Jacob Malik, introduced a new proposal that indicated a slightly greater willingness to make peace. It was now clear that Communist prospects on the battlefield were declining. Earlier, the Soviets had insisted that the Beijing government get nothing less than recognition as the legitimate occupant of China's seat in the UN; they now suggested that China merely be represented in some form at the Security Council. Representatives of both Korean governments would also be seated there to discuss the war; previously the Soviets had rejected the ROK government as illegitimate. But Malik rejected proposals that the North Koreans pull back to the 38th Parallel before talks began, and the Western powers showed little interest.[8]

MacArthur was lucky to be able to carry out his plans. He had already alienated Truman who had never had much use for him. Trouble developed over Taiwan rather than Korea. On July 31, MacArthur had gone to Taiwan to meet Jiang Jieshi. The two discussed arrangements for the defense of the island. MacArthur had informed the Joint Chiefs of Staff of the trip in advance and was not disobeying orders. But the administration, and especially Acheson, was nevertheless unhappy about the trip. The American leaders had no desire to be closely associated with Jiang or highlight the Taiwan issue, which involved a unilateral American policy and had the potential to split the United States from its allies. Moreover, MacArthur had not taken his State Department adviser with him and had delayed submitting a report about the meeting to Washington. These things fed unjustified suspicions that MacArthur had talked about political matters with Jiang or even had made some secret deal with him. Truman sent Averell Harriman to straighten out MacArthur about the basic features of his policy. However, a second and more serious incident followed. MacArthur had sent a message to the Veterans of Foreign Wars to be read at its convention on August 28. In it he played up the importance of Taiwan, grumbling that "nothing could be more fallacious than the threadbare argument by those who advocate appeasement and defeatism in the Pacific that if we defend Formosa we alienate continental Asia. Those who speak thus do not understand the Orient. They do not grant that it is in the pattern of the Oriental psychology to respect and follow aggressive, resolute and dynamic leadership, to quickly turn on a leadership characterized by timidity or vacillation, and they underestimate the Oriental mentality."

MacArthur had not cleared the message with the Defense or State Departments. General Frank Lowe, an assistant to Truman, had seen it in advance but ignored it as innocuous. Truman learned of it on August 26; but an attempt to get the message withdrawn was too late. Truman was furious, interpreting it (possibly wrongly), as a deliberate slap at him. The message certainly spoiled the effort to keep the Taiwan issue quiet and convince everyone that the United States only wanted to neutralize the island and had no ambitions there. Part of the speech, carelessly read or taken out of context, might suggest that the Americans wanted to use Taiwan as a military base. The U.S. Ambassador in the UN had just taken pains to refute Communist accusations about such plans. Asians also might not appreciate MacArthur's disquisitions about their supposedly special psychology. The embarrassment was worse because MacArthur's remarks coincided with several other unauthorized and even more irresponsible statements by American officials, as well as talk about "preventive war" outside the Administration.

On August 25, Secretary of the Navy Matthews spoke of beginning a war to compel cooperation for peace, remarking, "We would become the first aggressors for peace." On September 1, General Orvil Anderson, the commander of the Air War College, declared that the United States was already at war: "Give me the order to do it and I can break up Russia's five A-bomb nests in a week."

Anderson was fired, while Matthews was shunted off to become Ambassador to Ireland. Secretary of Defense Johnson, widely believed to have instigated Matthews' speech, was on the way out anyway. He was blamed for the lack of readiness of the armed forces (where he was deeply detested) and rightly suspected of intriguing with both the Republicans and the Chinese Nationalists. These episodes caused considerable embarrassment, and threatened to antagonize and worry the Chinese (though they do not seem to have affected Chinese decision-making, already hostile enough, in an important way.) Truman pondered replacing MacArthur as field commander in the Far East with Omar Bradley, leaving MacArthur in charge of the Occupation in Japan, but dropped the idea, perhaps because it seemed an excessive reaction, or was just too dangerous politically.[9]

5

Victory in South Korea

MacArthur planned to land in the enemy rear practically from the start of the war. Although several targets would be considered, from the first he focused on Inchon. A thrust from there could quickly retake Seoul and cut the enemy's main supply line. From a strategic point of view, this was so attractive as to be almost obvious. As noted earlier, Zhou Enlai spotted the possibility of a landing at Inchon almost as soon as MacArthur. But while strategy favored the idea, everything else was against it. Inchon involved so many practical difficulties that, MacArthur had a hard time getting the operation accepted. Among other things, it had to be planned and mounted in a fantastically short time for a major landing. Inchon involved a triple risk: First, that the formidable natural difficulties could be turned, by even a small defending force, into insuperable obstacles; second, that the forces withheld from the Pusan Perimeter to mount the landing would not make the difference between defeat and success there; third, that the Soviets would not attack a Japan stripped of the last remaining American ground forces. MacArthur's Chief of Staff Edward Almond, who wound up commanding Inchon, at one point remarked that "Inchon may have been the worst possible place we could bring in an amphibious assault, but it was also the only place where our assault would carry out its purpose: to cut off and destroy the enemy." Another officer remarked, "we drew up a list of every conceivable natural and geographical handicap, and Inchon had them all."

It was not, in fact, a good base because; it was too small and lacked enough piers. Only two narrow, easily mined, deep-water channels (just one suited for large ships) led from the open sea into the harbor. Tides at Inchon were tremendous; and much of the time the port was largely sealed off by impassable mud flats. The water was deep enough for tank landing ships (LSTs) to pass over the flats in daylight on just a few days a month. Even then, they would be stuck for hours before the water rose again and they could back out. A small fortified island, Wolmi, controlled the approaches to the inner harbor. There were no open beaches. The attackers would have to land in the city itself (population 250,000) after they vaulted over a sea wall. That feature alone horrified amphibious experts and was unpleasantly reminiscent of the disastrous Canadian attack on Dieppe in 1942. Landing at Inchon, in fact, meant "throwing away the book" and virtually ignoring most of the hard-won lessons of amphibious operations from World War II. Minefields, especially of the latest, hard-to-sweep mines, and well-manned shore batteries might make an attack on Inchon a disaster even if the defenders were relatively small in number. Everything depended on Inchon remaining very lightly defended. The Communists learning of the operation in advance, or even just taking serious precautions, was a nightmare for the Americans right up to September 15. Further, the deadline for Inchon was close. After September, the weather might well be too bad for it go forward on the next day the tides were right.

MacArthur had originally hoped to hold the North Koreans far north of the Pusan Perimeter and use the 1st Cavalry Division in an early landing at Inchon (Operation Bluehearts). It had quickly become clear this was not practical, and the Cavalry Division went to the Perimeter instead. So did the 2nd Division and the Marine Brigade, which MacArthur had hoped to use in a landing.

At that point, while MacArthur continued to aim at landing in the enemy rear, he may not have been dogmatic about Inchon as the target, although he expressed a preference for Inchon to General Collins when the Army Chief of Staff visited Tokyo in mid–July. Several alternatives were considered, including Wonsan and Chumunjin on Korea's east coast, and Chinnampo (the port of Pyongyang) and Kunsan on the west coast. The last place was 130 miles south of Inchon and was nearer the Pusan Perimeter. The beaches there were good, but MacArthur decided the routes inland were poor and a landing at Kunsan would just outflank the enemy, not cut him off. He settled on Inchon. Almond may have convinced MacArthur that he had been right the first time, but many people were tougher to win over.

The plan for the operation was finished by August 12; with September 15 the next suitable date. The 1st Marine Division would land on a two regiment front, drive inland to seize Kimpo airfield, cross the Han river and take Seoul. The Army's 7th Division, following it ashore, would wheel south to cover the right flank. The two divisions and Walker's forces, breaking out of the Pusan Perimeter, would trap the enemy between them. Selling the plan to the Navy, Marines and the Joint Chiefs of Staff took considerable time. Collins, who may have been unenthusiastic about any amphibious operation, had not liked Inchon when he first heard about it in July. Like the Navy, he was impressed by the horrendous tidal conditions. Oliver P. Smith, the very able commander of the Marine Division, was horrified at having to land in a built-up area. Even the principal planner, Admiral James Doyle, clearly disliked Inchon. He suggested a September 22 landing on open beaches at Posung-Myon, 20 miles south of Inchon. Undefended, it lacked the obstacles of Inchon. MacArthur's headquarters rejected this apparently highly attractive alternative because the area lacked a road net suited for heavy vehicles.

On August 19, General Collins returned to Tokyo, accompanied by the Chief of Naval Operations Admiral Forrest Sherman. Both were inclined to oppose an Inchon operation and preferred a landing at Kunsan. MacArthur had to use all his formidable theatrical talents to sell Inchon at meetings on August 23 and 24. Doyle's tepid endorsement was that "the best I can say is that Inchon is not impossible." In a memorable speech (which unfortunately was not properly recorded), MacArthur likened the plan to General Wolfe's capture of Quebec in 1759. He argued eloquently that the very difficulty of Inchon would assure that the enemy would continue to leave it without a proper defense. The enemy was so tied up around the Pusan Perimeter that it had nothing to spare for Inchon, and taking Seoul would assure a quick and decisive victory that would rock Communism in Asia. "The history of war proves that, nine times out of ten, an army has been destroyed because its supply line has been severed," MacArthur contended.

The amphibious landing was one of the most powerful weapons in the U.S. arsenal and should be used to strike deep. He convinced Collins and Sherman to let him go ahead, although it seems that Collins still preferred Kunsan. Doyle and the Marine generals had General Shepherd, who commanded all Marines in the Pacific, approach MacArthur to argue once more for Posung-Myon. Seemingly Admiral Sherman agreed, but he and Collins did not intervene. MacArthur turned the idea down.

On August 28, the Joint Chiefs formally approved the Inchon operation, but even then they were clearly uneasy. There was considerable criticism of MacArthur's command arrangements for Inchon. On August 26, he decided to form a new X Corps headquarters to control the operation and gave the command to Almond. Moreover, Almond would retain his position as MacArthur's Chief of Staff, although General Doyle Hickey would be acting Chief of Staff in his place. It was then expected that

Almond's tenure of command would be brief. After X Corps and Eighth Army joined up, the latter would take control of the Corps (or perhaps even dissolve the X Corps headquarters), and Almond would return to Tokyo and resume his post as Chief of Staff. There was much opposition to this. Many thought it a mistake to form X Corps at all. General Shepherd's experienced well-established Fleet Marine Force Pacific should get the job, as recommended by General Wright, MacArthur's chief planner. Others thought commanding a corps and acting as theater Chief of Staff was an impossible burden for one man. (Contrary to what is often supposed, however, Almond did not actually exercise power as Chief of Staff after taking over X Corps.) Lastly, there were considerable misgivings about Almond, one of the most controversial and interesting figures of the Korean War. There is no doubt that he was an extremely able staff officer and a valuable addition to the ingrown circle around MacArthur. His merits as a field commander were more arguable. General Matthew Ridgway, a good judge, shared MacArthur's high opinion of Almond and thought that he was the best corps commander in Korea. But Almond was a quarrelsome individual widely disliked in the Army. Already on very bad terms with Walton Walker, he became bitterly hated by the Marines and disliked by the ROKs. An imaginative tactician and hard-driving commander, he shared MacArthur's vogue for unorthodox organization. His divisional commanders, who usually disliked him, thought he intervened too far down the chain of command. Unfortunately, Almond strongly opposed racial integration and played a considerable role in delaying it in Far East Command. His attitudes were hardly unusual for a Southerner born in 1892, but Almond who had a bad experience commanding the black 92nd Division in World War II, seems to have been unusually stubborn about his views, insisting that integration was a bad idea long after men from similar backgrounds had changed their minds. His racial attitudes seem to have warped his judgment in dealing with some units in X Corps.

Fitting out X Corps involved serious problems. The 1st Marine Division was being rebuilt with men scrounged from all over the world. Its 5th Regiment, already in Korea, would have to be withdrawn from combat at the last possible minute. The 7th Division, which had been greatly weakened by transfers to fill out other divisions, had to be rebuilt largely with KATUSAs. No one liked the results. Many thought that Almond had managed to corner an excessive number of supporting units for his corps. He and Walker quarreled bitterly over the three battalions of the 5th Artillery Group, which Walker desperately wanted for the Perimeter. There were not enough Navy ships, so Inchon depended heavily on commercial merchant ships and repossessed tank landing ships that had been loaned to the Japanese. In fact, 37 of the 47 LSTs carrying the Marines would be Japanese-manned. Loading took place amid a typhoon.

Many people — at least other than MacArthur — worried about the defenses at Inchon. Fortunately, there was a way to keep a close eye on the area. Anti-Communists still held out on small offshore islands nearby. A U.S. Navy officer, Lieutenant Eugene Clark, landed on one island on August 31 to collect data on sea conditions and the approaches to Inchon. He sent agents into the city and was even able to rig navigation lights to help ships sailing up the channel. The Americans estimated that the enemy had just 1,000 men in and around Inchon, and that they could not be reinforced quickly. Their estimates proved slightly overoptimistic, and they were lucky. The enemy nearly learned of the plan, which was an open secret among newsmen. A Communist spy ring in Japan was captured with plans for Inchon in its possession just a week before the landing.

As it was, the Chinese had deduced American intentions without this. Zhou Enlai's was not an isolated view. The Chinese leaders were distressed by events in Korea and by late July perceived that North Korea's chances of victory were limited. Learning in Japan of obvious preparations for some sort of amphibious attack, and studying American operations in the Pacific during World War II, their General Staff's Operations Bureau in a meeting on August 23 chaired by Zhou Enlai's military secretary estimated that the Americans would land at one of five ports, with Inchon being the likeliest target. Mao found their reasoning convincing (independently, the senior commanders of the 13th Army Group in Manchuria had concluded that the Americans would make an amphibious move either against Seoul or Pyongyang). Mao personally told North Korea's representative of the Chinese estimate. Although the Chinese leaders were men of long military experience and sound judgment, Kim ignored them, apparently backed by his Soviet advisers. He, and probably Stalin, staked all on overrunning the Pusan Perimeter before the Americans could mount a landing. Even the North Koreans were aware that some sort of amphibious attack was coming, but they apparently estimated that the likeliest target was not Inchon but Wonsan. Receiving Soviet mines and instructors from Vladivostok, they concentrated on mining Wonsan and Chinnampo before the southern ports. Only a few mines of the least dangerous type were laid at Inchon before the invasion. The Marines captured a flatcar full of deadly "ground mines" that had not yet been planted. Inchon was defended only by two battalions of recently drafted, poorly trained men of the 226th Marine Regiment and two batteries of 76-mm guns.[1]

The Communists could easily have made Inchon's harbor largely useless to the UN forces in advance. In the retreat of January 1951, a dozen Americans with a few hundred pounds of TNT made Inchon unusable for nine months by blasting the tidal basin locks that gave access to the ship basin. Like the Nazis in Western Europe before D-Day, the Communists could easily have wrecked the few ports that their enemies *had* to have before an invasion. But the North Korean high command and its Soviet patrons lacked the foresight and courage to admit that Inchon might well be lost. The Communists in the Korean War, like the enemies of the Western seapowers in many other conflicts, proved unable to accurately gauge the latter's true capabilities. Either they belittled them, or, as the Communists were to do after Inchon, overestimated their ability and feared they could both force their way ashore and supply their forces (without permanent port facilities) at almost any point, pinning down many troops at places not suitable for a landing.

The UN forces expended much effort in mounting feints against various targets, especially Kunsan. The commanders of Task Force 77 devoted 40 percent of the carrier air effort to the Inchon-Seoul area, while the Far East Air Force blasted airfields and marshalling yards on the main line to Seoul. On September 13, American destroyers entered the channel leading to Inchon. They destroyed a small minefield and provoked the five 76-mm guns on Wolmi island into opening fire and revealing their positions. They were then blasted at the cost of one American killed. Wolmi was blanketed with napalm by carrier planes.

Now, when it was too late, even the North Korean command was convinced. On September 14, it started reinforcements for the Inchon-Seoul area.

On September 15, the invasion fleet of 260 ships carrying 70,000 men arrived off Inchon. Covered by a terrific bombardment, a Marine battalion seized Wolmi on the morning tide with relative ease. The Marines found two 76-mm guns still intact, but the inexperienced gunners had been too shaken to man them. The main attack went in at 5:30 in the afternoon. The 5th Marine Regiment hit "Red Beach," just 300 yards wide, on the left. Carried by landing craft, they stormed over the sea wall on ladders. The 1st Marine Regiment rode into "Blue Beach" to the south on "amtracs" (amphibious tractors.) Neither beach resembled what would ordinarily be called a beach. Although only a few hours of daylight remained the Marines easily entered the city. The next day, they completed securing it and started eastward, smashing a whole series of small forces of infantry and tanks that clumsily tried to counterattack or block them, or which simply ran into Marine ambushes. They quickly recovered a huge dump of American equipment and ammunition, and took Kimpo airfield, which provided a stream of airlifted supplies.

The North Koreans reinforced the Seoul area faster than expected, bringing back the 18th Division, which had just left Seoul for the Naktong front, and they assembled elements of their 31st and 9th Divisions, the 70th, 78th and 87th Regiments, the 107th Security Regiment, and the 25th Brigade. They sent the 44th Tank Regiment down from Wonsan, but it was almost entirely destroyed enroute by U.S. planes. The enemy facing X Corps amounted to about 20,000 men in the Seoul area proper, with about 10,000 more below the Han down to Suwon. But, although elements of this force would offer formidable defenses, they would not be assembled in one place or in time to do the Communists much good. A mere fraction of this force might have wrecked the invasion had it been at Inchon on September 15.

On September 20, the Marines advanced on Seoul as the Army's 7th Division followed behind them. The 5th Marines crossed the Han, amtracs swimming under fire from small arms, automatic weapons, antitank rifles and an antitank gun. The 1st Marines battled through Yongdungpo. Both regiments encountered tough resistance. North of the Han, the enemy's 25th Brigade, which was exceptionally heavily armed, and 78th Independent Regiment put up strong resistance in a chain of hills west of Seoul that the Japanese had fortified as a training ground. The 7th Marines joined the 5th on their northern flank. Almond was dissatisfied with the Marines' progress and plans. He wanted Smith to send the 1st Marines on a wide flanking maneuver through the eastern outskirts of Seoul. Smith demurred. He wanted a concentrated punch with his whole division in line. He expected a tough block-by-block fight through Seoul and did not believe that Almond's proposed maneuver would help much. He opposed it even when Almond decided on September 24 to let Smith attack on a narrow front while he brought in the Army's 32nd Regiment, with the 17th ROK Regiment attached, to make the southeastern attack. The Marines thought he was pressing for an unreasonable rate of progress. MacArthur hoped to liberate Seoul on September 25 for its supposed political effects (Almond, however, seems to have told him that he would only promise to liberate the city within two weeks of Inchon).

On September 25, the Marines finally cracked the tough enemy defense west of Seoul and drove into the built-up area. On the same day, the 32nd Regiment crossed the Han in borrowed Marine amtracs. It quickly took South Mountain, the hill dominating the city, and cut the routes eastward out of Seoul. It may have caused the North Korean commander to realize that he would have to retreat, but the enemy did not pull out abruptly. Instead, they launched a strong counterattack to cover the withdrawal, and violent street fighting followed. Shifting the Army regiment to the Han crossing left the blocking force to the south relatively weak. But the 31st Infantry Regiment pushed south to Suwon, and, skillfully led, routed a counterattack by the North Korean 105th Armored Division coming up from the Naktong front. Soon after, it linked up with American forces following the North Koreans north.

Despite the flanking maneuver, bitter street fighting continued in Seoul. The North Koreans barricaded intersections with mines and sandbags, covered by antitank guns, machineguns and infantrymen firing from inside buildings. The battle for Seoul lasted until September 28, although MacArthur, as had been his custom in World War II, had prematurely announced that the city had been liberated on September 25. (On the other side, Kim did not admit to Stalin that Seoul had fallen until September 30) The Communists had put up a good fight for Seoul at the expense of the South Korean civilians. They had murdered political prisoners and stripped the city of industrial equipment right up to the last minute. The able commanding general later received a typical Stalinist reward: Kim Il Sung had him purged. X Corps had lost 536 dead, 2,550 wounded and 65 missing, while the North Koreans had lost 14,000 killed and 7,000 captured, and a large amount of equipment. They had lost some 50 T-34s. The T-34, which two months before had terrorized the ROKs and Americans, was now regarded about as casually as an enemy tank could be. And the trap was closing on the North Korean army.

Contrary to what was widely supposed at the time, and even later, Inchon did not save the Eighth Army from being driven into the sea. The battle of the Pusan Perimeter had been won before Inchon. It would have been won more swiftly and surely had MacArthur poured the available forces into Pusan instead of withholding them for his masterstroke. Inchon did not make the difference between defeat and victory, but made the liberation of South Korea much quicker and cheaper. Later, others argued that Inchon was a mistake that had succeeded by a fluke or that it had little effect, with the North Koreans having been defeated by air-ground action around the Perimeter. The last claim was at best wildly exaggerated. X Corps had disrupted the enemy rear and cut his lines of supply and retreat far more completely than any frontal advance and air interdiction could have.[2] And, although Inchon did not save the UN forces from immediate defeat, crushing the North Koreans as quickly and completely as possible before the Chinese could join them was even more important than MacArthur realized.

The North Koreans and the Soviets on the spot seem to have been slower to realize the importance of Inchon than either Stalin or the Chinese leaders. (Curiously, although the latter had predicted an Inchon landing at an early date, they still found it a shock. Perhaps they had not expected it so soon. They were disgusted with Kim's failure to heed them.) Either Kim and the Soviet advisers were genuinely dense or so emotionally focused on driving the Eighth Army into the sea that Inchon just did not register. Or perhaps they were so terrified of Stalin's wrath that they were clinging to the desperate hope that victory in the southeast would even now save the situation and rehabilitate them in the tyrant's eyes. On September 18, Stalin, himself acting belatedly, had ordered the redeployment of four divisions from the Perimeter to the Seoul area, but they still dragged their feet about executing this order. Breaking with the very cautious policy he had followed toward any direct Soviet involvement in combat, he also ordered his Air Force to send a Soviet fighter regiment (propeller-driven), preceded by the necessary ground staff, radar, and an air defense battalion, to defend the Pyongyang area. The Air Force reported, however, that this would take until October 5. The snowballing Communist collapse evidently aborted this effort. Stalin also sent a special mission under General M.V. Zakharov to report on the situation and straighten things out. Only on September 25 did Kim Il Sung, who had kept the news of the Inchon landing secret for a whole week from the North Koreans on the southern front, finally give up the fantasy of breaking through to Pusan. By then the Americans had long since broken out of the Perimeter.[3]

The Eighth Army went over to the attack on September 26. It outnumbered the enemy forces by perhaps 2-to-1, but found it hard to get going. It suffered from worrisome shortages, especially of bridging equipment, nor could it concentrate a large force at a central point. In some places the enemy was still attacking, and it was a tough fight even to get to the Naktong, much less over it. The enemy held the high ground and had enough mortars left to make seizing it costly. Walker had just recently acquired two U.S. corps headquarters, reducing the fantastic burden of directly controlling four U.S. divisions on such a long front. The main effort was to be made by General Frank Milburn's I Corps, which included the 1st Cavalry and 24th Divisions. Walker and others rated Milburn the more able of his two corps commanders.

The 1st Cavalry, with the 5th Regimental Combat Team attached, would drive north along the Naktong to Waegwan and seize a bridgehead across the river there. The 24th Division, with the British Brigade under command, was to follow up and drive on Taejon. The 1st ROK Division had an important role protecting the Cavalry's right flank. Milburn had enough confidence in General Paik to permanently attach American howitzer, antiaircraft and heavy mortar battalions to his division, giving it almost the firepower of its U.S. counterparts. His trust was amply rewarded.

In the southwest, General John Coulter's IX Corps, which became operational only on September 23 would drive west and northwest to Kunsan with the 2nd and 25th Divisions. The rest of the ROK Army would go north. There was tough fighting all along the front. For a time MacArthur was so worried at the lack of progress that he even considered taking forces from the perimeter for a second amphibious landing at Kunsan. On September 19, the enemy began to break. With Waegwan taken, I Corps began crossing the Naktong on September 20. On September 22, the Communists seemed to be cracking, and pulling back despite Kim's crazy orders. Learning of the Inchon landing seems to have been the main factor in demoralizing the enemy. The advance turned into a pursuit. The 1st Cavalry Division played a bigger role than expected in this phase. Its Task Force Lynch, an infantry battalion with tank, artillery and supporting units, set out from the Naktong crossing on September 24 and drove 105 miles in less than three days. The leading element of Task Force Lynch encountered the 7th Division's 31st Infantry Regiment north of Osan late on the evening of September 26. After a battle with some North Korean tanks, the rest of Task Force Lynch reached the 31st's front the next day. Eighth Army and X Corps had joined hands, albeit loosely.

General Zakharov had just reported to Stalin that the North Koreans had suffered heavy losses, including almost all their tanks and most of their artillery. Ammunition and fuel was no longer being delivered, and signals communications were a mess. The Communist troops fled in every direction, pursued by motorized columns, and under a hail of bombs and rockets. The advancing Americans and ROKs found roads and fields littered with tanks, vehicles, guns, and other equipment and supplies, often intact but abandoned because they could no longer be moved. Some of the bypassed enemy fled into the Chin mountains in the southwest to fight as guerrillas. Many more surrendered (one group to an American plane) or were captured. The prisoner total reached 30,000 by October. The trap could not be completely shut, but probably not more than 25,000 to 30,000 men, escaped to the North, badly disorganized with practically no heavy weapons or tanks. The Front headquarters and one corps headquarters reached the "Iron Triangle" area just above the 38th Parallel to direct guerrilla action there. The ROKs in the east moved as fast as anyone, despite their lack of tanks and trucks, the rugged terrain and lack of roads. By the end of September, they were almost on the 38th Parallel.[4] On September 26, the Americans had terminated the strategic bombing of North Korean industry.

The advancing UN forces uncovered many atrocities. Killing, sometimes with mutilation, of American prisoners had been a common practice among North Korean front-line troops despite the North Korean high command's disapproval. Particularly during the retreat, many planned large-scale massacres were carried out by the Communist secret police, occasionally with army help. During the occupation of the South, the Communists killed 26,000 civilians as well as captured soldiers, although many of the people they most wanted to kill were safe behind UN lines. Many of the killings took place just before or during the Communist withdrawal. But as early as August 7, the American fleet sailing off the southwest coast had passed through bundles of floating corpses lashed together. A large-scale massacre of ROK prisoners of war reportedly took place in North Korea on September 10. At Taejon, the returning Americans and ROKs found a grave containing 500 ROK soldiers massacred at the airstrip, while other graves around the city contained 5,000 to 7,000 civilians, 42 Americans and 17 more ROK soldiers, killed between September 23 and 27. Six Americans and South Koreans, by a fluke, survived being buried alive. Similar smaller massacres were common. Fifty-three Southern civilians were killed in the Inchon police station when the Marines landed. A small-scale version of the Bataan Death March was endured by 376 Americans marched from Seoul to Pyongyang starting on September 26. Thirty-three Americans escaped, and just 296 reached Pyongyang alive. In June 1950, the Communists had still had a fair number of supporters in the South, mostly among students and industrial workers. The people of Seoul were at first impressed by the occupying forces' vigor and efficiency. But the Northern officials arrogance and brutality alienated people.

The Communists' behavior was not, unfortunately, unique. Already, in the Pusan Perimeter, the South Korean forces had been notorious for ruthless treatment of Communist supporters. Returning ROK soldiers and police, and sometimes civilians, took brutal revenge against real and supposed collaborators, arousing much criticism outside Korea, although their behavior was no worse than that of some elements of the resistance in Europe in 1944–1945, and did not approach that of the Communists. At Inchon, U.S. Marines occasionally had to intervene to stop killings. The British Brigade in Eighth Army later acted more decisively, ending all executions in the area under its control.[5]

The Drive North

Victory in the South opened the way for the invasion of North Korea. The United States had entered the war to repel the North Korean invasion, not fulfill the long-standing objective of a united independent Korea. However, within a few weeks just restoring the prewar situation became unacceptable to American officials and the public.

They forgot that Josef Stalin was not a good loser.

The South Koreans, of course, had favored liberating the North from the first: Rhee had declared he would not be bound by any settlement that left Korea divided. MacArthur had indicated to Collins and Vandenberg on July 13 that he expected to pursue the enemy north and unify Korea. John Foster Dulles summarized the basic arguments for such a course on July 14. He pointed out that the 38th Parallel had never been intended to be a political dividing line. Equity and justice called for a united Korea, while it was folly to let the North Koreans rebuild their strength for another invasion. To deter a renewed attack would require a permanent American military commitment. It was desirable to inflict a penalty on an aggressor. Dulles was not dogmatic. He conceded that "expediency" might make it wise to stop at the 38th Parallel, and doubted that the provinces bordering the USSR and China could be included in a united Korea. Others were less cautious. John Allison, the Director of the State Department's Office of Northeastern Asian Affairs, and Assistant Secretary of State Dean Rusk were more enthusiastic about liberating North Korea. They emphasized the moral arguments for uniting Korea, punishing aggression and preventing a renewed North Korean attack. Acheson found their arguments convincing.

They belittled or even ignored a consideration that worried the Soviet experts and the Policy Planning Staff—how the major Communist powers would react. (Attention focused, it should be noted, on the Soviets, not the Chinese.) George Kennan and Charles Bohlen opposed crossing the 38th Parallel. They were sure that, one way or another, Stalin would act to prevent the loss of a satellite state. Kennan, in particular, maintained that the Soviets might push China into intervening, and they might even commit their own forces to stop the UN from uniting Korea. From Moscow, Ambassador Kirk also advised caution. Yet Kirk and the Soviet specialists still believed that the Soviets neither wanted nor were ready for all-out war. To other observers that seemed to rule out direct Soviet intervention in Korea. That it might not rule out *Chinese* action with Soviet support was often lost sight of. There was a curious aversion to considering the possibility of what actually happened. The Policy Planners tended to agree with Kennan and Bohlen, and held that the risks of bringing on a major conflict outweighed any advantages to be gained from liberating North Korea. Even they, however, allowed that if the North Korean forces disintegrated and the major Communist powers took no action, UN forces might move into North Korea.

The CIA was cautious. On August 18, it warned that "grave risks" would be involved in an invasion of North Korea, suggesting, wrongly, that America's allies would probably not support it. It drew attention to the danger of Chinese intervention and seemed to take Soviet willingness to embark on hostilities more seriously than Kennan and Bohlen, although it did not commit itself on the probability of Soviet or Chinese intervention. Even without that, the Communist powers would harass an occupation of North Korea. It even suggested that the Communists might win control of an all–Korean government in a free election — an idea other observers dismissed with justified contempt.

But even the CIA admitted that many advantages would result if Korea were united. The Defense Department had neatly summarized these benefits on July 31. The Koreans desperately wanted unification, and the ROK was the legitimate government. The Korean situation provided the free world with its first chance to "displace part of the Soviet orbit." Liberating all of Korea would hurt the Soviet position in the Far East and show the Japanese that Soviet power could be checked. "Elements in the Chinese Communist regime, and particularly important segments of its population, might be inclined to question their exclusive dependence on the Kremlin. Skillfully manipulated, the Chinese Communists might prefer different arrangements and a new orientation. Throughout Asia, those who foresee only inevitable Soviet conquest would take hope."

The National Security Council and the State Department accepted this reasoning. As it became clear in August and September that the Chinese were not intervening in the battle for South Korea, many policymakers slipped into thinking they were not likely to move in Korea, period. They also blurred the distinction between Soviet and Chinese action, assuming that if it was unlikely that the Soviets would intervene, the Chinese probably would not act either. They believed, and continued to believe, that the Chinese would estimate that intervention in Korea would be costly and bring China no real advantage (just how great a misunderstanding of Mao this was will be seen later).

Nor did they think much of the effectiveness of the Chinese forces. While the Chinese Communist troops were obviously superior to the Chinese Nationalists, they had such a low opinion of the latter that this did not mean much. (It should be noted that this was based on a somewhat one-eyed view of the Nationalist forces; some Nationalist troops, notably those trained and equipped by the Americans under Stilwell and those commanded by General Li Zonggren [Li Tsung-jen] — in other words troops *not* under the direct control of Jiang Jieshi and his pet generals — had fought well against the Japanese.) While they feared in the desperate days of August and early September that the Chinese could tip the balance in favor of the North Koreans, they thought that Chinese entry into the war once the North Koreans were beaten was so likely to end in failure as to be improbable.

On August 17, the American Ambassador to the UN declared that no opportunity should be allowed for another invasion, and all of Korea should be free. National Security Council Paper 81/1, submitted to the President on September 9, did not explicitly commit the United States to liberate all of Korea, but assumed that it would try to do this unless the USSR or China intervened. NSC-81/1 admitted that it was "possible that Chinese Communist forces might be used to occupy North Korea, even though the Soviet Union probably regards Korea as being in its own direct sphere of interest," but rated this as "unlikely." If either major Communist power entered North Korea after UN forces crossed the 38th Parallel, MacArthur was to stop and consult Washington. In any case, he was to stay clear of the Soviet and Chinese borders. However, contrary to what was later widely supposed, NSC 81/1 did *not* exclude air or naval actions against China if it intervened. If anything, it assumed that such action would be authorized. Truman approved the recommendations on September 11. On September 27, MacArthur received a directive based on NSC 81/1. It designated his military objective as "the destruction of the North Korean Armed Forces" and authorized him to operate above the 38th Parallel if "major Soviet or Chinese Communist" forces had not entered North Korea. It forbade him to operate against Manchuria or Soviet territory.

It would have been hard for Truman to stop at the 38th Parallel even had he realized that would be wise. The American public overwhelmingly supported liberating North Korea, expecting the total defeat and punishment of the aggressor in line with the experience of World War II and American tradition. (Although later critics argued that few American wars have been "crusades," few have been limited to restoring the status quo either.) In 1950, the dividing lines of the Cold War were still new; they had not been given a spurious legitimacy by the passage of a generation. The Soviet satellite system was still regarded as an outrageous act of aggression, not accepted as a fact of life as it would be 10 or 20 years later. Destroying the North Korean regime was a proper response to an open attack by the Soviet bloc. After years of Soviet hostility even people who cared nothing about Korea found handing the Communists a beating emotionally satisfying.

The British and most members of the UN (India was an outstanding exception) agreed with American policy. The British introduced a vaguely worded resolution calling for elections under UN auspices to create a democratic all–Korean government. It did not directly call for occupying all of Korea but certainly implied it. The General Assembly approved the resolution on October 7 as American patrols crossed the 38th Parallel. ROK units advancing up the east coast had already crossed the frontier while MacArthur called on the North Koreans to surrender. They did not even bother to reply.[6]

The UN forces faced difficult terrain and supply problems. The Taebaek range cut North Korea into eastern and western compartments, and there were few east-west roads. It was believed that supplying a deep advance would require taking Wonsan, and there were grave differences of opinion about how to do that. The long controversy over Inchon may have contributed to the failure to develop a sound plan of campaign for the North at an early date. (A similar lapse, also due to prolonged quarrels about where to land, had harmed the planning of the Sicilian campaign in 1943.)

General Walker and most officers in Asia and Washington expected that the Eighth Army would take over X Corps and that headquarters would be dissolved, while Almond would return to Tokyo and his duties as Chief of Staff. (Walker and Almond were on such bad terms that it was undesirable to have Almond serve under Walker.) Walker planned to have X Corps, already concentrated around Seoul, strike north toward Pyongyang at the first possible moment, followed by the rest of Eighth Army, which would be concentrated in western Korea. The ROK I Corps would continue moving up the east coast.

Once Pyongyang fell, X Corps would attack east to Wonsan to trap the remaining North Korean forces. Alternatively, if it looked like the ROKs alone could not take Wonsan, Eighth Army's I Corps would strike from Seoul toward Wonsan and then attack from Wonsan northwest toward Pyongyang.

But the plan of campaign that was adopted differed radically from anything anyone had expected. Almost all the Army and Navy officers, in Far East Command recognized that it was a bad one. To everyone's surprise (including Almond), MacArthur decided to keep Almond in charge of X Corps and X Corps independent of Eighth Army. It would be carried around Korea by sea to land at Wonsan. From there, it would attack toward Pyongyang, cutting behind the enemy's main line of defense. This would assure the capture of Wonsan, avoid a frontal attack on what might be formidable defenses, and avert the wear and tear an overland march to Wonsan would inflict on men and vehicles.

But the scheme was a mistake. It proved a classic case of what Clausewitz had seen as the kind of error at the start of a campaign that could never be made good. The plan split the UN Command into two widely separated forces for the rest of the campaign in North Korea. It delayed the pursuit of the North Koreans and jammed the port of Inchon, worsening Walker's already bad supply problems. (As it turned out, all of X Corps could not even go out via Inchon. Only the Marines embarked there. The 7th Division had go all the way to Pusan to be picked up by ships.) MacArthur and most others had overestimated North Korean resistance and perhaps the importance of Wonsan. As the Eighth Army's G-3 had warned, the ROKs got there well ahead of X Corps. Moving with remarkable speed, they took Wonsan on October 11. The Marines had been scheduled to land there on October 20. Aided by Soviet advisers, the North Koreans had mined the harbor so heavily that it took two weeks and the loss of four minesweepers to open it. The Marines got ashore only on October 26. The 7th Division landed at Iwon farther up the coast. The 3rd Division, newly arrived from the United States, was to land at Wonsan and Hungnam. (This raised the American force in Korea to its maximum strength of seven divisions: six Army and one Marine.) Meanwhile, on October 9, the Eighth Army had begun its advance. The North Koreans had dug in north of the 38th Parallel, and, after several days of hard fighting, they broke. On October 19, Walker's forces took Pyongyang, but the enemy escaped destruction.

MacArthur had already laid plans for the occupation of North Korea. He told Truman on October 15 that he hoped to hold elections there by January 1 and withdraw soon after. The United States and the UN had agreed, much to Rhee's irritation, that the ROK government would not automatically take control of North Korea. ROK officials and troops would act as instruments of the UN until a new UN Commission for Korea supervised elections. X Corps would control the occupation forces, which would consist of the American 3rd Division, the other UN units in Korea and the ROK forces. Eighth Army, with the rest of the American troops, would return to Japan. The occupation would last just a few months. The 3rd Division was scheduled to leave MacArthur's theater in May 1951. There were no plans to keep American bases in Korea after the occupation ended. During October, previous plans to reinforce MacArthur were cut back. Bombers that had been supporting him returned to the United States, and ships carrying supplies and ammunition turned around.[7]

6

Chinese and Soviet Intervention

The Americans had recklessly ignored increasingly strong indications that China was likely to intervene in the Korean War. They did not realize it had already done so, in a small way, in the defense of Sinuiju. There is perhaps some slight excuse for their mistake since the Communist powers were not absolutely certain about what to do, though Mao Zedong was far readier to fight in Korea than would be realized in the West until the 1990s. They failed to do the only things that would almost certainly have deterred the Americans from trying to liberate North Korea: that was to openly move Chinese forces into North Korea before the Americans crossed the 38th Parallel, or issue a clear-cut declaration of their intention to intervene if that took place.

Instead, the Chinese sent veiled warnings, and communicated through indirect and unreliable channels. On September 25, General Nie Zhongren (Nieh Jung-chen) the Chinese Army's chief of staff, told K.M. Panikkar, India's Ambassador in Beijing, that China would not accept American aggression without resistance. But he referred directly only to incidents where American planes had mistakenly attacked Manchuria. Panikkar interpreted this, and remarks made earlier by Zhou Enlai and the Polish Ambassador to China as meaning that China planned to intervene in Korea. But he was hardly certain of this. He described his views as a "strong impression" and did not even report them to New Delhi until September 27. Nehru immediately passed Panikkar's messages on to the British. But while Nehru took the warnings seriously, none of the Western powers did. Panikkar was known to be sympathetic to the Communist powers and was deemed an unreliable reporter — with reason since even Indian officials had a low opinion of him. But vague reports from the Dutch Embassy in Beijing that seemed to support Panikkar were also discounted. On September 29, the U.S. ambassador in Moscow dismissed all this as an effort to bluff the UN into stopping at the 38th Parallel. Expressing a common view, he remarked that the logical moment for Chinese intervention had been when the UN forces were in the Pusan Perimeter. On September 30, Zhou Enlai declared "the Chinese people absolutely will not tolerate foreign aggression, nor will they supinely tolerate seeing their neighbors invaded by imperialists."

On October 2, he met Panikkar again, telling him that should American forces enter North Korea China would enter the war. He indicated that a move by South Korean troops would not cause China to intervene. These statements also were read as a bluff by most Western officials.

The Soviets got into the act. While opposing any UN entry into North Korea in public, they hinted at a different policy in private. On October 5, Vassili Kasaniev, a Soviet employee of the UN, told a member of Norway's UN delegation that the Soviets could not accept American troops occupying North Korea. But if UN forces halted at the 38th Parallel, the North Koreans would "lay down their arms" and let a UN Commission into the North to hold elections. Kasaniev showed some interest in the Norwegian's suggestion that it might be arranged to use only Asian troops in an occupation of North Korea. However, the Norwegian concluded that the Soviets did not accept the idea of the North Koreans actually surrendering. It was just another ploy to save the North Korean regime.

Complacency reigned. On October 12, the CIA declared that despite Zhou's statement there were no "convincing indications of an actual Chinese Communist intention to resort to full-scale intervention in Korea." Although recognizing that creating a non–Communist Korea would be a major setback for the Communist cause, it concluded that fear of war with the United States would outweigh that for the Chinese leaders. The CIA suggested that without Soviet help intervention would be costly for China, but "acceptance of Soviet aid would make Peiping more dependent on Soviet help and increase Soviet control in Manchuria to (a) point probably unwelcome to the Chinese Communists." Yet again, it argued that the best time for a Chinese intervention had passed. It concluded that "barring a Soviet decision for global war, such action is not probable in 1950."[1] After the Chinese intervened, this sort of thinking led many people to jump to the conclusion that World War III was at hand.

Victory, not a new war, seemed near. Truman met MacArthur at Wake Island on October 15 in a conference probably designed to aid the Democrats in the coming mid-term elections rather than to transact serious business. Despite Truman and MacArthur's basic distaste for each other, the meeting was very friendly. In a private encounter, MacArthur apologized for the Veterans of Foreign Wars incident. At the general session, he said that he expected "formal resistance" to end by about Thanksgiving, although the North Koreans were estimated to still have 100,000 poorly trained men. He explained his plans for occupation and reconstruction, praised State Department plans for a Japanese peace treaty and acidly criticized the French performance in Indochina. In response to a question from General Bradley, he assured those present that he could release a division for transfer to Europe by January. When Truman asked about Soviet or Chinese intervention, MacArthur declared that the chances of this were "very little. Had they interfered in the first or second months it would have been decisive. We are no longer fearful of their intervention. We no longer stand hat in hand." Only 50–60,000 [of the 300,000 Chinese troops in Manchuria] could be gotten across the Yalu. They have no Air Force. Now that we have bases for our air force in Korea, if the Chinese tried to get down to Pyongyang there would be the greatest slaughter."

Even if the Soviet air force was thrown in, the Americans could handle it, and it could not effectively cooperate with or support the Chinese. MacArthur later insisted — and Admiral Radford supported him — that his remarks were based on the assumption that if China intervened the Americans would automatically retaliate by bombing Manchuria. That is likely, but he did not make this clear at the Wake Island meeting.[2] Unknown to anyone there, the Chinese were about to enter Korea in force.

The Chinese and Soviet Decisions to Intervene

During July and August, Chinese preparations for possible intervention in Korea had gone ahead. Troops poured into Manchuria. Chinese internal propaganda, quite violently anti–American even in July, began during August to prepare people for some sort of unspecified action. Stalin continued to promise Soviet air cover and arranged to train Chinese jet fighter pilots and equip a whole fighter division.

Mao, by late July, was already quite worried about the situation in Korea. He and the other Chinese leaders were furious at being denied Taiwan. Mao himself seems to have expected that some armed clash with the United States was inevitable, if not over Korea, than over Taiwan or Indochina. He even seems to have regarded the Korean War as an opportunity to meet the Americans on a battlefield favorable to China. Chinese supply lines would be short and it would be easier to get Soviet help. The Chinese leaders, however, were not united on what to do. There seems to have been at least three factions, very likely with shifting memberships, in relation to the Korean War. At least some leaders favored early intervention in Korea as soon as it became clear that a North Korean victory was in doubt. Mao, and at least for a time Zhou Enlai, appear to have thought along these lines. For them, the question of whether the UN forces of any contingent crossed the 38th Parallel was not of paramount importance. In any case, they and the other Chinese leaders simply assumed that the other side would invade North Korea if it could. It was the ponderousness of the Chinese military machine, aside from the disagreements of the leaders, that prevented an early intervention in Korea of the sort the Americans had most feared. Indeed, some Chinese troops were still unprepared in critical respects even when they crossed into Korea. Resistance at the lower levels of the Chinese leadership and also perhaps the fact that the Chinese did not expect an American counterstroke at such an early date may also have helped to delay action. That may have been fortunate for the UN forces. Had the Chinese moved faster, or had they conceived the problem a bit differently, a comparatively small but heavily armed force, emphasizing artillery rather than infantry, sent to the Inchon area might have caused the UN a great deal of trouble.

At the other extreme, many of the second line Chinese leaders did not want to intervene in Korea at all, even if North Korea was completely lost. In between, China's military leaders, except for Lin Biao (Lin Piao), favored intervention if the tide turned against the North Koreans and the Americans, as expected, crossed the 38th Parallel. The commanders of the 13th Army Group in Manchuria concluded that China's chances of success in Korea were good: they would have superior numbers, higher morale and shorter supply lines than their enemy. The atomic bomb could not be decisive, and North Korea was the best place to fight the Americans before they became well-established there. However, they wanted still more men and equipment.

At a meeting of the Chinese Politiburo on August 4, Mao and Zhou indicated that they expected China to intervene. Indeed, they favored outright intervention with the Chinese operating under the guise of volunteers. Preparations to fight in Korea were accelerated and were to be completed by the end of August. By the middle of the month, however, it was clear they could not be finished that soon. Mao postponed the deadline until the end of September. The buildup continued. The "Northeast Border Defense Army" was to reach 36 divisions and 700,000 men. But the desired tank and airborne units were not nearly ready when war came.[3]

After Inchon, the Chinese and Soviets readily agreed the situation was disastrous. The Chinese were acidly critical of Kim Il Sung for ignoring their advice and his reluctance to give them information. Stalin defended Kim, blaming the mess on poor communications between Kim and his front-line commanders, then on the commanders themselves (to his own Politiburo he blamed the Soviet advisers). Pak Il-yu and Pak Hon-yong, who led the "Chinese" and "Southern" factions of the Korean Communists, came to Beijing to seek help, Kim being too busy to go or reluctant to face the Chinese, who were already fed up with him. The two Paks may have angled for Chinese support in overthrowing Kim, but they did not get it. Mao perhaps regarded such a move as too dangerous given the military situation, or feared Stalin's reaction to what the Soviet ruler would likely interpret as a Chinese intrusion in his sphere. This may have been unfortunate for the Communist cause; it was almost certainly unfortunate for the Koreans, since it seems likely that almost anyone would have been better than Kim Il Sung. The Chinese already had an indirect role in the war, and, contrary to their statement to Panikkar, they almost certainly did not intend to let even a ROK occupation of North Korea go unmolested, even if they did not intervene there. During September and October most of the ROK prisoners of war held by the North Koreans were herded into Manchuria where they were indoctrinated, hastily trained and formed into new divisions alongside newly drafted northerners.[4]

Kim had modestly taken the position of Minister of Defense into his own hands, and accepted Soviet-dictated changes in tactics and reorganization of the North Korean commands. The Soviets were particularly critical of the North Koreans throwing away tanks by not using them in coordination with preliminary artillery fire. Kim admitted to the Soviets on September 29 that his forces in the South were in bad shape and if the enemy crossed the 38th Parallel he could not stop them. The next day he frankly begged for help. He was forming six new divisions and rebuilding nine others, but implied that he would not have the time to complete this task without help. He asked for "direct military help from the Soviet Union" and, if that was impossible, from China or other Communist countries.

On this same day (September 30), the Soviet Politburo agreed, not surprisingly, that it was necessary to avoid a direct military clash with the United States. It agreed to furnish equipment for six new North Korean divisions and suggested that Kim get truck drivers, of whom he was very short (the North Koreans actually forced American prisoners to drive their trucks), from the Chinese. (It was only after this that Stalin received the North Korean admission that Seoul had fallen.) Very early on October 1, Stalin sent a message to the Chinese. Recounting the desperate situation of the Korean Communists, he asked Mao to immediately send at least five to six divisions, designated "volunteers," toward the 38th Parallel to give the North Koreans a chance to regroup. It was characteristic that Stalin did not openly propose a full-scale military campaign, although the action he wanted was bound to lead to one. The next few days would show just how devious and difficult relations between the two tyrants could be, even when they basically agreed on what should be done.

Chinese Decision-Making

On October 2, Mao ordered the Northeast Border Defense Army to finish preparations ahead of the previous schedule. He convened an enlarged meeting of the Politburo's Standing Committee. There he strongly argued that it was necessary to enter the war. The meeting endorsed this and Mao's proposal that Peng Dehuai (Peng Teh-huai) take command of the Chinese "volunteers." Mao did not, however, inform Stalin of the decision (and there is some disagreement among Chinese historians as to just how final this decision really was). Instead, on October 3, he informed Stalin through the Soviet Ambassador that China had planned to send several volunteer divisions to help the Korean Communists when the enemy had advanced north of the 38th Parallel, but many of his colleagues were more cautious. The Chinese Army was poorly armed, ill-prepared and had no confidence in success against the Americans. Moreover, such a move would probably lead to open war with the United States, and the Soviets would be dragged in. There would be much domestic opposition, which would turn against his government.

But a final decision had not been taken, and he was willing to send Zhou Enlai and Lin Biao to consult with Stalin. The North Koreans should wage a guerrilla war. Ambassador Roschin noted that this contradicted earlier Chinese assurances that their army was ready and even eager to fight the Americans. Roschin hinted that the Chinese had lost their nerve, but Stalin apparently concluded that the Chinese were simply bargaining.

On October 4, Mao convened another enlarged meeting of the full Chinese Politburo, including many senior officers and officials. Here he ran into more resistance. A majority of those present were reluctant to enter the war. Taking the plunge seems to have frightened even some who had earlier favored intervention, notably Zhou Enlai. The opposition pointed to China's difficult economic situation and there were many domestic enemies still at large that war would make more dangerous. Others argued that the Chinese would be no match for the better-equipped Americans and would be bound to suffer massive losses. The geographical situation in Korea would be vastly different from the vast spaces of China in which the People's Liberation Army had been so successful. Mao argued that the issue ran far beyond Korea. If the Communists were defeated in Korea, the prospects for revolution in Asia and the rest of the world would be worsened. If the enemy occupied Korea, there would be a permanent military commitment in the northeast.

In any case, conflict with the Americans, if not over Korea then over Taiwan and Indochina, was inevitable, and Korea was the best battleground for China. There, Soviet help would be available, Chinese supply lines would be short and the mountainous terrain would favor the Chinese over the Americans. The Soviet alliance and military presence in Manchuria would deter the Americans from bombing China at all, much less using nuclear weapons. He did not anticipate a long war or that the Korean War would develop into a world war. And he envisaged total victory in Korea where he and the other Chinese leaders thought in terms of fighting for the control of the whole country, not of restoring the prewar status quo and stopping at the 38th Parallel. Nor does anyone seem to have feared an immediate American ground invasion of Manchuria (a fear sometimes attributed to the Chinese leaders by Westerners). The meeting adjourned without reaching a conclusion.

Peng Dehuai, the most respected Chinese military leader who had reached the meeting late, conferred with Mao. The next day, he took an active part in the resumed Politburo session. Strongly backing Mao, he won over most of the opposition and Mao got his way.

On the same day, the Soviet Politburo again agreed that a direct clash with the United States in Korea must be avoided. If necessary, North Korea would be abandoned, but a renewed attempt would be made to get China to enter the war. Stalin sent a message to Mao strongly urging the Chinese to act. He argued that the Americans were not yet ready for a major war, nor was Japan yet rearmed. The Chinese would win in Korea and force the Americans to abandon Taiwan and plans for a separate peace with Japan. Stalin claimed that he was not afraid of war with the United States, and that the USSR and China together would be stronger than the United States and Britain. None of the other capitalist states had any military power at all. "If a war is inevitable, then let it be waged now, and not in a few years when Japanese militarism will be restored as an ally of the USA," he said, also warning that a united anti–Communist Korea would be an enemy bridgehead.

On October 7, Mao replied, indicating that he would send nine divisions to Korea, not right away, but soon. He asked to send Zhou Enlai to consult. In the meantime, both Stalin and Mao urged Kim Il Sung to hang on. Mao also ordered his forces to enter Korea.

On October 10, Zhou reached Stalin's villa on the Black Sea. Zhou told

Stalin that the Chinese Politburo had decided not to send troops to Korea, because China lacked money, modern arms and sufficient transport, and feared that the United States would declare war on China, while domestic reactionaries had not yet been dealt with. Zhou's misrepresentation of the actual decision of the Chinese leadership up to this point very likely represented a strategy agreed on with Mao to improve China's bargaining position with Stalin. But what happened later suggests that Zhou personally opposed intervention and was not above using the circumstances to sabotage the decision. Stalin now said that it would be very difficult for the Soviets to fight a large-scale war so soon after World War II, but he was ready to do so, if necessary. At the moment, however, the Americans were in a weak strategic position and were unlikely to risk war with both China and the USSR. The Soviet-Chinese alliance should deter them from striking China, so the Chinese need not fear retaliation. Stalin stressed China's interest in keeping a friendly government in Korea.

Zhou seemed refractory, so a visibly angry Stalin shifted to arguing that the Soviets and Chinese must at least provide a sanctuary for the North Koreans in which they could prepare to reenter Korea. Zhou, a bit shaken, seemed to back down and asked Stalin if the Soviets could provide air cover for the Chinese in Korea. Stalin assured him that he would do so, as well as provide weapons and equipment to the Chinese. On October 11, Zhou apparently misinformed Beijing that Stalin had refused to provide air cover, at least immediately. This lie greatly upset the Chinese leaders and caused a serious crisis. Mao put preparations for intervention in Korea on hold. On October 13, Stalin, thinking that the Chinese would not act to stop the rapidly advancing UN Command, told Kim to prepare to retreat to Chinese and Soviet territory. Kim was about to implement this order and prepare for guerrilla warfare when Stalin reversed himself. After much anxious thought and argument, Mao had decided to go in even if he could not get a promise of immediate Soviet air cover and secured Politburo agreement to this. Early on October 14, Stalin received a message from Mao informing him of this decision.

Stalin was mightily pleased and cancelled the evacuation of North Korea, assuring Kim that China would rescue him.[5] In this fantastically devious manner, the course was set.

Just how much they could depend on the deterrent effect of the Soviet alliance and Soviet air defenses seems to have bothered the Chinese leaders. They were by no means sure the Americans would not retaliate against China. Some may have expected that Manchuria at least would be bombed and insisted on costly preparations against this. The Chinese moved industrial machinery, petroleum, ammunition and supplies from South to North

Manchuria, and removed some important machinery and materials from Manchuria entirely. Zhou Enlai told some officials that coastal areas of southern China might have to be evacuated during a long war.[6] Two Soviet air divisions that had been stationed in China for some time went home, turning over their planes to the Chinese, while the Soviet air force in China was built up to 13 air divisions—nine fighter, three ground-attack and one bomber. Beginning in November, the Soviets' 151st Fighter Division and 29th Fighter Regiment would enter combat over Korea. But these pilots were not well trained and probably had only a small effect on the Korean situation.[7]

The Chinese Forces

On the night of October 19–20, Chinese troops began crossing the Yalu river into Korea (advance parties may have preceded the main body by a few days). While the Americans were well-informed about the buildup of forces in Manchuria, which had gone on for months, the movement into Korea went completely undetected.

The forces committed in Korea were the cream of the People's Liberation Army, but were lightly equipped compared to the North Korean attackers in June. The Chinese army was primarily armed with rifles, machine guns and mortars. It had only a few hundred tanks (mostly Japanese-built) and relatively little artillery, mostly light Japanese guns with a few American medium howitzers. The units crossing the Yalu had no tanks and little artillery at all. The Chinese infantry (and a few cavalry units) depended primarily on support from mortars. They were equipped largely with a mixture of Japanese and American equipment; they were just beginning to receive some Soviet weapons—submachineguns, heavy 120-mm mortars and truck-mounted Katyusha rocket launchers. The officers and NCOs were experienced veterans of many years of fighting, and machine-gunners and mortar men were well trained. Many of the men, sometimes most of the personnel of whole armies (a Chinese army was actually the equivalent of a Western corps) were ex–Nationalists who had either defected in entire units, surrendered or been captured. The three categories were treated differently. The Communists still depended heavily on ex–Nationalist technicians, gunners and tank drivers. All Chinese soldiers had been strongly indoctrinated and morale was high, though a minority was very fearful of the heavily armed Americans. The Party's propaganda emphasized that the ROKs had started the war and that if the enemy won in Korea they would invade China, which especially impressed the Manchurians who formed a large proportion of the 13th Army Group.

When the Chinese soldiers learned from Koreans that it was the Communists who had started the war and they suffered heavy losses, the indoctrination recoiled on its authors. But now most were confident that superior numbers and morale in the service of a just cause would triumph. One notable difference between the Chinese and their Korean Communist allies was in their treatment of prisoners. Chinese combat troops were vastly more humane in their treatment of prisoners than the North Koreans. The difference was less when the UN captives reached the prisoner of war camps, but even there the behavior of the Chinese was not as bad.

Although the Chinese forces might be lightly armed, they were very skilled at making use of terrain, at infiltration, night fighting, reconnaissance and camouflage. This last characteristic was the key to the events of the next six weeks. The UN forces had to find the Chinese the hard way. Marching at night, avoiding the main routes and using secondary roads and mountain trails, the Chinese halted and hid by day.[8]

The ROK dash up the east coast was far advanced when the UN forces crossed the 38th Parallel in the center and west. The American I Corps led the drive north, while the 1st Cavalry Division had a tough fight on October 7–8 breaking through the enemy defenses at Kumchon. It trapped a large enemy force in the "Kumchon pocket." Even though many North Koreans got away before trap was shut, it ended a coordinated Communist defense in the west. The advance to Pyongyang became a sort of race between the Cavalry Division and the ROKs, perhaps to the exclusion of trapping the fleeing enemy. Some units nevertheless had some tough fighting. The British and Australians had strange encounters with some North Korean units, taking them by surprise and capturing thousands of prisoners who at first thought that Westerners not wearing American uniforms must be Soviet soldiers who had come to their rescue.

On October 19, the 1st Cavalry Division entered Pyongyang. There was great pleasure in the West, not to mention Korea at the liberation of the "first Iron Curtain capital." Few foresaw that the liberation would soon be undone, and no one in 1950 would have guessed that Communist totalitarianism would survive in North Korea long after it had ended in East-Central Europe and the USSR itself. An attempt to cut off the enemy retreating from Pyongyang and liberate their American prisoners by dropping the paratroopers of the 187th Airborne Regimental Team at Sukchon failed. The jump went well, but the whole operation was just too late. The North Koreans were fleeing too fast, and only a single regiment was caught between the paratroopers and the British Brigade coming up from the south. Later moves did rescue some U.S. prisoners who were in horrible shape, but many were massacred before the UN forces reached them. The

Americans continued to pursue north, crossing the Chongchon river. They aimed to prevent the North Koreans from falling back into the almost roadless mountain area near the Yalu around Kangye and Manpojin where they would be very hard to root out. North Korean resistance was now very weak, but the UN forces had advanced 300 miles in six weeks. Their supply lines were very stretched. With great difficulty, engineers opened the railroads as far as the Imjin river near the 38th Parallel, but long hauls by truck, supplemented by an airlift, were needed to get supplies to the front. The Americans' 2nd and 25th Divisions were largely immobilized so the rest of the Eighth Army could advance. In the east, the easy drive up the Sea of Japan had continued. The 7th Infantry Division landed at Iwon on October 29, well north of Wonsan, its original destination. The ROKs reached Hungnam and Hamhung on foot.[9]

MacArthur was bent on driving right up to the Chinese frontier. On October 17, he moved the restraining line beyond which non–ROK troops were forbidden to move farther north. On October 24, he abolished it altogether. The Joint Chiefs of Staff questioned this action which at least at first sight, violated their directive of September 27. MacArthur, arguing that the ROKs alone could not do the job, cited a message Secretary of Defense Marshall had sent him on September 30 as modifying the directive: "We want you to feel unhampered tactically and strategically to proceed north of the parallel." Although that gave the message a twist Marshall had not intended, the Joint Chiefs were indulgent.

The Eighth Army was advancing toward the Yalu on a broad front on October 25 when ROK units ran into Chinese troops in both the Eighth Army and X Corps sectors. In both areas they took Chinese prisoners, but the high command reacted remarkably slightly. The Eighth Army was driving north and northwest on divergent axes. The U.S. I Corps with the 24th Division and the 27th Commonwealth Brigade was on the left, with the ROK 1st Division on the corps' right: The three divisions of ROK II Corps were on the army's right. A severe but successful fight went on in the coastal sector where the American and Commonwealth units were advancing against the North Koreans. On October 26, ROK II Corps was attacked by two of the three Chinese armies— the 38th and 40th — operating on the Western front. (The 13th Army Group's 42nd Army was facing X Corps in the east.) By the end of October 29, ROK II Corps had collapsed; the ROK 6th Division and a regiment of the 8th Division were largely destroyed. The Chinese 39th Army had hit the 1st ROK Division in the center of the Eighth Army front.

The 1st ROK Division was surrounded with its supporting American tank, artillery and antiaircraft units. But it held out. It was supplied by air and reopened the blocked supply route on the ground. Paik Sun Yup insisted that he faced strong Chinese units, not just a few elements supporting the North Koreans as Eighth Army's G-2 at first declared. Eighth Army headquarters was slow to react to what was going on. On October 28, Walker ordered the 1st Cavalry Division north to pass through the 1st ROK Division and continue the drive to the Yalu. The 1st ROK Division's own attack north on October 29 encountered stubborn, well dug-in Chinese. It became apparent that resuming the offensive would not be easy and, on October 31, Walker ordered the U.S. 2nd Division to Sunchon to hold that road junction in the rear of ROK II Corps. The next day a force of engineers and ordnance units was hastily formed to protect the now open right flank of I Corps and the vital bridges over the Chongchon, while a battalion of the 5th Cavalry Regiment was sent to bolster the ROK Corps. The Cavalry Division's commander, General Hobart Gay, was unhappy. His division was already weak, with one regiment still held south of the Chongchon. He wanted to pull back and concentrate his units, but was turned down.

On November 1, the Chinese moved under the cover of the smoke from the forest fires they had set. That night, Chinese infantry supported by mortars and Katyusha rockets attacked the 8th Cavalry Regiment north of Unsan and the ROK 15th Regiment to its northeast. The ROKs were overrun, some fleeing into the Americans' rear. The 1st and 2nd Battalions of the 8th Cavalry were forced back as the Chinese infiltrated into Unsan behind them, amid the fleeing ROKs. An extremely confused situation developed. Part of the retreating forces bypassed Unsan to the east. Some U.S. tanks bulled their way right through the enemy-held town, while other tanks and vehicles were trapped there. The Chinese cut the road southeast, and the disorganized Americans could not break the block. Scattered groups got out around it. The 3rd Battalion, holding a position southwest of Unsan and guarding a bridge over the Kuryong river, was also attacked. Its command post was temporarily overrun, and the battalion commander was never seen again. The battalion's escape route was cut. The 5th Cavalry Regiment and a battalion of the 7th tried but were unable to break through to it. The smoke from the forest fires still obstructed air strikes. Gay had to order the relief force to withdraw, but part of the encircled battalion broke out in small groups. In the end, the 8th Cavalry Regiment and its supporting units lost over 600 men and most of their heavy equipment.

The Eighth Army pulled back to the Chongchon; the 27th Commonwealth Brigade and the U.S. 19th Infantry Regiment held a bridgehead over the river. On the right, the 5th Regimental Combat Team, hastily switched from the Army's left, and the few ROK battalions still capable of fighting prevented the Chinese from driving into the Eighth Army's rear while the rest of ROK II Corps reassembled at Kunu-ri. The Chinese attacked the Chongchon bridgehead strongly, but were beaten off. On November 6 they broke off action and withdrew — they seemed to disappear. The Americans were mystified by this, but the Chinese had simply run out of supplies and ammunition.

Mao was extremely pleased with this battle, although Peng had more reservations about the Chinese performance. The Chinese were impressed by American firepower, but considered the American infantry poor, unfamiliar with night fighting and close combat. Mao even persuaded himself that American tanks were not too much trouble, at least at night. However, Peng wanted reinforcements. On November 1, Mao ordered the 9th Army Group of the Third Field Army to Korea. On November 8, it was decided to assign it to the northeastern sector where it would replace the 42nd Army, which would join the main body of the 13th Army Group on the western front. Two more armies, the 50th and the 66th, would be committed to the west.

In the northeast, the Chinese had had more trouble. At Sudong, a ROK regiment driving northwest from Hungnam toward the Chosin (Changjin) Reservoir had run into the Chinese 124th Division, supported by North Korean tanks. The ROKs took heavy losses, but did not collapse. The 1st Marine Division's 7th Regiment came up to relieve the ROKs on November 2. In tough fighting the Marines largely destroyed the Chinese division, along with its supporting armor. On November 7, the Chinese withdrew on the eastern front as well.[10]

A very serious situation seemed to develop in the air. On November 1, Soviet MIG-15 jets based at Dandong began crossing the Yalu to attack American planes. Yak propeller-driven fighters, piloted by North Koreans who had not been seen in the air lately, joined them. The Red fighters dashed across the river to attack, then took refuge in what became known as the "sanctuary" of Manchuria where the Americans were forbidden to follow. Despite this advantage, the Yaks suffered heavy losses. But the MIGs were something else. They were clearly superior to any U.S. jet fighter then in East Asia. The MIG-15 was a hundred miles an hour faster than the F-80 and could climb right away from it.

At first, MacArthur himself had not seemed too concerned by the Chinese intervention. On November 5, for reasons never satisfactorily explained, he suddenly became far more worried. He now ordered all-out air attacks on targets near the Yalu and especially against the bridges spanning the river. He authorized mass fire-bomb attacks by B-29s on cities and towns in the part of Korea still held by the enemy, similar to those on Japanese cities in 1945. That tactic had previously been forbidden in Korea, as had all attacks within five miles of the border. In World War II, MacArthur had been one of the American commanders most careful about air operations that might hurt civilians. This decision showed how apprehensive he was.

Some South Korean officials were privately upset at the bombings, but, oddly, they attracted little criticism elsewhere. (After assuming command of the Soviet air units supporting the Chinese, General Lobov organized tours of his pilots to the bombed towns to rouse their enthusiasm.) There was much greater upset over attacking the Yalu bridges—another example of the way in which the use of air power, not only in the Korean War, could become politically controversial in a way that had no genuine relationship to alleged concerns with civilian lives. After considering the matter, Truman turned down attacks on the bridges. MacArthur objected violently since large forces were pouring across the bridges. "This movement not only jeopardizes but threatens the ultimate destruction of the forces under my command."

This jolted Washington. It seemed inconsistent with MacArthur's initial calm appraisal of the Chinese move that Washington had shared. MacArthur did not, however, ask to bomb Chinese territory. Truman and the Joint Chiefs relented, letting him bomb the Korean ends of the bridges as long as the attacking planes did not enter Chinese air space.

This restriction made it hard to hit the bridges. Bombers usually attacked bridges by flying along their long axes, and the refusal to let them cross Chinese territory forced them to attack the bridges from the side. Bends in the Yalu made things more difficult, rendering one bridge completely immune to attack. To bomb the other bridges, the U.S. planes had to fly predictable paths exposed to antiaircraft fire and fighters dashing across the Yalu. MacArthur's air commander muttered, "It cannot be done—Washington must have known that it cannot be done."

The Air Force began attacking the bridges on November 8 without much success. Navy carrier planes, starting the next day, did better. The F9F Panthers that escorted the strikes found that the MIGs were not only faster in level flight, but outclimbed, outdived and out-turned them. Only the fact that the American pilots were better trained saved them. A Navy pilot, Lieutenant Commander William Amen, was nevertheless the first American pilot to get a MIG-15. But the Navy concluded that had the enemy fighter pilots been well trained and properly used their superior planes, losses would have been heavy. The Air Force concurred. Despite their bad gunnery, the MIGs did drive the RB-29 reconnaissance planes out of the Yalu area, leaving the Air Force dependent on the few reconnaissance jets. Antiaircraft fire got worse. The Communists, perceiving that "flak-suppression" attacks were limited to the Korean side, actually moved most of their guns to Manchuria. By the end of November when the Navy and Air Force shifted to other targets, the Americans had destroyed five of the twelve frontier bridges and damaged some others. But the Chinese had laid four pontoon bridges across the Yalu, which began to freeze on November 19. (Japanese engineers told the Americans that when the river froze it was possible to lay railroad tracks on the ice.) On December 5, attacks on the bridges were stopped. The campaign in any case was too late. By the time the attacks began, most of the Chinese forces were in Korea.

MacArthur, on November 7, had requested that his fighters be allowed "hot pursuit" of enemy planes for a short distance into China. The Joint Chiefs, the President, and Secretary Acheson were all favorable, but when Acheson asked the NATO allies about the idea, the latter were so hostile that it was dropped. This may have been an important precedent for "limiting" the war that became influential later on. It was clear that MacArthur's Air Force needed reinforcement with newer fighters. On November 8, two wings of F-84 Thunderjets and F-86 Sabrejets were ordered across the Pacific.[11]

Evaluating the Chinese Intervention

By early November, it was obvious that China was intervening in the war. But it was not at all clear in the West why or how many troops had been committed. On November 2, the Chinese announced that "volunteers" were organizing to aid Korea, while the North Korean radio declared that a volunteer corps had come to defend the "hydroelectric zone." The Chinese did not employ this theme, but many optimistic Westerners thought that their aim was merely to protect the important Korean hydroelectric plants that supplied much of Manchuria's electric power. On November 11, the Chinese government declared that the volunteers were already aiding the Koreans.

Chinese prisoners were surprised to learn they were volunteers. Interrogation seemed to indicate that, while not volunteers, they did belong to specially formed "task units" drawn from the various Chinese armies for service in Korea. The Americans apparently mistook a system of code names for actual unit designations. For example, the "55th Unit" was thought to be drawn from the 39th Army in Manchuria, when in fact it was the code name for the whole of that Army, and the "1st Battalion of the 55th Unit" actually meant not a battalion, but the whole of the 39th Army 's 115th Division. This may have been part of a deception scheme in which some prisoners were actually plants coached to mislead the Americans. An additional element of the deception scheme may have been radio signals designed to indicate that only a small part of the Chinese force in Manchuria had crossed the Yalu. General Charles Willoughby, MacArthur's erratic intelligence chief, may have squeezed the evidence to fit his commander's preconceptions. Along with the inability of reconnaissance planes to find evidence of large numbers of enemy troops, this led to the welcome conclusion that the Chinese force was still small and probably had some limited aim. The American leaders did not realize that the Air Force was not well-equipped to conduct reconnaissance in support of a ground campaign, a task neglected since 1945. Few air crews were properly trained for such work, and there were few competent photographic interpreters; this was a specialized job carried out mostly by draftees during World War II. Moreover, the RF-80s now carrying the reconnaissance burden concentrated on surveying the main roads, not the secondary routes the Chinese actually used.

On November 8, the CIA estimated that while 700,000 Chinese troops were in Manchuria, there were just 30–40,000 in Korea (in fact, there were at least 180,000 in the country). Chinese aims were unclear, but there was a grave risk of general war, and they could easily commit more forces. A stalemate might result. The Chinese might only want to protect the North Korean power plants, or hold a limited area of North Korea as a foothold for the North Korean government and a base for guerrilla operations. They might also be part of a long-lasting, limited operation to tie down U.S. forces as part of some scheme serving Soviet interests.

But MacArthur and the officials in Washington soon recovered their nerve. Walker's explanation of the defeat of early November, given to MacArthur on November 6, was that Eighth Army had been advancing in pursuit on a broad front in widely separated columns, based on a "calculated logistical risk." Its supplies had been just enough to support one reinforced U.S. division and four ROK divisions against light opposition. An ambush and surprise attack by fresh units— only some of which were Chinese — had triggered the complete collapse of ROK II Corps, which had been infected by a fear of the Chinese that hit particularly hard precisely because of earlier overconfidence. The ROK II Corps was now only about 50 percent effective. Resuming the advance, as he intended, required extending railroad service to Pyongyang and opening its port of Chinnampo to shipping. Some also seem to have blamed the 8th Cavalry

Regiment's leadership. Willoughby told General Almond that it had failed to put out the proper security.

MacArthur now concluded, as he had told Ambassador Muccio on November 14, that there couldn't be more than 30,000 Chinese in Korea. Otherwise, air reconnaissance would have found them. He was still sure that any large Chinese force would be spotted and destroyed, or air power would at least isolate the battlefield. His confidence in the ability of his air force to find the enemy and cut his supply lines was probably the most important factor in his thinking and the disaster that followed. His view was that the Chinese were unlikely to be engaged in a major campaign. They would be afraid to fight the United States without all-out Soviet support, which was unlikely since the Soviets were just not ready for World War III and the best chance for their intervention had already passed. He estimated that they were engaging in diplomatic blackmail. General Almond was also confident. He appears to have been especially contemptuous of the Chinese, due to his study of reports on the downfall of the Chinese Nationalists. It has also been suggested that racial bias played a role in his thinking. Not everyone in Korea was complacent. Some Eighth Army staff officers and the Marines were more cautious. The ROK Minister of Defense, Shin Sung Mo, openly urged halting the advance and taking up a defensive position.

Some in Washington and London had more serious misgivings than the commanders in East Asia. George Marshall disliked the dispersion of X Corps, although General Bradley thought it reasonable. The Joint Chiefs of Staff seriously considered changing MacArthur's mission, an idea to which he violently objected and that was finally rejected on November 9. They failed to reach a definite conclusion about Chinese intentions. They thought the Chinese could not drive the UN Command out of Korea without overt Soviet air and naval help, but the Chinese might tie down American forces there at Soviet instigation. They considered having MacArthur dig in for a time, perhaps along a shorter line at the "neck" of the peninsula. Bradley opposed this as demoralizing, especially to the South Koreans. The Joint Chiefs favored reassuring the Chinese about American intentions in case their actions stemmed from real fears for the power plants and the Manchurian border.

Over the next few days, vigorous efforts were made to reassure the Chinese. On November 10, a draft resolution was presented to the UN Security Council calling on the Chinese to withdraw, and assuring them that the UN would hold their frontiers inviolate and protect their legitimate interests in the border area. (A Chinese delegation was already enroute to New York to discuss the issue of Taiwan.) But the Chinese

6. Chinese and Soviet Intervention 113

expressed contempt for the resolution, and the Soviets vetoed it. In speeches on November 15 and 16, Acheson, Assistant Secretary of State Rusk and Truman himself tried to reassure the Chinese. The Chinese showed no interest in a British proposal to establish a buffer zone along the frontier. But the idea was discussed right up to the disaster in late November, much to MacArthur's irritation. He absurdly compared the idea to Munich.

The United States's allies were more worried than the American leaders, several warning that the Chinese were deadset on intervening. The British, especially Field Marshal Slim, one of the ablest World War II commanders, favored a retreat to a stronger defensive position at the "neck" of Korea. Less realistically, they were obsessed with the hope of creating a buffer zone. Some of the State Department's China experts— O. Edmund Clubb, the Director of the Office of Chinese Affairs, and John Paton Davies of the Policy Planning Staff— were deeply worried. (Both, ironically, were being fiercely attacked by McCarthyites, and later were equally unjustifiably praised, for allegedly favoring the Chinese Communists.) Both doubted that Chinese aims in Korea were limited. Clubb, who had warned at an early date that the Chinese were not bluffing, suggested, as did Davies, that the Chinese move was part of a plan to lure the West into a war with China as a prelude to World War III. Davies urged retreating to the neck of Korea and increasing the tempo of rearmament. Other American officials, notably the head of the CIA, feared that the Soviets were willing to risk a war or were considering launching one. Some of what anxiety existed was thus focused on possible Soviet moves outside Korea rather than what the Communists might do there.

The CIA did not draw clear conclusions about either Soviet or Chinese intentions, but decided that the Chinese aims were probably not limited to securing the power plants or a buffer zone. However, the Chinese pretense that their men were just volunteers, the failure to detect large numbers of troops and their apparent passivity after early November all encouraged the idea that no major campaign was intended. Many American officials and officers *later* said they had grave misgivings about resuming the offensive in Korea. Some did, probably though contemporary evidence for such qualms is hard to find. When State and Defense Department officials met on November 21 the tone was complacent. Secretary Marshall and others seemed confident in the success of MacArthur's next offensive, which was to jump off November 24. Acheson was a shade less optimistic, but even he envisioned at worst only a partial success. Admiral Sherman and General Vandenberg agreed that if the offensive bogged down or the Chinese kept on fighting, "we would probably have to tell the

Chinese Communists that they must either quit or we would have to hit them in Manchuria." This paralleled views MacArthur had expressed on November 14. A main topic of the November 21 meeting was whether MacArthur should announce that on completing his advance he would hold the high ground overlooking the Yalu with ROK units and send the other UN units to the rear. MacArthur continued to bitterly oppose a "buffer zone" and any suggestion that he stop short of the river line.[12]

His forces were about to suffer a disaster that made the whole issue academic.

7

The Immediate Consequences of the Korean War

A contemporary observer, Peter Calvocoressi, justly remarked that the Korean War was "not so much a local war as a localized general war." As shall be seen later, this remark was even truer than he supposed. Korea changed the international climate tremendously, leading to a rearmament drive in the West and an intensified struggle over Germany and Japan. The Western powers moved slowly and tentatively to bring the former Axis powers into a worldwide defensive system.

American conventional military forces were so weak that a major buildup was needed just to fight in Korea, and the war amply confirmed the heightened perception of the Soviet threat registered in NSC-68. During late June and early July, the National Security Council staff doubted the Soviets would start a major war in the short run, but admitted this was not certain and that further moves by Chinese or satellite forces in Southeast Asia or against Yugoslavia were possible. So was a Soviet move against Iran employing the Iranian Communists. Charles Bohlen took a similar view. George Kennan was nearly alone in being sure that the Korean War would stay an isolated incident. Acheson, skeptical in any case about determining Soviet intentions, considered the present situation one of the "gravest danger." He stressed that the Europeans were scared. NSC-68 now became the blueprint for a massive military buildup. The draft was extended, and the military budget practically doubled in the first months of the war. The replacement of discredited Secretary of Defense Louis Johnson — undoubtedly, for all his faults, a scapegoat for the failure of the Administration as a whole — by George C. Marshall ensured that the money would be well spent. As usual when Marshall was at the center of national affairs, things went more smoothly. By the end of 1950, expenditures on defense and foreign aid for the 1951 fiscal year were set as $53.4 billion. They had originally been planned to reach only $18.5 billion. On July 19, the President submitted his first budget increase, and called up part of the inactive reserves and four National Guard divisions. The recall of many men who had served in World War II while many reservists drawing pay stayed at home contributed to the administration's unpopularity, but proved a wise move by assuring that the armed forces would get some experienced men while preserving a mobilization base for an future emergency. NSC-68 set targets for the expansion of the armed forces. By July 1954, the Air Force would grow from 48 wings to 95, the Army from 10 weak divisions to 20 full-strength ones, the Navy from 15 aircraft carriers and two skeletal Marine divisions to 27 carriers and two full-strength Marine divisions. Its planes, mostly propeller-driven in 1950, would be largely replaced by jets. The American overseas base system, previously limited to NATO, the occupied countries and the Philippines, began to expand. The United States quickly gained rights to bases in Morocco, Libya and Saudi Arabia.[1]

In a parallel set of decisions announced on September 12, the British government began a three-year military buildup costing ƒ 3.6 billion, while the NATO Council resolved in August that rearmament must now get priority over economic recovery. This greatly complicated the last stages of the Marshall Plan, and in 1951 led to serious political crises in Europe as rearmament strained fragile economies. In the same month, Truman obtained authorization for price and wage controls. He did not put them into effect immediately, but his handling of the economy was yet another respect in which the Korean War differed drastically from the Second Indochina War. Non-defense government expenditures were pared and taxes increased to pay for the war. In December 1950, Truman finally imposed controls over the economy and raw material allocations. These measures did not increase his popularity, and the administration of controls by the Office of Defense Mobilization caused bitter quarrels between government, business and labor. But the productivity of American workers continued to increase dramatically in the early 1950s, much in contrast to later phases of the postwar era. Thanks to this, tax increases and controls, inflation was limited to one sharp spurt in early 1951 that did not disrupt the civilian standard of living. There was a steady boom. Increased American purchases of raw materials, however, injured European and especially British economic recovery.[2]

After the Soviets recovered from their initial shock at the American entry into the Korean War, they cautiously exploited the Communist victories, indulging in veiled threats about what might happen elsewhere, especially in Germany. In an early pronouncement on the war, Deputy Foreign Minister Gromyko, harping on the theme that it was really a civil war, spoke of a general right of divided countries to unify themselves. The East Germans, who could always be disavowed, went further. On August 3, Walter Ulbricht suggested that West Germany might share the fate of South Korea. But these hints, perhaps no more than crude attempts to exploit the North Korean successes for psychological purposes, backfired and weakened opposition to West German rearmament.

The Soviets also exploited a local crisis in Austria, which suffered serious economic trouble. Inflation and a shortage of food, along with a government decision to end subsidies and let food prices rise caused considerable suffering among Austrian workers. Bargaining between the unions and the government deadlocked during the summer. The usually weak Austrian Communists gained popularity. On September 26, wildcat strikes and demonstrations by the workers led to violence. In the Soviet Zone, the strikers, assisted by Soviet troops who interfered with the Austrian police, occupied railroad stations and postal and communications offices. The Socialist rank and file, although not their leaders, backed the strikes while the Communists inspired rumors that Czech troops might intervene. They apparently did not aim at overthrowing the Austrian government—hardly a possibility given the Western occupation of most of Austria—but at gaining control of the unions and forcing the Communist Party's admission to a coalition government. But once the Communists' manipulations became clear, many workers dropped out. An attempt to launch a general strike on October 4 misfired because of Socialist and union opposition. Violence by Communist strong-arm squads was defeated by the workers themselves, and the original issues were settled.[3]

German Rearmament

The Korean War led the American and British political leaders to end their opposition to rearming the West Germans, an idea their military men had favored for some time. Although Truman at first resisted the idea, it was also clear to most officers that major American and British military reinforcements were needed on the European mainland, something the French and Germans strongly desired. NATO had only 14 divisions of very uneven quality, and 1,000 planes facing an estimated 25 Soviet divisions and 6,000 planes in forward positions alone. NATO planners over the next few months concluded they would require 95 and ⅓ divisions (three months after a mobilization), 556 major warships, and 9,212 planes to defend Europe.

It would not be easy to defend Western Europe without West German troops, if it could be done at all. On July 3, Truman and Acheson agreed the issue was no longer whether, but how to bring the Germans into the European defense effort. They opposed creating a German national army and instead favored a German contribution to a multinational European force. A European army was discussed in the Council of Europe in August 1950. Churchill gave an impressive endorsement of the idea. But the British government did not wish to take part in it.

As High Commissioner John McCloy and the National Security Council noted, the Germans themselves did not want a national army and indeed were reluctant to arm at all. McCloy observed that forming a German national army would create a serious risk that the Germans would play off east and west, and ultimately join the Soviets—an interesting example of the intense distrust of the Germans still common in 1950 (and McCloy was widely considered, then and later, to be soft on the Germans). Chancellor Adenauer, who had been reluctant about rearmament, now urged building up the German police force to counter the "Bereitschaften" (the nucleus of the East German Army). He did not expect a Soviet attack in the near future, but thought the Soviets might use the Bereitschaften in some sort of aggressive action. McCloy deemed a Korea-type attack unlikely in Germany, but thought the Soviets might use the East German forces in a coup against West Berlin. In a few months they would be strong enough to overwhelm Western forces there. On August 30, Adenauer formally requested that the Allied forces occupying his country be reinforced and that the West German police be strengthened. He offered West German participation in an European army. The British agreed as Foreign Secretary Bevin shared fears of a move against Berlin.

McCloy and other optimists hoped that with an early start a significant German force might be ready by the spring of 1952, or even earlier. Deputy Secretary of Defense Robert Lovett thought that 10 German regimental combat teams might be available in the summer of 1951.

There was considerable opposition, especially in France, to German rearmament in any framework, while there was little enthusiasm for the idea anywhere, including Germany. Just five years after the defeat of the Nazis, it was about as popular as a diagnosis of cancer. West German rearmament was the most unpopular Western policy of the two decades after World War II. Even American intervention in the Second Indochina War did not at first arouse as much opposition. Opponents argued that the Germans could not be trusted, and creating a German armed force in any form would revive militarism and undermine democracy in Germany, something many German-haters had no faith in anyway. Once armed, the West Germans might turn to the Soviets and make a deal for a reunited Germany allied to the USSR. Although dead wrong, such arguments could not be laughed off in 1950. As has been seen, even some proponents of a German role in Europe's defense privately shared these fears. And the Soviets might react to West German rearmament by attacking before it became effective — evoking the very danger it was meant to counter. Although this defeatist argument would have applied equally to any other endeavor to strengthen Western Europe's defenses, it impressed many people and the Soviets exploited the fears behind it.

Advocates of arming West Germany pointed out that without it Western Europe would remain defenseless, that in the existing situation Germany was not a danger, and that it was the Soviets who had begun the game of arming the Germans. The West Germans had to be brought into play if only to counterbalance the East Germans. The extent to which these arguments, although true, lacked emotional impact is suggested by the fact that the last one seemed to simply bounce off the consciousness of many Westerners. Although the Soviets' arming of the Bereitschaften was well known and frequently discussed in 1950, many people tacitly assumed (and still do) that "German rearmament" was something involving only West Germany and initiated by the Western powers. (And there were widespread assumptions — usually but not always hidden — that, unlike the West, the Soviets could be trusted to control "their" Germans, or were somehow "really" more anti–Nazi or anti–German than the Western democracies, or that the East Germans had, unlike the Western ones, been rendered innocuous.) Although the Western governments would nominally agree to arm the West Germans, the opposition was strong enough to prevent the decision becoming effective for five years.

During August 1950, the Defense Department devised a proposal for European defense, a "package deal" to be accepted in toto or not at all. The Americans would reinforce Europe with the equivalent of 5½ divisions, 8 tactical air groups and supporting naval forces, if Britain and France substantially increased their own forces in Europe, and agreed to a single Supreme Commander and a West German role in a European army. The Germans would contribute just individual divisions; no German national army or general staff would be formed. The Secretary of State disliked this plan, favoring a more gradual approach to win over the French. He thought that once an integrated command and other measures were agreed on, the force of circumstances would make the French agree to arm the Germans. But many of his subordinates agreed with the Defense

Department. Against his better judgment, Acheson caved in and Truman approved the program on September 8. The next day, the president announced that American reinforcements would go to Europe, warning that American plans were based on similar action by the Western Europeans.

The British and the smaller NATO allies, except Norway, liked the package deal. The French welcomed U.S. reinforcements and a unified command, but balked at a German role in defense, although at first they obscured this by insisting that other powers build up their strength before letting the Germans join in a very subordinate role. Foreign Minister Schuman revealed their basic attitude when on September 22 he suggested that discussing the raising of German forces should be put off for nine months. Reluctantly, the French agreed to consider German participation, but not a German army. As an interim measure, it was agreed that German industry could make light military equipment, and the German police would get automatic weapons and mortars. The Western foreign ministers agreed to end the state of war with Germany and revise occupation arrangements to give greater powers to the German government.

Under pressure from their allies, the French during the fall of 1950 devised the "Pleven Plan" for a (continental) European army composed of contingents from national armies except for Germany, which would not have one. No German unit bigger than a battalion would be formed. Everyone else regarded it as unworkable, and the Germans objected to the subordinate status it implied.

The Americans modified the "package deal," offering their contribution in return for an "agreement in principle" on German participation, and sought to improve the Pleven Plan to make it practical. Privately, General Marshall pondered "going it alone," raising small German units of up to battalion size and incorporating them in U.S. divisions if nothing else could be arranged with the allied countries. In mid–December 1950 at a foreign ministers' meeting in Brussels, a compromise was agreed on. The European army would consist of national "combat groups" similar to the regimental combat teams of the U.S. Army. The French agreed that West German rearmament could start in the not too distant future, and the German contribution would be just a fifth of the Allied total. The Germans would provide only defensive air forces and light naval craft, and get the lowest priority for receiving American supplies. On December 15, an integrated headquarters for NATO (SHAPE) was formed. On December 19, Truman named Eisenhower commander of American forces in Europe and Supreme Allied Commander, Europe. But by the end of 1950 an effective German contribution was still a long way off. The more the

French brooded over their own proposal for a European army, the less they liked it. This ultimately led to its defeat in 1954 and ironically to the creation of a West German national army, which they liked even less.[4]

The attempt to rearm West Germany was paralleled by a pair of somewhat less controversial decisions: to reach a peace treaty with the Japanese and give them a role in their own defense. The latter posed a delicate problem since the Pacific countries disliked it almost as much as Europeans disliked German rearmament, and it was hard to reconcile with the renunciation of war written into the Japanese Constitution in 1946. The Japanese themselves disliked the idea. Since 1949, the Joint Chiefs of Staff had favored eventually rearming Japan to a limited extent, but no steps toward this were taken before the Korean War. That war made the issue pressing. With American troops leaving for Korea, there was little in the way of ground forces for internal security or defense against a Soviet invasion from the north (after Inchon no ground combat troops remained at all). The Korean War, although partly fought to avert a long-term threat to Japan, thus resulted in increasing the invasion threat in the short run. That was a particular worry in late 1950 and early 1951.

On July 9, 1950, MacArthur established a "Japanese National Police Reserve" (NPR) of 75,000 men, armed with American-made small arms since all Japanese military equipment had long since been destroyed in the demilitarization phase of the Occupation. At first, it was only a lightly-armed constabulary that MacArthur and Prime Minister Yoshida did not see as the start of full-scale rearmament. Many Americans and Japanese, however, did see it as the cadre for an army. Events in Korea forced the pace. As late as December 1950, the Joint Chiefs of Staff felt that simultaneously rearming both West Germany and Japan would provoke the Soviets excessively, but they quickly reversed themselves. In early 1951, the NPR was reorganized into four lightly equipped infantry divisions and built up to 110,000 men. Plans were laid to give it medium tanks and artillery (they were not actually issued until the Japanese peace treaty went into effect in 1952). In May 1951, Truman approved building the NPR (the "police" designation was absurdly retained, proving euphemism in such matters was not only a Communist vice) into a 10-division force by July 1952. A small air force and navy were planned. It was hoped that the task of defending Japan could be left to the Japanese, and no one contemplated an expeditionary force for service elsewhere. But the Japanese government regarded further expansion of the NPR with a jaundiced eye. The Japanese public disliked it, and Prime Minister Yoshida may already have resolved to base Japan's defense primarily on American help, with Japan for political and economic reasons doing as little as possible. The first stages of Japanese rearmament went much more smoothly and quickly than the arming of West Germany, with less international opposition than might have been expected. But the process then stalled and had little effect on the world balance of power.

After the Korean War began, the Defense Department still disliked an early peace treaty with Japan, but the alliance between the State Department and MacArthur in favor of an early peace got its way. In July 1950, serious work on a treaty began. On September 7, Acheson and Secretary of Defense Johnson agreed on the basic principles to govern a treaty. The Defense Department still opposed having the peace treaty go into effect before the end of the Korean War, but Acheson and John Foster Dulles, the chief architect of the Japanese peace treaty, finally persuaded General Marshall to alter this stand. Getting the mild and nonpunitive treaty the Americans wanted, and an accompanying security pact that would let American forces stay in Japan as allies would be difficult. The Americans were determined to push ahead despite Soviet hostility. But they also faced opposition from other countries that wanted heavy reparations from Japan and sought restrictions on the Japanese economy. Not only the Soviets and Chinese, but some neutrals, opposed American plans to retain control over the Ryukyu and Bonin islands and keep bases in Japan itself.

On October 26, the Americans presented an outline of a peace treaty to the Soviets. Dulles suggested to Ambassador Malik that the Soviets would lose nothing and reduce tensions by accepting it. Malik found the proposal highly resistible. He grumbled that the Soviet Union was now surrounded by American bases and professed peaceful intentions. Remarks of this sort were now the regular theme song of the Soviets when they were asked to state their grievances.[5]

The Soviets did not take the Western moves in Germany and Japan lying down, although they did not say anything for nearly a month after the Western foreign ministers had agreed to some sort of German participation in defense. They may have been waiting to ensure that Chinese forces would enter Korea, an event that would put teeth in their protests. On October 19, they sent an extremely sharp note to the Western powers. Ostensibly it was a reply to a Western protest made nearly five months before against the creation of the Bereitschaften. The Soviet tone was as arrogant as the delay in "responding." They insisted the German force in their zone was no more than a normal police force and denounced the Western protest as a device to cover the rearmament of West Germany, which it claimed had already taken place. "The Soviet government states that they will not tolerate such measures of the United States, Great Britain and France which aim at reviving the German regular army in Western Germany" the response stated.

7. The Immediate Consequences of the Korean War 123

In traditional diplomatic language, this was a threat of war, only just short of an ultimatum. On October 21, Soviet and satellite ministers meeting in Prague issued a proclamation calling for forbidding German rearmament, and the creation of an all–German Constituent Council composed of equal numbers of representatives from West and East Germany to prepare the formation of an all–German government. It repeated the call for an early peace treaty with Germany and the departure of all occupation forces within a year as stated in the Warsaw Declaration two years earlier. On October 28, Acheson rejected this. He repeated his earlier denunciation of the East German Army and complained about the threats Ulbricht had made in August. He acidly noted that unlike the Soviets the Western powers had carried out the Potsdam agreement on demilitarizing Germany. He demanded free all–German elections and the removal of restraints on German trade, and ridiculed the proposal for a Constituent Council.

On November 3, the Soviets sent another note to the Western powers proposing a four-power conference of foreign ministers to discuss fulfilling the Potsdam agreements regarding the demilitarization of Germany. Acheson flatly refused to discuss only Germany. He did not really want a conference at all, especially one held under the shadow of the threat made in October. However British and French public opinion prevented an outright rejection of the idea. The Soviets combined the proposed negotiations that would encourage more delays in mobilizing the West Germans with more threatening talk. On November 6, Deputy Premier Bulganin made a speech with particularly menacing overtones, declaring among other things that the American and British governments intended to unleash a new war. France's exemption from this charge was presumably designed to hint that the French and Soviets had a common interest in opposing West German rearmament.

On November 20, the Soviets angrily rejected the American proposal for a Japanese peace treaty. They opposed the continued American control of the Ryukyus and Bonins, demanded the withdrawal of occupation troops by a definite date and the complete disarmament of Japan—all ideas with wide appeal in the Pacific basin and indeed in Japan itself. Soon the Soviet press charged that the Americans were readying a Japanese force of half a million men. The Soviets grumbled about Japanese participation in the Korean War. While exaggerated, their complaints had some basis. The Americans had used Japanese-manned minesweepers and landing craft, and Japanese technicians in Korea, trying ineffectively to keep this secret.[6]

There was already considerable fear in the West. The events of the next months increased it and produced the second great war scare of the Cold War.

8

Disaster in North Korea

MacArthur had planned to resume the drive to the Yalu in mid–November, but Eighth Army's supply problems forced a postponement until November 24. Walker and his staff did not realize how strong the Chinese were, but were nevertheless uneasy. In the east, General Oliver P. Smith, whose 1st Marine Division had the most critical task in X Corps, was far more cautious than General Almond, who had dangerously dispersed his corps. During mid–November, the Marines pushed very slowly up a single bad mountain road to the Chosin Reservoir. Smith was acutely aware that his left flank was wide open. Suspecting that the enemy was far stronger than his superiors realized, he deliberately slowed the advance. He built a base and airfield at Hagaru-ri, just below the Reservoir, a wise move that may have saved X Corps.

On November 24, MacArthur's intelligence estimated that the enemy in Korea numbered 83,000 North Koreans and 40,000–71,000 Chinese. The strength of the North Koreans, who played a surprisingly small role in the coming battle, may have been inflated. But the numbers of the Chinese were grossly underestimated. Two army groups with over 300,00 men were now in Korea. The 9th Army Group, under General Song Shihlun (Sung Shi-lung), with three armies (each of four divisions rather than the usual three) had crossed into Korea and relieved 42nd Army, which joined the main body of the 13th Army Group in the west. Two more armies, the 50th and 66th, joined the 13th Army Group. The new Army Group in the northeast suffered a grave weakness. It was not properly clothed for winter. Unlike the 13th Army Group, which consisted mostly of northerners and had fought in Manchuria during the Civil War, its men came from warm areas and had fought in the eastern coastal region. Their lack of experience with or preparation for extreme cold proved disastrous. The

8. Disaster in North Korea

Chinese expected the UN forces to resume the offensive. In fact, they depended on it, planning to lure them into traps in both east and west.

The plan for the "final" offensive was for Walker's army to advance with three corps abreast on a 70-mile front: the American I Corps on the west, IX Corps (the strongest) in the center, and the still shaky ROK II Corps, which had not been properly rebuilt, on the right. Walker kept only most of the 1st Cavalry Division in reserve, while its artillery was forward supporting IX Corps. The terrain was difficult. The hills were not high but there were so many of them it was hard to find flat areas to set up the artillery, and radio reception was bad. On November 27, X Corps would join in the attack. While much of Almond's strength was expended on eccentric moves north and northeast, the Marines, supported by an Army regimental combat team, would attack west from the Chosin reservoir to cut the supply line of the forces facing the Eighth Army. Many people worried about the 30–35 mile wide gap between Eighth Army and X Corps. Only a single patrol had crossed the mountainous terrain there. MacArthur's defeat was often later blamed on his supposed neglect of the gap; in fact, he himself worried about it and ordered special attention paid to the area by air reconnaissance. Both the worry and the blame were unjustified. The terrain was so rugged that it offered no practical passage for an enemy force. The enemy did not attack out of or through the gap, but crushed Eighth Army's right with a frontal attack. The real culprits were MacArthur's assumptions that the Chinese were only one fourth of their real strength and that their supply lines had been effectively interdicted by air attack.

On the day the offensive began, MacArthur himself flew over the enemy-held area just south of the Yalu. Seeing nothing, he assumed nothing much was there. This epitomized the cause of the disaster. A reporter overheard MacArthur joke to the 24th Division's commander that if things went fast enough, some of the men might be "home by Christmas." Idiotically, the news media reported this as a "promise," and the attack was dubbed the "Home by Christmas offensive," a name thrown in MacArthur's face when things went wrong. An officer in the Pentagon made a more pointed comment when he noted that the general had been out of the United States so long that he now thought of Japan as home.

The Eighth Army, with about 118,000 men, jumped off in temperatures below freezing. Walker thought he faced only about 50,000 enemy, about half Chinese, on his immediate front concentrated around Unsan opposite his center. In reality, he faced over 200,000 men. The reinforced 13th Army Group was concentrated around Huichon in front of ROK II Corps.

For a day and a half, Eighth Army made progress. Only the ROK Corps ran into tough opposition. Then the roof fell in. The Chinese attacked the ROKs and IX Corps. The Chinese 38th and 42nd Armies struck the ROKs with much the same results as a month earlier, while the 40th Army hit the U.S. 2nd Division. The rest of the Chinese attack fell on the 25th Division and the 1st ROK Division in I Corps.

The Chinese did not overwhelm the UN units by main force. Contrary to myth, there were no massive charges or "human wave" attacks. The Chinese were masters of infiltration tactics. At least at this point, Chinese commanders were canny and cautious. They had not gotten where they were in many years of fighting against stronger foes by throwing men away. They infiltrated the front through the low ground, outflanking the company perimeters formed for night defense and came against their rear, seeking to destroy their supporting weapons. They moved in columns, seeking soft spots and attacking when necessary on a narrow front, supported by very effective machine guns and mortars. After trying to get the defenders to exhaust their ammunition, the Chinese infantrymen, supported by submachine gun fire, tried to get close enough to throw grenades. In fact, many men seem to have been armed only with grenades. Luckily for the UN forces their grenades were not very effective and the average Chinese did not throw very well. The Chinese had almost no artillery support; American planes reportedly destroyed most of their guns before they reached the front. In a few cases, the Chinese were supported by North Korean tank fire, but this seems to have had little impact on the battle.

The ROK Corps collapsed almost immediately, while the 1st ROK Division and the Americans, though under heavy pressure, hung on tenaciously. The 25th Division was caught in an awkward situation. In its center, a strong tank-infantry task force, Task Force Dolvin (later Task Force Wilson), was leading the division's advance but out of contact with the regiments on either flank. Luckily, the divisional commander had reinforced the task force with an infantry battalion late on November 25. It was able to fight its way back out on November 27. The 2nd Division, on what was now the Army's right, was in the toughest position. On the division's left, the 23rd Infantry Regiment had been about to attack through the 9th Infantry's front when the Chinese hit. Two of the 9th's companies were destroyed, but the Chinese were prevented from getting at the artillery units. However, they occupied a formidable position on Hill 329, "Chinaman's Hat," behind the Americans, from which they brought down mortar and machinegun fire on the supply route and from which they could not be driven. On the right, the 38th Infantry, along with the 3rd Regiment of the 7th ROK Division, (the only unit in ROK II Corps that was still effective) faced east in a desperate effort to prevent the Chinese from rolling up the whole front. In a critical struggle, the defenders had important support from antiaircraft vehicles—twin 40-mm pom-poms and quadruple .50-caliber machineguns. Apparently even the 2nd Division's commander, General Keiser, did not yet realize how bad things were on November 26. Certainly Coulter at IX Corps headquarters and Walker did not. I Corps did halt its advance to support the 1st ROK Division, and Walker did alert the Cavalry Division. But only the Turkish Brigade (which was less well-armed than an American regiment) was sent east. It was expected not only to block the road from Tokchon to Kunu-ri in the rear of the 2nd Division, but to retake Tokchon from the Chinese. This has been likened to "applying an aspirin bottle cork to the hole in a beer barrel." The Turks, heading east, did win a battle—against a retreating force of ROKs they mistook for Chinese. It took considerable time for the American command to find out what had actually happened. (Then the facts were suppressed, with surprising success. The Turks, badly led and not always easy to deal with, enjoyed remarkably friendly news coverage, which was better than they deserved.) On November 27, the Turks tried to attack east. They ran into an overwhelming Chinese force. That day, Walker finally realized the seriousness of the situation: he faced a major counteroffensive, not just a troublesome local counterattack. The 25th Division was now shifted to Milburn's I Corps to simplify control, and Walker put what was left of ROK II Corps under IX Corps command. Coulter was given the 1st Cavalry Division, the ROK 6th Division (which was attached to the Cavalry Division) and the 27th Commonwealth Brigade. These units were committed to prevent the Chinese coming from the ROK II Corps area from reaching Sunchon on the road south from Kunu-ri, far in the 2nd Division's rear, and even driving all the way to the coast to cut off the entire army. The next day Walker ordered a withdrawal to the Chongchon. The whole right flank of the army was under terrific pressure. The ROK 6th Division panicked under attack, and the Turks were beginning to disintegrate. A general withdrawal was now urgent. On November 29, the Chinese reached not only the Kunu-ri–Sunchon road, but the Anju-Sunchon road to the west, the main road used by I Corps.

The 24th Division managed to clear the small Chinese force that had reached the Anju-Sunchon road. The force blocking the Kunu-ri-Sunchon road on the planned line of withdrawal of the 2nd Division and the Turks was a bigger problem, but it did not *seem* to be really strong. The 2nd Division's Reconnaissance Company failed to dislodge it, nor did another attack when a company from the 38th Infantry joined the reconnaissance unit. Tanks, however, had run the roadblock. Unfortunately the tankers did not, or because of radio trouble could not, report the depth of the block. Turks who had survived an ambush of a supply convoy earlier did not tell the Americans that they had been ambushed not once, but twice on the road. The roadblock, originally imposed by no more than a battalion, was becoming stronger. The Chinese, now moving by day as well as night, pushed their whole 113th Division forward to dig in for six miles along the narrow pass between Kunu-ri and Sunchon. About ten mortars and 30–40 machineguns were bearing on the road. A British battalion was supposed to be near and about to clear the roadblock from the south, although it was reported to have been stopped. General Keiser, who was not in direct communications with the British, may have thought the British force was stronger and closer than it really was. In fact, the British had not attacked at all, but had repelled a small Chinese attack. Lacking tanks and artillery support, and far from any supporting units, the British battalion commander did not think it safe to venture further. Keiser apparently assumed that the British, in conjunction with a relatively modest effort by his incredibly hard-pressed division, would open the way south. But the British were apparently not even asked to attack unless Keiser specifically requested this, and they remained inert.

General Milburn had offered to let Keiser pull out to the west and then move south over the Anju-Sunchon road in his I Corps area. But Coulter—perhaps fearing traffic jams—would not let Keiser do that. (Apparently some service units, supply vehicles and others used the Anju-Sunchon road anyway.) With the help of an unusually successful night strike by B-26 light bombers, the 38th Infantry Regiment and the Turks—who were now useless and not even replying to American orders—got away from the Chinese. The 23rd Regimental Combat Team was to function as the division's rearguard in the withdrawal. But the tanks and antiaircraft vehicles, instead of being concentrated for a breakout along with the whole infantry battalion that was riding on them, were scattered widely through the divisional column.

On November 30, the 9th Infantry Regiment and the 3rd ROK Regiment attacked south, running into the enemy farther north than had been expected. The attack broke down. The British battalion, whose actual position seems to have been unknown to either its own brigade or higher headquarters, was asked to attack, but never did so. An attempt by the 38th Regiment, which was very tired from fighting the previous night, to renew the attack, failed. (All three of the 2nd Division's infantry regiments were down to a few hundred men each.) Then the American road column tried to barrel out, everyone assuming they had just a short distance to go. Some vehicles got through, but others were caught. Finally, the organized withdrawal just broke down, resulting in an enormous slaughter of Americans, ROKs and Turks. Colonel Freeman, commanding the 23rd Regimental Combat Team, finally got permission from the Assistant Division Commander (Keiser was out of touch) to take his men out via the Anju-Sunchon road. That proved fortunate, although very controversial, for it did expose artillery and engineer units—now the rearguard—to even heavier losses. The 2nd Division alone lost over 4,000 men in the Chongchon battle, and Keiser was unjustly made a scapegoat. Walker now insisted on a long retreat, breaking contact with the Chinese.[1]

The Chosin Reservoir Campaign

Thanks to Almond and MacArthur, X Corps was in a far more perilous position than Walker's army. It narrowly escaped an even worse defeat than the Chongchon, but inflicted severe losses on the opposing Chinese. Almond's whole corps was badly scattered. Almond was not satisfied with either of his Army divisions since both had been hastily rebuilt with a large number of KATUSAs and the recently arrived 3rd Division also had a large number of blacks and Puerto Ricans. Nor did Almond trust the judgment of General Barr, the 7th Division's commander. It is generally conceded that he was correct on that point. On the corps' left, the 3rd Division and a Korean Marine Regiment held Wonsan, while on the right most of the 7th Division and two divisions of I ROK Corps were spread over a wide area of doubtful strategic value. In the center, the 1st Marine Division and part of the 7th Division were in the Chosin Reservoir area.

On November 27, the Marines were to strike west while a task force of the 7th Division east of the Reservoir struck north. The Marines and even some on Almond's own staff disliked this plan. Such an attack, involving a drive of 55 miles by a pair of Marine regiments across bad terrain on a narrow front, would be very difficult even against the small Chinese forces and scattered North Korean remnants Almond imagined that he faced. He seems to have thought he was still opposed by the three divisions, one badly battered, of the 42nd Army with just 20,000 enemy on his front. (Some Chinese prisoners taken on November 25 and 26 identified themselves as belonging to units from other armies and revealed part of the enemy plan, but this information was not processed in time.) His corps faced a fresh army group six times as strong, although the Chinese commander was unable to bring his full forces to bear in any relevant time in the ensuing battle. The Marine G-2 does not seem to have differed from Almond's views, but Smith, the quiet and more than capable Marine commander, suspected that they seriously underestimated the enemy. Smith, rather than the higher commanders, prevented a major disaster.

Despite General Smith's best efforts, his division was badly strung out on the steep road running 78 miles from Hungnam on the sea to the Chosin Reservoir, which was the only overland supply route for the Marines and the Army task force east of the Reservoir. The three battalions of the 1st Marine Regiment held a series of bases at Chinhung-ni, Koto-ri and Hagaru-ri, where Smith had his command post. The last place, just below the Reservoir, was the most critical point at all. Here the Americans were building an airstrip capable of handling C-47 transports (the military version of the old DC-3 airliner). Hagaru-ri, however, was terribly vulnerable. The 3rd Battalion, 1st Marines, minus one company down at Koto-ri, held a four-mile perimeter overlooked by higher ground that would have needed two full regiments for a proper defense. The Marines did have support from Army engineers, service troops and their own tanks, which had simply been unable to get farther up the ice-coated road. At Hagaru-ri, the road forked. The left-hand fork ran up to Yudam-ni, west of the Reservoir, on a plateau 3,400 feet higher. Here the 5th and 7th Marines, with most of the artillery and the only tank that had gotten that far, were to carry out the attack west. F Company of the 7th Marines held an isolated perimeter at Toktong Pass south of Yudam-ni. The right-hand fork of the road led up the east side of the Reservoir. There the 7th Division's Task Force Maclean (later renamed Task Force Faith), with two infantry battalions from different regiments and a weak artillery battalion (but with vital tanks and antiaircraft vehicles), had just taken over positions vacated by the 5th Marines. It expected to occupy these positions—laid out for much stronger units—only briefly before an additional infantry battalion arrived and it attacked north. That unit never arrived, and the badly scattered force lacked the stockpiles of fuel, ammunition and other items the Marines had carefully accumulated. It did not even have proper cold weather gear.

The coming battle would be fought in the worst terrain and weather of the whole Korean War. It was far colder than the region east of the Taebaek range, and grew colder. The Americans were at the edge of their endurance. They cursed the "shoepac," their inadequate footgear, that trapped moisture and without extreme precautions often caused frostbite. Without explosives, they could not dig in the frozen ground. Batteries worked poorly, while vehicle engines had to be run constantly. Weapons worked erratically. The M1 rifle fortunately proved dependable, but carbines often jammed; the Browning automatic rifle sometimes worked, depending apparently on the technique of lubrication used. Light machineguns had to be fired frequently to keep them in working order. Grenade pins often stuck, and no one dared to remove their mittens to work them out. Even when the pins could be pulled, grenades were often duds. Bazooka ammunition often broke open, while mortar base plates wore out or simply broke against the ground. Artillery fired, but slowly as the recoiling tubes crept back instead of jumping back into position. Medical supplies had to be carefully warmed. But, although the Americans could hardly appreciate it at the time, the weather worked in their favor. The Chinese of the 9th Army Group were far worse off. As noted earlier, the blundering Chinese high command had sent in men with no experience in such cold and without proper gear. Many lacked gloves and wore tennis shoes.

The Chinese had originally planned to attack on November 25, but circumstances forced Song to delay for two days. He planned to crush the Marines and Task Force Maclean, then the rest of the 7th Division. The 59th, 79th and 89th Divisions (only part of the last reached the battlefield in time) would destroy the Marines at Yudam-ni, while the 58th and 80th Divisions crushed the Americans east of the Reservoir and struck Hagaru-ri. The 60th Division was to cut the road south of Hagaru-ri. Song's supply situation was so tenuous that he could not commit his 26th Army in the initial attack and held its divisions back too long.

The Americans actually struck first. Although by the evening of November 26 Almond knew that the Eighth Army had suffered a reverse, it still seemed to be only a temporary one. Even if it was worse than that, he believed the X Corps attack would aid Walker's forces. This was a horrible blunder. The Marines attacking from Yudam-ni the next day met strong resistance, advancing only a mile. Luckily, the Chinese did not adopt a more yielding defense and let them rush farther into a trap. That night the Chinese offensive began, except at Hagaru-ri. It was doubly fortunate the Chinese concentrated their efforts against the strongest Marine force, while the 58th Division, slated to hit Hagaru-ri, was not quite ready to strike.

The 80th Division ran into Task Force Maclean. The Marines at Yudam-ni held out in fierce fighting. The Chinese were able to attack at Hagaru-ri only on the night of November 28–29. The Marines there enjoyed excellent intelligence thanks to a pair of Korean agents who had mingled with civilians and Chinese troops outside the perimeter. Their inadequate forces were thus disposed at the most threatened points, which were East Hill, overlooking the perimeter from the east, and a draw on the southwest that gave the Chinese a covered approach. The Chinese were supported by four mountain guns that were silenced by Marine artillery. But, attacking at the same points over and over, the Chinese finally took East Hill and held it against counterattacks.

Almond himself visited the hard-pressed force east of the Reservoir, which was holding down the enemy's 80th Division. Whatever his other faults, he was a courageous and active man who regularly went to the front. But he did not recognize how bad the situation was there or in the rest of his corps. Smith was left to direct what reserves he had and reunite his division. All he could do immediately was to order a force to fight up the road from Koto-ri to reinforce Hagaru-ri. Task Force Drysdale, a motorized column of 922 men with 29 tanks set out early on November 29, composed of a British Marine Commando unit, G Company of the 1st Marines and an Army Infantry company. At "Hellfire Valley" it ran into the same sort of gauntlet the 2nd Division met on the Kunu-ri-Sunchon road a day later. Against the advice of Lt. Colonel Drysdale, the tank commander put all of his tanks at the head of the column. Drysdale had little control over the armor. When the column came under fire, the tanks stopped to shoot; the unarmored vehicles were forced to halt and exposed to enemy fire. The Chinese chopped the task force up. At Smith's insistence, Drysdale pressed on. The results were not quite as bad as at Kunu-ri; 400 men and 16 tanks reached Hagaru-ri. Smith rightly thought they were so badly needed that the costly operation was justified. During the night of November 29–30 the Chinese killed or captured most of the men left along the road. A few made it back to Koto-ri. Artillery and night-flying fighter-bombers broke up the Chinese attack on Hagaru-ri that night before it got started. On November 30, the 31st Infantry Regiment's tank company and rearmost elements, which had been part of Task Force Maclean, got to Hagaru-ri, further reinforcing the defenders. They helped fight off the second big attack on the Hagaru-ri perimeter on the night of November 30–December 1.

East of the Reservoir, the rest of Task Force Maclean were undergoing perhaps the worst battle of the Korean War and perhaps the worst experience undergone by American soldiers in combat in the whole of the twentieth century. Maclean's force, spread over 10 miles, was in a desperate situation from the moment the Chinese struck. The road to Hagaru-ri was promptly blocked, and there were virtually no communications with headquarters. In an incredible muddle, no one provided the Task Force with a common radio frequency with the Marines. A Marine Forward Air Controller with the Task Force called down air strikes with his radio, but otherwise this channel was not used. However, the Marines were so hard-pressed they had little other help to offer. Almond should have ordered Maclean to fall back on Hagaru-ri on the morning of November 28 at the latest, but even after he flew in by helicopter that same day he still expected Task Force Maclean to resume its attack north.

8. Disaster in North Korea

That night, Maclean himself belatedly decided to pull back. His most advanced battalion fought its way back down the road to join the other infantry battalion and the artillery at an inlet of the Reservoir. But enroute Maclean was wounded and captured, dying a few days later. Lt.Colonel Don Faith took over. The battered force barely hung on at the inlet, surviving thanks to the antiaircraft vehicles and their incredible blanket of fire. But ammunition was running out and, apparently on Smith's order, the 31st Regimental Rear and the regimental tank company whose attempts to reach the main body had failed, was ordered to pull back to Hagaru-ri. On December 1, Faith tried to break out. The artillery fired its last shells and destroyed the guns while the force tried to fight its way to Hagaru-ri. Unless their trucks full of wounded were abandoned, they could not get off the only road. The ice on the Reservoir would bear the weight of a man in some places, but could not take the weight of a truck. In fact, it was not yet completely frozen, and there was enough open water for flying boats to land, take out the wounded and bring in supplies, but this was not done. The breakout had some success at first, but the going became tougher and tougher. The truck convoy came under attack. Already shaken after a misdirected napalm attack had killed some Americans, the men became demoralized. When Faith was killed, control broke down completely. The convoy was destroyed. At least 1,500 men had been lost. A few hundred men got away or were picked up by heroic rescue efforts mounted by the Marines. Many of the survivors were badly wounded. Only 385 reached Hagaru-ri in good enough shape to be put in a provisional Army battalion; mentally, they were so beaten down they were not very effective. The disaster was totally unnecessary because had the whole Task Force fought back to Hagaru-ri as soon as the Chinese offensive began, it would probably have survived and also averted the crisis at Hagaru-ri. The destruction of the Army force had at least tied down and exhausted the Chinese 80th Division. The fighting of the last few days and the worsening cold also had taken its toll of other Chinese units.

Almond, who seems to have been denser than MacArthur, only recognized the full extent of the crisis on November 30 under the latter's influence. MacArthur on November 29 had ordered him to concentrate his corps around Hungnam and Wonsan. (Later, under Almond's advice, he decided to abandon Wonsan.) On December 4, the 3rd Division moved by road and sea from Wonsan to Hungnam. By dusk on December 5, most of the 7th Division had also reached the Hungnam perimeter. ROK I Corps fell back to the coast for evacuation by sea; part of it was dropped off at Hungnam but most of the corps went on to South Korea. MacArthur at the beginning of December was considering keeping

X Corps in a beachhead around Hungnam more or less permanently, in the hope that it would threaten the enemy's communications. Washington, however, disliked the idea. It was doubted that it would have the desired effect, and fearing the imminent outbreak of World War III far more than MacArthur, officials saw beachhead so close to Soviet air bases as far too exposed. Even a modest intervention by Soviet planes could have practically eliminated the Americans' close air support and disrupted movement along the road between the Reservoir and the sea, and made evacuation by sea a costly battle rather than the orderly "administrative" operation that took place.

The effectiveness of the Chinese forces was fast ebbing in the dreadful cold. After December 1, they no longer attacked the American perimeters, but tried to keep the Marines from fighting their way out. Now it was the Americans who were attacking, with plenty of air support. There were never less than 24 Corsairs overhead and sometimes as many as 60. The planes acted as "ambush-busters." It was so cold that their 20-mm cannons sometimes jammed, but napalm bombs could be dropped closer than usual to the Marines.

On the night of November 30–December 1, the Yudam-ni force prepared to break out. The first step was to reach F Company at Toktong Pass, which incredibly still held out. A battalion of the 7th Marines surprised the enemy by making a silent cross-country night march to relieve F Company. The rest of the Yudam-ni force pushed along either side of the road at daylight, led by the only tank. On December 3, the vanguard reached Hagaru-ri. Carefully resting his men there, Smith planned the next stage of the breakout. Now most of his division was together in a place where planes could land and take off (over 4,000 wounded Marines and soldiers were flown out). On December 6, the Marines started out from Hagaru-ri. There was tough fighting to clear a roadblock. The head of the column entered Koto-ri early on December 7. Here there was only a small strip suited for cub planes, but obsolete Avenger torpedo bombers converted into transports flew in to pick up the wounded.

Although the Chinese were weakening fast, the last stage of the breakout was in some ways the most difficult. The Funchilin Pass area, between Koto-ri and Chinhung-ni, was 10 twisting miles through exceptionally rugged terrain.

The road spanned a tremendous chasm where pipes carried water from the Reservoir down to a power plant. The enemy had blown the original bridge there and destroyed the replacement the Americans had installed. The gap was crossed by a gatehouse on the uphill side of the road so men could walk over it. But without a bridge, no vehicles could cross. An Army engineer company with the Marines had the special equipment needed to erect treadway bridges, but not the bridging itself. The necessary sections were airdropped into Koto-ri.

On December 8, the breakout began from Koto-ri. Chunks of at least three Chinese divisions were still along the road. They were suffering from the cold, but did not have to move around much. They had spattered the road with craters and manned bunkers similar to those used by the Japanese in World War II. Stoutly constructed of heavy logs and sandbags, and covered with dirt, they could only be wrecked by a direct hit by a bomb or a rocket.

An attack was coming from the south to meet the division. On December 7, Task Force Dog of the 3rd Division relieved the 1st Battalion of the 1st Marines at Chinghung-ni, freeing it, with the help of Army engineers and anti-aircraft vehicles, to take vital terrain far up Funchilin Pass. Patrols had found the most critical enemy position on Hill 1081. The Marines pushed relentlessly along treacherous, icy ridges where there was just one usable path; heavy snow helped protect them on the coldest day yet. The Chinese still held the crest of Hill 1081 on December 9, where they enjoyed a wide field of fire. While Corsairs blasted the crest, the lead Marine company worked a platoon around behind the Chinese, under cover of a shelf that stuck out below the crest. The hill was captured in one of the most important small-unit actions of the war. Over 500 Chinese had been killed, while less than half the attacking Marines were still alive and unwounded.

On the road, the 7th Marines reached the great gap. By the time they took the gatehouse, the Chinese there could no longer fight. Fifty men just gave up, and their weapons had to be pried out of their frozen hands. The trucks came down with the bridging — they were driven back for a time by mortar fire — and the engineers went to work. It turned out that the gap was a bit wider than expected, and cribbing was set up using railroad ties that chanced to be stacked nearby and the help of some of the fitter Chinese prisoners. The first vehicles crossed the gap at 6 P.M. On December 9, the last early on December 11. When the engineers destroyed the bridge, Korean refugees were still pouring through the gatehouse.

The whole of X Corps was now safe in the Hungnam perimeter. Planes, artillery and naval guns could lay down a wall of firepower there. The Marines were rewarded by being the first unit to board ship, having suffered 718 dead, 3,500 wounded, 200 missing, and 7,338 "nonbattle casualties" (mostly frostbite). The Chinese and the North Koreans, who had belatedly reached the perimeter, made only a few modest attacks on the defenses. The Chinese were hardly fit to fight, and neither Communist force had the heavy weapons needed for a serious attack on the beachhead. An orderly evacuation went ahead, ending on Christmas. A small amount of supplies had to be destroyed, but 105,000 troops left with all their equipment, along with 86,000 Korean refugees (12,000 other refugees were brought out of other northern ports). The Koreans were horribly crowded, often on open decks in terrible weather. The cargo ships *Meredith Victory* and *Virginia Victory* were each loaded with 14,500 people, while one tank landing ship carried 10,500 people south.

Behind them the Chinese 9th Army Group had been shattered. No less than a third of its men suffered frostbite. It was not fit to join the drive into South Korea and would not reappear at the front until March 1951. The Chinese were dissatisfied with their performance, recognizing they had suffered from lack of adequate firepower, transport, communications and food. They had only narrowly failed to destroy the Marine division and much of X Corps (Almond's units were so dispersed, and many so close to the sea, that it would have been hard for the Communists to have moved fast enough to have gobbled up all of them). The Americans had experienced a near escape from catastrophe. The Marines could not have escaped destruction if the Chinese been better dressed or had they been able to bring a bit more firepower to the battlefield. Even given the limitations they worked under, the Chinese might well have won. They could easily have concentrated greater forces against Hagaru-ri rather than Yudam-ni. The survival of the American force at Hagaru-ri against the attacks the Chinese did launch was a near thing. The 58th Division alone might have overrun Hagaru-ri had it struck the first night as planned. Moreover, the 80th Division might have been able to bypass Task Force Maclean and join in the attack on Hagaru-ri. The loss of Hagaru-ri would have doomed the 1st Marine Division and the 7th Division.[2] Chinese chances later on were lessened by the delay in bringing down reinforcements. It is not clear why the North Koreans, who were much better clothed than their allies, played so small a part in the critical fighting either here or in the west.

Despite the wonderful performance of the Marines and the success of X Corps evacuation, the United States and its allies had suffered a terrible disaster. As S.L.A. Marshall observed as early as 1953, the defeat along the Chongchon was one of the decisive battles of the century. Along with later decisions in Washington, the defeat in North Korea ensured the survival of the North Korean regime and the indefinite prolongation of the Korean War. As we shall be seen, it came very close to triggering World War III. The United States had lost battles before, but this defeat would not be redeemed by later victory.

The critical and immediate causes of the defeat were MacArthur's false assumption that the Chinese were far weaker than they were, and that the Air Force had "isolated the battlefield" and cut off most of the enemy's supplies. Officials at all levels had shared the belief that the Chinese were not really bent on a major campaign. The defeat in North Korea was not inevitable because of the balance of forces. Had MacArthur realized what he was up against or simply been more prudent, he could have pulled back to the "neck" of Korea and formed a strong defensive position along a short front near his supply base. The UN forces would then have stood a good chance of smashing a Chinese attack. The dispersion of X Corps contributed to defeat, as did to a smaller extent Washington's insistence that American planes bomb the Yalu bridges without entering Chinese airspace. More remote causes of the defeat were MacArthur's decision to invade North Korea with his forces split into two widely separated commands, the Air Force's post–World War II neglect of reconnaissance, and a defect of U.S. Army as opposed to Marine, tactics. Army units formed company perimeters for all-around night defense. Along the Chongchon, the Chinese were able to overcome such perimeters. In contrast, the Marines in the Chosin Reservoir campaign normally consolidated into battalion perimeters, which had a staying power several times greater. Had the Eighth Army used the same tactics, the Chinese attack on the Chongchon would probably have failed.[3]

The Long Retreat

While X Corps had gathered in the safety of the Hungnam beachhead, Walker's army had broken contact with the enemy. On December 3, he ordered the evacuation of Pyongyang — too early in the opinion of many because the abrupt retreat forced the abandonment of much equipment and supplies that could have been saved with a delay of even a day or two. The U.S. 2nd Division, the Turks and ROK II Corps had been beaten to a pulp, and were being rushed far to the rear to rest and reorganize. The 1st Cavalry Division and the 25th Division had taken heavy losses. It may nevertheless be that, as some have maintained, in terms of material strength the Eighth Army should have been able to hold Pyongyang, or at least some line in the neck or waist of Korea.

But the morale was not there. The Americans were badly shaken. Except perhaps for General Walker, they expected to lose not just North Korea but to evacuate Korea entirely. Even the best of the ROK troops and their leaders were in a mood of black despair such as Americans can hardly imagine. Their hopes to free the northern part of their country from Stalinist tyranny had ended in a nightmarish disaster. They now knew that at best they could save the south only at the cost of another long and bitter struggle. The British Commonwealth units, which had not suffered seriously in the Chongchon battle, alone were unshaken. Serving valiantly as the rearguard in the retreat, they even regarded the whole business as something of an unnecessary fuss. They often salvaged vehicles and supplies unnecessarily left by the Americans (the Indian medical unit attached to the British even saved a whole freight train). But the mental state of the rest of the UN force meant that any stand must be made far to the south.[4] While Walker and Almond may have been confident of the probable results, few others were.

To most of the rest of the world, it seemed likely that the UN Command was going to be forced out of Korea, and probably sooner rather than later. And it appeared all too likely that would be the prelude to World War III — if it had not already started.

9

The War Scare of 1950–1951

On November 28, MacArthur warned Washington that "we now face an entirely new war." He estimated that he faced 200,000 Chinese and 50,000 North Koreans, and the enemy aimed to destroy the UN forces in Korea. He now warned that the Air Force could not interdict the enemy's supply lines, and that his present strength was "not sufficient to meet this undeclared war by the Chinese with the inherent advantages which accrue thereby to them."

A shaken National Security Council convened that afternoon. At this very important meeting the tentative decision was made to limit the war to Korea.

General Bradley explained that the Joint Chiefs of Staff did not favor air attacks on China. The enemy had too many planes in Manchuria that could hit the overcrowded UN airfields in Korea and Japan, causing heavy losses and disrupting airlift operations. No defense against enemy air attack was possible without bombing the enemy air bases or sending planes back to Japan. But the reasons for limiting the war went beyond this perhaps temporary, tactical consideration as Marshall and Acheson stressed. Marshall endorsed a memorandum drawn up by the secretaries of all three armed services. It argued that the UN must avoid getting into a general war with China because "to do this would be to fall into a carefully laid Russian trap."

It was inadvisable to attack Chinese territory or use Chinese Nationalist troops. A faster military buildup in the West was needed, and more troops for Korea should be obtained from other UN members. Secretary Acheson and General Bradley agreed. Acheson warned that the danger of a general war was now much greater, a point he had made to the Senate Foreign Relations Committee earlier that day. The Chinese Communists must be charged with aggression in the UN and pressure should be brought against them, but Nationalist troops should not be employed. Acheson glumly remarked, "we can't defeat the Chinese in Korea, they can put in more than we can."

It might be necessary to take air action against Manchuria, but Acheson thought if such attacks succeeded the Soviets would probably come in to aid the Chinese. He remarked curiously that they would not consider this a war with the United States. (According to Truman's memoirs, Acheson remarked that if we bombed Manchuria, "Russia would cheerfully get into it" and that the Soviets had tried to lure us into traps time and again. "This one differs only in being bigger than the earlier ones," he said. The President's version seems to be more probable and consistent with the Secretary of State's usual pattern of thinking than the obscure official account of what Acheson said.) Truman accepted these arguments. At this point, the American leaders considered it both possible and desirable to hold a line in Korea, although doubts about this grew as the magnitude of MacArthur's defeat sank in and even became exaggerated.[1]

The ultimate policy of the United States in the Korean War — to save South Korea while limiting the war to Korea, and giving up the aim of uniting the country — was not explicitly formulated for several months. But it was already implicit in the thinking expressed at this meeting. So was the war scare of the next few months.

American officials had generally thought full-scale Chinese intervention in Korea unlikely unless the Soviets had decided to start a general war — something previously regarded as improbable. Now that China had intervened, they and many other people throughout the world jumped to the conclusion that World War III might be imminent. The Soviets' menacing talk in October and November strongly contributed to this idea, as did the serious defeat the French had experienced in Indochina in the fall and China's invasion of Tibet. It was widely feared that the Chinese attack in Korea might be part of a plan to divert American forces to East Asia, while splitting the Western alliance as a preliminary to World War III. Alternatively, the Communist powers might open "another Korea" elsewhere. O. Edmund Clubb, who had been the most articulate advocate of the unfashionable view that the Chinese would attack in Korea, had expected something of the sort all along. The Soviet experts like Kennan and Bohlen, who had also feared Chinese intervention, did not share such ideas, which were hard to square with the "normal" pattern of Soviet behavior. But there was a curious tendency to skip over the possibility that the Soviet and Chinese immediate goals were limited to Korea — although this was probably the case at that time. (Nevertheless, Clubb's hypothesis may have borne some relation to what Stalin was thinking, or to plans that were as yet only forming in his mind.)

On November 29, MacArthur suggested using Chinese Nationalist forces in Korea. The Joint Chiefs did not flatly reject the idea, but warned him that it involved all sorts of political difficulties with America's allies. On November 30, MacArthur told them that combining the Eighth Army and X Corps to hold a line across the "neck" was not practical. Such a line was too long for the available forces. He hoped that X Corps — he optimistically insisted that its position was not as bad as it looked — would threaten the supply lines of the enemy forces attacking the Eighth Army and help brake the enemy advance south. But he did not expect the Eighth Army to make a stand in the foreseeable future. He sent an even gloomier assessment on December 3. His command was "facing the entire Chinese nation in an undeclared war and, unless some positive and immediate action is taken, hope for success cannot be justified and steady attrition leading to final destruction can reasonably be contemplated."

By then the war scare in the Western world had become full-blown, fed by an unfortunate episode at Truman's press conference on November 30. Truman said, "We will take whatever steps are necessary to meet the military situation just as we always have." When asked if that included the atomic bomb, Truman replied, "That includes every weapon we have." In reply to another question, he stumbled, saying "It is a matter that the military people will have to decide," and "The military commander in the field will have charge of the use of weapons, as he always has." It is possible, though not likely, that Truman was consciously trying to bluff the enemy into restraint, an idea Winston Churchill for one thought there was much to be said for. But his clumsy remarks seemed to imply that it might be up to MacArthur to decide whether to use the bomb against China.

The whole exchange was often given a misleading twist, especially outside the United States. Some newspapers in Europe gave the impression that American planes were about to drop nuclear bombs on China. There was near panic, and Prime Minister Attlee promptly arranged to visit Washington. Truman had, in fact, ordered 10 B-29s equipped to carry nuclear bombs from the United States to Guam, with the bombs but without their nuclear cores. This was largely a precaution against Soviet attack. There was little feeling in the administration that the bomb should be used except in case of World War III. Apart from anything else, few saw any suitable targets in either Korea or China.

Distrust of the Americans grew along with the fear of world war. Many Europeans and Asians began acting as though the Americans, not the Soviets and Chinese, were the real menace to peace. Many people blamed MacArthur, whose reputation was now tarnished even in the United States, for the whole conflict with the Chinese. A myth arose that only his insistence on driving right to the Yalu had provoked Chinese intervention, and some people blamed the whole decision to liberate North Korea either on MacArthur or the United States. (That the Chinese might have intervened even had the UN never tried to liberate North Korea was not considered.) Criticism of American policy in general rose to a crescendo. Often the Americans were convenient scapegoats for unpopular policies of the European governments. West German rearmament, and even policies toward Germany and Japan in general (often absurdly regarded as "reactionary"), the Americans' friendliness toward the Chinese Nationalists (which was often exaggerated) and their allegedly excessive concentration on military factors became targets for attack. Even at the official level there were fears that the Americans would plunge into an all-out struggle with China unless restrained by "older and wiser heads." Where Europeans got the idea that they were wiser than Americans, a view for which the first half of the twentieth century could not have afforded much evidence, is a mystery.

Such attitudes were not universal. The Belgian Ambassador in Washington, Baron Silvercruys, calmly told American officials that he saw no particular value in using atomic bombs on Chinese cities—why not go a little further and destroy the Soviet facilities for making atomic bombs? But this refreshingly tough reaction was unusual. The Americans were shocked to find even the British inclined to oppose a UN resolution declaring the Chinese guilty of aggression, if only because they feared that it entailed a commitment to fight China before Western Europe was strong enough to defend itself against the Soviets. At a meeting of high State and Defense Department officials on December 1, Acheson commented that there was a "virtual state of panic" among our friends in New York who were blaming everything on the Americans. But the conferees shared the growing fear of war. The Director of the CIA declared that his agency was preparing a memorandum that made a better case that an early world war was likely than had been supposed, and, while the Soviets "probably do not plan on war now" they were "willing to have if they can bog us down in Asia." He thought the United States should get out of Korea. That view was not generally accepted, but it was beginning to seem likely that the Americans would be forced out instead. The meeting reaffirmed the earlier decision not to retaliate against China.[2]

The CIA estimate submitted the next day declared that when the Chinese intervened in Korea the enemy alliance had accepted the risk of general war, and perhaps had acted in expectation of one. Whether the Soviets now intended to start a war was unclear, but they might well prefer to start one via the Far Eastern theater to divert American forces and divide the United States from its allies. A later estimate, issued on December 11, admitted that it could not be determined whether the Soviets had decided on war, but stressed that they regarded their present situation as one of great strength. They definitely aimed to get the UN forces out of Korea, force withdrawal of the American fleet from the Taiwan Straits and make China a leading power in the Far East, as well as reducing Western control over Japan and blocking West German rearmament.

Ambassador Kirk, visiting Washington, told the President on December 19 that the Soviets were not likely to march immediately, but might do so if the West declared war on China or suffered a disaster in Korea. But the chances of war were three to two, against.

Some considered that too optimistic. On December 1, O. Edmund Clubb, apparently vindicated by the Chinese attack, argued that it was "largely meaningless" except as part of a global Soviet plan. The Soviets were probably ready to start a world war by several routes: by provoking UN action against China, defeating the United States in Korea or attacking elsewhere. Clubb warned that the United States had to expect to be surprised. He even suggested the Soviets might launch an airborne invasion of North America, which had been largely stripped of troops and tactical air units. Admittedly, intelligence estimates did not support this idea, but, as he tactfully put it, our intelligence had "serious gaps." Clubb urged holding on in Korea if possible. He did not favor carrying the war to China just then, but raised the possibility of a blockade of China and of atomic attacks on the Yalu dam and other power installations in North Korea if things went badly. The weight of his advice, however, was in favor of caution and trying to win time while avoiding defeat in Korea. He was pessimistic about avoiding world war.[3]

Opinions within the United States government about the likelihood of war crystallized into three forms during December. Clubb and some others feared that the Soviets had *already* decided to launch a war in a few months or were likely to do so. At the "other extreme," Kennan, Bohlen and MacArthur thought there was little danger of Stalin starting a general war unless the odds were squarely in his favor, and this was not yet the case. In between, Truman, Acheson, most State Department officials and the Joint Chiefs of Staff did not expect war in the near future, but did not think that the danger could be disregarded. They feared that if the Americans retaliated against China, the Soviets might resort to war — either to "honor" their alliance, or, more likely, because Stalin would calculate that an American concentration on East Asia was just what he wanted. They also thought that the peak of danger NSC-68 had projected in 1954 would now arrive earlier in 1952. The military buildup must be speeded up, and some precautions taken against an early Soviet attack that might be encouraged by either defeat in Korea or an overcommitment of American strength in East Asia.

When Acheson, Marshall and their subordinates met again on December 3, the Korean situation seemed even worse. So did relations with the Allies. Acheson was ready for a cease-fire on the 38th Parallel, but did not expect to get one on reasonable terms. He believed the Chinese would demand Taiwan and a UN seat at least. If the Koreans were abandoned, the results would be bad, and noted that the "present tendency among other countries is to criticize us rather than the Chinese Communists." Even the even-tempered Marshall was bitter, saying "the attitude in the UN was illogical, amounting almost to bad faith." Admiral Sherman opposed asking for a cease-fire, while Omar Bradley doubted the Chinese would agree to one. Acheson warned that if the United States got into a "general war" with China, "many of our allies would quit us and deal with the Soviet Union." At a later meeting, it was generally agreed that Korea would have to be evacuated. Acheson opposed asking for a cease-fire until Attlee had been consulted and it became absolutely necessary. He believed that the Chinese would demand total withdrawal from Korea, the abandonment of Taiwan, and the negotiation of a peace treaty with Japan by a conference of foreign ministers including the Beijing government.

Acheson's mood was already tougher than the military. He was further stiffened by the advice of George Kennan and Dean Rusk. Kennan, who had been on leave, visited the State Department on December 3. He was unhappy with talk of seeking a cease-fire or negotiating with the Soviets. He sharply disagreed with the CIA and doubted either World War III or "another Korea" was likely. He insisted that the United States had suffered a defeat, but it must bear up under it and fight back. On December 4, he and Rusk met Acheson, and Kennan observed that the worst possible time to negotiate with the Soviets was from a position of defeat. Rusk strongly favored holding on in Korea, though he thought that the military were excessively dejected. They impressed Acheson, who found that Marshall agreed with the proviso that it was necessary to see what happened to X Corps and that the Americans must not dig themselves into a "hole without an exit." Although the military was more inclined to expect withdrawal from Korea, they were also more inclined to leave the way open to attacks on China even if they did not favor immediate action. They rejected using Chinese Nationalist forces on several grounds: it might precipitate all-out war, it would be unacceptable to at least some allies, and, if a general war did develop, it would be better to use the Nationalist forces in China rather than Korea, which would then have to be evacuated anyway. The CIA doubted that the Nationalists would be useful. Observers on Taiwan warned that they would be in poor shape and were in no condition to invade the mainland.[4] Fear of global war was dominant. On December 6, all military commanders were warned that the danger of war had greatly increased.

Attlee's delegation arrived the same day. Like Churchill on his first wartime visit to Washington in December 1941, he aimed to impress the Americans with the priority of Europe. In a less Churchillian vein, he wanted them to negotiate with the Chinese even on matters beyond Korea and to get a cease-fire there while limiting the war. He was willing to have the Americans give up their protection of Taiwan, as well as let the Communists get China's UN seat. But he does not seem to have regarded the former idea with much enthusiasm. The British believed that the policies they favored might yet promote an early split between the Chinese and the Soviets, which the Americans dismissed. Several days of discussion followed in which the two sides "agreed to disagree."

Both sides' fears about the others possible intentions were exaggerated. The British were privately resolved to stick by the Americans even if they plunged into an all-out struggle with China, while it became clear that the American leaders planned nothing of the sort and thoroughly agreed that Europe must have priority. Although the British shared fears that the Soviets might start a world war, they were actually more confident than the Americans about the probable course of the campaign in Korea. Field Marshal Slim, the Chief of the Imperial General Staff, was sure the Americans could hold a line at some point simply because the Chinese could not supply an indefinite advance. The other British military leaders agreed. Although serious difficulties remained between the two countries about the priority given to reaching a cease-fire and the concessions permissible to obtain one, the British went home content.[5]

Dealing with MacArthur

Truman, showing a forbearance he later regretted, did not fire MacArthur. He may have overestimated the trouble that would cause, MacArthur's reputation had temporarily suffered considerable damage, and Truman might have gotten rid of him in December with less fuss than when MacArthur forced him to act in the spring of 1951. But he and others naturally distrusted MacArthur's judgment. They were disgusted by his ridiculous attempts to explain away his defeat. MacArthur claimed that his November 24 attack had been just a "reconnaissance in force" that had saved his forces from disaster by springing a planned enemy trap prematurely and that he had executed a planned withdrawal. This was nonsense.

Graver, if more understandable, were MacArthur's well-publicized complaints that he was hampered by restrictions preventing operations against China (without saying so directly, he led people to wrongly imagine that he had opposed those restrictions all along). His statements were widely taken outside the United States as a sign that the government did not control him. On December 5, the administration finally clamped down on all public statements by officials. Meanwhile, the Army Chief of Staff had flown out to MacArthur's command to determine the chances of holding on in Korea and MacArthur's views on a cease-fire.

Collins found Walker and Almond quite confident. Walker did not think he could hold the Seoul area without serious loss, but he might hold the old Pusan Perimeter almost indefinitely if reinforced with X Corps. Almond thought his corps could stay at Hungnam indefinitely. On December 6, Collins met MacArthur along with the top Air Force and Navy commanders in the Far East. They considered possible courses of action. MacArthur badly wanted to bomb and blockade China, and use Chinese Nationalist forces. He warned that without these measures and lacking reinforcements—which, Collins said, would not be available until April—he would have to evacuate Korea. Collins discussed the use of the atomic bomb, but MacArthur did not seem to think that it would be decisive.

MacArthur thought that the UN should accept an armistice if the Chinese agreed to halt on the 38th Parallel. Only now did he finally decide to evacuate X Corps and add it to Eighth Army instead of hanging on to a separate beachhead at Hungnam.

This belated decision was vital if South Korea was to be saved. MacArthur's judgment about the immediate tactical situation had blown hot and cold in early December. His toying with the odd concept of holding on permanently at Hungnam, and his suggestion at one point that Walker fight a major battle for Seoul consorted oddly with his long run pessimism about holding any line in Korea.

Collins' report to the Joint Chiefs indicated that things in Korea were not as bad as had been feared, but still reflected MacArthur's pessimism rather than Walker's greater confidence. Marshall and the Joint Chiefs continued to talk of withdrawal. They were impressed by Soviet threats against Japan and the fear of general war. Vandenberg and Sherman wondered if it might be wise to get out of Korea just to save Japan. Chairman Bradley and the Army opposed this, but even they seriously considered (but ultimately rejected) telling MacArthur to detach a division from X Corps for Japan's defense instead of moving the whole force to South Korea. (A few weeks later, in early January, they suggested that MacArthur transfer some troops from Korea to Hokkaido.) They rejected MacArthur's request to send the four National Guard divisions mobilized earlier and still training to Japan. They discussed the prospects of world war in gloomy terms.[6]

National Emergency

Fear of war was widespread. Polls showed that over half the American people believed that World War III was near; Europeans were even more frightened. On December 14, Truman approved accelerating the program agreed on in September 1950 so that the forces originally planned for July 1954 would be ready by July 1952, along with a production and mobilization base to augment them further. Two more National Guard divisions would be mobilized in January. On December 15, Truman proclaimed a national emergency, a move harking back to Roosevelt's similar declaration in May 1941. He announced the expansion of economic controls and the curtailment of the production of some civilian items. He appointed Charles E. Wilson, who had done a similar job in World War II, to head the Office of Defense Mobilization.[7]

The Soviets and Chinese were not slow to exploit events in Korea. On November 28, even before the full extent of victory was clear, General Wu Ziuquan (Wu Hsiu-chuan), Beijing's envoy to the UN Security Council, took an arrogant and unyielding tone. He denounced any compromise on Taiwan, such as neutralizing it or putting it under UN trusteeship. It had to be handed to Beijing. He demanded that the Americans withdraw from Korea, and that the UN condemn American aggression in Korea and Taiwan. The Chinese now took the lead in attacking Western plans for Japan. On December 1, Beijing radio announced that China would not tolerate a unilateral peace treaty between the United States and Japan (as the Soviets had earlier declared that they would not tolerate West German rearmament.)

On December 3, both Communist powers denounced the rearmament of Japan. Zhou Enlai followed this with an even more violent denunciation of the United States for making Japan a "colony" and a base for aggression. On December 15, the Soviets accused the British and French of violating the terms of the alliances they had made with the USSR during World War II by rearming the Germans. Acheson noted that the atmosphere of the mid-December Brussels conference was tinged with fear — the Soviet gambit had worked. In fact, the Western Europeans were not yielding on matters related to Europe, but East Asia was a different matter. But Acheson agreed to a friendlier reply than he would have liked to the Soviet proposal of November 3 for a Conference of Foreign Ministers on Germany. He later wrote that he and Marshall agreed that negotiations on Germany could only be a "spoiling operation." On December 22, the Western powers rejected the Soviets' specific proposals and the Prague Declaration as a basis for settlement, and pointed out that the only existing German military force was the one that the Soviets themselves had created. They called again for all–German elections. But, while unwilling to only discuss Germany, they would talk about the international situation in general. They suggested that representatives formulate a basis for a foreign ministers meeting. The Soviets accepted this on December 30.[8]

In the UN, allied and neutral nations combined to press for a cease-fire, although Wu did nothing to encourage them. As at several other points in the Korean War, there was a pitiful spectacle as the non–Communist world rushed to placate the Communists, dreaming up opportunities to negotiate and attributing "moderate" aims to them that had never occurred to the Communists themselves and in which they had not the slightest interest. Mao had never even considered halting on the 38th Parallel and was bent on taking all of Korea. He prodded Peng, against the latter's inclination and the judgment of his subordinate commanders, to push forward as fast and far as possible, and hoped for a quick victory. If that did not materialize, a more carefully prepared offensive should secure Korea in 1951. The Soviets actually had to caution the Chinese against revealing all their prohibitive conditions for a cease-fire too soon.

The Chinese ignored a request from a 13-nation Arab-Asian bloc on December 5 that they stop on the 38th Parallel. The Asians outlined a detailed plan for mutual Chinese-American withdrawal from Korea and an American withdrawal from Taiwan. While both the North and South Koreans laid down their arms, a 50,000-man force of other UN troops would oversee all–Korean elections and the formation of a new Korean government. The Americans disliked the political conditions involved, and it was singularly naïve to imagine that the Communists would allow a genuinely free election. Finally the Asians, led by India, sponsored a dual resolution for a simple cease-fire to be arranged by a group of three representatives and a political conference on Far Eastern political matters. The Americans disliked the latter idea and were divided even on the merits of a cease-fire. But they reluctantly endorsed the proposal, and worked out terms calling for a demilitarized zone along the 38th Parallel, an exchange of prisoners and supervision of the truce by a UN commission. The General Assembly passed a resolution in favor of this on December

14, over the opposition of the Soviet bloc. Mao denounced it as a trick. Wu would not even meet the three representatives, who offered to go to Beijing if necessary. On December 22, Zhou Enlai declared the whole resolution illegal since the legitimate Chinese government had not participated in the UN when it was passed. He demanded withdrawal of all foreign forces from Korea and Taiwan, and that Beijing get China's UN seat. He jeered at the call for a cease-fire and declared that the UN crossing of the 38th Parallel had "thoroughly destroyed" it as a demarcation line.[9]

The Americans were unhappy to find out that even after this most UN members were reluctant to condemn the Chinese as aggressors. Americans were furious at the Chinese Communists. Part of the public was becoming even more hostile to the Chinese than the Soviets, a strange state of mind that was to persist into the 1960s. Although the Truman administration was hardly inclined to ignore the fact that the Soviets were the main enemy, even Acheson and Marshall were disgusted at what they rightly saw as a disposition to appease the Chinese. There was general anger at the idea of "Red China shooting its way into the UN." Whether the Beijing government was seated in the UN perhaps could not have mattered less, but to refuse to condemn an attack on a UN army seemed utterly fantastic, and still does.

Neo-Isolationism and American Morale

At home, the Truman administration suffered a different sort of attack from critics on its right. In contrast to the situation in Indochina in the 1960s, it was elements of the right, not the left (the far left, of course, was very weak) that were inclined to throw in the towel. The domestic critics shared one feature with their foreign counterparts: few offered a plausible alternative to the policies being pursued. The Republican victory in the fall elections had already been taken as a repudiation of an administration that had never been very popular. With the world widely believed to be on the brink of World War III, American policy was damned as a failure. Feeling against the Chinese was violent; veterans organizations and some congressmen urged using the atomic bomb, although their ideas of where to drop it were hazy. The defeat in North Korea lent at least superficial plausibility and topicality to recriminations over the defeat of the Chinese Nationalists. Acheson was more unpopular than ever. The Republican members of the House and Senate collectively demanded his replacement.

Led by Senator William Knowland, a few Republicans who genuinely favored tougher policies toward the Communist bloc urged bombing and blockading China.

Strangely, this line of attack was largely eclipsed by a noisy, although not really popular resurgence of old-style isolationism, often thinly disguised as what can only be regarded as a sort of pseudo-anti–Communism, a phenomenon of the post–World War II era that has not been sufficiently studied. Despite a good deal of posturing, ritual denunciations of appeasement and anti–Communist verbiage, most of the opposition favored *reducing* the American effort, not stronger policies. Even some who professed to favor General MacArthur's ideas favored decreasing support to NATO while becoming more deeply involved in Asia and were lukewarm about the military buildup. (MacArthur, by contrast, favored all-out rearmament.) Senator Taft reacted to the defeat in November by calling for withdrawal from Korea. When Truman conferred with the leaders of Congress on December 13, he found the Republicans reluctant even to associate themselves with his proclamation of a national emergency.

Not all of Truman's enemies were Republicans. As before Pearl Harbor, some conservative Democrats were actually more extreme than mainstream Republicans. On December 12, the prominent "conservative" Democrat Joseph Kennedy, a strong supporter of Joe McCarthy and an unrepentant isolationist, made a nasty and well-publicized denunciation of the United States' allies and the Truman administration. He called for withdrawing not just from Korea, but all positions outside the Western Hemisphere. Former President Hoover put forward a somewhat more moderate and plausible program on December 20. Hoover argued that the UN forces had been defeated in Korea, and any sort of land campaign against the Soviets was hopeless. He proposed that the United States concentrate on developing air and sea forces, and confine its efforts to holding the Western Hemisphere and island positions such as Britain, Japan, the Philippines and Taiwan. The United States should aid Western Europe only if its efforts to develop forces for its own defense were well-advanced. *Pravda* joyfully reprinted Hoover's speech. The Soviets had much reason to be pleased with such antics.

Senator Taft took a similar line, grumbling that "the defense plan should not be one in which, in an effort to protect Europe, we would destroy the economic life of this country." The administration, and moderate Republicans like Thomas Dewey, John Foster Dulles and Henry Cabot Lodge attacked such ideas as futile and suicidal, as did Knowland and the genuine hard-liners. A so-called "Great Debate" began, with many Republicans and some Democrats attacking the plan to send reinforcements to Europe. Senator Taft fired the opening gun on January 5. He suggested dissolving the UN and replacing it with a more effective organization (in itself not a bad idea) and advocated a program similar to Hoover's. He again attacked Truman's dispatching forces to Korea as an usurpation of Congress' power to declare war, and denied that the president had the right to send troops abroad in any circumstances without Congressional authorization. In a confused and contradictory argument, he suggested that the projected reinforcements for Europe were too few to be effective but might provoke a Soviet attack. There was much support for this line among congressional Republicans. On January 8, Senator Wherry introduced a resolution that U.S. ground troops should not go to Europe without Congress' authorization. Lengthy hearings followed in which Marshall and Eisenhower effectively defended the administration's policy. On April 4, the Senate passed a resolution that was nominally a compromise. It endorsed Eisenhower's appointment to NATO but suggested that no more than the four divisions already assigned go to Europe without congressional approval. Like the antics of Joe McCarthy, but with more reason, the importance of the Taft-Wherry school was magnified across the Atlantic and caused much worry in Europe.

It did not reflect the mood of the American people, although they were neither happy with the situation nor supportive of the Truman Administration. (Harry Truman was not a national hero until well after he left office.) There was a widespread feeling that the Korean War was a "mistake." Support for the war had crashed after the defeat in North Korea. But there would be no further decline after early 1951. In fact support for the war increased a bit after Eisenhower became President. And there was much support for stronger measures than those taken by the administration, while there was no sympathy whatever for the other side. Quite the contrary: hatred of the Communists remained strong and bitter. No one doubted they had started the war or that they were evil. People were not satisfied with the way things were going. They might not agree with or even understand the policy of limiting the war, but the feeling of stark incomprehension of the whole business or any feeling that the war was "immoral" was completely lacking — a total contrast to the situation in the next war. So, despite mounting casualty lists and unhappiness with their leaders, Americans would stick it out.

The Korean War never had the terrific demoralizing impact of the Second Indochina War, and support for the war effort did not collapse.[10]

10

Nadir and Recovery

The military situation was not as bad as it seemed despite the gloom in Tokyo, the West and Korea that persisted until mid-January 1951. The Chinese 9th Army Group was unfit to fight, a fact that the Americans did not realize, and the Chinese in the west had great difficulty even in following the Eighth Army. The Chinese suffered severe supply problems even though they had captured plenty of American supplies, and the civilian transportation system of northeastern China had been stripped of trucks and buses for the sake of Peng's forces. Peng, acutely aware of this, did not really want to pursue the Americans closely. He and the other field commanders were uneasy about a deep advance. Peng preferred to let the enemy remain well north on the 38th Parallel and launch a carefully prepared offensive in 1951. Mao, however, was anxious to push as far south as soon as possible and take Seoul. He hoped for an early total victory in Korea. If only because of the state of mind of his enemies, he may have been nearly right. One big, successful push might have panicked the UN into evacuating Korea. Mao told Peng on December 11 that it was believed that General Collins had told MacArthur to be prepared to evacuate the country.

Traveling mostly on foot and accompanied by every sort of draft animal, including camels, the Chinese moved south. Neglecting the camouflage and other precautions taken earlier, they rashly rushed over main roads in broad daylight, and trucks drove with lights on at night. This proved costly as they were slaughtered by American fighters and light bombers. In mid-December the Chinese reverted to moving by night and careful concealment. The Americans then lost track of them.[1]

At about the same time, new American jet fighters reached Korea. The 27th Fighter Escort Wing's F-84 Thunderjets proved fine fighter-

10. Nadir and Recovery

bombers but a disappointment in air combat. Initially they had some success against the poorly selected Soviet pilots of the 151st Fighter Division, but the straight-winged, under-powered F-84 was really no match for the MIG-15 unless combat took place below 15,000 feet, a rare event. Maintaining air superiority, without which the UN Command could not remain in Korea, depended on the elite 4th Fighter Wing's dangerously few F-86 Sabrejets, which, had swept wings like the MIGs. The Sabrejet pilots soon demonstrated their ascendancy. Moving into Kimpo air base, they began patrols along the Yalu, flying a screen or barrier to stop the MIGs from interfering with the fighters and bombers working farther south.

This was the start of a battle for the sky over Korea that lasted until the armistice. It would sometimes be a near thing. Until late 1951 there were less than 100 F-86s in East Asia facing several hundred MIGs. The MIG-15 outperformed every other Western plane it would meet over Korea and, in some characteristics, surpassed even the F-86. (The reader should be warned that comparing the Soviet and American fighters is a tricky business, complicated by the fact that two different models of the MIG-15 fought against no less than three different models of the F-86.) Lighter, it could fly higher than the F-86, outclimb it and accelerate faster. It could outturn the Sabrejet, at least at high altitude, and apparently was faster in level flight at those heights, or at least was faster than the F-86A (later Sabrejets did better in this respect). However, the MIG lacked range, had a slow rate of roll and was much less stable, especially at high speed. It had a tendency to go into uncontrollable spins. The F-86 was a safer, more stable plane with better controls and easier to fly. More rugged, it could outdive the MIG-15, was faster at most altitudes, and had better cockpit visibility. Neither plane was well-armed for fighter versus fighter combat. The MIGs armament of one 37-mm and two 23-mm cannons, all slow-firing, was deadly against bombers (the MIG had been designed as an interceptor) but was not especially effective against fighters. The F-86 carried the same armament of six .50-caliber machineguns used by most American fighters in World War II. They were faster-firing than the Soviet cannon and more likely to score hits in fighter versus fighter combat, but did not do enough damage when they did strike. The Americans enjoyed better gunsights than their enemies. Soviet pilots were generally satisfied with the MIG and inclined to think that it was about equal to the F-86. Americans often over-rated the MIG-15 during the war, but those who had a chance to fly one delivered by a defector in 1953 generally did not think much of it. Whether the Sabrejet and the superiority of American pilots would compensate for the vastly superior numbers of the enemy would, however, sometimes be an open question. In some degree, the MIG-Sabrejet battle proved a prototype for the competition in conventional weapons during the whole Cold War. The very latest Western equipment, from tanks to jets, would usually be at least a bit better than its Soviet counterparts. But the Soviets enjoyed longer production runs, and, in the mass of older models that always formed the bulk of each side's equipment, there was often little to choose between the two sides.

The F-86s, for the moment, had little difficulty in handling their Communist counterparts. A few hastily trained Chinese pilots were introduced into combat in December, but, although carefully shepherded by the Soviets, the results were disastrous. They were soon withdrawn. The enemy jets were unable to interfere seriously with the American air interdiction program, begun in mid-December, and the whole Communist MIG force stood down for the first 10 days of January 1951. The Navy's carriers, freed of the task of giving close air support to X Corps, joined the Air Force in blasting bridges, tunnels, marshalling yards and supply centers in a belt across Korea. Contrary to what was sometimes said later, it is clear that interdiction at this point caused the enemy a great deal of trouble. Their supply lines were now much longer and exposed than in the fall, nor was there a static front of the sort that later reduced their supply requirements and made countermeasures against air attack easier. The UN did not suffer from air attacks. The short range of the MIG-15 would now have made it hard for the enemy to mount attacks from the Manchurian air bases against the now distant UN targets, while throughout the war the Soviets were very cautious about launching any offensive air operations from that sanctuary.[2]

The main UN force had retreated to the vicinity of the 38th Parallel. Morale remained awful. There was a panicky fear of "Red hordes" (widely supposed to be "drug-crazed"), and an expectation of defeat and evacuation. The Americans had lost track of the Chinese, overestimated their strength and underestimated their own. Washington had acted quickly to replace the heavy loss of material, rushing almost a complete set of equipment and supplies for an infantry division across the Pacific. The Eighth Army was also getting some reinforcements. X Corps was reaching South Korea just in time, and new UN units were now available. Unlike the Turks who had been oversold, they were a real contribution to the UN's strength. (The Turks were in a particularly bad mood. Angry at the Americans, they had massacred some Korean refugees trying to cross the Han. Like many other atrocities committed by non-Westerners against other non-Westerners, this got remarkably little publicity.) A Canadian battalion, although still training, would reinforce the British Commonwealth force. The French and Dutch battalions had boosted the U.S. 2nd Division's strength and would fight very well in the coming battles. A Greek battalion joined the 1st Cavalry Division (in a bit of luck, one of the Cavalry regimental commanders was a Greek-American). Ethiopian, Filipino and Thai battalions still needed training and acclimatization, which was not successful in the Thai case.

The ominous lull that followed the long retreat ended on December 20, but it was the North Koreans not the Chinese who showed up. The North Koreans had no less than 14 very weak divisions grouped in II, V, and III Corps (the last not yet at the front), supported by a huge train of 6,000 pack horses. The "divisions" were so small that the fighting force numbered only 61,500 men. These units had been hastily formed or rebuilt with new draftees and dragooned ROK prisoners of war in a sinister masterpiece of Stalinist reorganization. They were far from the well-trained, heavily armed forces that had invaded in June 1950. Now armed only with rifles, automatic weapons and mortars, they were not too different from their Chinese allies, though better dressed. (Even after the North Korean armored units were rebuilt, they were largely held back to counter possible amphibious landings in the Communist rear.) But they were a serious threat. Later Mao badgered Stalin into finally getting Kim Il Sung to consolidate his forces into a smaller number of strong divisions.

Striking a ROK division north of Chunchon in the central mountains, the North Koreans began to outflank, it, forcing the commitment of American forces to the area. From Chunchon, the most important north-south road through central Korea, Route 28, led to Wonju, where a lateral road, Route 20, crossed the peninsula. In all, five main roads met at Wonju, and the central railroad line from Pusan to Seoul passed through the place. The war began to assume a new pattern. From this point on the Communists directed their main attacks whenever possible against ROK units, a practice that had already worked well in November. More lightly equipped than the other UN units, they had a superstitious fear of the Chinese. And the Communists also tended to concentrate their efforts in the central corridor where their lightly armed forces could operate in relatively favorable terrain that minimized the UN advantage in firepower and vehicles.

On December 23, General Walker died in a jeep crash. General Matthew Ridgway, the Deputy Chief of Staff of the Army and a brilliant field commander in World War II, flew in to replace him. Walker had been a good general, but Ridgway was a superb one. MacArthur had far more confidence in Ridgway than he had in Walker. When they met on December 25, he assured the new Eighth Army commander of a free hand, and warned that the Chinese were a dangerous foe and not to be underestimated.[3]

No decision had yet been made on whether to hold Korea or evacuate. It was Ridgway's leadership that tipped the balance in favor of holding. By so doing, he probably contributed more than any other American military leader to the defeat of the Communist side in the Cold War.

Washington expected the worst. On December 29, the Joint Chiefs of Staff told MacArthur that "it appears from all estimates available that the Chinese Communists possess the capability of forcing the United Nations forces out of Korea if they choose to exercise it." They again warned that he would not get important American reinforcements and stated, "Korea is not the place to fight a major war. Further, we believe that we should not commit our remaining available ground forces to action against Chinese Communist ground forces in Korea in face of the increased threat of general war."

It was, however, desirable to resist the enemy's aggression at some position in Korea and deflate his prestige if it could be done without serious losses. MacArthur was to defend in "successive positions" subject to the primary consideration of the threat to Japan: "It seems to us that if you are forced back to a position in the vicinity of the Kum river and a line generally eastward there from, and if thereafter the Chinese Communists mass large forces against your positions with an evident capability of forcing us out of Korea, it then would be necessary under these conditions to commence a withdrawal to Japan."

On December 30, MacArthur replied with the best case he ever made for extending the war. "It is quite clear now that the entire military resources of the Chinese Nation, with logistic support from the Soviet, is committed to a maximum effort against the United Nations Command," he said. "In implementation of this commitment, a major concentration of the Chinese forces in the Korean-Manchurian area will increasingly leave China vulnerable in areas whence troops to support Korean operations have been drawn. Meanwhile under existing restrictions our naval and air potential are being only partially utilized and the great potential of Chinese Nationalist forces on Formosa and guerrilla action on the Mainland are being ignored."

MacArthur argued that if the United States or the UN recognized the "state of war which has been forced on us by the Chinese authorities" and took retaliatory actions, we could:

> [1] Blockade the coast of China; [2] Destroy through naval gunfire and air bombardment China's industrial capacity to wage war; [3] Secure reinforcements from the Nationalist garrison on Formosa to strengthen our position in Korea if we decided to continue the fight for that peninsula; and [4] Release existing restrictions upon the Formosan garrison for diversionary action

10. Nadir and Recovery

[possibly leading to a counter-invasion] against vulnerable areas of the Chinese mainland. I believe that by the foregoing measures we could severely cripple and largely neutralize China's capability to wage aggressive war and thus save Asia from the engulfment otherwise facing it. I believe furthermore that we could do so with but a relatively small part of our overall military potential committed to the purpose. There is no slightest doubt but that action would at once release the pressure upon our forces in Korea, thereupon determination could be reached as to whether to maintain the fight in that area or to effect a strategic displacement of our forces with the view to strengthening our defenses of the Littoral Island chain while continuing our naval and air pressure upon China's military potential. I am fully conscious of the fact that this course of action has been rejected in [the] past for fear of provoking China into a major war effort but we must now realistically recognize that China's commitment there has already been fully unequivocally made and that nothing we can do would further aggravate the situation as far as China is concerned. Whether defending ourselves by way of military retaliation would bring on Soviet military intervention or not is a matter of speculation. I have always felt that a Soviet decision to precipitate a general war would depend solely upon the Soviets' own estimate of relative strengths and capabilities with little regard for other factors.

He stressed that the forces he wanted — the four National Guard divisions — were to defend Japan, not Korea.

MacArthur warned that evacuation from Korea would release the bulk of Chinese forces "for action elsewhere — quite probably in areas of far greater importance than Korea itself," as well as having disastrous political results. Continued action in Korea by pinning down enemy resources protected areas to the south. He remarked that "I understand thoroughly the demand for European security and fully concur in doing everything possible in that sector, but not to the point of accepting defeat anywhere else — an acceptance which I am sure could not fail to insure later defeat in Europe itself. The preparations for the defense of Europe, however, by the most optimistic estimate are aimed at a condition of readiness two years hence. The use of forces in the present emergency in the Far East would not in any way prejudice this basic concept. To the contrary it would insure thoroughly seasoned forces for later commitment in Europe synchronously with Europe's own development of military resource."

Without reinforcements and under the existing restrictions, he indicated, he would be forced back to the Pusan Perimeter and finally into evacuation. Over the next few days he made clear that he thought the decision could be deferred until reaching the Pusan line rather than the Kum.

MacArthur's message was seemingly based on the false premise — which the Eighth Army was about to explode — that operations against China were vital if his forces were to stay in Korea. However, it expressed a basic viewpoint that remained valid in his eyes after that particular idea was shown to be wrong. MacArthur doubted that the Soviets would embark on a general war in the near future. Ironically, his ideas on that point were close to that of George Kennan and later critics who regarded Western fears of Soviet attack in 1950–1951 as wildly exaggerated. Nor did he believe that the Soviets would take major risks just to honor their alliance with China if they were otherwise unready for war. On the other hand, MacArthur not only rated Asia as more important than Washington did, but regarded China as a menace by itself that could and should be defeated. Unlike the China bloc and most conservative Republicans (with whom he is often carelessly lumped), MacArthur did not regard the Chinese as Soviet puppets. He told David Lilienthal in March 1951 that "China today can't be explained by saying it is a pawn of Russia" and the Communist regime there would stay with the Soviets only as long as their interests coincided. He feared, however, they would remain allied for many years. Eventually they would clash, "but that clash will not come in our lifetime."

The Joint Chiefs were not unsympathetic to MacArthur. This was especially true of Admiral Sherman who told his colleagues on January 3 that, as far as he was concerned, open hostilities already existed with China. On his initiative, the Joint Chiefs recommended on January 12 that if the UN Command could stay in Korea MacArthur should get two National Guard divisions for the defense of Japan. If he had to evacuate Korea or if the situation there was stabilized, a naval blockade should be imposed on China. Restrictions on the operations of the Chinese Nationalists and on air reconnaissance of Manchuria and the Chinese coast should be removed. But targets in China should be bombed only if the Chinese attacked American forces outside Korea. However, on January 9, the Joint Chiefs had warned MacArthur that there was little chance of a policy change. A blockade would await evacuation or stabilization, and needed UN agreement. He would not get Nationalist reinforcements, nor could he attack China unless the Chinese attacked outside Korea.

MacArthur responded by complaining that his missions, to hold in Korea and defend Japan, were contradictory. He was not strong enough to do both. He could hold a beachhead in Korea for a limited time, but with the continued restrictions and no reinforcements the enemy would eventually make it untenable. In the absence of overriding political considerations, the UN Command should withdraw from Korea. He evidently wished to evade deciding whether to order an evacuation and thus force Washington to take the blame for one.

The president now intervened. On January 13, he sent a long personal message to MacArthur stressing the great political and strategic importance of holding on in Korea if possible. Even if the UN was driven out of Korea, continued resistance should be maintained on the offshore islands. Truman carefully expounded the basic principles behind the restraints on MacArthur. The American course of action had to be such as "to consolidate the great majority of the United Nations. This majority is not merely part of the organization but is also the nations which we would desperately need to count on as allies in the event the Soviet Union moves against us. Further, pending the build-up of our national strength, we must act with great prudence in so far as extending the area of hostilities is concerned. Steps which might in themselves be fully justified and which might lend some assistance to the campaign in Korea would not be beneficial if they thereby involved Japan or Western Europe in large-scale hostilities."[4]

General Ridgway arrived in Korea believing that it would not be necessary to evacuate, but that Eighth Army needed a shake up. However, he was shocked to find out how bad morale was and was dismayed by how few artillery battalions the Eighth Army had. He wanted to replace some commanders, encourage a more aggressive attitude and improve its tactics, which, as the renowned expert S.L.A. Marshall had found, were "deplorable." He wanted more effective use of infantry firepower, patrolling and night operations, and a less roadbound approach with more attention to the importance of securing high ground. Major attacks were to be made with units closely aligned, methodically reaching phase lines and "mopping up" before moving on to prevent enemy infiltration.

Ridgway was just getting started when the Chinese began their "Third Phase Offensive" on New Year's Eve. He had not had time to make any changes in the Eighth Army's deployment. I Corps, on the west, stood before Seoul, with the U.S. 25th Division, the Turkish Brigade and the 1st ROK Division on the Imjin river, with the British 29th Brigade in reserve. To the east, IX Corps had the 6th ROK Division and the U.S. 24th Division in line, to oppose an attack on Seoul from the northeast, with the 1st Cavalry Division and the 27th Commonwealth Brigade in reserve. Letting his corps commanders put the two ROK divisions side by side was a bad mistake by Walker that Ridgway did not have time correct. To the right of IX Corps, ROK III Corps was deployed with three divisions, the 2nd, 5th, and 8th in line and the 7th Division in reserve. But east of IX Corps the "front line" was a theoretical concept that bore little relation to the situation on the ground. Conditions there resembled those on the German front in Russia in the winter of 1941–1942. There was no continuous line or even alignment. Widely separated ROK units, whose positions and situations were only vaguely known at Eighth Army headquarters, tried to block the North Koreans from getting onto vital arteries of communications. The

U.S. 2nd Division was moving to backstop the ROKs in the central corridor. Ridgway planned to commit X Corps there to take over the whole sector. Still further east, ROK I Corps with two divisions, with a wide gap between them, held the east coast.

As expected, the Communists main blow was in the west. The North Koreans launched a secondary attack in the east. The Chinese expected to meet prepared defenses including minefields and bunkers. They had brought up artillery, hardly used in their earlier offensives. The carefully prepared attack broke right through the ROK 1st and 6th Divisions, and hit the 24th Division hard. Ridgway had known that he could not hold in place, but hoped for a time to keep a bridgehead around Seoul. With the ROKs panicking and the whole army exposed to an outflanking force from the east where it was clear that ROK III Corps was in bad shape, Ridgway ordered a withdrawal over the Han on January 3. There was a difficult evacuation over the Han on pontoon bridges that were endangered by ice floes as well as enemy action, combined with a humiliating mess when the Chinese overran part of the British 29th Brigade that was acting as a rearguard for the U.S. 25th Division. With 300 men lost, Ridgway ordered that UN units would no longer serve as rearguards for American units. On January 4, the Communists took Seoul. Another long retreat followed. Inchon, Kimpo and Suwon airfields were abandoned, forcing the F-86s and many close-support air units back to Japan. The demolitions at Inchon were excessive, rendering the port almost useless for many months after the UN forces later recaptured it.

Peng was surprised that the UN Command had pulled back so far. He exploited the victory cautiously, sending forward only his 50th Army and the North Korean I Corps, which served under Chinese command on the western flank. He did not want to plunge too far south in the western sector, fearing overextension and an Inchon-type landing in his rear, while the North Koreans and Stalin complained about his failure to pursue all out. On January 7–8, a 25th Division patrol found that the Chinese were not keeping up an all-out drive south. This confirmed Ridgway's view that the real threat was now in the center.

The morale of the UN forces had hit rock bottom. The Communist offensive, by driving the F-86s and eventually most of the U.S. fighter force back to Japan, gave the Soviets air superiority over northwest Korea by default. Only fast reconnaissance planes dared to fly north of the Chongchon. Bombers and fighter-bombers generally stayed well south of that river, and northwest Korea became known as "MIG Alley." During January the Communists embarked on a step-by-step plan to gain air superiority over all of Korea. The Chinese planned to rehabilitate old airfields and build new ones, all heavily defended by flak batteries, first in MIG Alley and then farther south. When they were finished, fighters and then ground-attack planes would move in. From North Korean bases they could range far south without provoking retaliation against Manchuria.[5]

Even before the Chinese struck, the North Korean V Corps had hit ROK III Corps "frontally" in the central corridor, driving down Route 29 toward Wonju, while their II Corps circled round the ROKs right flank through high mountains where a huge gap had been completely undefended. A regiment from II Corps established a roadblock on Route 29 between Hongchon and Hoengsong, cutting the ROKs main supply route while the rest of II Corps pushed still farther south into the UN rear. The still shaky U.S. 2nd Division was sent to hold Wonju, with one of its regiments heading farther south to reduce the enemy roadblock south of Hongchon. With ROK help, it smashed the roadblock on January 2. This had hardly been accomplished when, on January 3, other elements of the Communist II Corps pushing farther east and south cut the Pusan-Wonju-Seoul road and the main supply route of Almond's X Corps, which was trying to shore up Eighth Army's eastern flank. Almond's command now included the U.S. 2nd and 7th Divisions, the 187th Airborne Regimental Combat Team, and the battered ROK 2nd, 5th and 8th Divisions. The ROK III Corps, with the 7th and 9th ROK Divisions, tried to form a front farther east as ROK I Corps retreated along the east coast. Almond had given up the U.S. 3rd Division and some artillery battalions to I Corps, and the 1st Marine Division, no longer under his command, was fighting guerrillas and establishing a blocking position far to the south around Andong. O.P. Smith had flatly refused to serve under Almond again. Ridgway tacitly went along with this since no one wanted to lose Smith's services, or deal with the stink the resignation or relief of this outstanding general would cause. But in this fantastic situation, with friends and enemies scattered all over the map, Almond performed far better than he had in northeast Korea.

While the U.S. 7th Division and the ROKs moved to reopen X Corps' main supply route and block and cut off the North Korean II Corps, the 2nd Division tried to hold Wonju against V Corps. The Americans and their allies were in an awkward salient, with the enemy's II Corps on the east and part of V Corps outflanking them to the west. Wonju itself was in a bowl-like valley and hard to defend. On January 7, the North Koreans infiltrated a battalion-sized force into the town while other troops attacked the American defenses outside the built-up area. The North Koreans were stopped, but the divisional commander went along with the request of Colonel Freeman, still commanding the 23rd Infantry, to be allowed to pull back from Wonju to high ground south of the town. There, the Americans would still dominate the vital crossroads. Although some 2nd Division officers thought this movement unnecessary, Almond allowed it. But the division pulled back much farther than he had authorized.

This was a crucial moment. The loss of the Wonju area could easily force another retreat by the whole of the Eighth Army, and the tendency to retreat was gaining a momentum of its own. Infuriated, Almond ordered the 2nd Division to turn around and retake Wonju. He probably also decided to fire its commander, although he did not actually do so for a few more days. The counterattack went forward in ghastly weather. There was no air support, and fierce fighting took place in terrible cold. At one point a ROK regiment protecting the American flank broke under attack. But on January 11, the Air Force got into the air again. In tough fighting, the Americans, Dutch and French stopped North Korean attacks. The Communists finally broke off, pulling back to positions around Hoengsong. On January 19, Wonju, or what was left of it after air bombardment, was reoccupied. Meanwhile, the North Korean II Corps had been stopped. It was not smashed in a big battle, but ground down as the Americans and ROKs blocked one route of advance after another, forcing the North Koreans to turn aside and seek a new path for infiltration. The Communists ran into constant patrols, small fights and air attacks; they were exhausted and out of supplies. X Corps and ROK III Corps began to form a more coherent front.[6]

Reconnaissance in Force

As fighting raged in the center and east, the western front was quiet. Ridgway ordered I Corps to launch a large-scale "reconnaissance in force" in the Osan-Suwon area to determine the enemy's position and intentions. The Americans would then withdraw. On January 15, following a big air strike, the 27th Infantry Regiment attacked, supported by diversions by the 3rd Division and the 1st ROK Division. It found many dead civilians killed by an earlier air attack, but did not meet serious resistance until it reached Suwon. There it suffered few losses while air strikes and artillery inflicted heavy casualties on the enemy. The Chinese had proved weaker than expected, and a similar operation by IX Corps confirmed that a similar situation existed on its front.

Ridgway decided to launch a bigger reconnaissance in force, "Operation Thunderbolt." On January 25, I and IX Corps each sent a reinforced division north toward the Han, X Corps protecting the right flank of the advance. I Corps quickly secured Suwon. The Soviets had warned the Chinese that the UN Command would attack, but the Chinese disbelieved this and were taken by surprise. Their 50th Army was badly battered during the last few day of January, although it was reinforced by the 38th Army in the east. The Chinese leaders may not have minded the losses of the 50th Army all that much, for it was an ex–Nationalist force that had defected to them en masse during the civil war. Peng, however, later paid tribute to its fighting ability. Worrying about a landing in his rear, he urged as early as January 27 pulling back above the 38th Parallel and even belatedly accepting the UN cease-fire offer of January 13. But Mao would not listen.

On February 1, the reconnaissance in force turned into a full-scale advance to the Han. Ridgway dictated a slow, careful advance, securing the high ground, with units keeping in alignment and maintaining defense perimeters at night with constant patrolling. The Navy bombarded the enemy from the sea and tried to reinforce the Communists' fears of an amphibious outflanking move. An unusual feature of the drive to the Han was "Operation Punch." Two task forces from the 25th Division, "Bartlett" and "Dolvin," each composed of roughly one infantry battalion and one tank battalion with supporting elements, drove up the main highway from Suwon to Seoul and a secondary road to the west. The main Chinese defense position, Hill 440, lay between the two roads. The Chinese positions were methodically blasted by tanks, antiaircraft vehicles and artillery. The infantry took the enemy held hills during the day, but retired each night, letting the Chinese reoccupy the abandoned ground. The tactic was repeated for three consecutive days. By the end, the Americans estimated they had killed 4,251 Chinese with less than 70 UN dead. Under such pressure, the enemy withdrew to the Han on the night of February 8–9. Inchon and Kimpo airfield were now back in UN hands. Ridgway had told MacArthur on February 3 that he did not intend to take Seoul and that he did not recommend advancing beyond the 38th Parallel with his present forces. MacArthur thoroughly agreed with him on the latter point unless the war was carried to China, but favored taking Seoul. Seoul, he noted, was a vital supply hub.[7] An advance beyond the Han was desirable, if only to protect Inchon and Kimpo.

By the end of January, Ridgway's leadership, obvious success at the front, and the institution of five-day rest and recuperation leaves in Japan had vastly improved morale. The Eighth Army could not only defend but attack successfully.

Battles for the Central Corridor — Wonju and Chipyong-ni

However, as Ridgway already suspected, the enemy's main strength was not in the west at all. And the Communists were far from giving up the dream of throwing the UN forces out of Korea. Taking over from the North Koreans in the central corridor, the Chinese were readying a "fourth phase" offensive there.

X Corps had also launched a reconnaissance in force toward the northeast. On January 29, a large patrol mounted jointly by the 2nd and 7th Divisions encountered the Chinese 42nd Army at the "twin tunnels" area three miles southeast of Chipyong-ni. This town, northwest of Wonju, was a junction of five roads and controlled entry from the east into the Han valley. At the "twin tunnels," the railroad from Wonju to Seoul dived through two tunnels, with a bridge between them. The main road, Route 24, serving Chipyong-ni from the south passed through the valley between the hills pierced by the tunnels.

The patrol fought a terrific battle against a superior force of Chinese for two days and suffered heavy losses. It was lucky to escape at all. Ridgway told Almond to send a strong blocking force to the tunnels. A battalion of the 2nd Division's 23rd Regiment and the French Battalion found the place unoccupied and took up positions on high ground nearby. Most of the force occupied a single hill, but one French company held a detached position on Hill 453, the highest ground in the area. The 42nd Army now sent the whole 125th Division against the French and Americans. There was desperate fighting during the night of January 31–February 1. Luckily the Chinese ran short of mortar ammunition and the allied force was saved by strong attacks by USAF and Marine fighter-bombers that arrived after dawn. The Chinese withdrew with enormous losses and on February 3 the Americans occupied Chipyong-ni without difficulty.

Ridgway now ordered an offensive in the central corridor, a spoiling attack to disrupt the expected enemy attack there. Almond planned a coordinated offensive by his own corps and ROK III Corps called "Operation Roundup." The main burden of the attack was to be borne by the ROK 5th and 8th Divisions. They would drive north from Hoengsong and envelope Hongchon, the next large town to the north on Route 29 from east and west respectively. They would be backstopped by the U.S. 2nd Division, the 187th Airborne Regimental Combat Team, and the 7th Division. A peculiarity of the offensive was that quite large supporting forces from the U.S. 2nd and 7th Divisions would operate intermingled with the ROKs. The 2nd Division supplied Support Force 21, composed of artillery, tank and infantry battalions to support the ROK 8th Division, while the 7th Division's Support Force 7 fought with the ROK 5th Division. Smaller "support teams" composed of tank and infantry companies would also operate in support of the ROKs. The chain of command over these support forces was not entirely clear. This was the first time Americans had

10. Nadir and Recovery

been put under the control of ordinary ROK units, as opposed to the elite 1st Division, and even Paik Sun Yup had never been given control over U.S. infantry units. This move did not command universal enthusiasm among the Americans and did not prove to be one of Almond's better ideas.

On February 5, the UN attack began. It enjoyed some success against North Korean units, although the advance in the east by the 5th Division had to be strengthened by bringing in the ROK 3rd Division. In the west, the 8th Division had gotten spread out, with wide gaps between its regiments. The attack had produced a broad salient, 25 miles across and a convenient target for the Chinese attack.

Eighth Army had predicted a Chinese offensive, but it came a bit sooner than expected. Peng apparently hurried his attack after the Americans took Chipyong-ni. Almond, however, apparently underestimated the extent to which the Chinese had shifted their strength east. A wary Ridgway ordered the UN attack to stop on February 11. But by the time this order was given, the Chinese had struck.

They had assembled their 39th, 40th, 42nd and 66th Armies in the central region, with the North Korean III and V Corps in support to the east. The Chinese broke right through and quickly destroyed the ROK 8th Division. In the east they drove back the ROK 3rd and 5th Divisions with considerable losses. The Chinese, however, were surprised at their failure to destroy the 3rd Division and thought that it fought relatively well. Support Force 7 was able to pull out and reached safety relatively intact. Support Force 21 was not so lucky. It could not get clear orders, but after a dangerous delay set out south on Route 29, joined by Support Team "Baker" and many ROKs, the latter so demoralized as to be useless. Falling back under heavy attack, it broke through a roadblock to join the 3rd Battalion, 38th Infantry at Saemal where Route 2, the lateral transpeninsular road, crossed Route 29. The infantry battalion managed to collect the ROKs and got them to fight. There the whole force was cut off together. A small force sent to relieve them was beaten back with heavy losses when it was taken by surprise by Chinese whom the Americans mistook for ROKs. Under pressure, the American-ROK force broke out. Part of it reached the Dutch battalion holding Hoengsong, after appalling losses at what became known as "Massacre Valley."

The destruction of the ROK 8th Division and the withdrawal of the other ROK divisions, which drifted south and east pursued by the North Koreans, left a huge gap of 12 miles in the X Corps line, which what there was of it, now faced northeast. The Chinese poured through the hole.

Ridgway had the headquarters of I ROK Corps flown in from the east coast to take over the 5th Division and what was left of the 8th. Almond was given control of the ROK corps. The 27th Commonwealth Brigade and the 6th ROK Division were ordered transferred from IX Corps to help Almond fill the gap. But the forces already at Chipyong-ni and Wonju would have to brake the enemy drive.

At Chipyong-ni, the 23rd Regimental Combat Team and the attached French held low hills around the town. Attempts to force the Chinese off the higher ground to the northeast and southwest had failed and, on February 11, enemy preparations for an attack were seen. As the seriousness of the situation finally sank in on February 12, Almond had been ready to let the 2nd Division commander and Colonel Freeman withdraw from Chipyong-ni. Ridgway intervened, insisting that it be held. That was fortunate, since the Chinese were already getting across the 23rd Regimental Combat Team's line of retreat. Had it pulled out as the Chinese expected, it probably would have been caught in the process of moving and destroyed. The Chinese underestimated the size of the UN force at just over 3,000 men instead of twice that, and their attack on the Americans and French in place apparently had to be hastily mounted by three divisions from three different armies. One division was only able to bring four battalions into the battle. However, when the Chinese attacked on the night of February 13–14, they had plenty of fire support from 76-mm guns, pack howitzers and 120-mm mortars, and the ground was so hard that the Western soldiers could not dig in properly. The defenders were aided by flare-dropping planes that lit up the Chinese, whose initial infantry attacks were not well-directed. As in the first Chipyong-ni battle, the fire of the antiaircraft vehicles was a major factor in the successful defense. After dawn, planes spotted a large number of Chinese trying to hide out for the day in the "twin tunnels" area and inflicted heavy losses on them. Otherwise, low cloud hampered air operations, including the dropping of supplies. The second night the defenders were even more hard-pressed. The Chinese attack, better conducted, broke into G Company's position and the Chinese could not be dislodged, while a relief attempt by the Commonwealth Brigade along Route 24 was not going well.

To the west, IX Corps mounted its own relief effort over Route 24A, using the 1st Cavalry Division's 5th Regiment. It went too slowly. The regimental commander, Colonel Crombez, then decided to ram through an armored task force, with 23 tanks carrying 160 men of his L Company. For infantry to ride atop tanks in action was not usually a good idea. When the relief column ran into tough opposition most of the men had to jump off, and most of those were killed or wounded. Despite this, most of the tanks got through, reaching Chipyong-ni on the afternoon of February 15 as small arms and mortar ammunition was running low. The rest of the

10. Nadir and Recovery

5th Cavalry followed the task force in. Unexpectedly, the Chinese did not attack that night. They had suffered enormous losses (the Americans estimated over 5,500) and were pulling out.

While the Chipyong-ni battle was fought, most of the rest of the 2nd Division, the 187th Airborne Regimental Combat Team and the ROK 18th Regiment were winning an even more important battle at Wonju to the southeast. The allied force was less well placed than the one at Chipyong-ni, having assumed that the Chinese—contrary to their usual practice—would launch their main attack astride Route 29. And the too-long perimeter was overlooked by enemy-held higher ground. The Chinese 40th Army slid two divisions to the west through a river valley to attack the UN left in the early hours of February 14. The Chinese struck the 3rd Battalion, 38th Infantry and the Dutch. There was desperate fighting. After daylight, the weather cleared, exposing the Chinese to massive air strikes and a huge artillery bombardment. The legendary "Wonju shoot" by the big guns killed perhaps 5,000 Chinese. Transport planes dropped supplies. The Chinese, however, had gained important ground. One position, Hill 342, changed hands three times before they had enough and pulled out toward Hoengsong.

Farther southeast, the North Koreans had pushed back the ROK 3rd and 5th Divisions. Though shaken, the ROKs did not break, and the U.S. 7th Division's 31st Infantry came up to support them. The Communists' "Fourth Phase" offensive had failed. Even then they recognized that it was a serious reverse, and it has been cogently argued that the battles for Wonju and Chipyong-ni were the turning point of the Korean War.[8] Ridgway now began planning a quick counteroffensive to take advantage of the Chinese discomfiture.

It was now clear that the UN forces would not soon or easily be driven from Korea. MacArthur's bungling in November and the subsequent panic had hidden facts that should have been obvious. Air support aside, the artillery and tanks of the UN units, other than the ROKs, gave them far greater firepower than the Communists. If deployed with reasonable care, they could not be overwhelmed. Collins and Vandenberg, visiting MacArthur's command, were greatly relieved. Even MacArthur had admitted by January 18 that things looked brighter and that his forces could stay in Korea indefinitely. The problem of whether to carry the war to China now receded, as far as Washington was concerned.

Fear of global war in the fairly near future persisted, although it was less intense than in December. The Joint Chiefs of Staff on January 15 warned Secretary Marshall that "the United States faces today one of the greatest dangers in its history. The Korean War could be the first phase of a global war between the United States and the USSR." Existing Western forces remained relatively weak. Soviet strength and readiness were not fully known but they were in "advanced stages of preparation for war." They pointed to grave dangers in Indochina and Iran as well as Korea. At a conference between the Joint Chiefs and the State Department the military warned that, while the U.S. position would greatly improve in 18 to 24 months, the Soviets would be able to overrun Western Europe during the next two or three years.

They concluded: "In general, from a military point of view, time is on our side, and our prospects for victory in the event war comes are steadily improving. The critical period, in terms of relative military strength, is the period of the next two or three years. If war comes during this period, though we would probably not lose it, we would have a difficult time winning it." On January 30, the Joint Chiefs gave MacArthur two National Guard divisions for the defense of Japan (he was forbidden to use them in Korea). Some State Department officials still feared an early world war or a succession of local attacks designed to split the Western alliance. John Paton Davies expressed the view that the Chinese Communists would attack Taiwan and perhaps also Indochina. He and others on the Policy Planning Staff surmised that the Soviets might be tempted to precipitate war in 1951–1952. While tying down the Americans in Asia, they would send the European satellites against Yugoslavia. Should the United States fail to do anything and Yugoslavia fell, they thought the Western Europeans would seek an accommodation with the Soviets. Yet the same thing might happen if the Americans reacted strongly, and in either case war might begin in conditions favorable to the Soviets.[9]

Fear of a larger war strongly influenced the renewed UN attempt to secure a cease-fire and the belated condemnation of China as an aggressor. The Chinese had hardly rejected the first cease-fire attempt when a new one started, to the irritation of the Americans. On January 11, a new cease-fire resolution was introduced, calling for a cease-fire to be followed immediately by a conference on Far Eastern problems including Taiwan and China's representation in the UN, a withdrawal of non–Korean forces from Korea, and — although this point was exceedingly vague — arrangements for a new Korean government. The General Assembly passed the resolution by a vote of 50–7 on January 13. The United States voted for the resolution, a highly unpopular move at home. Secretary Acheson feared that the conference it called for would lead to a cave-in on Taiwan and the UN seat. But he believed that it was necessary to pay deference to the views of the European allies, and rightly calculated that the Chinese would again overreach themselves and reject it. The Soviet bloc voted against the resolution and on January 17 the Chinese contemptuously rejected it. They insisted that negotiations start before a cease-fire, that all foreign forces leave Korea and Taiwan, that they be seated in the UN, and that a seven nation conference — stacked in their favor by including the "neutrals" most unfriendly to the West — meet in China to deal with Far Eastern problems. The Chinese then saw that they had gone too far and on January 22 conceded that agreeing on a cease-fire would be the first item on the agenda of the proposed conference. But the Americans would not be put off. They finally pressured the UN into condemning China's aggression. They had to promise the British and other allies that they would not carry the war to China. A resolution condemning Communist China as an aggressor was finally passed on February 1. Burma and India joined the Soviet bloc in opposing it and most neutrals abstained.[10] The gesture demonstrated the divisions in the UN rather than moral unity in the face of aggression.

11

Stalin's Decision for World War III

The war scare of late 1950 had an odd relation to reality. Many people in the West feared that Stalin had already decided to start a war in a few weeks or months. The belief that 1951 and 1952 would be a period of maximum danger, which later seemed quaint and wrong, was accompanied by a dangerous converse supposition — that if the West got past the next year or so, the worst of the danger would be over.

But Stalin's mind worked on different lines. Although his threats and actions had led to the war scare, he probably had not decided on war when it started. He was merely in the process of doing so.

And he had no intention of rushing into a poorly planned, head-on attack against an alert, united Western world. Stalin may have been completely mad by this time. But even when he was mad he had no use for the childish, slam-bang approach of a Hitler to whom many Westerners simplistically compared him. He remained cunning and methodical to the end; so much so that his plans were only revealed in 1977 by the Czech historian Karel Kaplan who learned of them by accident from the former Czech Minister of Defense Alexej Cepicka.

In January 1951, Stalin summoned the rulers and defense ministers of his European satellites to a conference in the Kremlin. After listening to reports on the state of their armies, Stalin announced that he planned to occupy all Europe. He stressed that such a move must be very carefully prepared. He explained that the Korean War had shown that the United States was weak in spite of its use of the most advanced military techniques, and it was possible to profit from this weakness in Europe. No

European army could resist the Soviet Army; quite possibly an invasion would meet no resistance at all. The existing American military forces were not very large, so the Soviet camp, therefore, had a temporary net superiority. (Whether Stalin meant a superiority of force in Europe alone or in the world as a whole was, perhaps deliberately, left unclear.) Stalin admitted that this superiority was a provisional one. It would last only three to four years. After that, the Americans could rapidly reinforce Europe and attain full superiority in atomic armaments. Consequently, he said, a brief delay was desirable to complete preparations for war. All of the Soviet bloc's capabilities had to be mobilized. During the next three to four years, all international and internal policies would be subordinated to this objective. Only total mobilization would permit seizing a unique occasion to bring "socialism" to all of Europe. He then adjourned the meeting. The next day the satellite ministers met the Soviet General Staff, and the forces they were to supply and the missions they were to carry out were fixed. If anyone thought the plan was a mistake, they had the sense to keep this to themselves. It is a comment on the sort of men that Stalin had installed in East-Central Europe that even many years later Cepicka still deplored the fact that Stalin' successors had abandoned the plan.[1]

Cepicka's account is not the only evidence that Stalin planned a third world war in his last years. In 1954, Vladimir Petrov, the chief of Soviet intelligence in Australia, defected, bringing with him documents detailing Soviet secret operations there. A document dated June 6, 1952, called for a radical reorganization of all intelligence work in Australia to create an apparatus that could function effectively under any conditions, and cautioning that this should be done gradually and in such a way as not to panic agents or cause them to "interpret our preparations as a sign of inevitable war in the near future." Petrov himself interpreted this a warning that war was in fact on the way. Some Soviet officers, notably the Air Force General Ostroumov, although not in on the secret, deduced during 1952 that Stalin was bent on war.[2]

Another piece of supporting evidence appeared in documents published by the Italian Communists in 1970. They indicate that the Italian Communist leaders had the impression at the end of 1950 that Stalin thought an early outbreak of war was a serious possibility. In January 1951, Stalin unsuccessfully urged Togliatti, the head of the Italian Communist Party, to move to Bucharest to take charge of the Cominform. He made clear to the Italian Communist leaders that he considered the danger of general war to be "great and imminent."[3] It is noticeable that he did not reveal his decision. Instead he implied that there was a danger of war developing in the existing situation and that he expected war right away in 1951.

Obviously he either distrusted them or feared that they might let the secret leak out. (Why he deliberately misled them in the matter of timing will be discussed later.)

Armaments expenditures increased enormously in 1951–1952. The satellites spent considerable effort stockpiling food, already short which ultimately helped to trigger the East German uprising in 1953.[4] Some outside observers, notably the well-known Russian Menshevik "kremlinologist" Boris Nicolaevsky, deduced in 1951 that Stalin had shifted from policies assuming that war was possible only in the indefinite future to a policy based on an early war. He argued that the purge of Rudolf Slansky, the General Secretary of the Czech Communist Party and the most prominent victim of the late Stalinist purges in East-Central Europe, and the dismissal of the Soviet Minister of Security Viktor Abakumov were connected to a decision to prepare for world war. Abakumov's fall was part of a series of lengthy, complicated and typically Stalinist maneuvers that began in 1951 and were aimed at undermining the position of Lavrenti Beria, the deputy Prime Minister in charge of security. Beria's policies in the intelligence field had been geared to the idea that a world war would not take place for a long time, which Stalin now deemed treasonable. Stalin may have blamed Beria for the at least partial paralysis of Soviet intelligence in the United States, a product of a series of defections and the Americans' breaking of Soviet codes. He may also have blamed Beria, who was in charge of nuclear development, for delays in developing the H-bomb.

Work on the limited power "layer cake" H-bomb went on. (This weapon was quite different from the theoretically unlimited thermonuclear weapons sought by the Americans, but the "layer cake" was the only type that anyone in 1950–1951 could be sure would work.) But the machines to carry it were something else. Unlike the Americans, the Soviets had early begun and stuck with an imaginative program to develop intercontinental ballistic missiles, but they were still a long way off. And because of the limitations of Soviet aircraft engines and later errors in their initial ICBM program, the development of Soviet intercontinental delivery systems was much slower than could have reasonably been expected — one of the more important lucky breaks the West would enjoy in the Cold War. Korean experience indicated that the planned intercontinental bomber, the piston-engine Tupolev-85, developed from the Soviet copy of the B-29, was too vulnerable. It was cancelled. Stalin wanted a pure jet plane to replace it, but Tupolev, the leading Soviet designer, maintained that the turbojet engines in prospect were not adequate. He courageously declined to undertake the project. He was allowed to proceed with a turbo-prop development, the Tupolev-95 ("Bear" in Western designation) that, although appearing belatedly, proved an adequate aircraft. Against advice, Stalin insisted on a turbojet counterpart, giving the job to the untried Myasischev design bureau. Tupolev had been right. The first version of the Mya-4 (NATO designation "Bison"), delivered late, had too short a range. Later versions with better engines came close to living up to Stalin's expectations, but few were built. The clumsiness and inadequacy of the Soviet strategic bombers and early ICBMs would have far-reaching consequences, helping to lead Khrushchev to the gamble that basing shorter-range missiles in Cuba would radically change the strategic balance.[5]

Stalin's explanations to his puppets in January 1951 left many questions unresolved as they were told only the minimum they had to know in order to execute the tasks assigned their countries. Nothing was revealed about the grand strategy of the coming war. Stalin did not explain how he expected to finish the United States or otherwise end the war, or what would happen in Asia. Whether the Chinese knew of the plan was left unsaid. Stalin's explanation that a delay was needed to finish preparations for a campaign in Europe did not make sense, at least in terms of the framework in which it was posed. The Soviets were already capable of taking continental Western Europe on short notice. With a Western buildup taking place, and American and perhaps West German reinforcements on the way, the odds on the ground in Europe were not likely to get better, although a further increase in Soviet and satellite forces might counterbalance the Western buildup in the theater. Had the ability to take Western Europe been the only issue, there would have been every reason to act at once. The real problem was not seizing the European mainland in the first stages of a war, but what would happen after that. Japan, also, was more vulnerable to an immediate attack than was likely to be the case even in a year or so.

The real reason for waiting must have been elsewhere. It seems likely that Stalin was waiting to accumulate more nuclear weapons and delivery capabilities, and carry out political measures to split the enemy alliance and bring the rest of the world over to the Soviet side. The three to four year period may have been geared to the expected progress of the H-bomb project and intercontinental bombers. His calculations may also have been influenced by an estimate that he could only count on delaying West German rearmament for so long. By 1954 it might be a serious factor. He could not know that the French obstruction of their own proposal for a European Defense Community would delay German rearmament to the point that it could not interfere with his plans. (However, there is reason to think that Stalin believed the West Germans would not be loyal and effective members of the Western coalition.)

The decision to start a world war in the near future — no matter how carefully prepared — was insane. It was based on a fundamentally mistaken conception of the real power balance in the world and probably the general political situation, which lacked the fluidity that had characterized it in the late 1940s and offered less scope for Soviet maneuvering. The USSR had no real chance of winning a war in the early or mid-1950s even if it began in the most favorable circumstances. The much bigger American nuclear stockpile and strategic air force, and industrial complex behind them, were advantages that no clever stratagem or political manipulation could overcome. Even a long lead in the race for the H-bomb would not have overcome the American advantages. Had there been a war, the Soviets might have been defeated more easily than anyone realized at the time. Although Westerners underestimated Soviet industrial capabilities in the early 1950s, they did not realize — and Stalin averted his eyes from — the disastrous state to which Soviet agriculture had sunk.[6] War might well have led to famine and complete collapse within a short time.

The decision for war was not totally without precedent or precursors. Stalin's readiness to intervene in Czechoslovakia in 1948 (although it proved unnecessary), the Berlin blockade, and the decisions to invade South Korea and Yugoslavia showed a growing predilection for risk-taking and using military force. He had also become more and more stubborn in pursuing his objectives even in a losing situation, as in the Berlin crisis and the Greek civil war. There is little to be said for the view that Stalin was ever a pragmatist or realist, and, contrary to what is widely maintained, he was not always cautious. Even before his mental decline in the post–World War II years he had indulged in bouts of over-optimism, recklessness and downright irrationality. Those defects were spectacularly expressed in the Great Purges of the 1930s, his confidence in 1940–1941 that Hitler would continue to work with him, and his refusal to believe warnings of the Nazi attack. Stalin had sometimes been grossly over-optimistic in military matters, most notably in his belief in 1939 that Finland would quickly collapse under Soviet attack, and his supposition in late 1941 and early 1942 that the Nazi forces in Russia would soon be routed. Nevertheless, to start a world war before the world political situation and power balance had clearly and unmistakably turned in favor of the Soviets was a radical departure from Soviet theory and practice, and the concept of the future that Stalin had entertained earlier. As late as June 1950 he had reacted to the American intervention in the Korean War in a typical way — by becoming more cautious. It is not surprising that most observers — Nicolaevsky was an outstanding exception — did not detect the decision for war. It was an act of madness not explainable in terms of

11. Stalin's Decision for World War III   175

precedent or the real world situation, although it was probably not totally unrelated to the latter.

Stalin probably told the satellite leaders of his decision soon after he made it; he had no reason to delay. It is probable, therefore, that he decided to embark on war no later than December 1950. (That the decision was made then is hinted by the Italian Communist report mentioned earlier.) The timing suggests the reasoning behind it. It followed a major success in Korea. Stalin might not have been impressed by a single military victory, but the Chinese success, coupled with the American failure to retaliate against China and the evident disarray in the Western camp, may have led him to think that the Americans must be far weaker and the Western alliance more brittle than he had supposed. The general Soviet outlook already predisposed Stalin to wishful thinking about the weakness of intracapitalist alliances, and in late 1950 there were plenty of conflicts that disguised the basic solidity of NATO. It was apparent that West German rearmament was not imminent and was a divisive issue in the West. The wars in Korea, Indochina and Malaya would tie down substantial Western forces for years. The Korean War in particular seemed a major source of tension between the Western allies. Even if there was no complete Communist victory in Korea, the war might, if properly manipulated, be used to split the Western alliance further, and embitter relations between the West and the ex-colonial countries.

That Mao's regime would bear a heavy burden may have been a source of satisfaction for Stalin. Arranging the diversion of enemy forces against another opponent and the mutual exhaustion of his enemies had always been a particular preoccupation of Stalin. In late 1950 this was achieved at little cost. Stalin usually did not make major decisions abruptly however bizarre. Perhaps he had been turning the idea of an early world war over in his mind as a possible course of action if the Chinese proved very successful ever since he had started to press them to intervene in Korea, even if the main and immediate reason was to rescue North Korea. It is interesting to note that Sir Girja Bajpai, the top permanent official of the Indian Foreign Office, and some French officials had speculated as early as the summer of 1950 that the Soviets sought to bring about a Chinese-American war, although they had no hard evidence for this idea. [7] There may have been something after all to the ideas advanced by O. Edmund Clubb in late 1950, although Clubb's time-scale, like that of most observers was badly off.

At bottom, however, such considerations may have been food for rationalization rather than rational analysis. Egomania and a desire to finish the world revolution before his death were probably the true reasons for Stalin's decision. He had no faith in his successors. According to Khrushchev, he once grumbled, "When I'm gone, the imperialists will wring your necks like chickens."[8]

Stalin's decision for war was probably not the product of a need to counter a perceived threat or the product of the "interacting spiral of mutual anxiety and rearmament" that some have seen as the crucial factor in this and other periods of the Cold War.[9] At the meeting with the satellite leaders, he spoke not of dangers to the Soviet bloc but of exploiting an opportunity afforded by the enemy's weakness. The decision followed a victory over the West and not an increase in any Western threat. It is true that Stalin had rated West German rearmament as sufficiently important to bring to bear an overt threat of war in October 1950. Later, in May 1951, he responded to American plans for a separate peace with Japan with a similar threat. But the relation of these overt threats to the decision for war was probably remote at best. It is not likely that Stalin felt compelled to head off an offensive danger from a rearmed West Germany and Japan. His policies toward those countries in 1951 and 1952 seem to have been determined not by fears that they would overturn the balance of power against the Soviet Union in favor of the West or that they would be unleashed in war against the USSR. Rather, he seems to have indulged in wishful thinking that German and Japanese nationalism could be steered against the Western powers.

Stalin's first concern after deciding on war, of course, was to hide the decision from the Western powers, in which he was remarkably successful. His first steps involved a dazzling deception on two levels in which he moved to both defuse the ongoing war scare and exploit it to further confuse the Western powers. On the level of diplomacy, he sought the four-power conference on demilitarizing Germany first raised on November 3, 1950. With an appearance of reluctance, he agreed on December 30 to the West's insistence on holding a preliminary conference to prepare an agenda, and, on February 5, that it could consider issues other than the German question.

From this time on Stalin seemed anxious to maintain reasonably steady negotiations with the West, whether over Germany or Korea or some other issue, though he seemed not at all concerned that they lead to any result (which they did not). During 1951 and 1952, grumblings over the Japanese peace treaty, the German issue and rough spots in the Korean armistice talks, were interspersed with Soviet "peace offensives" in a way that bewildered Westerners. On February 16, 1951, Stalin tried to reassure the West or, at least, its more gullible elements. In one of his increasingly rare "interviews" with *Pravda*, he made an exceptionally bitter personal attack on the British Prime Minister, but not Truman or any other Western leader, and stated the Korean War "can end only in the defeat of the interventionists." But he used the less harsh and emotional Communist characterization of the UN war effort — as an "intervention" comparable to the Allied intervention in the Russian Civil War rather than "aggression." He insisted that the Soviet Union had not increased its military forces and, contrary to Western claims, had demobilized after World War II. In reply to the question of whether a new world war was inevitable, he declared, "No. At least at the present time it cannot be regarded as inevitable."[10] The qualifying phrase suggests that he had not lost a sinister sense of humor.

While issuing these reassurances, however, Stalin also operated a second, more bizarre deception. The Italian Communists were led to expect war in the very near future. A Chinese who contacted the U.S. government in January 1951 told the Americans that a pro–Soviet faction within the Chinese Communist Party had been told that a world war would start that spring.[11] It remains unclear whether this man was a Maoist agent or, as he claimed, was acting on behalf of a non–Communist underground group allied to an anti–Soviet Communist faction. But in either case Stalin may have been using the Chinese and Italian Communists to mislead the Western powers into fearing an immediate war. The purpose of these strange moves may have been to put over an elaborate double-bluff. When war failed to break out in 1951, the Western powers would be inclined to relax their efforts and scorn further warnings, even if well-founded. In the short run, it might help to deter or delay German rearmament and a Japanese peace treaty. Stalin had used phony war scares before: in 1927–1928 he had pretended that Britain and France were plotting war against the USSR to create a suitable atmosphere for the elimination of Bukharin, and the start of collectivization and industrialization.

These deception measures were just the first and simplest moves undertaken to prepare for war. During the remainder of Stalin's life the Soviets pursued several major policies that helped set the stage for war (although their purposes were not clear to contemporaries, and the Soviets might have followed some of them under other circumstances). The common thread behind them was forming a world-wide anti–American bloc — or, more exactly, anti–British and anti–American. Stalin regarded British ties with the United States as unbreakable. The Soviets continued to oppose West German rearmament, and any treaty with Japan that let the Americans maintain bases there or form an alliance with that country. Further, they aimed to turn the Germans and the Japanese against the Western powers. Stalin seems to have convinced himself that nationalism would cause both countries to revolt against the Western occupying powers, a hope expressed in 1952 in his last published work, *Economic Problems of Socialism*. In Japan, although apparently not in Germany, he hoped that the local Communists would lead the nationalist upsurge. During 1951–1952, he tried to further split the West by playing on differences between the "Anglo-American bloc" and the continental European countries, especially France. He also tried to drive a wedge between the West and the ex-colonial countries. He moderated his hostility to "neutralism" and made friendly gestures toward India, Indonesia, Burma, Egypt and Syria. The aim of splitting the Western camp and isolating the West were linked in the promotion of the violent "Hate America" campaign, which also served to get people in the Communist countries into a mental state suitable for war. The centerpiece of the campaign was the claim that the United States was waging germ warfare against North Korea and China as the first step in a program of genocide against the peoples of Asia, as well as the Germans.

Stalin seems to have wanted the Korean War to continue indefinitely in order to tie down Western forces and provide a stage for faked atrocities. This proved a difficult and dangerous course, for he had to keep the Chinese fighting but avoid a major expansion of the war. There seems to be no good reason to suppose that the Chinese were ever told of his plans. Unfortunately, it is impossible to be absolutely certain that Stalin never wanted an armistice in Korea at all. It is difficult to determine from the available record whether or when either of the big Communist powers wanted an armistice, or, just as important, the exact price they were willing to pay for one. After Stalin's death, both clearly wanted an armistice, but before then things are not clear. American negotiators at Kaesong and Panmunjom were sometimes sure their Chinese counterparts genuinely sought to end the war, but often were equally sure that they did not. Although painfully slow, there was some progress toward an agreement in 1951–1952. But that may proceed from the nature of the case. Total intransigence would have caused a breakdown of the talks and a violent reaction by the Americans. Moreover, Stalin had to manipulate a Chinese "ally" probably unaware of his plans for world war and which, by June 1951, probably wanted peace in Korea. Conveniently for him, Mao was in no rush to conclude an armistice. For some time Mao planned a new offensive in Korea, and, at least by mid–November 1951, expected the negotiations to drag on for another six months to a year. And Mao envisaged *renewing* the war in three to five years.[12] Stalin, however, acted at least twice, in November 1951 and November 1952, to force the Chinese to take up negotiating positions unacceptable to the West. In 1952, he had Foreign Minister Vyshinsky publicly torpedo a face-saving compromise on the crucial issue of voluntary repatriation of prisoners of war that the Chinese clearly favored. It is conceivable, though not likely, that he did this only because he found voluntary repatriation genuinely repellent. The principle was certainly distasteful to Communist minds, and the Chinese swallowed it only with the greatest reluctance. Whether American insistence on voluntary repatriation prolonged the Korean War, as has been widely believed, thus remains uncertain. Whatever its moral validity, however, it may have simplified Stalin's task of keeping the Chinese fighting. As it was, Stalin had to make major changes in his policy toward China. During the Korean War, if not before, he dropped the aim of replacing Mao with Gao Gang, and he conceded more equality to the Chinese and their concepts of revolutionary strategy.

The Soviets and the Chinese subtly changed their policy toward the ongoing struggle for Southeast Asia, which, outside of Indochina, had begun to turn against the local Communists. They clearly wanted the wars in Indochina and Malaya that tied down Western troops to go on. But the struggles against the neutralist regimes governing Burma and Indonesia now cut across the aim of building a worldwide front against "Anglo-American imperialism." Iran was perhaps a partial exception to the policy of stressing alliances with the neutralists over promoting Communist takeovers. While the Soviets tried to befriend Mossadegh's anti–British government, the strength of the Iranian Communists, and Iran's economic and strategic importance made a Communist seizure of power there a tempting possibility.

As noted earlier, Stalin's policies in his last years were based on a mistaken appreciation of the military balance, and wishful thinking about Germans and Japanese. He was also wrong if he thought that continuing the Korean War would further his plans. The best way to get the West to relax its guard and efforts to rearm would have been to make peace in Korea as quickly as possible. The war's encouragement of rearmament and anti–Communist feeling more than offset the diversion of Western forces to a secondary theater and the chances it provided to exploit differences between the Western countries. But that was not obvious at the time. The Joint Chiefs of Staff and many others in the West thought that Korea was a major drain on Western strength and, for that reason as well as the obvious ones, were eager to end the war as soon as possible. They tended to ignore the fact that without the stimulus of the war there would have been little or no rearmament after June 1950. It would have been hard even for professional soldiers— perhaps especially hard for them — to see that prolonging a bloody war in which victory could not be expected might be in the interests of their country. In retrospect, this perverse situation seems to have obtained in 1951–1952. Curiously, both sides sought something contrary to their own interests: the West to end the war, Stalin to spin it out. But, even if the Korean War's impact was basically unfavorable to his plans, Stalin nevertheless managed to use it for his purposes. Although Soviet diplomacy was stiff and poorly conducted in 1951 and 1952, Stalin had not lost his old ability to lead his enemies around by the nose. His efforts to put the Western powers off guard, and turn Asians and Africans against them were not entirely ineffective.

The Cold War from January 1951 to Stalin's death in 1953 took place on two levels. On the surface, international tensions seemed to decrease, while in truth war drew closer. The West was even more thoroughly confused than usual. Its initial, unfounded fear of an early attack was replaced by a growing and even more unfounded conviction that war was not likely in the near future. Rather, the Cold War would go on as usual, with only limited and local military engagements. It was thought that Stalin was not planning all-out war, and the danger of one was not too great. The belief became widespread that the West should not aim to build up its strength by a definite date. It should "stretch out" its efforts, following "long-haul" policies aimed at maintaining a more modest and economically supportable state of readiness over many years, and devote more attention to the political and economic struggle for the underdeveloped countries. People were increasingly aware that the triad of Western concerns in the Cold War—building forces to deter world war, countering local aggressions of the Korean type, and building political and economic structures in the backward countries that would resist local Communist efforts—were, inevitably, competitive. After Stalin's death, some of the criticisms of Western policies that were developing in the early 1950s may have been quite justified. But before March 1953 they were a bit premature.

In reality, the West was in a deadly race against time, but few sensed this. Despite the warnings of a few people, notably General Marshall and Paul Nitze, the Western rearmament effort ebbed. Despite the efforts of Acheson and Eisenhower, bickering over West German rearmament dragged on. NATO did not get German troops in any time relevant to countering Stalin's plans. Western Europe remained vulnerable. Even in 1954, only 16 Western divisions faced 97 slightly smaller Soviet and satellite divisions on the vital central front. The West's blunders would not have given the Soviets victory had war come. But had Stalin lived a year or two longer, the Western peoples—and especially the Western Europeans—would have rued the decisions that were made.

However in early 1951 the situation was fluid enough that it was not certain that Stalin would be free to prepare for war undisturbed. Whether the Korean War would be limited to Korea and who would win it was not yet decided. Even a major reversal of alliances was perhaps not out of the question.

The Concubine of General Yi

China's entry into the Korean War may not have strained only the Western alliance. Despite the victory in North Korea, some of China's rulers may have feared all-out war with the United States so much that they seriously considered breaking with the Soviets and overthrowing Mao.

In early January 1951, a Chinese contacted the State Department using an American private citizen as an intermediary. He was apparently a member of one of the non–Communist coalition partners serving with General Wu's delegation to the UN (his identity remains secret) In contacts continuing to early March, Charles Burton Marshall and John Paton Davies of the Policy Planning Staff sought to sound out "Third Party," as the Chinese envoy was called, and promote a Chinese rupture with the Soviets. They stressed there was no real reason for conflict between the United States and China.

In the first series of exchanges from January 6 through 17, the Chinese emissary explained that his government was split into three factions. One was a pro–Soviet "Stalinist" faction led by Liu Shaoqi: Lin Biao was its strongest military supporter. Mao was currently aligned with it, although "Third Party" intimated that he was trying to limit Soviet penetration and might be won over by the second faction, a nationalist or "patriotic" group willing to break with the Soviets. Zhou Enlai and the important General Chen Yi belonged to this group. Non-Communist elements in the government formed a third faction that "Third Party" insisted had its own underground organization, which included some ex–Nationalist generals who had defected to the Communists and still controlled some troops. Their current aim was to work within the Communist regime to persuade Mao to avoid involving China in a world war or, failing that, back a coup by the nationalist faction of the Communists. They preferred a new civil war to fighting the United States and had secured an alliance with Chen Yi by giving him a "nifty concubine and a fine new car." "Third Party" warned the Americans that the Chinese "Stalinists" had been told that a world war was coming in the spring. Liu Shaoqi strongly favored war, which might begin with an attack in the Taiwan Straits or a Soviet attack on Japan. There was a hint that the "Stalinists" calculated that the

United States would be so preoccupied with the Soviets that China would not suffer much harm when war broke out.

"Third Party" wanted assurances that the United States would not support Jiang Jieshi and that ultimately the Taiwan issue would be settled. It was necessary to convince the "patriotic" Communists that the Americans were willing to be friendly. He urged the Americans to let the Beijing government enter the UN, and warned against bombing China or too obviously embracing the anti-Stalinist forces. Either would endanger the prospects of the anti-Soviet groups. The Taiwan issue could be put aside for a time. Although Jiang must be gotten rid of, the forces on Taiwan should be strengthened. They might be useful if fighting began on the mainland.

The Americans explained they could not let Beijing into the UN while fighting went on in Korea. Later, things could be different, and the same consideration applied to American recognition. The United States was not tied to Jiang and the Cairo Declaration promising China that Taiwan was still valid. America's policy toward Tito showed how it would react to a Chinese break with the Soviets. Beijing must make the first move; the Americans had already shown their reasonableness by not striking back at China. "Third Party" noted that the Chinese Communists—with some reason—had attributed this to fear of Soviet reaction. The Americans warned they might lose patience and cut loose from the UN. If China joined the Soviets in a world war, it must not count on gaining immunity because the Americans would concentrate their efforts against the Soviets, or on changing sides as Italy had in 1943. They also warned "Third Party" that they had learned that the Communists planned to purge the non-Communist elements from their regime.

The State Department was excited about these contacts, believing that "Third Party" was genuine. Other information seemed to confirm what he said. The Americans had gotten feelers from purported emissaries of Chen Yi as early as January 1950 indicating his readiness to back a break with the Soviets. But the results proved disappointing. On January 29, a message from "Third Party" indicated that the leaders in Beijing wanted to show their desire for a settlement. They wished to withdraw from Korea. Their first step would be to abandon Seoul and pull back to the 38th Parallel. In return, they wanted the UN resolution condemning China as an aggressor withdrawn. The message arrived too late to act on the suggestion, and, in any case, the promised withdrawal did not occur. Assistant Secretary of State Rusk suggested that the Chinese make a lesser gesture by releasing an imprisoned American missionary. On February 1, "Third Party" reported that Mao seemed about to veer from Moscow. On February

5, he warned that an attack on Taiwan was probable in March or April. But Washington received a report that the missionary had died. On March 5, "Third Party" reported that there was now no prospect of Mao breaking with Stalin; the only course left was a coup. That was his last message. In June 1951, the Americans concluded that "Third Party" might have been just a Chinese Communist agent.[13] No coup, of course, materialized.

This strange episode is still perplexing. Some of this individual's story was compatible with a Maoist effort at "disinformation" to influence the Americans against striking at China. There does not seem to be any confirmation from other sources that the non–Communists in the Beijing government had the sort of organization he claimed. The existence of such a group was unlikely given Communist police measures, although perhaps possible if it was protected by some faction within the Communist Party. On the other hand, while there is ample precedence for Communist regimes using phony anti–Communist underground groups as devices in intelligence and security matters, they were very reluctant to admit the existence of divisions within the ruling party except during an actual purge. Curiously, "Third Party" did not allude to Gao Gang, the real "Stalinist" in the Party leadership; yet there is reason to think that Liu Shaoqi and Chen Yi held the views he ascribed to them.

Stalin could hardly have approved such revelations, but they may have served a number of purposes for Mao. He may have hoped to at least discourage the Americans from acting against China, while an actual offer from them might at least improve his bargaining position with Stalin. And he may even have considered changing sides if the Americans offered a big enough inducement and Stalin engaged in some enterprise hostile to or too dangerous for China. But the Soviet ability to intervene in Manchuria probably rendered a real reversal of alliances too difficult. "Third Party's" report that the Communists planned to attack Taiwan may have fit in with a scheme (evident later) to divert American forces from Korea. His report that the Soviets planned all-out war in the spring is less easy to understand, but may have been a result of Soviet "disinformation" planted with the Chinese Communists. Whether "Third Party" was a genuine non–Communist or a Maoist agent, he may have been an indirect tool in Stalin's program to mislead the West into fearing an imminent war.

12

The Chinese Are Defeated: February to June 1951

Although no one in Korea knew it, Stalin's decision for world war had transformed the war there from a local, if critical engagement in the Cold War into the preliminary phase of a never-fought World War III. The late winter and spring of 1951 saw seesaw fighting across the middle of the Korean peninsula and the biggest battles of the war.

The Communist "Fourth Phase Offensive" had been defeated. The Communists already feared an even more serious strategic reverse and an amphibious landing behind them.

General Ridgway now moved to exploit the overextension of the battered Communist forces on the central front. He planned roughly parallel drives by IX and X Corps to cut off the salient they had driven in the UN line and clear Route 20 running east across Korea from Wonju to Kangnung. The offensive was titled "Operation Killer," a name that provoked much unfavorable reaction. Even General Collins was unhappy with it. Ridgway characteristically commented that he was "by nature opposed to any effort to 'sell' war to people as only a mildly unpleasant business that requires very little in the way of blood." The 1st Marine Division, returning to the front after a month of fighting guerrillas around Andong, was put under IX Corps. (O.P. Smith briefly took over the Corps when its commander, General Moore, died of a heart attack during "Killer.") On February 21, it advanced from Wonju astride Route 29 north and northeast toward Hoengsong, and through X Corps' 2nd Division, which was edging eastward. The rest of IX Corps, the ROK 6th Division, the 27th Commonwealth Brigade and the 1st Cavalry Division cleared the moun-

12. The Chinese Are Defeated

tains between the Marines and the Han river, while X Corps' U.S. 7th and the ROK 3rd Division attacked in the east toward Pyongchong to meet IX Corps and close the trap. The 2nd Division joined in the attack a day later. The advance was hampered by bad weather. A thaw had begun, producing floods, but enemy opposition was relatively light. The Communists had foreseen the UN's intentions and pulled out before they could be cut off. After all the fuss about its bloody name, "Killer" killed few Communist soldiers.

On the central front where the main effort continued, "Killer" transitioned into "Operation Ripper," a bigger attack to take Hongchon and Chunchon and reach the vicinity of the 38th Parallel. But "Ripper" included a major attack in the west by I Corps to regain Seoul by a flanking maneuver designed to get the enemy to withdraw without a battle in the city. Deception measures led the Communists to expect an attack over the Han to the west of Seoul while I Corps struck east of the capital. On March 7, six years to the day since the U.S. Army had crossed the Rhine, the 25th Division crossed the Han in a carefully prepared operation that was a model of its kind. Under a heavy bombardment, tanks forded the river while assault boats carried the infantry across. DUKW amphibious trucks followed with supplies and evacuated the wounded. Opposition to the passage over the river was not great, but there was some tough fighting above the north bank. As the UN Command had hoped, the attack levered the Communists out of Seoul. On March 12, they began to withdraw, and ROK patrols found Seoul largely deserted on March 14. Only a few enemy soldiers who wanted to give up were left, along with perhaps as few as 135,000 people of a prewar population of over a million. The Communists had carried off thousands of young people to the north as they pulled out. In the center, after some tough fighting in which it was hard to keep units in the mountains supplied, the enemy had begun withdrawing again. It was clear they would not stand below the 38th Parallel, although it was also evident that the units from the 9th Army Group were finally arriving from northeast Korea and that a whole new army, the 60th, had come from Manchuria. There was little doubt that the current planned withdrawal was a prelude to a new enemy offensive. The Communists were fighting a delaying action; they had not been routed.

On March 15, the Marines, having outflanked Hongchon, found the place deserted. Chunchon, also deserted, fell to the 1st Cavalry Division on March 21. In the east, the ROKs had reached the planned objective line. But they were unable to keep the 10th North Korean Division or what was left of (it was down to less than a thousand men) from breaking out on March 17–18 and regaining the Communist lines after roaming about in the UN rear for months.

Ridgway had kept his sole paratroop unit in reserve, hoping for an opportunity to use it on the central front to cut off an enemy force. But the enemy's rapid withdrawal foiled this. He discerned, however, an opportunity in the west to trap the North Korean I Corps, which was retreating from the Han toward the lower Imjin. On March 23, the 187th Airborne Regimental Combat Team dropped at Munsan-ni to cut off the North Koreans in conjunction with the ground advance of the U.S. I Corps. An armored task force driving from Seoul through the 1st ROK Division attacked to join up with the paratroopers. The second and last airborne operation in Korea, like the first, was a misfire. The drop did not go especially well — all the men fell in the drop zone allotted to one battalion and the operation was just too late. The paratroopers, "Task Force Growdon," and the ROKs found that the enemy was already gone. The 187th and Task Force Growdon turned east to try to cut off the retreat of Chinese units on Route 33. Rain, landslides and delays in getting fuel to the tanks slowed the advance. The Chinese were able to hold open their line of retreat.[1]

The results of "Killer" and "Ripper" had been disappointing in terms of destroying enemy forces and material. The enemy had been shoved back, but not badly damaged, although Chinese morale was none too good. The UN had only gained a cushion of territory.

The fighting of late 1950 and early 1951 had exposed some of Mao Zedong's limitations as a war leader. Like Hitler and Jiang Jieshi, he was prone to overcontrolling things from a remote headquarters, overruling his field commander (although his judgment in such matters was far better than Jiang's) and was apt to overextend his forces. But, unlike them, he was not fixated on holding territory and was realistic enough to recognize his mistakes. He let Peng retreat in time. So, while Mao was apt to get his army into a jam, he was, unfortunately, flexible enough to get it out again. The UN Command was painfully aware that the real showdown with the Chinese was still to come, and it and the Western world worried about what the Soviets might do to support China.

On the east coast the ROKs had crossed the 38th Parallel on March 24, while in the extreme west other South Koreans crossed it on March 27 and Americans crossed it on the central front on March 30. Whether to go over the prewar boundary once more had been a controversial issue. During February, the consensus in favor of confining the war to Korea had hardened. It was agreed that the United States could not unite Korea militarily, although, as Acheson stressed, it could not accept anything less than the prewar status quo. MacArthur had advised on February 11 that major operations in North Korea were impractical without bombing Manchuria, a view he maintained up to his relief. During February, the

12. The Chinese Are Defeated

Joint Chiefs of Staff even rejected his request to bomb the North Korean port of Rashin and the North Korean power installations. But both MacArthur and the Joint Chiefs wanted a free hand to recross the 38th Parallel if only for local, tactical purposes. Acheson had mildly opposed a "general advance" across the parallel; he thought that the Allies would strongly object. But Marshall persuaded him to forego an explicit prohibition of such a move. But MacArthur did not get an explicit directive on the issue, or indeed, any matter related to Korea.

In mid–March, as the success of the UN offensive became clear, some in Washington became bolder — bolder than MacArthur in a way. Admiral Sherman, always the toughest member of the Joint Chiefs where Korean matters were concerned, proposed driving to the Pyongyang-Wonsan line, an idea that he favored for several months. That would put 85 percent of the Korean people and most of North Korea's food supply under ROK control. Whether the North Korean regime would have been viable had an armistice been reached on that line is doubtful. General Collins seemed to like the idea, but soon became more cautious. For a time the Joint Chiefs favored reaching a line running from the Imjin in the west to just north of Wonsan in the east. Marshall, however, doubted that such a line would be secure, and Ridgway favored advancing only to the Imjin-Chorwon-Hwachon line. Taking the latter places, not too deep in North Korea, would cut into the "Iron Triangle" and complicate the enemy's supply situation. But he expected to have to fall back from that area in a short time to meet the expected enemy spring offensive, and all speculations about where the UN should halt any advance were subject to the condition that the Soviets would not intervene — or rather intervene more than they already had.[2]

The next UN offensive, "Operation Rugged," began April 3 with the main effort by I Corps in the west. The UN forces aimed to reach the "Kansas line," the first good defensive position north of the 38th Parallel. It became, more or less, the main UN line for the rest of the war. It ran from the lower Imjin river to the Hwachon Reservoir in central Korea, and from there to Yangyang on the east coast. Most of the Eighth Army reached the line by April 9, with X Corps and ROK III Corps closing in on their part of the line on April 20. The Hwachon Reservoir posed a special problem, reminiscent of that presented by the Roer river dams in Germany in 1944–1945. Formed by the Hwachon dam on the Pukhan tributary of the Han, it was the main source of water and power for Seoul. If the Communists opened its sluice gates, they could flood the area downstream, washing out bridges and splitting IX Corps. The dam was too strong to be broken by conventional bombs and was hard to get at on the ground. The 1st Cavalry Division approached the dam from the south. On April 9, it attacked on a narrow isthmus only half a mile wide between the Pukhan and an arm of the reservoir, and was stopped. The Chinese opened some of the gates. Although the effect was less than feared, they did break some bridges. Renewed efforts against the dam from the south failed. A Ranger company and a company of the 7th Cavalry then tried a night amphibious landing with assault boats behind the enemy. They got ashore unopposed, but determined Chinese counterattacks forced them to re-embark. The dam was still in enemy hands as the I and IX Corps drive transitioned on April 11 into "Operation Dauntless." They were to reach the "Utah Line," then, if possible, the "Wyoming Line" and threaten the Iron Triangle that was the centerpiece of Communist supply efforts. The two corps reached the Utah Line, pushing a salient in the middle of the enemy front. ROK Marines took the Hwachon dam on April 16. By then it was clear that the enemy was fast preparing its own spring offensive.[3]

Sea and Air

The struggle for Korea continued to be powerfully affected, if not determined, by the control of the sea and air around and above the peninsula.

The Communists were acutely aware of the danger of an amphibious landing in their rear, and in late January Mao informed Stalin of Peng's worries about the state of coastal defenses. The Americans learned in early February that the Chinese feared a landing either at Inchon or somewhere on the "waist." Another naval demonstration was carried out. In March, the Chinese still feared a landing either in the west at Chinnampo or in the east at Wonsan. Peng was anxious to get the spring offensive underway to forestall a UN landing at Wonsan or nearby Tongchon, which he expected to be in conjunction with a UN land attack at the eastern end of the front. Mao agreed, and suggested stationing the Chinese 42nd Army, relieved at the front in mid-March by fresh units from China, to back up the North Koreans around Wonsan. Much Communist strength during the rest of the Korean War would be devoted to guarding against another Inchon. That great victory continued to pay dividends. The Communists' anxiety was heightened by moves undertaken by the U.S. Navy for other reasons. On February 16, it had begun the "siege of Wonsan" by landing ROK Marines on islands in Wonsan harbor. This move was designed to enable ships to operate safely further inshore and provide advanced positions if the UN forces ever advanced north again to Wonsan, as many still hoped. To the communists, it seemed to increase the threat of a major landing. The "siege" pinned down a growing number of shore batteries and antiaircraft guns around Wonsan. Similar "sieges" followed against other North Korean ports.[4] Islands off North Korea would also be occupied to provide advanced radar stations to support air operations and bases for the partisans operating behind Communist lines in the North.

USAF, U.S. and Royal Navy carrier planes waged a continuing effort to interdict the movement of enemy supplies from Manchuria to the front. The Air Force was given the job of interdicting enemy communications on the western side of Korea. A British or American light carrier operating in the Yellow Sea supplemented Air Force operations in the west. The fleet carriers of the U.S. Navy's Task Force 77 operating in the Sea of Japan handled the eastern side of the peninsula. While in areas subject to air attack the enemy moved, when possible, only at night, the task had become more difficult with Soviet air intervention and the removal of U.S. jets to distant bases. The Soviet domination of MIG Alley meant that the highest priority targets, north of the Chongchon and especially the Yalu river crossings, were free of attack for most of the first quarter of 1951. The B-29 Superfortresses were really too few to fulfill the assigned task of blasting North Korean bridges and marshalling yards, and growing enemy flak defenses forced them to bomb from higher altitudes with less accuracy. Fighter-bombers, usually dive-bombing, attacked rail lines. But only one sortie in four secured the direct hit on a track with a 500-pound bomb necessary to stop traffic for the eight or nine hours required for repairs. North Korea had an enormous number of railroad tunnels, that provided shelter for trains and supplies. The UN air forces did not have the special bombs needed to destroy tunnels (although the RAF had such weapons as the "Tallboy" and "Grand Slam" bombs late in World War II). Fighter-bombers and Navy attack planes did go after tunnels by hurling delayed action-bombs and firing rockets into tunnel mouths to destroy trains, supplies and personnel hiding there during the day, but could not seriously harm the tunnels themselves. Other fighter-bombers carried out "truck-hunting" missions, searching from the lowest possible heights for the daytime hiding places of enemy trucks. In February, fighter units were assigned specific areas in which to operate, so the pilots could become familiar with the terrain. At night, B-26 light bombers, and Navy and Marine night fighters tried to catch road convoys and trains in movement.

North Korea's railroads were the core of the enemy supply system. Six lines entered the country from the north (a seventh line entered Korea from the Soviet Far East, but terminated at Rashin in the far northeast, which had no direct rail connection with the rest of Korea). These lines formed two largely separate networks, one western and eastern, with little lateral connection between them. The western network had a pre-attack capacity of some 6,000 tons daily, the eastern 5,000. The eastern network was rather more vulnerable. All three of its lines converged at Kilchu in the northeast. Just one line continued over many bridges down the coast through Wonsan, and in many spots it was exposed to naval gunfire as well as air attack. The North Korean road network could carry about 1,500 tons a day by truck to supplement the railroads.

The Communists' wants, however, were few. They were operating a comparatively lightly-armed infantry army without the massive requirements of British or American-style divisions. Their forces could get by with no more than 3,000 tons of supplies a day. They developed an effective organization to keep supplies moving. In February, the Chinese established a special logistical command that was amply supported by the North Koreans. This included seven "branch units" that each had ordnance, support and transport sections with four truck regiments (120 trucks) each and a porter battalion, as well as aircraft-spotting units. Depots were given their own truck companies. Two Chinese railroad engineering divisions were sent to support the North Koreans, whose Railroad Bureau largely operated the railroads while the Department of Military Highways maintained the roads. Civilians were drafted to help the soldiers in repair and construction when needed. In February–April 1951, 500,000 soldiers and civilians were estimated to be working on the Communist supply system. There was a continuing duel between Western planes and Communist countermeasures.

The UN forces did confine train and truck movements to the night. Attacks on the eastern rail network were particularly effective. Rail traffic there was beaten down to under 500 tons a day, and sometimes to nothing at all. There was a particularly dramatic series of strikes against a series of bridges near Kilchu at "Carlson's Canyon," an episode that inspired James Michener's *The Bridges at Toko-ri*. This seemed to be an especially weak spot, but the Communists finally abandoned the original route entirely to build a whole new line that was less vulnerable. By early April only a few short stretches of the eastern network were operating. But then Task Force 77 had to withdraw from the interdiction effort for a whole month, first to defend Taiwan against an apparent threat of invasion and then to provide close air support for the UN ground forces facing the Chinese spring offensive. The light carriers usually operating in the Yellow Sea took its place but could not make up the difference. When Task Force 77 returned, the eastern rail network had recovered to a considerable extent. Although the swings in fortune were less dramatic, the story was similar in the west. Rail deliveries were beaten down to 500 to 1,500 tons a day, but this and the cargo carried by trucks proved enough to keep the Communists going, although not without difficulty, and enabled them to get ready for the spring offensive. It was tiring and costly to get supplies to the front, but it was done.

Success was due to a mixture of defenses, warning systems and elaborate precautions in moving, concealment and repair. While the heavier flak guns forced the B-29s to fly higher, a growing number of automatic weapons made low-level attacks such as "truck-hunting" more difficult and dangerous. "Flak traps" were established, with dummies in parachutes hanging from trees or simulated targets—dummy trains, trucks tanks, and soldiers, and fake bunkers—to entice planes into antiaircraft fire. Aircraft spotters were stationed at 300–400 meter intervals along the main supply routes. By mid–1951 over 1,650 specially prepared spotter posts were in use. They would signal when planes were in the area. Trains and trucks then stopped immediately.

The Communists learned to avoid moving trains, if possible, under a full moon, or between the hours from ten to midnight, when UN planes were most active. When necessary, trains were run close together in defiance of normal safety rules. As early in the war, they were run over very short stretches of open track. Even damaged bridges could sometimes be used; freight cars could be pushed or towed over spans that could not bear the weight of a locomotive. Some bridges were kept in operation only at night; spans were lifted in and out of place and they were made to look damaged and out of operation by day. The Communists also learned to fake broken railroad tracks, with debris and straw strewn across a line. Bypasses were built around normal routes, often even before the old route was knocked out. Repair equipment and materials were pre-positioned near important points and likely targets. Trucks drove without lights in moonlight, and only the lead truck in a convoy drove with its lights on at all. Lights were strung along mountainsides, and steel cable across narrow valleys to decoy and destroy night-flying planes. Real trains and trucks were carefully camouflaged by day. Stockpiles of supplies were widely dispersed as well as camouflaged. In addition to dummies, damaged trains and trucks were used as decoys. Vehicle tracks were made into empty buildings to lead pilots to think trucks were hiding there. Trucks were hidden in ravines by day. Later the Communists tended to move them into a growing number of strongly-built bunkers, then later still into mines, caves, and railroad tunnels, which were the usual shelters for trains. Truckers carried oily rags to be set on fire so attacking pilots would think they had destroyed their targets even when they had not.

The American commanders were eager to get back into MIG Alley to attack transportation targets and airfields. They had hoped to start escorting bombers there at the beginning of March, but Suwon airfield was too badly damaged. The first B-29 mission to MIG Alley on March 1 was escorted by F-80s rather than Sabrejets and was roughly handled. No planes were lost, but some were badly shot up. An F-86 squadron was able to move into Suwon only on March 10. Space there was limited; the rest of the 4th Fighter Wing had to stay at Taegu, using Suwon as a staging base. The Sabrejets again patrolled along the Yalu while the bombers and fighter-bombers went to work. (Some fighter-bomber units had moved back to Korea, but others were still based in Japan and staged through Korean fields.) The Soviet 151st Fighter Division was relieved in March, and the 303rd and 324th Divisions, whose pilots were better selected and trained, entered combat. The new Soviet pilots thought their predecessors seemed demoralized. Although badly outnumbered, the Sabrejets were nevertheless able to deal with the MIGs.

On March 30, the B-29s successfully attacked the middle Yalu bridges (the river was now thawing). Getting the most important bridges at Sinuiju across the river from the main MIG base proved tougher. On April 7, the Superfortresses, escorted by Thunderjets while the Sabrejets flew a screen, attacked Sinuiju. They hit the bridges but did not destroy them, and the MIGs got one B-29. A return to the same target on April 12 proved disastrous. Enough MIGs from the 324th Fighter Division got through the Sabrejet screen to shoot down two B-29s, while a third staggered back to Suwon but never flew again. The escorting F-84s were just too slow to compete with the MIGs. Henceforth, the Sinuiju area was off-limit to the B-29s, the first important Soviet success in the air over Korea. The Sabrejets, however, maintained control over the rest of MIG Alley and helped foil the Communists' plans to support their spring offensive.

The Americans kept track of work on the North Korean airfields. An enemy air offensive was a worrisome prospect. South Korea's ports, airfields and supply dumps presented concentrated and vulnerable targets, and were defended by few antiaircraft guns. The Americans held their hand until the enemy bases were nearly ready. On April 17, just a few days before the Communist spring offensive, the bombers stopped attacking enemy supply lines and went to work on the airfields. A week of attacks reduced them to a mass of craters. The UN forces thus maintained control of the air, except just across the Yalu from Andong. The enemy would have to operate without any important air support unless the Soviets took an open part in the campaign.[5]

There was considerable fear of just that.

The Relief of MacArthur

The UN offensive had coincided with the final showdown between MacArthur and his superiors. Although the fears that had originally prompted his program to carry the war to China had proven unfounded, the general remained unhappy. Since Ridgway's arrival, he had little to do directly with the campaign in Korea and plenty of time to brood over the situation. As MacArthur saw it, the Truman administration had no plan or will to undo the defeat in North Korea, much less solve what he regarded as the basic problem in East Asia: China's capacity for aggression. He rightly suspected that without a new offensive strategy the war might drag on indecisively for years. And he seems to have believed that the Joint Chiefs held views fairly close to his own and might be prodded to get the policy changed. During February he drew up a plan for victory that might get around the administrations desire to avoid action outside Korea. Once the Eighth Army reached a line covering Seoul, he envisaged laying a barrier of "radioactive waste" along the south bank of the Yalu, rendering the area impassable. With the enemy's supply lines completely cut, the UN forces, reinforced with Chinese Nationalist troops, would carry out a super–Inchon operation with simultaneous amphibious and airborne landings on both coasts of North Korea. While the "radioactive waste" scheme involved all sorts of technical difficulties and the idea of releasing so much radiation is repulsive, it might have been cheaper in human life than the course actually followed.

But perhaps because this plan would not eliminate the Chinese Communist regime, MacArthur shelved it and did not submit it to the Joint Chiefs. Instead, on February 13, he resumed advocating the measures he had urged in December. On February 22, he urged the Joint Chiefs to support the anti–Communist guerrillas in China and prepare for an eventual Nationalist landing near Shanghai. He publicly grumbled more and more often about the limitations imposed on his forces and his lack of specific directives. On March 7, he gave the press an interview implicitly critical of the administration during which he complained that "critical decisions have yet to be made" and spoke of the "abnormal military inhibitions" under which he operated. He stressed that a stalemate would inevitably be reached in Korea. He also imprudently revealed that he did not expect serious reinforcements. On March 15, he opposed dropping the unification of Korea.

More serious transgressions followed. MacArthur must almost certainly have known that they would provoke Truman into firing him, although he may have calculated that his position as an "international" officer would protect him for a while. On March 20, he learned that the President planned to propose a cease-fire in Korea. MacArthur insolently sabotaged the plan. On March 24, he offered to meet the enemy commander in Korea in person to arrange an end to the war. The offer was preceded by contemptuous and threatening remarks. MacArthur spoke of "the clear revelation that this new enemy, Red China, of such exaggerated and vaunted military power, lacks the industrial capacity to provide adequately many critical items essential to the conduct of modern war." Further, he said, "The enemy therefore must by now be painfully aware that a decision of the United Nations to depart from its tolerant effort to contain the war to the area of Korea through expansion of our military operations to his coastal areas and interior bases would doom Red China to the risk of imminent military collapse."

The Chinese rejected this "offer," as they probably would have rejected Truman's proposed statement, which now could not be made. The Joint Chiefs of Staff were reluctant to do more than reprimand MacArthur, but Truman privately resolved to fire him at the first opportune moment. He may already have decided to do so because of another issue that could not be publicly revealed. Decoded Spanish and Portuguese diplomatic messages had disclosed that MacArthur had spoken critically of administration policy to diplomats of those countries. A clear-cut occasion for getting rid of MacArthur soon appeared. Joseph Martin, the Republican leader in the House of Representatives, had asked MacArthur to comment on a speech in which Martin demanded that the Chinese Nationalists open a "second front" on the mainland. On April 5, Martin read MacArthur's reply, written on March 20, on the House floor. It was vintage MacArthur, a full expression of ideas that the administration had firmly rejected. MacArthur described his views as following "the conventional pattern of meeting force with maximum counterforce, as we have never failed to do in the past. Your view with respect to the utilization of the Chinese forces on Formosa is in conflict with neither logic nor this tradition. It seems strangely difficult for some to realize that here in Asia is where the Communist conspirators have elected to make their play for global conquest, and that we have joined the issue thus raised on the battlefield, that here we fight Europe's war with arms, while the diplomats there still fight it with words, that if we lost the war to Communism in Asia, the fall of Europe is inevitable; win it, and Europe most probably would avoid war and yet preserve freedom. As you point out, we must win. There is no substitute for victory."

Eloquent as the message was, it was also dishonest. MacArthur knew perfectly well that, as he admitted later, the Nationalist forces on Taiwan were far from ready to assault the mainland. Another indiscreet and shifty

12. The Chinese Are Defeated

communication came to light a bit later. In a letter to the conservative magazine *Freeman*, MacArthur had blamed Washington for not arming additional ROK troops, although he himself had advised against doing that in January. He had preferred sending the arms available to the Japanese National Police Reserve. He and other American generals deemed the ROK officer corps inadequate for the existing units, much less new ones.

The Martin letter was enough to enrage Truman. He conferred with his advisers the next day. They urged caution. General Marshall was surprisingly reluctant to fire MacArthur; he favored ordering him back to the States for consultation before doing anything else. Truman wished to make sure that the Joint Chiefs of Staff were united firmly behind him. They unanimously recommended MacArthur's relief on April 9. They did not consider him technically guilty of insubordination since they held that he had not violated a direct order; but he *had* violated Truman's December 1950 directive on clearing speeches. Further, he had shown a lack of sympathy for the administration's policy and jeopardized civilian control over the military. The last point, of course, was the crucial one. Even had Truman now decided that MacArthur's strategy was right, he would have had to fire him. On April 11, MacArthur was relieved and replaced by Ridgway.

An explosion followed. Disgust with the restrictions on the American forces, genuine and not necessarily unreasonable misgivings about the adequacy of containment, and the general atmosphere of tension contributed to an unprecedented blast of public fury. MacArthur, while widely disliked (especially by men who had served under him), was a national hero. No one regarded Harry Truman as one, not in 1951 at any rate. The Democrats and some moderate Republicans rallied behind Truman, albeit without much enthusiasm. Senator Knowland's description of MacArthur's relief as a "Far Eastern Munich" was one of the milder comments from the opposition. Representative Martin talked of impeaching Truman. Others suggested MacArthur had been fired because of a Communist plot, or that Truman had been drunk or drugged. The more irresponsible Republicans even questioned Truman's right to fire MacArthur — something MacArthur himself never contested. MacArthur's departure caused general relief in Western Europe where he had few admirers. It posed a potential propaganda problem for the Communists, but they rose to the occasion. *Izvestiya*, on April 20 explained that MacArthur had been fired as a scapegoat for military failure and as a sacrifice to placate demands for peace.

MacArthur returned to a hero's welcome. On April 19 he spoke before a joint session of Congress. In a moving speech he brilliantly summarized the case for carrying the war to China. The Democrats had to agree to hearings on the "military situation in the Far East" by joint sessions of the Senate Committees on Foreign Relations and Armed Services. Public debate on whether the war should be "expanded" went on.[6]

The War Scare Revives

It was not clear that that decision lay solely in American hands. As spring began the war scare rose again. There was considerable fear that the Soviets would intervene massively to support the expected Chinese spring offensive. Even if the Soviets wished to confine the resulting fighting to Korea, it was generally believed that would lead to all-out war. There was no question that the Soviets, who were known to have been strengthening their forces in the Far East since December, could commit enough forces to drive the UN Command out of Korea — or worse, trap it there, leaving Japan ill-defended. The Americans trembled at the thought of a Soviet atomic bomb destroying Pusan; the port and its dumps were vulnerable even to conventional air attack.

Several remarkably and perhaps suspiciously detailed reports on alleged Soviet plans for action in April or May fell into American hands. Some warned of a full-scale Soviet attack in East Asia, while others indicated that the Soviets planned a more limited, disguised move using Soviet planes and Soviet Asian "volunteers" on the ground. The CIA could not confirm any of these reports, which smack of plants, and clearly doubted their validity. But given the CIA's record that provided little comfort. Some of the worry became public. Sam Rayburn, the respected Speaker of the House of Representatives, warned Americans that the danger of world war was greater than at any time since 1945. President Truman did not gainsay him, commenting that "the Speaker is a truthful man." On April 6, additional Strategic Air Command bombers were ordered to the western Pacific, and nine atomic bombs were prepared on Guam. The fear was not limited to the United States. Continental European officials grumbled that they could not understand why Washington was so much more optimistic about war not breaking out in 1951. The British, however, seem to have been more skeptical.[7]

There seemed to be a lesser, more local threat that the Chinese would attack Taiwan or Indochina, a fear they cleverly played on. On February 3, Zhou Enlai warned Ambassador Panikkar that because of the UN resolution condemning China as an aggressor the war was likely to spread. In January, "Third Party" had warned that an invasion of Taiwan was planned for the spring. Concentrations of troops and junks in Chinese ports pointed toward an invasion in April. Although the intelligence agencies were skeptical, the threat seemed serious enough to take the carriers of Task Force 77 from Korea for a "show of force" and reconnaissance mission along the coast of China from April 8 to 14. The invasion scare was almost certainly a clever and successful feint. It diverted a sizable American force just before the spring offensive, relieving pressure on the Communist supply lines in Korea. It may be no coincidence that one of the occasional Chinese raids into Indochina also occurred in this period.[8] At least on the level of grand strategy, the Communists had ably prepared for their coming "Fifth Phase Offensive," and the biggest battles of the Korean War.

The Communist Spring Offensive

The Eighth Army, now ably led by General James Van Fleet, was in good shape. In Korea 505,000 UN troops faced 542,000 Chinese and nearly 200,000 North Koreans.

For some days the Chinese forward units had broken contact. The long withdrawals of March and April had brought them back to their main forward base in the Iron Triangle. Their forces in Korea in the late winter and spring had been built up to four army groups, one drawn from each of China's four field armies. The newly arrived 3rd and 19th Army Groups, equipped with Soviet weapons, would carry the main burden in the spring offensive. The older 9th Army Group, only lightly engaged in March, had been rebuilt and reorganized, It had resumed the standard Chinese organization, in that the "extra" fourth division once attached to each of its armies had been broken up to supply men for the remaining units. It was allotted relatively simple tasks. The 13th Army Group, which had borne most of the burden of the fighting from November through March, was now far understrength and played only a small role. Nine North Korean divisions, still far understrength, would support the Chinese.

The UN forces kept their main strength under U.S. I Corps in the west where the Chinese main blow was expected. There the ROK 1st Division and the U.S. 3rd Division, with the British 29th Brigade under its command, were nevertheless stretched. Farther east the Turkish Brigade, and the U.S. 25th and 24th Divisions completed the corps line. IX Corps had the 6th ROK Division and the 1st Marine Division in line, with the 27th Commonwealth Brigade in reserve. X Corps had the U.S. 2nd and 7th Divisions and the 5th ROK Division in line. The Eighth Army had the 1st Cavalry Division and the 187th Airborne Regimental Combat Team in reserve. ROK III Corps with the 7th and 3rd ROK Divisions, and ROK I Corps with the Capital and 11th Divisions, held the eastern mountains and coastal corridor.

The Communists main effort was to be a double envelopment of the whole of U.S. I Corps and the capture of Seoul, using the same routes taken by the North Koreans in June 1950. North Korean I Corps in the west coastal sector would advance through Munsan-ni, but depended on the Chinese 19th Army Group opening the way by smashing through the ROK 1st Division and the British 29th Brigade. The 3rd Army Group would strike along the Uijongbu axis (Route 33) crushing the U.S. 3rd Division, the Turks and the 25th Division. The 9th Army Group would hit the U.S. 24th and ROK 6th Divisions while the 13th Army Group launched a holding attack on the Marines. The North Korean III and V Corps would strike east of the Hwachon Reservoir, hoping for a breakthrough that would enable them to cut into the coastal corridor from the northwest.

Air reconnaissance and talkative Chinese prisoners had alerted the UN Command to the coming attack. The Chinese set forest fires to cover their movements but could not entirely hide them from the air. They attacked on the night of April 22–23. The UN forces were surprised by the intensity of the opening bombardment, and the Chinese brought a few T-34 tanks into action against the 25th Division but relied on mass infantry assaults supported by automatic weapons and mortars. Unlike their earlier operations, these were close to the much talked about "human sea" attacks, and they were very costly. Except for taking place at night, they reminded older observers of the opening British attacks in the Battle of the Somme in July 1916. Sheer weight drove I Corps back. The Chinese forced a crossing of the Imjin against the ROK 1st Division, which fought well. The 3rd Division's front included a long stretch along the Imjin, which ran nearly parallel to Route 33, its main supply route. The British 29th Brigade held perhaps the most crucial sector of all. It was attacked by the whole 63rd Army. Here the Imjin was low and easy to ford, and the Belgian Battalion, attached to the British, was awkwardly situated across the river. The Belgians succeeded in getting out of their exposed position, and the first Chinese attacks were thrown back. But finally the Chinese broke through. The Gloucester Battalion was cut off. It rallied on Hill 235 ("Gloucester Hill"). Further east, the Chinese had broken through the Turks, endangering the 3rd Division, and still further east had routed the poorly prepared ROK 6th Division, which fled in panic. This left a 10-mile gap between the 24th Division and the Marines. The American and New Zealand artillery units supporting the ROKs lost much of their equipment. The Chinese threatened to cut IX Corps' supply route, which ran nearly parallel to the front and even outflank the defenders of Seoul. The Marines, already under pressure from attacks on their front, refused their left flank and prevented the Chinese breaking into their rear, which some thought they might have done had they moved faster. After April 25 the Chinese broke off their attacks on the Marines.

On April 23, Van Fleet ordered I and IX Corps to fall back to the Kansas Line. The 24th Division was shifted to IX Corps while the 27th Commonwealth Brigade and part of the 1st Cavalry Division, which Van Fleet had wanted to use in a counterattack on the western front, rushed to fill the gap left by the collapse of the 6th ROK Division. The 27th Brigade, and an American tank company, artillery unit, and engineers succeeded in blocking the Chinese advance at a critical point at Kapyong. An attempt by a much too weak relief force — the Philippine Battalion (part of the U.S. 3rd Division) and a few British tanks—failed to reach the trapped Gloucesters. A second, larger effort was overtaken by the retreat. The Gloucesters tried to break out, but only a few men reached the UN lines. Their heroic stand, however, had helped cost the Chinese victory. The retreat to the Kansas Line was largely successful, although the 25th Division's 5th Regimental Combat Team ran into a classic Chinese ambush and suffered heavy losses. On April 26, Van Fleet decided to have IX and X Corps pull back further, to the oddly designated "No Name Line." The Chinese had gotten within four miles of Seoul, whose fall had been widely expected in both the West and Communist worlds. Tanks and artillery in the streets blasted at them. That day, however, the Chinese seemed to weaken. After days of suffering murderous air attacks, especially in front of I Corps, they began moving much more cautiously during the day. Peng wanted to stop the offensive on April 26, but Mao overruled him. The attack went on for a few more days, but finally the Chinese halted and began to pull back. The North Koreans had scored some successes against the ROK 3rd Division on the right of X Corps and ROK III Corps. Both corps fell back about 20 miles. In the west, the Chinese had advanced about 35 miles at tremendous cost. The UN forces estimated communist losses at about 70,000 compared to a tenth of that on the UN side. The UN now pushed back, although it was certain that the Communists would renew their offensive.

The Hwachon dam was now back under Communist control, but the threat it posed was dealt with from the air. On May 1, U.S. Navy Skyraiders torpedoed the sluice gates. Although the Communists' air campaign had not gone well, they moved propeller-driven Yak fighters and Stormovik ground-attack planes into Sinuiju airfield just across the Yalu from the MIG base at Andong, presumably to support the "Second Impulse" of the "Fifth Phase Offensive." On May 9, the Americans responded with a massive attack by over 300 planes that wrecked the Sinuiju base and destroyed all 38 planes there.

Van Fleet expected a renewed attack, probably in the west. Ridgway at first agreed, but began to suspect the enemy might also strike well to the east if only as a secondary effort. He advised a shift of reserves eastward. Although a movement of Chinese forces to the east was detected, a major attack in the eastern mountains was widely discounted on the grounds that it would be too tough for the enemy to supply forces there.

Peng had no intention of going back over the same ground again. On May 10, he had begun moving five Chinese armies from the 9th and 3rd Army Groups east of the Hwachon Reservoir. Although the terrain would be difficult, it might reduce the effect of the UN's greater firepower and mobility. Peng aimed to destroy the whole of the ROK force on the eastern front and the U.S. 2nd Division with it. Four Chinese divisions and half a dozen North Korean divisions would hit the ROK corps, while 11 Chinese divisions fell on X Corps. A holding attack would hit the Marines who were now the leftmost division in X Corps (O.P. Smith had left Korea, so his men could now serve under Almond again). The Eighth Army's Western units stood behind formidable defensive positions, manning bunkers protected by mines and "fougasses" — 55-gallon drums of napalm detonated by remote control.

The attack began on May 16. The ROK 5th and 7th Divisions collapsed in the worst South Korean defeat of the war. The divisions of ROK III Corps folded rapidly during the following day and night. Farther east, ROK I Corps managed to hold with the help of naval gunfire. The 2nd Division was under heavy pressure, and its Dutch battalion failed to obey an order to counterattack and a quasi-mutiny developed. The 23rd Infantry Regiment tried to shore up the right flank but was forced to withdraw under strong attacks. The Chinese had gotten across its line of withdrawal. It ran into an ambush and had to get out across country, abandoning heavy weapons and vehicles. The Marines had shifted to the east to take over part of the 2nd Division's front, while Van Fleet shifted the U.S. 3rd Division, the ROK 8th Division and artillery units to X Corps. The 187th Airborne Regimental Combat Team followed. Van Fleet had authorized exceptional expenditures of artillery shells, five times the standard rate. The fantastic bombardments were a great strain on guns, trucks and the men who operated them but were a major factor in stopping the attack. I and IX Corps and part of the Marine Division went over to the attack to threaten the enemy's supply lines in the Iron Triangle. Van Fleet was confident that the enemy's supply difficulties would cause it to fail. He was right; the Chinese could not even get enough food to their men. By May 19, the 2nd Division still seemed badly stretched, but the Chinese seemed to be losing impetus. In addition to the titanic shelling, the Chinese in front of the

12. The Chinese Are Defeated

Marines and the 2nd Division suffered heavily from newly effective night bombing directed by MPQ radars. The system had been in use for some time but was only now working well. Although as late as May 21 the ROKs were still falling back, the U.S. 3rd Division now protected the far southern flank of X Corps and the enemy was now under pressure elsewhere. The UN Command deactivated ROK III Corps, distributing its units between X Corps and ROK I Corps, which had performed well. The ROK corps was now under direct Eighth Army command. On May 23, the enemy broke off the offensive. By that time Peng realized his forces were spent. His 12th and 15th armies, which had tangled with the Marines and the 2nd Division, were especially mangled. He now ordered his forces to fall back rapidly, planning to bring his Chinese forces back to the area west of the Hwachon Reservoir, leaving the area east of the reservoir to the North Koreans. To avoid jamming the roads in the east, some of the Chinese units in the west had to pull out to the northwest below the reservoir. The Americans would try to intercept this move.

The UN now went over to the attack in the fastest shift to the offensive following a major enemy assault in the war. A limited counterattack had begun on the X Corps front on May 22. Almond was apparently the first to see the possibility of chopping off the big salient created by the ROK defeat by a drive using the Marines and the 2nd Division northeast up Route 24 to the Soyang river, and over that river to the road center of Inje — and, if possible, all the way to Kansong on the east coast. The 187th Airborne Regimental Combat Team was put under the 2nd Division. "Task Force Gerhardt," formed from part of the 187th, and the 2nd Division's tank, antiaircraft and engineer units led the attack. Its operations were closely watched by Almond who characteristically bullied and lashed on its commanders. Supported by jets, it quickly reached the Soyang river bridgehead on May 24 and struck for Inje. There it ran into stiff opposition, suffered heavy losses and was forced back. The next day a bigger "Task Force Baker" was formed of the whole 187th Airborne, a tank battalion and attached troops near the Soyang crossing. It readied a renewed drive for Inje, linking up with Task Force Gerhardt. But determined Chinese rearguards tied up the U.S. 23rd Infantry Regiment and the attached French for a whole day of bitter fighting. Task Force Baker did not get really started until May 27. It got to Inje that day, but took time to clear high ground there. It was another 52 miles to the ultimate objective on the coast. Already, on May 26, the North Koreans had taken over the delaying action, letting the Chinese slip away.

IX Corps' 7th and 24th Divisions, advancing in the central corridor, trapped almost the entire 180th Chinese Division between them. But it was already becoming likely that I and IX Corps would not catch really big enemy forces, although by forcing large-scale enemy movements over roads in daylight they made the Communists run a gauntlet of air attacks and sometimes long range artillery fire, which took an enormous toll of men and vehicles. The 7th Division, taking Chunchon, did find an unexpected prize, freeing 19 Americans. They had been captured in the Chosin Reservoir campaign in December and had accompanied a Chinese unit since instead of being sent to a prisoner of war camp. Although no large units other than the 180th Division were destroyed, the enemy retreat was costly. Many smaller groups of Chinese, bypassed by the armored drives that led the I and IX Corps attacks, were quite willing to surrender. They were in bad shape and short of food. Much enemy equipment was captured. The Chinese were obviously worried. On June 1 they even issued an anguished public complaint about their lack of equipment and supplies, which was widely believed to be directed against the Soviets. Stalin may have been anxious enough about the prospects of a complete Chinese collapse to prepare to commit a limited Soviet ground force of five divisions to Korea.

The North Koreans whom the UN forces generally considered inferior soldiers to the Chinese, had fought hard. Their determined efforts, the mountainous terrain and the speed of the enemy withdrawal prevented the great victory hoped for. Still, the enemy, or at least the forces that had been engaged, seemed badly battered. Van Fleet and Almond were very optimistic, and thought for a while that the enemy had been so weakened that a continued UN counteroffensive could destroy the Communist forces and liberate much of North Korea. On May 28, Van Fleet proposed mounting a major amphibious operation on June 6, using the 1st Marine Division for a short-range "amphibious hook." It would land at Tongchon where it would join up with an overland drive. Ridgway considered the idea excessively risky given the UN's limited aims and rejected it. By the time Van Fleet advanced the proposal the enemy had gotten out of the danger zone east of the Hwachon Reservoir and resistance was stiffening.

The UN estimated that the May offensive had cost the Communists as many as 105,000 casualties—10,000, mostly Chinese, had been captured. How many men the Communists really lost is uncertain. Chinese sources insist that they (not counting the North Koreans) had lost "only" 85,000 men — still a staggering number — in April and May. But given the unreliability of other Communist casualty statistics it would be unwise to rely on this either. The UN Command in May had lost casualities of 21,758 men, with 2,037 killed. The missing totaled 10,532 — the vast majority South Koreans.

12. The Chinese Are Defeated

Although Ridgway rightly considered Van Fleet and Almond overoptimistic, he did wish to keep up the pressure if only long enough to regain the Kansas Line and a cushion of territory beyond. He launched "Operation Piledriver" to try to seize Chorwon and Kumwha in the Iron Triangle. The offensive began June 3, encountering stubborn resistance from both the Chinese and North Koreans, but especially the latter. On June 11–12, patrols reached Chorwon and Kumwha. There was tough fighting for the high ground around them, while the 1st Marine Division and the ROKs hit the "Punchbowl," an extinct volcano that was strongly held by North Korean units. There was exceptionally fierce fighting there. The Americans eventually took Pyonggang, the northern tip of the Iron Triangle. But it was overlooked by enemy-held higher ground, and they soon abandoned it.

The UN victory had ended the Communist dream of driving the UN Command out of Korea. But the hope that the UN could liberate most of Korea without expanding the war outside it was also a dream, although it impressed some later writers on the Korean War. It had warned the Chinese and Soviet leaders for a time. Although the UN forces could have forced the enemy far to the north, they lacked the strength to liberate the country. Van Fleet soon concluded the enemy still had numerical superiority and would even be able to launch another offensive within two months. He could push the enemy forces back but did not have enough troops to destroy them by maneuver, and as the enemy fell back his supply lines would be shortened. Although Van Fleet drew up plans for a major advance to the Pyongyang-Wonsan line, he did not, contrary to impressions he later fostered, actually favor carrying them out. And the likely cost of such an offensive steadily increased. The Communists actually resumed the offensive in the sky during June, trying to gain control of the air. "Night heckler" light planes bombed South Korean airfields, and MIGs using better tactics flew far south of the Yalu. But the Sabrejets coped with them, and a new series of attacks kept the North Korean airfields inoperable. The enemy air offensive ended on July 12, just as the armistice talks began.

On May 17, the National Security Council had finally settled on NSC-48/5, a general statement of current policy in Asia. The United States would seek a united and free Korea, but only by political means, and recognized that achieving that aim was probably not now possible. An end to the war would be sought. It would be expanded to China only if the Chinese attacked outside Korea or if the UN Command had to evacuate Korea. On May 31, Ridgway received a directive reflecting the new policy. All older restrictions on his operations remained. He was to create conditions for an armistice and the eventual withdrawal of non–Korean forces by building up ROK power to repel any new North Korean attack.[9]

13

The Truman-MacArthur Conflict Continues

The Truman administration's decision to limit the war to Korea remained bitterly controversial in the United States. The hearings prompted by MacArthur's recall began May 3. They marked the effective end of the fight between MacArthur and the administration. They are intensely interesting as the climax of public debate about the only serious proposals ever advanced to turn the tide of the Cold War in favor of the West by military means.

MacArthur was the first witness. He ably expounded his views, arguing that national tradition and sound policy alike called for decisive action to win the war and unite Korea. China should be bombed and blockaded, and Chinese Nationalist forces should be employed both in Korea and against the Chinese mainland. MacArthur stressed that China was a major threat in itself, not just as a Soviet ally. He conceded that the United States was not particularly well-prepared for all-out war — he urged the biggest possible military buildup — and admitted that Europe was vulnerable. But time was not necessarily on our side in the conflict with the Soviet-Chinese alliance. As time passed the enemy's strength might increase more than our own, an implicit argument for taking drastic action while the balance of power still favored the West.

MacArthur argued that the Soviets were not likely to be provoked into war by anything we did in Korea or China unless they were otherwise ready and willing to fight. Even if the Soviets intervened, their forces in the Far East were not really strong and were at the end of a long and strained supply line. MacArthur stressed that the Soviets could not take

13. The Truman-MacArthur Conflict Continues

Japan. The Chinese were at full stretch and could not do much more to hurt us; they lacked the capability to respond to attacks on Manchuria with attacks on Japan. The best way to deter the Soviets was to win in Korea. MacArthur even expressed the view that the Chinese might be reluctant to call on the Soviets for troops. Our allies were not likely to break with us over any offensive action we took against the enemy in the Far East. At most, only a small increase in forces would be needed to carry out his program. Any additional commitment of forces, in any case, would not endanger Europe, which would not be defensible for another two years. China was especially vulnerable to a blockade, and the already strained Trans-Siberian railroad could not replace seaborne traffic.[1]

Senator MacMahon, however, extracted the damaging admission from MacArthur that he was, after all, just a theater commander, not privy to everything known to the authorities in Washington who had to take a global view. Secretary of State Acheson, General Marshall and the Joint Chiefs of Staff were an impressive force of witnesses against MacArthur, mustering strong arguments against his ideas and putting up a strong defense of the containment policy.

They stressed that MacArthur's program would provoke war with the Soviets, or, at best, their reaction would be dangerously unpredictable. The actions he proposed could be used by Stalin as a diversion. With American strength sucked into East Asia, the Soviets could start a world war in relatively favorable circumstances. And since the other NATO countries opposed MacArthur's program, it could dangerously split the Western alliance and perhaps lead to the loss of vital overseas bases. MacArthur, who had remarked that he favored the United States going ahead alone if necessary, was accused of willfully risking or even preferring "unilateralism." (This accusation was unjust.)

General Bradley stressed, "As long as we keep the conflict within its present scope, we are holding to a minimum the forces we must commit and tie down. The strategic alternative, enlargement of the war in Korea to include Red China, would probably delight the Kremlin more than anything else we could do. It would necessarily tie down additional forces, especially our sea power and air power, while the Soviet Union would not be obliged to put a single man into the conflict. Red China is not the powerful nation seeking to dominate the world. Frankly, in the opinion of the Joint Chiefs of Staff, this strategy would involve us in the wrong war, at the wrong place, at the wrong time, and with the wrong enemy."[2]

MacArthur's proposals were also attacked on narrower military grounds. The Air Force Chief of Staff pointed out that the true source of the enemy's material in Korea was in the Soviet Union. He was in no position to wage a strategic air campaign against China without incurring dangerous losses that might impair the Strategic Air Command's ability to deal with the Soviets in all-out war. "While we can lay the industrial potential of Russia to waste, in my opinion, or we can lay the Manchurian countryside to waste, as well as the principal cities of China, we cannot do both, again because we have a shoestring air force," he stated.

China was not too vulnerable to the actions proposed. It was too backward to be powerfully affected by blockade and bombing, while the Trans-Siberian railroad and the Soviet-controlled ports in Manchuria would be holes in any blockade. The Soviets would be tempted to break a unilateral American blockade, while a UN blockade was probably unobtainable. Moreover, if China was bombed, the enemy might retaliate by attacking installations in South Korea, Japan and Okinawa. The Chinese Nationalist troops would not be of much use in Korea and would involve political complications with our allies. The Nationalists were in no position to invade the Chinese mainland at present and could never do so without major American help, which would not be commensurate with the costs. (MacArthur himself now admitted that the Nationalists were not ready for an invasion, although he maintained that they could send a useful force to Korea.) The Joint Chiefs suggested that MacArthur's program would require larger forces than he envisioned and rated Soviet capabilities in the Far East higher than he did. In secret testimony the Joint Chiefs warned that the Soviets could probably gain air superiority over Japan in the first stages of a world war.[3]

The "MacArthur Hearings" were a success for the Truman administration. They did not make its policies popular, for contrary to what is often claimed most of the public continued to favor MacArthur's ideas. It should be noted also that positions in the Truman-MacArthur controversy did not reduce to a simple clash between right and left in American politics, any more than disputes over other Cold War issues in this period did. Conservative Southern Democrats backed Truman as they did on most Cold War issues, while the Republicans split. The socialist journal *New Leader* favored firing MacArthur as a threat to civilian authority, *and* implementing his program. Some people endorsed part of MacArthur's program and rejected the rest of it. In May 1951, the able liberal Senator Paul Douglas opposed bombing China or backing a Nationalist invasion of the Chinese mainland, but called for blockading China and using Nationalist forces in Korea.[4]

The administration had not won everyone over, but had shown there was at least a reasonable case to be made for its policies and had fended off the attack of MacArthur and the opposition. (Although Truman became even more unpopular than he had been before.) To some extent it also bought off the opposition. Acheson and Marshall made clear they would never let Taiwan come under Communist rule. Military aid and advisers were again going to the Chinese Nationalists. In May, Assistant Secretary of State Rusk made an oft-quoted speech that wrongly seemed to suggest that the administration had swallowed the China Bloc's view of the world. He declared that the "Peiping (the Nationalist name for Beijing) regime may be a colonial Russian government—a Slavic Manchukuo on a large scale. It is not the Government of China. It does not pass the first test. It is not Chinese." These apparent absurdities may have been at least partly designed to taunt anti–Soviet elements in China into acting. As the Chinese leaders had reason to know, Rusk's remarks had some basis in Stalin's aspirations, if not current reality.

The administration had not in fact come to love Jiang Jieshi. In late 1952, it reportedly laid a plot to overthrow him and replace him with reform-minded elements among the Nationalists. But the plan misfired.[5]

Most of the administration's prominent enemies—Senator Knowland was an exception—had actually shown little interest in serious alternatives to existing policies or winning the Korean War. Rather than serious discussion of Cold War policies, the Republicans in the hearings wasted much time beating the dead horse of the administration's supposed responsibility for the defeat of the Chinese Nationalists, while much of the opposition preferred harping on the issue of subversion at home. Fortunately for the Truman administration, the opposition showed little skill or interest in ferreting out differences of opinion within the administration as well as the discrepancies and weak points in its case, which were not minor. The differences between the Joint Chiefs of Staff as a group and MacArthur's position were less than they were made to seem, while there were serious conflicts or potential conflicts of opinion apparent even in the open testimony. Under questioning, the Secretary of State admitted that no allied country had actually threatened to pull its troops out of the war if MacArthur's program was implemented, much less break with the United States. There was, in fact, little evidence that the Western alliance was that fragile. Secretary Marshall and General Bradley admitted that they would have favored bombing Manchuria had they been sure the Soviets would not intervene. Evidently they did not fully share General Vandenberg's view that the Air Force was too weak for the operations MacArthur wanted. In contrast to most administration witnesses, Admiral Sherman maintained that China was quite vulnerable to a blockade, and Marshall tended to agree. Sherman in fact privately favored a unilateral blockade. The thesis that refraining from action against China prevented the Chinese from retaliating against UN bases in Korea and offshore — that the "privileged sanctuary" about which MacArthur complained really worked both ways — was much cited by later writers. But in 1951 it was only advanced by General Bradley and was not taken too seriously by other witnesses. Vandenberg seems to have dismissed it. The idea was in fact spurious. The Chinese, without larger, overt Soviet intervention could not attack even South Korean targets on a serious scale. As was seen, their own program to do so failed because their Soviet allies could not gain air superiority over North Korea. There is little reason to think they could have successfully escorted bombers into UN territory. In the existing circumstances the restraints enabled the MIGs to attack American planes in uniquely favorable conditions and shielded enemy bases from attack. The advantages of sanctuary were purely one-sided.[6] But the truly gaping holes in the administration's position were the facts that in January the Joint Chiefs had favored implementing at least some of MacArthur's ideas if the UN was forced out of Korea, that they still favored those measures if the Chinese attacked American forces elsewhere, and that during 1951 and later they were to recommend retaliation against China if an armistice in Korea was broken. The logic of arguing that it was justifiable to take the risk of striking against China in those cases, but not in the existing circumstances, might have escaped most people. The caliber of Truman's enemies, however, was such that they hardly noticed this.

In fact, the Joint Chiefs and some other elements of the administration changed their minds about some of MacArthur's ideas in 1951–1952. Contrary to a widespread assumption, the end of public debate in 1951 did not end consideration of taking the war to China. General Marshall himself, after visiting Korea in June 1951, considered recommending that Zhou Enlai be told that unless the Chinese agreed to an armistice, "we are going to give them a taste of the atom." During 1951 and 1952, the restrictions on bombing Rashin and the power installations were lifted. In September 1951, the Joint Chiefs urged allowing "hot pursuit' of enemy planes into China (but dropped the idea later when the tactical situation changed). During 1952 they came to favor using Chinese Nationalist forces in Korea. They recommended that if armistice talks broke down, a naval blockade should be imposed on China. In 1952, even George Kennan suggested selective bombing of targets in southern and central China to force agreement on an armistice.[7]

The administration's own intelligence evaluations of the situation in China were surprisingly optimistic and supported MacArthur's claims for the effectiveness of his program. Even overthrowing the Communist regime was a real possibility. Its hold on the country was weaker than it seemed;

13. The Truman-MacArthur Conflict Continues 209

its cruelty and its economic problems had reduced its popularity. Contemporary American estimates (very likely exaggerated) held that there were still 600,000 or more anti–Communist guerrillas only half loyal to the Nationalists at large in southern China. They could easily be strengthened, although they were unlikely to overthrow Mao's regime by themselves. But, just as MacArthur said, China's economy was extremely dependent on overseas and coastal trade, and peculiarly vulnerable to bombing and blockade. Such measures would greatly reduce China's military capability and even endanger the stability of the regime, making a Nationalist invasion possible. A long stretch of coast south of Shanghai offered a good target for a landing. All-out American air and naval attacks (excluding only ground forces) and aid to the guerrillas, culminating in a properly prepared Nationalist landing, might even lead to the defeat of the Communist regime. The Nationalists were of course totally unready for an invasion in early 1951, but in some months could be greatly strengthened — and the Americans studying the problem assumed that the United States would do nine-tenths of the work anyway.

The crucial question in relation to a decisive blow against China was how the Soviets would react. And about that no one in the Administration was optimistic. The CIA believed that the Soviets would regard a Nationalist invasion as a serious threat to their security interests. If one was successful enough to endanger Chinese Communist rule, the Soviets would intervene (if they had not done so before), risking war with the United States if necessary.[8] The tempting possibility of overthrowing Mao's regime was thus ruled out by the fear of Soviet reaction — the controlling factor in the rejection of all of MacArthur's program. No one else was as sure as the general that the Soviets would remain passive if his plans were implemented.

The emotion and confusion of the Truman-MacArthur controversy derived not just from the complexity of the issues but the fact that the protagonists viewed what was going on from quite different standpoints. From MacArthur's point of view — and probably that of most Americans in 1951 — American policy in the Korean War, if not the whole policy of containment, was a disastrous departure from the national tradition of winning wars. By indecisive action, the United States was storing up trouble for the future and would not even stop the Korean War from dragging on endlessly.

From the perspective of the administration, the Korean War and all Asian issues were just part, albeit an important part, of a far larger struggle to which they had to be subordinated just as the fighting in the Pacific theater had had to be subordinated to defeating Germany in World War

II. That there was no war in Europe in 1951 and the administration hoped to avoid one, mattered less than the strategic similarity between the two situations. From this standpoint, MacArthur was just a theater commander suffering from "localities," as Marshall and Eisenhower had called it during World War II. Measures that Truman himself would have liked to take against the Chinese (as the president himself pointed out to MacArthur) had to be foregone to avoid prejudicing the West's chances in a larger war.

What is now known of Stalin's plans amply justifies most of Truman's policies. Given Stalin's decision for war, the West could not afford MacArthur's program. (If successfully carried out, it might have dislocated Stalin's plans or caused him to change his mind about war, but it would have been reckless to gamble on such an outcome.) Ironically, the hard core of Truman's position in 1951, the danger of world war, was often played down by fashionable later commentators, however hostile they were to MacArthur. Wrongly supposing that the administration's fears of Soviet aggression had been exaggerated — ironically putting them in agreement with MacArthur — they preferred to stress less important and often unconvincing elements of the administration case. (For example, the "mutual sanctuary" thesis and China's supposed lack of vulnerability to the actions MacArthur wanted.) They often projected post–Korean War ideas about the supposed necessity of waging only limited wars in the nuclear age, and the elaborate theorizing about such wars common later in the 1950s and the 1960s onto the situation of the early 1950s, and the very different ideas that in reality dominated that era and guided the actions of the American government. The Korean War was fought in a political and strategic framework, and a mental and moral atmosphere much closer to that of World War II than to that of the Second Indochina War.

Yet, MacArthur and his supporters had much right on their side. They were right in thinking that the administration's policies would not end the Korean War, right in thinking that at best they would perpetuate an ugly and unstable status quo in East Asia with the risk of further dreadful conflicts, right in regarding the Korean example as a poor way to run a war, right in seeing the concession of immunity to a Chinese "privileged sanctuary" as a dangerous precedent for the future, right in regarding the outcome of the war as a compromise with aggression and tyranny. The North Korean regime would survive its Soviet creators and with the threat of acquiring mass destruction weapons pose an even bigger danger than it had as a Soviet satellite. And the habit of "not winning" would persist into the 1990s, even after the reasons for it were gone. As General Dave Palmer has sardonically noted, many people would sneer at General

MacArthur's famous remark that "there is no substitute for victory," but no one would ever explain what that substitute was.

Truman, to be sure, had little real choice in acting as he did. He faced a situation in which there were no good alternatives, and even the right choice had a terrible price.

14

Armistice Talks Begin

The shattering defeats of April and May 1951 showed the Communists that they could not overrun Korea, at least in the near future, and seemed to open the way to a truce based on the continued division of the country. From the narrow standpoint of Korean affairs, the Communist powers needed at least a breathing space until Peng's command recovered from the heavy losses of the spring, if not an actual end to the war. That would have been in the interests of the Chinese and North Koreans. But Mao may have been ambivalent, at least hoping that a pause in the fighting, more Soviet material and victory in the air might yet allow defeating the UN forces.

From the point of view of Stalin's grand strategy to which the Chinese probably were not privy, it was desirable for the war to go on. But it was also desirable not to exasperate the Western powers. Although the MacArthur hearings and other evidence showed that the Americans did not want to extend the war to China, opening armistice talks—even endless, exasperating talks—would keep hope alive in the West and deter inconvenient offensive actions. It might also provide opportunities to divide the anti–Communist alliance.

Despite the obvious problems of the Chinese and Koreans (about which the former had even complained publicly), Stalin cheerily wrote to Mao on June 5 that he favored a drawn out war; it would give the Chinese troops experience in modern warfare and hurt the Americans. He offered to provide the Chinese with more artillery if they needed it. Noting Peng's report that Chinese morale was low, he suggested that successful local attacks on UN forces might cure that.

On the same day, Mao told him that the situation was difficult and that he was sending Gao Gang and Kim Il Sung to Moscow. The East Asians

14. Armistice Talks Begin

made it clear they wanted an armistice; Stalin, on June 13, conceded that one was now advantageous. The Chinese, however, were clearly not desperate. Mao outlined the terms he envisaged for an armistice: Restoring the 38th Parallel as the boundary between the two Koreas, with a minor neutral zone on both sides of the line. The Chinese would not make a UN seat for Beijing an issue. They did wish to raise the question of Taiwan, but would drop it if necessary. Mao considered launching an offensive in August, and, in other messages, sought more Soviet advisers and equipment.

The Chinese position — and there may have been significant differences within their government — is difficult to make out. Mao personally may have hoped that an armistice, or even just negotiations as in the Chinese Civil War, would be just a brief respite to gain time for a new grand offensive. By mid–August, while ready to conclude an armistice, he did not see it as a de facto peace (as the West did) but saw it as *lasting just three to five years*. Then the North Koreans, at least, would resume the war. This expectation was clearly alluded to in a cable to Stalin on August 13, and the Soviet leader apparently let Mao assume he agreed with it. (Just when Mao dropped the idea of renewing the war is one of those things that would be useful to know but is not yet clear.) Moreover, he always seems to have anticipated launching a major attack just *before* any armistice was concluded for psychological reasons: to give the world the impression that the Communists had forced the UN Command to sue for peace. The imminence of an armistice never, for the Communists, excluded launching major military operations.[1]

Characteristically, Stalin, had already been responding to American feelers even as he had encouraged Mao to fight a long war. The Americans had made unsuccessful exploratory contacts with the Soviets in Paris, and through the American and Swedish Embassies in Moscow. Charles Burton Marshall visited Hong Kong to contact the Chinese government and perhaps revive contact with "Third Party," but these efforts failed. In mid–May, the State Department commissioned George Kennan, on leave at the Institute of Advanced Study, to get in touch with Jacob Malik, the Soviet Ambassador to the UN. Kennan was not to try to negotiate, but make clear the Americans' purposes and intentions. He met Malik on May 31 and raised the issue circuitously. In the next few days, Secretary Acheson and UN Secretary General Lie both declared they favored an armistice approximately along the 38th Parallel. At a second meeting on June 5, Malik, having evidently obtained instructions from Moscow, told Kennan that the Soviets wanted peace in Korea but could not take part in cease-fire talks. He advised approaching the Chinese and North Koreans. In a radio address on June 23, Malik gave a clearer signal. After the usual denunciation of the Western powers, he declared that the Soviets believed that the Korean conflict could be settled peacefully, and as a "first step discussion should be started between the belligerents for a cease-fire and an armistice providing for the mutual withdrawal of forces from the 38th Parallel." This seemed to indicate (misleadingly) that the Communist powers had dropped their demands that all foreign forces withdraw from Korea, that the Americans withdraw from Taiwan and that the Beijing government be admitted to the UN as prerequisites for a truce. In Moscow the Soviets told Ambassador Kirk that the armistice should not involve political or territorial issues. It should be a strictly military arrangement. The Americans accepted this idea. In fact, talks between the UN and Communist military commands seemed the safest and simplest course since they had no diplomatic relations with the Chinese or Korean Communists, wished to exclude Taiwan and China's UN seat from discussion, and the Chinese in Korea still claimed to be "volunteers" rather than part of China's own armed forces.[2]

On June 29, the Joint Chiefs of Staff advised General Ridgway of the requirements for an armistice. A demilitarized zone 20 miles wide should be created along the front line when the armistice was signed. A military armistice commission should be formed with equal representation from both sides and unlimited rights of inspection throughout Korea to ensure that the armistice terms were carried out. No reinforcements or material were to be brought into Korea by either side except for one-for-one replacements. Prisoners were to be exchanged on a one-for-one basis. That would favor the UN forces, which held far more prisoners than the Communists. Probably some in Washington already suspected that many enemy prisoners did not want to return to their side. On that day, Ridgway radioed the enemy command offering to discuss an armistice. He proposed to meet on a Danish UN hospital ship off Wonsan. Mao and Stalin both agreed to accept the talks, but vigorously rejected the site. Stalin graciously declined Mao's proposal that he direct the negotiations. On June 30, Ridgway received a message from Peng and Kim Il Sung. The Communists agreed to meet and proposed conferring at Kaesong, a former capital of Korea just south of the 38th Parallel.

Ridgway was puzzled to get several versions of this message, one of which stated "we agree to suspend military activities." He warned the Joint Chiefs on July 2 that, as he read them, the Communist "intent is clear that military action shall be suspended from the beginning of armistice negotiations. Such action might gravely prejudice (the) safety and security of United Nations forces." He warned that the enemy seemed to be building up for a new offensive. The Joint Chiefs told him that the English-language version of the enemy reply from Beijing, which they deemed authoritative, indicated that the enemy did not bank on a "preliminary cessation of action." The Communists may in fact have wanted this, but evidently decided not to press the point. Superficially, a "preliminary cease-fire" seemed an attractive, life-saving idea. But the Americans rightly saw it as a trap. By stopping the bombing and blockade of North Korea it would immediately ease the Communists' supply problems, and let them rebuild the North Korean airfields and fill them with planes. Such an informal understanding would bind the UN Command but could be denounced by the Communists at their convenience, probably without evoking much adverse reaction. The UN Command consistently opposed such arrangements.

Over the next few days, preparations for negotiations at Kaesong were finished. On July 6, Ridgway dispatched instructions to the UN delegation. He warned that the enemy would indulge in propagandistic speeches, and the best way to handle this was to ignore them. Patience was required, and the other side should be allowed to save face. If a chance arose to detach China from the Soviets or increase tension between the Communist powers, the delegation should exploit it. (This should be yet another corrective to the notion that the Americans thought that the Soviet-Chinese axis was unbreakable or that the Chinese were Soviet puppets.) Ridgway nursed particular hopes for such a move. On July 9, he suggested that he make a public statement aimed at helping to detach China from the Soviets. The proposed statement bitterly attacked Communist imperialism, and cuttingly referred to Soviet encroachments on Chinese territory in Manchuria, Sinkiang and Mongolia along the same lines Dean Acheson had pursued in his speech of January 12, 1950. The Joint Chiefs rejected the idea lest it cause a breakdown of the talks.[3]

Mao had informed Stalin on July 3 that he envisaged five main points for an armistice, including a cease-fire with a buffer zone of 10 miles on either side of the 38th Parallel, neither side being allowed to bring in reinforcements and a control commission of neutral states. All non–Korean troops were to leave Korea. Stalin accepted this position in general, but opposed bringing up the idea of a control commission, which Mao had not regarded with enthusiasm but had included because he expected the Americans to raise a similar idea.

On July 10, the two sides finally met at Kaesong. Pessimistic Western observers thought the talks might take six weeks.

They dragged on for two years.

The UN delegation was led by Admiral C. Turner Joy, the American naval commander in the Far East. Ridgway would often be at odds with Washington over policy at the armistice talks since he usually favored a harder line. Joy was even more disgruntled. A supporter of MacArthur, he wanted to win the war, not reach a truce, and often disagreed with his instructions on crucial points. Nevertheless, he performed patiently and capably. At first, even Joy may have expected an early armistice. Later, he concluded bitterly that "it was a mistake to assume, or even to hope, that the enemy was capable of acting in good faith," and maintained the UN should have continued the offensive during the summer of 1951. Save for General Paik Sun Yup, who played no role in the talks—Rhee opposed an armistice—the UN delegates were all Americans.

The Communist delegation was nominally headed by the Soviet-Korean General Nam Il, the North Korean vice premier and chief of staff. But the UN delegation soon decided that Joy's true opposite number was the Chinese Major General Xie Fang (Hsieh Fang), Peng's chief of staff and an officer specializing in political affairs, even though he was not even the ranking Chinese member of the Communist delegation. In fact, the Communist military men were directed by a civilian, China's Deputy Foreign Minister Li Kenong. From the start the Communists indulged in often childish propaganda antics, giving the UN delegation chairs whose legs had been sawn off and insisting that their flags stand higher than the UN's. The North Koreans seem to have been to blame for the most insulting moves; the Chinese, by comparison, were comparatively civil.

Admiral Joy stressed that the UN wished to discuss only military matters related to Korea, and hostilities would go on until complete armistice terms were agreed on. He proposed a nine-point agenda that stipulated this. Its first concrete point was to arrange Red Cross visits to prisoner of war camps. Other points called for agreement on a demilitarized zone, arrangements for a military armistice commission, agreement on inspection by military observer teams and arrangements to exchange prisoners. Nam Il responded by calling for both sides to withdraw to the 38th Parallel, and the removal of all foreign troops from Korea. There should be an immediate cease-fire, including air and naval operations, and the creation of a 20-kilometer wide demilitarized zone. Only then should prisoners be discussed. He rejected the UN agenda and especially to its call for visits to the POW camps. His own proposed agenda included agreement on the 38th Parallel as the demarcation line and withdrawal of all foreign forces. In other words, the Communists sought to load the agenda to get agreement on their major demands in advance. The UN delegation absolutely rejected this.

A battle of the agenda began that lasted over two weeks, interrupted by floods that prevented meeting on one day and a three-day suspension of the talks when the UN demanded that the Communists allow equal access to Kaesong for newsmen accredited to the UN Command. On July 15, the UN offered a simpler condensed version of its agenda that omitted Red Cross visits to POW camps as a specific item. The Communists agreed to omit reference to the 38th Parallel from the agenda, while warning they intended to insist that it become the demarcation line between the two sides when substantive talks began. They remained firm on their demands for the withdrawal of all non–Korean forces for several meetings. Admiral Joy acidly pointed out that the absence of such forces had not averted war in 1950. While the departure of the non–Korean elements on both sides was to be expected, it should be kept in "accurate phase" with the development of assurances that hostilities would not recur. In any case, the question lay beyond the scope of a military armistice and was unnecessary for one. The Communists finally agreed to place it under the heading of a final agenda item: recommendations to the governments of both sides for subjects to be considered at a post-armistice conference. Later events showed, however, that they had not dropped the idea of securing withdrawal through the armistice terms, albeit via an indirect route. On July 26, a five-point agenda was finally agreed on. The adoption of the agenda itself constituted completion of Item 1. Item 2 was the fixing of a military demarcation line between the two sides, Item 3 the arrangements for supervising the armistice, Item 4 arrangements relating to prisoners of war, and Item 5 recommendations to governments.[4] Progress through this short list proved agonizingly slow.

The agenda had hardly been agreed on when the Communists resumed insisting on the 38th Parallel as the military demarcation line between the two sides. They observed that both sides held areas north and south of the line; both would give up territory and this would restore the prewar dividing line. But such a deal involved the UN Command giving up much more ground than the Communists and trading a formidable defensive position for a worthless one. There was no precedent for an army that had only recently been advancing voluntarily yielding territory this way. It is hard to believe the Communists thought that the Americans would accept the idea. They may have deemed Acheson and Lie's references to the 38th Parallel as some sort of entering wedge. If they were stubborn enough, the Americans might just give in. It is possible, although less likely, that they regarded Acheson and Lie's remarks as a promise that the UN Command was trying to welsh on. In any case, Mao was bent on gaining the 38th Parallel and planned to get it by launching an offensive in August or September if necessary. Stalin did caution him not to let the armistice talks break down completely over this. The Americans were in no mood to yield any military advantage without due compensation. The armistice talks, like the war as a whole, had become a test of strength in which neither side was inclined to lose face. Both, of course, were entangled in inconsistencies. The West had fought over the Communists' original violation of the 38th Parallel in June 1950, although it had never regarded it as a legitimate political boundary. It had tried to abolish it in the fall and then tried to reestablish it as a boundary in December 1950 — only to have Zhou Enlai insist that it had been "thoroughly destroyed" — a remark that the Communists now forgot.

Admiral Joy argued that that the demarcation line should be based on the existing battle line. He pointed out that the UN had air and naval superiority in and around Korea, and argued that the Communists would gain more from an armistice than the UN Command in terms of a respite from air and naval pressure. Therefore, the Communists should offer compensation to the UN by conceding territory. He proposed a 20-mile demilitarized zone north of the UN front line. Joy did not expect the Communists to accept this position, but hoped to use it as a bargaining point. (It should be noted that the UN Command also held islands off North Korea that it expected to return to Communist control. But it held back this particular bargaining point until a later stage of the negotiations.) Nam Il insisted that the 38th Parallel really represented the true balance between the two sides. More coherently, he argued that the existing front line on the ground represented the total effectiveness of all the UN forces, so the UN did not deserve compensation. A deadlock developed that persisted for weeks. The Communists rejected the UN's suggestions to move on to the next item of the agenda and became increasingly insulting and arrogant, while Joy became coolly cutting. The atmosphere became bitter; the transcripts of these "peace talks" have to be read to be believed. The UN delegates inevitably responded to Communist unpleasantness by descending from the high plane envisaged by Ridgway, although Joy and his colleagues avoided the hysterical abuse and endless speeches favored by the enemy. On August 10, Joy refused to discuss the 38th Parallel any further. Ridgway wanted to issue an ultimatum, insisting that the Communists alter their position within 72 hours or the talks would be broken off. But Washington overruled him.

The deadlock began to break on August 18. The Communists considered that there could be "adjustments" so the demarcation line need not coincide exactly with the 38th Parallel. On August 19, the UN allowed that the existing battle line reflected the effect of its air and naval operations.

There seemed to be a chance to resolve Item 2 when the Communists abruptly disrupted the negotiations. They had charged the UN with violating the neutral zone around Kaesong several times. Most of the charges had been baseless, but the UN Command admitted that two of the incidents had been genuine, albeit inadvertent. The Communists themselves had also violated the zone by marching troops through it, which led the UN Command to suspend talks from August 5 to 9. On August 23, the Communists claimed that UN planes had bombed the conference site. They cut short an on the spot investigation by a member of the UN delegation, who quickly concluded that the "evidence" he was shown was faked. When he told the Chinese this, they suspended the negotiations, which were not resumed until late October. The Americans decided that the incident was an elaborate, if clumsy hoax that must have been planned well in advance. Admiral Joy thought the Communists hoped to bully the UN into giving them the 38th Parallel line.

A more likely explanation is that the Communist powers hoped to bring indirect pressure to bear on the San Francisco Peace Conference, which convened to conclude the peace treaty with Japan on September 4. The Communists had opposed the treaty, and the Chinese were particularly angry at being excluded from the conference. It is noteworthy that the Communists first indicated a readiness to resume the Korean talks on September 19; the peace treaty and the Japanese-American Security Pact had both been signed on September 8.[5] Probably related plans for an attack in Korea had fallen through. On August 17, Peng had ordered a ground offensive, but supply problems caused by bombing and severe floods, and the objections of lower-ranking commanders led to its postponement. While the Communists did resume the offensive in the air, it was the UN forces that launched a limited offensive on the ground.

The Communist decision to just suspend the talks rather than break them off proved prudent. The Americans were inclined to bring very heavy pressure to bear if the armistice talks collapsed completely. In that event, the Joint Chiefs of Staff favored lifting the restrictions on bombing the North Korean power plants, imposing a naval blockade on China, "hot pursuit" of planes into Manchuria and an advance to the "neck" or "waist" of Korea. And there seems to have been strong support for both measures in the State Department.[6]

Unfortunately, the Communists were growing in strength faster than the UN Command.

The UN's Last Offensive

Van Fleet had pondered a major offensive to reach the Pyongyang-Wonsan line. But such an attack required a formidable set of preconditions, including a major deterioration of or withdrawal by the enemy forces, or reinforcements for the Eighth Army, and a change in his mission. Ridgway showed no enthusiasm for any deep advance into North Korea or an amphibious landing near Wonsan. Van Fleet, however, did want to "improve" the UN line and, hopefully, bring pressure to bear on the enemy. He was especially anxious to obtain more depth to protect the Hwachon Reservoir (and Seoul's water and power supplies) and the Seoul-Chorwon road.

The first aim led to very bloody fighting to "straighten out the sag" in the eastern sector of the front where the North Koreans held high ground overlooking the UN line around the Punchbowl. The result was an exceptionally grim struggle in rugged terrain. It resembled the fighting in Italy in 1943–1944, an infantry and artillery war from hill to hill in which operations always seemed to take longer, require more forces and cost more lives than had been expected. The North Koreans had well-built bunkers behind minefields, and now had plenty of machineguns, mortars and artillery. The South Koreans began attacking on August 18, and failed. The American 2nd Division and the 1st Marine Division had to be committed to the fighting for the Punchbowl and the neighboring "Bloody Ridge." The size of the task was still underestimated. The Americans attacked with too small forces on too narrow a front. They had to apply more pressure on a broader area to make progress. There were constant enemy counterattacks at night, and the Americans were shocked to find that the enemy's ground firepower was now almost as great as their own. The North Koreans fought with skill and determination. Their bunkers withstood direct hits by 105-mm shells. Only the larger artillery pieces proved useful. The Marines badly needed their excellent close air support. They were also glad to have the armored vest, a new innovation without which many more men would have been killed. The Punchbowl and Bloody Ridge were taken only after heavy losses. Van Fleet cut down his offensive plans, but still hoped for a short-range amphibious operation if his next attack succeeded.

But the battle for "Heartbreak Ridge," just beyond Bloody Ridge, began on September 13 and was an even costlier repetition of the earlier battles. More and more units had to be committed on a wider front against an enemy that had been underestimated. The North Korean hold on Heartbreak Ridge began to crack when American tanks, attacking in Mundung-ni valley west of the Ridge using a track fixed up by engineers, took them by surprise and got into their rear. Finally, by mid–October, the Ridge was won. The North Korean V Corps showed signs of disintegration and had to be relieved by Chinese units. Van Fleet had cut down earlier plans for

14. Armistice Talks Begin

a more ambitious drive in the west; on October 3, I Corps, followed by IX Corps on October 13, began a more limited attack. These attacks were less costly than the fighting in the east. The "limited offensive" ended on October 23. It had seen the last major battles of maneuver in the Korean War. This last major offensive initiated by the UN may have helped cause the Communists to return to the conference table, but it had been very costly. The UN Command had suffered 60,000 casualties, while the Communists were believed to have lost 234,000 men — probably an overestimate. Ridgway, on November 12, restricted Van Fleet from launching attacks larger than battalion size. The Communists had used the lull from June to August to strengthen their position, and things got still worse after October. Van Fleet himself dropped any idea of launching a major offensive. On December 10, his planners estimated that a push to the Pyongyang-Wonsan line, without actions outside Korea, would cost nearly *200,000 casualties.*[7] (By way of comparison, Eisenhower's command had suffered 766,000 casualties in the whole campaign from Normandy to the Elbe in 1944–1945.)

During the summer of 1951 some changes had taken place in the military commands in Korea and Japan. The Americans had completed racial integration in Far East Command, an important contribution to military effectiveness. The British Commonwealth ground forces in Korea had belatedly, at American rather than British initiative, been concentrated into a single Commonwealth Division. A major effort began to improve the ROK forces, which now consisted of five active divisions with five more forming. The lull at the front allowed the UN Command to take one ROK division at a time out of combat and run it through a training camp. A proper training organization was established so that South Koreans would no longer be hurled into combat with as little as ten days preparation. More ROK officers went to American schools. The Americans also began upgrading the ROK Army's equipment with the activation of more artillery units, including some with 155-mm howitzers, and preparations began to provide the ROKs armor. They began training on old World War II tank destroyers. American ground forces in Korea remained at the same strength. In the winter of 1951–1952, the 40th and 45th National Guard Divisions, which had been sent to defend Japan, swapped places with the 1st Cavalry and 24th Divisions that had been in Korea since 1950. The defense of Japan remained a source of anxiety. In July 1951, the Air Force sent a National Guard unit flying F-84s, the 116th Fighter Bomber Wing, to Japan where it was reserved for air defense duties.[8]

Battle for the Air

In the fall of 1951, the UN faced serious trouble in the air. On July 12, after a series of battles in which the Sabrejets had again won, the Communists had stood down and even abandoned their effort to rebuild North Korean airfields. By contrast, Kimpo airfield was improved to the point that the whole 4th Fighter Wing (still comprising the entire F-86 force) could be concentrated at that forward base. It was now getting the new F-86E, that had hydraulic controls, that improved maneuverability, and a radar gunsight that greatly improved shooting. That was fortunate since the Soviet units were now receiving the MIG-15 bis, with a more powerful engine that could push it even higher and faster than the earlier model. Operations in August showed that the newly operational Meteor 8, flown by an Australian squadron, was no match for the MIG-15. The Sabrejet was still the only Western fighter able to deal with the Soviet jets.

On September 1, the Communists took the offensive in the sky, using new tactics. In late September Chinese units joined the battle for the first time since early 1951. There were now 525 MIGs based north of the Yalu, facing less than 90 F-86s. The Americans were hard pressed. The MIGs frequently harassed Western fighter-bombers. They did not shoot many down — at lower altitudes, the F-80s and F-84s were not hopelessly inferior to the MIGs — but often forced them to jettison their bombs and flee. After September 20, the fighter-bombers were driven out of MIG Alley; by October fighter-bombers flying north of Pyongyang were being attacked. The Communists had started rebuilding the air bases at Namsi, Saamchon and Taechon. When they were finished the MIGs would be able to push farther south.

Only the B-29s with their heavy bombloads could eliminate the enemy airfields economically. A first attempt to use the Shoran electronic guidance system to attack the airfields at night did not work well, so the difficult decision was made to send the B-29s in by day with F-84s flying close escort. Experience in April should have shown that this would not work. After some abortive missions, an attack on October 22 cost a B-29. The following day, the B-29s headed for Namsi. While Chinese and North Korean units tied up the Sabrejets flying a protective screen along the Yalu, 44 Soviet MIGs attacked the B-29 formation. They shot down one F-84 and three of the eight B-29s. The rest got back to base, but were so badly shot up they never flew again. There were just too many MIGs for the Sabrejets, and the Thunderjets were not equal to the job. Some pilots thought the speed differential between the B-29s and any escorting jets alone would have made escort too difficult. These were impossible losses

14. Armistice Talks Begin

for the small B-29 force. The big bombers switched to night operations. Beginning on November 4, they again tried Shoran-directed attacks. At first they were not too effective, but with more experience they were able to bomb accurately enough to keep the North Korean bases out of action. Meanwhile, it had become clear that control of the air in daylight was in serious jeopardy. One wing of F-86s could not stand off the whole MIG force. (In November the heavy RB-45 reconnaissance planes were also chased out of MIG Alley.)

On October 22, after repeated requests for help from the Far East Air Force, USAF Headquarters gave into requests for more Sabrejets. Seventy-five F-86Es with pilots and crew chiefs were sent from the States to reequip the Far East Air Force's 51st Fighter Wing. It entered combat on December 1. During December the reinforced Americans won a series of big air battles despite a shortage of spare parts and drop-tanks needed to keep the F-86s flying. In that month the enemy seemed to give up hope of gaining air superiority. From then on, the Communist powers used the sky over Korea as a training ground, as the Soviets had used the air fighting in the Spanish Civil War and the Sino-Japanese War back in the 1930s. The air fighting seemed to follow a regular cycle. As a new "class" of enemy pilots arrived, they flew high and fast and rarely engaged in combat. As they became more experienced, they flew lower and were more aggressive, finally "graduating" and seeking all-out battles that usually ended in heavy losses to the Communist fliers. Then another "class" would come and the cycle would resume. The Soviets were in fact rotating complete new units. Their methods proved blundering. They made no effort to provide continuity of experience, ease the transition of the newer men or transfer the hard-won experience of the older units to the newer ones whose training in the USSR seems to have been remarkably erratic. The 97th Air Division, which replaced the 324th Division in February 1952, proved so bad that it had to be taken out of combat and replaced by a recalled older unit. Moreover, relations with the Chinese air force apparently became worse. After June 1952, the Chinese units insisted on operating independently, without Soviet protection or even coordination. Even the friendliest Russian pilots thought their Chinese counterparts were poorly prepared.

The "stalemated" struggle for the daylight skies was now accompanied by a steadily more difficult effort to keep the old B-29s going at night. The Communists introduced more flak, radar and searchlights, and night fighters. The Americans tried to counter this. Both sides, however, were reluctant to bring their latest equipment into this duel, which resembled that fought between British Bomber Command and the Germans from 1942 to 1944. The Americans learned to avoid flying at heights where condensation trails were produced, avoid moonlit nights and make use of bad weather. They painted the undersides of the bombers black, and made use of feints and "chaff" to beat enemy radars. Reluctant to use their latest night fighters, they began using older, propeller-driven Marine night fighters to escort the B-29s in July 1952. Somewhat newer Navy F3D jets were brought in during November. Near the end of the war the Air Force reluctantly let its new F-94s accompany the bombers over enemy territory. These things proved just enough to enable the B-29s to survive. Only the Soviets' reluctance to commit their own radar-equipped late-model night fighters allowed the B-29s to last out the war.[9]

Interdiction

The Communist air offensive had interfered with the continuing "interdiction" campaign against their supply routes, an effort that resembled the campaign waged against the Germans' supply routes in Italy in 1944.

After the Communist offensive in May 1951 had been smashed, the Americans had shifted from attacking enemy railroads to trying to interrupt road movements in a narrow belt between the 39th Parallel. This effort, called "Operation Strangle," was a failure. The enemy was just not that dependent on trucks. Nor were the Americans very effective at catching trucks at night. (Only oxcarts hauled ammunition and supplies during the day.) In August 1951, the air effort returned to the railroads. Though officially designated the "Rail Interdiction Program," it too was generally called "Strangle." In August, Washington let Ridgway bomb the important port and supply center of Rashin, near the Soviet border. It had been off limits to attack since the summer of 1950. Beyond F-86 range, it was attacked on August 25 in a special mission by B-29s escorted by Navy carrier fighters.

The new railroad interdiction attacks had some success at first. Each fighter-bomber wing was assigned its own sector, with which the pilots became all too familiar. The attacks seriously impaired the movement of supplies, and much material piled up enroute to the front and was destroyed. But Communist countermeasures (many described earlier) improved. The Americans encountered more and more interference from MIGs, and more and more flak, that was increasingly concentrated around the most common targets. The effectiveness of Communist antiaircraft fire was increased by the growing use of proximity fuses for the heavy guns and radar fire control. Still, some railroad lines were completely unserviceable in October. Some people even hoped that supply problems would force the Communists to make a major withdrawal, perhaps even to the Pyongyang-Wonsan line. But bad weather gave the enemy a respite, and the nights grew longer. In winter, bombs became less effective. They tended to bounce off the frozen ground before exploding. The enemy's repair and rebuilding efforts (notably the use of temporary and prefabricated replacement bridges) were perfected. By December a complete bypass route had been completed for the vital Pyongyang-Sunchon line and in that month it became clear that "Strangle" alone would not defeat the enemy in Korea. The Americans had hammered rail traffic to just four or five percent of the prewar level, but that proved enough, with trucks and porters, to get adequate supplies forward to support a static front and even a growing number of heavy weapons.

Whether "Strangle" was worthwhile at all has been much discussed. Admiral Clark, the commander of Task Force 77, flatly condemned the interdiction effort as a failure. The Navy had never been enthusiastic about interdiction and had rated it as ineffective as early as June. It had never nursed much hope for "Strangle." General Ridgway and some others were more generous. It was probably a major factor in causing the Chinese to postpone the offensive originally planned for August until November, and then drop it entirely. It continued to cause frequent shortages and tied up an enormous enemy effort, but at a serious and growing cost in valuable pilots and planes. Interdiction nevertheless continued. In early 1952, the name "Strangle," which had become embarrassing, was replaced by "Saturate." The change in designation did in fact mark a change in strategy. "Saturate" aimed at concentrated attacks by fighter-bombers and light bombers on short stretches of track, while the B-29s concentrated on major bridges south of MIG Alley.

The Navy made increased efforts at night, using special versions of the Corsair and Skyraider. In an operation called "Moonlight Sonata," they hunted on moonlit winter nights, using the combination of moonlight and snow cover to pick out trains and trucks. This was succeeded by the more imaginative and successful "Insomnia," which did not aim so much at directly destroying trains as cutting the rails late at night to maroon them in the open where other planes would catch them after dawn. Rather surprisingly, it proved easier to find targets on dark rather than moonlit nights. Apparently, the Communists were more likely to be careless in complete darkness. Still, the few planes operating at night could not make much of a dent in the enemy's movements. The Air Force's only contribution to interdiction at night, the B-26 light bomber, was too big, unmaneuverable and poorly instrumented to be an effective night intruder.

The immediate reasons for the failure of the interdiction effort were:

(1) The enemy's consumption of supplies was low. This was partly due to the fact that the front was static, but also to the relatively primitive nature of the Chinese Army. A more mechanized enemy, requiring a bigger and more elaborate supply effort, would have been more vulnerable to air interdiction.

(2) The enemy was resilient, had plenty of manpower for repairs and was intelligently directed.

(3) Lack of enough aircraft.

(4) Lack of an effective ability to attack at night or in bad weather, or even effectively assess the damage done by attacks made at night.

(5) Interference by enemy active defenses, MIGs and flak. However, although the Soviet MIGs were a serious problem in the northwest, they were probably not decisive. The Communists kept supplies moving over the eastern railroad net as well, although the Navy carrier planes in that area rarely encountered enemy planes.

(6) An additional narrowly technical reason for the failure of interdiction was the lack of a weapon capable of destroying tunnels, which were not only vital for the operation of the Korean railroads but were the enemy's best hiding places for supplies and equipment.

Either an effective night attack capability or an anti-tunnel weapon would have changed the equation for interdiction in Korea considerably. With the available technology, however, the ability to interdict supplies was limited. And in Korea, as in Italy in 1944, air interdiction alone, without a major offensive on the ground that would increase the enemy's consumption of supplies and force him to move in daylight, could not force an enemy army to retreat.[10]

Incredibly, many Americans ignored these costly lessons, and in the Second Indochina War invested wildly exaggerated hopes in interdicting the Ho Chi Minh Trail, even though conditions in Indochina were much less favorable to interdiction than in Italy or Korea.

15

The Cold War Outside Korea, 1951–1952

While war raged in Korea, the struggle for Japan continued. As the Americans sought a peace settlement and a degree of Japanese rearmament, the Soviets aimed to overthrow the Japanese government. In spite of their weakness, the Japanese Communists still played a big role — if only in Stalin's mind. The Soviets and the Japanese Communists were convinced there would be a "people's democratic revolution" in Japan in the near future, a belief that helps explain Stalin's general overconfidence.

Given conditions in Japan and the attitudes of most Japanese, these hopes were bizarre. But there were precedents for such wildly over-optimistic assessments. They were not much sillier than the Soviet schemes to overthrow the Weimar Republic in the 1920s and 1930s. They were a culmination of an old misunderstanding of Japanese society. The Communists supposed that Japan's social structure was not entirely that of an advanced capitalist country. Rather, it had "feudal" remnants and, in many ways, resembled its underdeveloped Asian neighbors more than the advanced Western countries. The "bourgeois-democratic" revolution had never been finished in Japan. This analysis implied there was considerable revolutionary potential there. Some of the smarter Japanese Communists had long doubted it, but they were never able to convince Moscow. Unfortunately for the Communists, the real resemblances that had existed between Japanese rural society and that of pre-revolutionary China had been wiped out by the occupation land reform. Insofar as the "bourgeois-democratic" stage of the Marxist scheme had any reality, it had been completed by the occupation.

After the Korean War began, the Japanese Communists sabotaged transportation facilities to support the North Koreans and infiltrated agents into occupation and Japanese government offices. The occupation authorities banned the party's newspapers after it backed the North Koreans. The members of the "Directorate" that had taken over the open functions of the party's headquarters were put on the "purge" list in September 1950.

In the fall of 1950, the party became more radical. It described the "colonization of Japan" not as a threat but an ongoing reality. On October 12, its underground paper called for combined workers uprisings and rural guerrilla warfare after a long period of preparation. The armed struggle line was endorsed by the Fourth National Party Congress held in February 1951. The Communists started setting up a "self-defense corps" and formed military units in selected mountain villages, which were to establish guerrilla bases. The principal themes of the party's efforts were summarized in its "1951 Thesis" or "New Program"—the first since 1932, which was drafted in August 1951 and adopted by the Fifth Party Congress in October 1951. At least part of the "1951 Thesis" was written by Stalin himself. It was marked by violent anti–Americanism; the occupation was "slavery." Even Japanese capitalists were being ruined. Japan was a "colonial-dependent country" like China, and the terminology applied to the Japanese situation was similar to that used about the Communist seizure of power in China. The occupation land reform was attacked as a fake, and heavy use was made of "peace" slogans, likely to be particularly popular in Japan. A "broad-based united front," including even medium-sized businessmen would be formed, as the Japanese Communists almost entirely discarded anti-capitalist propaganda. But the "Japanese revolution" proved one of the worst fizzles in the history of the world Communist movement. Terrorism and sabotage in factories (some committed by the Internationalist faction, which the orthodox faction only gradually subdued) did not win converts. Most of the party's illegal operations were penetrated by government agents. By 1953, even many Communists saw that their policy was disastrous. Party membership fell off.[1]

The Japanese Peace Treaty

In reality, Japan was the most stable country in Asia. There the Western powers held the cards, and, if they played them with a minimum of common sense, Japan was bound to take their side. Nevertheless, devising a peace treaty presented knotty problems. There was much fear of Japanese rearmament. The British and French wished to extract commercial concessions from Japan, while the Australians, New Zealanders and

Southeast Asians wanted reparations. The Japanese themselves did not much like what would probably be a "separate peace" with the Western powers only. Last, but not least, were the threats made by the Soviets and Chinese, to which the fighting in Korea gave point. Already, in November 1950 the Soviets had taken a position toward Japan like that toward Germany. They demanded that their annexation of Sakhalin and the Kuriles, agreed on at Yalta, be registered in the peace treaty, which must cede Taiwan to the Beijing government. But, while pocketing their annexations, they went on to pose as defenders of Japan's sovereignty, opposing American bases in Japan and American plans to retain control over the Ryukyus and Bonins.

Despite the reverses in Korea and the war scare, Acheson insisted on a peace treaty and a defense arrangement with Japan, with or without Soviet or neutralist assent. The Americans were determined to keep bases in Japan itself, American military administration of the Ryukyus and Bonins, and to exclude reparations or commercial restrictions. Perhaps ironically in view of later developments, the American government, fully supported by business and labor, favored the maximum possible economic development in Japan. (In any case, given Japan's still shaky economic situation, the United States was likely to wind up financing reparations.)

John Foster Dulles, admitted by even his worst enemies to be an able negotiator, arrived in Japan on January 25 to start formal talks on a peace treaty with the Japanese and the other Pacific powers. A less publicized aspect of his mission was to win the Japanese over to larger-scale rearmament. In that task he failed. Prime Minister Yoshida made clear that he did not regard a really large effort as politically desirable or possible. Agreement on the peace settlement, however, proved easy to obtain. The Japanese knew that the Americans were their protectors not only against the Soviets but the other Allies. Quickly settling matters with the Japanese, Dulles went on to placate the Filipinos, Australians and New Zealanders with defense pacts to reconcile them to Japanese rearmament and the denial of reparations.

Dulles returned home to draft the peace treaty. By the end of March it was circulated to the former Allied powers. After returning to Japan to reassure the Japanese that MacArthur's removal had not changed things, Dulles tried to harmonize views with the Western Europeans. The British were persuaded to drop their hopes of restrictions on Japanese industry. They agreed with the Americans on other matters, but there was a serious clash over Taiwan. The British Cabinet, against Foreign Office advice, maintained that the Chinese Communists should take part in the peace negotiations and that Taiwan should be ceded to them. That was bound to be unacceptable to the Americans, and in the middle of the Korean War was a remarkably foolish idea regardless of the rights and wrongs of American China policy. The Cabinet finally accepted Dulles' and the Foreign Office's view that neither Chinese government should attend the peace conference. Japan would give up sovereignty over Taiwan, but not formally transfer it to anyone else. That left the way open to support an independent Taiwan, an alternative the United States held in reserve behind its public policy of backing the Nationalists until 1972. Dulles persuaded the British to let Japan choose which Chinese regime to recognize. But he had already gotten Yoshida to agree not to recognize Beijing against the inclination of most Japanese. The British later felt cheated on this point.[2]

The UN victories in the spring assisted Dulles since Japan no longer seemed as exposed as in December 1950. But the Soviets did not let progress on the treaty go undisturbed. On May 7 they sent a harsh note to the United States denouncing the American treaty draft. It included the second threat of war of the Cold War era, although perhaps less direct than the one in the Soviet note on Germany of October 19, 1950. Blaming the Americans for the failure to make peace earlier, it grumbled that "as a result of this, the occupation of Japan has impermissibly dragged on." The method of preparing the treaty violated the Potsdam agreement. The note spoke of the "impermissibility" of excluding China from the formulation of the treaty, and complained that the treaty draft did not explicitly transfer Taiwan to China or limit Japan's armed forces. The Soviets objected to American administration of the Ryukyus and Bonins and the continued presence of American forces in Japan, comparing the treaty draft unfavorably with the peace treaty with Italy, which had required the departure of troops in 90 days. They proposed a conference of Foreign Ministers in June or July to prepare a treaty that would limit Japan's armed forces, neutralize Japan and remove all foreign troops within a year. Some Westerners feared that the Soviets would go to war over the issue, although the Soviets' failure to follow up the threats made in 1950 ensured that most people were unimpressed. A bitter exchange of notes ensued. In one, the Americans tried to toss an apple of discord into the enemy camp by insinuating that the Soviet failure to mention the transfer of Manchuria back to China might be connected with Soviet schemes there.

The Soviets got support from an unexpected quarter. The Indians indicated that they opposed American administration of the Ryukyus and Bonins, and objected to the failure to cede Taiwan, the Kuriles and Sakhalin to the Communist powers (the Americans intended to merely force Japan to renounce sovereignty over them). In an ambiguously worded point they also insisted that American forces leave Japan after the occupation ended (a view shared by other neutralists, notably Egypt) while conceding that Japan might make a defense arrangement with the United States at a later date. The Americans learned that Nehru had privately declared that the current Japanese leaders represented the old military clique and would rearm as fast as possible, while the Americans seemed to be basing their plans on a world war. American diplomats, however, believed that Nehru's policy was really due to fear of the Communists and the calculation that he could afford to offend the Americans, but not the Soviets and Chinese. Many of Nehru's subordinates disagreed with his policy. The Indians finally decided not to attend the peace conference to avoid having to line up with the Soviets or seem grossly inconsistent. Burma and Yugoslavia followed their example.

To the surprise of many, the Soviets attended the San Francisco Peace Conference. The Communist powers may have orchestrated the break in the Kaesong talks to bring psychological pressure to bear on the coming meeting, but plans to accompany this with a ground offensive in Korea had to be given up.

The conference met on September 4. The Philippines, Australia and New Zealand had already been paid off with signature of formal alliances a few days before. It lasted just four days since the Americans had secured rules of procedure that severely limited the Soviets' opportunities for obstruction and, indeed, debate in general. Andrei Gromyko, the head of the Soviet delegation, seemed a bit befuddled to some observers and did not even seize the chances to make trouble that were open. On September 5, the Soviets proposed amendments to the treaty that stood no chance of adoption. The Soviets did not argue for a really harsh treaty, but seemed to aim both to win over Japanese public opinion and play on fears of Japanese rearmament and commercial competition. While demanding that Japan be neutralized and that foreign troops withdraw, they offered to let Japan rearm to a limited extent. Japan could have an army of 150,000 men, a defensive air force of 200 planes and a navy of 75,000 tons. That was hardly less than what the Japanese themselves planned. Neither the Japanese nor those who feared them were impressed.

The conference was a success, even though, as Acheson later observed, "Never was so good a treaty so little loved...." The Soviet bloc and Egypt refused to sign. On September 8, the same day that the treaty was signed by the rest of the participants, the Japanese-American Security Treaty was concluded. This peculiar agreement enabled the Americans to stay in Japan. But it was not a true bilateral alliance. The Americans undertook only a de facto guarantee to defend Japan. Moreover, it explicitly allowed American troops to intervene to suppress large-scale internal disorders instigated from the outside. This clause and the inequality of the obligations involved caused growing discontent in Japan, leading to riots and the revision of the treaty in 1960. Still, Japan was firmly on the Western side. The Soviets insisted that the occupation had not really ended. On December 31, 1951, Stalin sent a most unusual New Year's message to the Japanese, over the head of their government and expressing the "deep sympathy the Soviet people entertain for the Japanese people in the distress that has befallen them owing to a foreign occupation." But he assured them they would achieve "the regeneration and independence of their country, just as the peoples of the Soviet Union did."[3]

The Western Buildup Ebbs

During 1951 and 1952, there were no dramatic events in the Western world comparable to the Korean War or the Japanese peace treaty. Instead, there were tedious attempts to negotiate with the Soviets and an effort to build up Western defenses that was only partially successful. The West laid overambitious, yet insufficient plans that were inadequately executed and cut short before they were completed. Quarrels over West German rearmament dragged on without resolution. NATO was transformed from a political alliance to a rationally organized military command. The force defending Western Europe became something more than the corporal's guard it had been in 1950, but much less than what was needed to stop the attack that Stalin expected to launch in 1954 or 1955. Issues outside Europe not directly connected with the Cold War increasingly diverted the attention of the Western Europeans. The British were distracted by ugly and tense crises over Iran's nationalization of their oil holdings, and Egypt's desire to abrogate the Anglo-Egyptian treaty of 1936 and gain control of the Suez Canal and the Sudan. The Kikuyu ("Mau-Mau") rebellion in Kenya became yet another drain on British strength. Nationalist feelings spread in French North Africa as the greatest crisis of postwar French history loomed.

The Soviets continued their effort to disrupt Western and West German rearmament, using both threats and negotiations. The American government did not like negotiating with the Soviets at a low point of Western strength and morale, and especially objected to confining talks to the subject of Germany. But it could not resist the British and French governments, which were politically fragile and faced elections in the near future, and wanted talks. The French leaders in particular felt it vital to convince their people that every effort had been made to resolve the German question, and perhaps hoped that the Soviets might even change their policy when faced with West German rearmament.

15. The Cold War Outside Korea, 1951–1952

By late February 1951, the Western powers and the Soviets agreed on a preliminary meeting in Paris to prepare an agenda for a four-power meeting of foreign ministers. The agenda conference, held in Paris from March 5 to June 21, was an episode of dreary and useless wrangling of the sort that had become typical of dealings between the two sides. The Soviets wished to focus on German rearmament — that is West German rearmament — in which the Western governments were carrying out measures few in the West much liked. The Western powers insisted the German issue was just a local aspect of a general relationship between the major powers and wanted discussion of the larger issues. The negotiations became increasingly tangled. The British and French, softening their original position, became willing to accept some Soviet proposals for the sake of having a conference.

Soviet inflexibility, however, led to a deadlock on how to treat the subject of NATO and American bases in Europe and the Near East, which even the Americans were willing to discuss and which had not originally been an issue. Some contemporary observers suspected there had been a major shift of calculations in Moscow. Realizing that West German rearmament was not imminent, a fact actually obvious for some time, Stalin decided in March to strike at the Western alliance proper. Alternatively, failing to see obvious divisions on matters of substance in the West during the early discussions, he lost interest in having a major conference. Perhaps increasing arrogance and inflexibility got the best of him. The Soviets had blundered badly. Even a slightly more flexible approach would have given them the foreign ministers conference they had originally wanted, which would probably have hurt Western unity and resolve. As it was, the agenda meeting convinced the French government that it could not hope for an agreement with the Soviets. But it tended to defuse the fear of war in the West.[4]

The Western powers continued sluggishly and unsteadily to build up NATO. In late January 1951, after touring his new European command General Eisenhower returned to the United States in a surprisingly optimistic mood. He admitted to the president that if the Soviets attacked right then, all Europe would probably be lost. But he doubted that they would attack. He observed that 350 million people in Western Europe should not fear 190 million backward people. Neutralist sentiment, he maintained, was a greater danger than Communism in Europe. But every country supported the Western buildup, except for the Netherlands. He even expressed some confidence in the Italians, generally considered the weakest link in NATO. He needed 50 to 60 divisions to defend Western Europe. Such a force, too small to attack the Soviets, would not be provocative. In the short run, he hoped to get 10 to 12 American divisions, including the six already allotted. "Of course, we should not plan on keeping our divisions there forever," he remarked. "Once the Europeans build up an adequate force, and get some reserves trained, the Americans can come home." He thought the Americans should perhaps establish a time limit for their departure. He may have hoped to start removing American troops as early as 1954.

While few, if any, Americans expected that U.S. ground forces would stay in Europe as long as they did, the Defense Department at first shared Eisenhower's hope for a larger American force than actually materialized. Secretary Marshall hoped that Eisenhower would have 10 American divisions by the end of 1951. But, thanks to the continuation of the Korean War and cutbacks in the military buildup, only the four divisions already scheduled to go joined the two divisions already in Germany. Fighting the Korean War remained theoretically, and usually actually, subordinate to the military buildup it had spawned. But it nevertheless sometimes interfered with it.

After his "Supreme Headquarters Allied Powers Europe" (SHAPE) was activated in Paris on April 2, Eisenhower was disillusioned, especially with the French. He outlined plans that differed somewhat from those earlier mapped out by NATO planners and the Joint Chiefs of Staff. He favored a defensive stand well east of the Rhine — which would require major German forces — strongly and directly supported by naval forces. He agreed with earlier assessments that a standing force of 46 divisions would be adequate on the outbreak of a war, but wanted reserves mobilized far faster. A force of 97 divisions had to be ready on the thirtieth day after mobilization, instead of 95⅓ in three months. He soon learned he would not have more than the six American divisions already allotted. By the end of 1951, his forces had risen from less than 15 divisions and 1,000 planes to 24 divisions and 1,580 planes on a projected "D-Day," while 44 divisions could be available on the thirtieth day.[5] But by then the buildup was already slowing down. And there were quarrels over NATO's organization and who would hold NATO's Atlantic and Mediterranean Commands.

During World War II, similar issues were settled in weeks or days. In the twilight "peace" of 1951 they festered. The British objected to having the Atlantic command go to an American, although the United States was now the strongest power on that ocean. It was initially expected that the Mediterranean theater, as in World War II, would be separate from Eisenhower's command. It might have far-reaching responsibilities extending into the Middle East. The British wanted it, if they could not get the Atlantic post. But Eisenhower favored forming a southern command for

15. The Cold War Outside Korea, 1951–1952

the Mediterranean responsible to his headquarters. During 1951 the Western powers became interested in forming a Middle East Command based on an alliance with Egypt and other countries in the region, though, Egypt as well as Syria had chosen "neutralist" policies even before the revolution of 1952. The Middle East Command, which was formally proposed in October 1951, was regarded as a Western imperialist plot to keep British forces in Egypt, which denounced it in terms little less hostile than those used in Moscow. But the abortive Middle East scheme tipped the scales in favor of Eisenhower's ideas. The British were placated by the assurance that Admiral Mountbatten would command "Allied Forces Mediterranean."

Extending NATO's membership was also controversial. In early 1951, the United States came to favor Greece and Turkey joining the organization. But the smaller Northern European countries feared involvement in obscure Balkan and Middle Eastern problems (not without reason) and only reluctantly came to agree to this. The issue of Spain was even more divisive. Its strategic position at the entrance to the Mediterranean, and the possibility that Eisenhower's command, or part of it, might have to retreat there led the American military to favor inviting Spain to join NATO. Truman (who despised Franco) and Acheson saw that this would be unacceptable, but urged that Spain be allowed to "associate" with NATO, an idea Britain and France rejected. Contact with Franco was very unpopular in Europe and with American liberals refighting the battles of the 1930s. In any case, Franco's anti–Communism proved overrated. The Americans' own attempts to deal with him fared poorly thanks to his greed, arrogance and sluggish handling of the talks. He demanded considerable military aid and refused to let American forces enter Spain in peacetime. A Spanish role in Western defense was not arranged until the Eisenhower administration.[6]

The key and most contentious issue remained West German rearmament. As Peter Calvocoressi scornfully remarked, "Raising no more than twelve divisions assumed the force of an atom bomb." While it was perhaps not inconceivable that NATO could raise the forces to defend Western Europe without invoking German help, few opponents of German rearmament really favored that. It would be too great a strain. Those who feared the Soviets usually wound up swallowing West German rearmament in some form; those who just could not stomach the idea usually ended by insisting that there was no Soviet threat, if they had not held this view from the start. There was little middle ground.

In early 1951, parallel negotiations began in Bonn and Paris to arrange a West German contribution to defense and fit it into a European Defense Community (EDC) framework acceptable to France. Reconciling the two proved difficult. The German military representatives negotiating with the Allied High Commissioners in Bonn insisted on forming at least 12 all–German divisions, three of them armored and equipped with heavy tanks (which the Allies wanted to deny them), and supported by a tactical air force of 20 wings (1,960 planes) and a fleet of light ships. The High Commissioners had to admit these ideas were sound. The Germans asked for political concessions such as replacing the Occupation Statute by a new set of agreements with the Western occupiers. The French liked none of this. They had wanted a European Army of large mixed divisions formed from national contingents.

The American military was ready to bypass the EDC if necessary to get German forces. But Acheson, despite grave doubts that the EDC was practical, agreed with the British in September 1951 not to rearm West Germany until the EDC was set up. This concession actually meant indefinitely postponing West German rearmament. Apart from the danger of enraging the French and disrupting NATO, Acheson thought that the EDC or something like it was vital for long-run reasons. He looked forward to a time when there would be no substantial American forces in Europe. A European Army would be needed to prevent Germany from becoming dangerous, which was yet another demonstration that even in the early 1950s fear of a German threat had not yet vanished. Meanwhile, the Paris negotiations dragged on, the issues so tangled that few understood them. The French only reluctantly accepted a force of small national divisions (called "groupements" to save face). The smaller countries doubted that the EDC was workable and feared that even if it did, France or Germany would dominate it. Their fears would have been relieved by British participation. But while favoring measures of European integration, the British were not ready to join in them themselves. The main obstacle, however, was that the French wanted to keep the Germans subordinate, while the latter demanded political equality for all contributors to the EDC. The Germans gradually extracted concessions that only hurt support for the EDC in France. An agreement to form 41 "groupements" was reached in October 1951. But in January 1952, the French raised new issues— they wanted Germany banned from regular membership in NATO and a prohibition on Germans building heavy weapons. A compromise had to be arranged. The Germans were already forbidden to have nuclear, biological or chemical weapons, or make missiles or military aircraft. They also accepted that certain other weapons would not be built in exposed "forward areas."

The EDC agreement was signed on May 27, 1952, but its ratification was delayed. In 1954, the French Assembly rejected it. The French public

15. The Cold War Outside Korea, 1951–1952

believed the Soviet threat had diminished, and even non–Communists thought the EDC would increase East-West tension. Some wanted France to keep its army under purely national control. Most powerful of all was the wishful thinking that without the EDC there would be no German rearmament. West German rearmament had to be negotiated all over again. The EDC negotiations are arguably of more interest to students of international organization than to historians of the Cold War, as an example of how not to do things. The result of the time and energy invested in these bungled negotiations, and the decision to subordinate West German rearmament to the EDC's success, was that not one West German soldier would have been ready to oppose the attack that Stalin planned.[7]

Already, in mid–1951, the Western military buildup had run into heavy weather in other respects. By June, Acheson suspected that at least in Europe rearmament had gone faster than economic realities would permit. He read the serious divisions in the British Labour Party and the results of the French elections in June as warnings that European support for rearmament was under strain.

While the American effort had made progress, it suffered delays. Some people, notably Stuart Symington, the president of the National Security Resources Board, had warned all along that the 1952 target date for the NSC-68 buildup, set in December 1950, was unattainable. In April 1951, the National Security Council judged that even in the United States enthusiasm for the mobilization effort was waning. By July, it was clear that the targets set for 1952 would not be met. Pressure was building for a let-down in the defense effort. Secretary Marshall, increasingly worried, warned against this. Despite his efforts, the House of Representatives cut $1.5 billion from the proposed military budget. Suspecting that the current effort was a one-shot affair, Marshall differed with other officials about how to use the allotted funds. He favored using appropriations to spread weapons production over a longer period; that way, weapons designs could be improved and production lines would stay open longer. The Joint Chiefs and Paul Nitze of the Policy Planning Staff favored a policy leading to a faster payoff of weapons in hand. Marshall's policy should be distinguished from a deliberate reduction in effort, or, as it was confusingly called, a "stretchout," which he and Nitze both strongly opposed. In fact, Marshall was the most important foe of a "stretchout" in the sense of reducing the rearmament effort. This, and the indications, noted earlier, that he favored a tougher line toward China than that of the administration, suggest that his retirement in September 1951—for reasons of health, and not, as is sometimes said, the nasty attacks of Joe McCarthy—was of greater importance than generally realized.

Studies conducted for NSC-114, the Cold War policy statement that was to replace NSC-68, were not encouraging. In August 1951, NSC-114/1 warned that Soviet military production was of higher quality than had been expected. The growth of the European satellite forces, which was greater than had been expected in 1950, alone had probably offset the increase in strength in Western Europe. (The shock administered by the North Koreans may have led the Americans to overrate the reliability and effectiveness of these forces.) Forecasts of the growth of the Soviet nuclear stockpile now held that it would reach the level previously expected in mid–1954 by mid–1953 instead. "On all these counts, NSC-68 projected a prospect which was more favorable for the United States than now appears to have been warranted." While Western Europe's cohesion had increased since NSC 68 was drawn up, the situation in the Middle East, especially Iran, and some other parts of Asia was worse. The danger of war by miscalculation or a local conflict getting out of hand was acute. Forecasts of the probable results of a Soviet attack in the near future remained unchanged. The Soviets and their allies would overrun continental Europe, the Near and Middle East, and East and Southeast Asia despite American atomic attacks.

The American effort was falling short of plans. Assuming no further slippage in production, stable prices and an early end to the Korean War, Army units would be nominally ready by mid–1952. But they would not be fully manned or adequate to support mobilization or deployment of forces to some overseas areas. The Army would be able to sustain combat operations at the planned level in a global war early in 1953. If the Korean War went on, this date would be put off until late 1953. The Navy was on schedule, although its equipment could not be modernized, and a minimum level of war reserves would not be reached until 1953 or 1954. While the Air Force's planned 95 wings would be formed by mid–1952, certain types of equipment would not be available by then. Plane production had been delayed by shortages of machine tools and design changes. But the expected shortfalls would be made up in the year following December 1951.[8]

The Soviet military threat seemed more serious than before, while Western plans based on earlier, over-optimistic predictions were not being carried out. Nevertheless, pressures mounted in Europe and the United States to do less rather than more.

After the spring of 1951 there was a declining belief in the threat of war among most of the Western public and officials. No new and overt Soviet aggressive actions had taken place. Mere Soviet gestures, even without concessions, and negotiations, however empty of result, sufficed to quiet fears, especially in Europe. Americans were more keyed up, thanks to the Korean War, but even they were becoming more optimistic. In Korea, the Chinese had been stopped, and armistice talks were taking place. (That the UN was in danger of losing control of the air was not well known.) The very intensity of the fears of an imminent Soviet attack in late 1950 and early 1951 now rebounded against the West. Since no attack had taken place at what seemed to many to be the point of maximum danger, many people assumed that the threat of war was receding. As usual, short-run, long-run and middle-term dangers were confused. On December 30, 1951, in its summary of the year, the *New York Times* noted that "the black pessimism with which 1951 began has faded noticeably. The fear of the Big War is still real, but the calamity is not expected to happen in 1952. There is a growing conviction that the West, with the help of American economic and military power, and with patient resolution of its own differences, can strike a posture formidable enough to deter aggression from the East."

The rearmament drive had coincided with, complicated and delayed the last phase of Europe's recovery from World War II. The French and British economies, especially the latter, were running up against genuine limits. Rearmament was directly competitive with the production of vital British exports; Marshall Plan aid had already ended, perhaps prematurely. The Ottawa meeting of the NATO Council in September 1951, which admitted Greece and Turkey to NATO, created a "Temporary Council Committee" to close the gap between NATO expenditures and requirements that were raised by Eisenhower's assessment that reserves must be mobilized faster in the event of war. It was also apparent that the "infrastructure" of airfields and other installations needed to support the combat units were inadequate.[9]

But the Americans themselves slackened their efforts. In the fall of 1951, as the budget for the 1953 fiscal year was worked out, appreciations of Soviet aims became subtly more optimistic. On October 12, NSC-114/2, a follow-up report on the status of the NSC-114 programs, proposed a "stretch-out." The president, civilian officials in the Pentagon and the Bureau of the Budget favored such a move, although Leon Keyserling, the Chairman of the Council of Economic Advisers, joined Paul Nitze and the Policy Planning Staff in resisting the idea. Nitze, if anything, favored increasing the defense effort. But putting the effort on a "long-haul" basis, discarding the idea of achieving a state of readiness by a particular date, and maintaining reduced defense budgets (albeit still high by pre–Korea levels) over a long period had considerable support.

The Joint Chiefs of Staff now favored major changes in plans for the buildup, altering the balance between the services. This may have been a preparation for or a hedge against a stretch-out, which they did not want but expected. Increasing interest focused on tactical nuclear weapons as hopefully a cheap form of firepower that would compensate for fewer troops. The Joint Chiefs increased the target for the Air Force to 126 combat wings, with reduced average manpower. The Army's growth would be reduced, and the Navy would lose two carrier air groups. The new Secretary of Defense, Robert Lovett, energetically sought to cut the budget.

Truman's growing unhappiness at defense costs, which he feared would ruin the economy, ended in a decision at a poorly recorded meeting at the White House on December 28, 1951, to stretch out the buildup and impose a ceiling of $60 billion on military expenditures and foreign aid. The aim of an Air Force of 126 wings was maintained, but 30 wings would not be combat ready in the next fiscal year. The defense program of Truman's last year stressed lower budgets, a long-haul approach, airpower and tactical nuclear weapons, thus anticipating Eisenhower's "New Look" defense policies. On January 4, Lovett and the Joint Chiefs warned of the consequences: true readiness would be postponed until 1956. Truman had gauged political trends correctly. Congress sliced his reduced defense budget of $48.6 billion to $43.9 billion and resisted attempts to restore the cuts.

December 1951 had marked a general "running up against the limits" for the Western powers, although at least in the case of the United States those limits were self-imposed or due to political and psychological factors rather than objective economic constraints.

Reducing the overall defense effort meant that a radical change of course in Korea seemed out of the question. MacArthur's belief that only the will to lift existing restrictions and at most modest reinforcements were needed to win, perhaps valid in the spring of 1951, was clearly wrong by late 1951. In December 1951, the National Security Council endorsed continuing the current course in Korea. On the same day that Truman decided on the stretch-out, General Bolte, the Army's Deputy Chief of Staff for Plans, warned that the United States now had no certain military capability to reach a favorable decision in the Far East, and no knowledge of how long it would take to acquire one. Only a drastic change in America's global strategy or all-out mobilization of national resources could immediately increase our military capability. The first could endanger national security; the second would cause grave economic problems. Thus the United States was now locked into the Korean War, if Stalin's plans had not already ensured this. It is perhaps no coincidence that the UN position on "Item 3" of the Korean armistice talks—arrangements for a cease-fire — began collapsing during December 1951, although local circumstances were also involved.[10] Curiously, despite the immense impact of the stretch-out decision on the Korean War, not to mention immensely larger issues, it has never attracted much attention from historians, much less the criticism directed against both sides in the Truman-MacArthur controversy.

During 1952 the relaxation was increasingly rationalized by the argument that Western strength had reached a level that, although far from adequate to prevent Europe from being overrun or ensure an early Soviet defeat, would make war a terrible gamble for the Soviets. Admittedly at some risk, the Western powers could slacken their efforts, while maintaining sufficient strength to deter an attack that might come at any time in the future. This argument, registered in NSC-135/1 (the successor to NSC-68 and NSC-114), was deceptively plausible. War *was* an awful gamble for the Soviets, and Stalin would never have considered war given the existing balance in power in anything like his "normal" frame of mind.

Some people, especially Paul Nitze, continued to oppose a stretch-out as too risky. Nitze complained that the new policy statement wrongly assumed the risk of world war was far less than previously thought, while underestimating American capabilities. It too readily accepted a position of disadvantage vis-à-vis the Soviets, and wrongly rejected gaining a preponderance of power and either rolling back Soviet power or inducing a change in the Soviet regime. Nitze was particularly unhappy, as were many others, at the inadequacy of North America's air defenses and civil defense measures. Nitze himself regarded a policy of "rollback" as too dangerous, at least at that time, but thought that it would be desirable for the West to clearly gain the upper hand. While more alarmist than his opponents about war in the near-term, he was more optimistic about the chances of improving the situation in the long run.

Nitze, one of the ablest public servants of the postwar era, was right, but he had no real inkling of what Stalin was planning and his arguments lacked decisive force. NSC 135, despite serious qualifications, registered the victory of the opposing view and showed the sort of perceptions of the Soviet threat that would dominate American policy for most of the rest of the Cold War. "Although there is continuing danger of general war, the most immediate danger facing the United States is that a progressive and cumulative loss of positions of importance to the United States (either as a result of deterioration within the free nations or of Communist cold war actions or a process involving both) could eventually reduce the United States, short of general war, to an isolated and critically vulnerable position," NSC-135 said. Loss of the Cold War over the long run by general erosion was the main danger, not world war in the near future. This appraisal was not necessarily an optimistic one, for NSC-135 recognized more explicitly than NSC-68 that in many areas the situation was unfavorable to the West. But the CIA's November 1952 "Estimate of the World Situation Through 1954" suggested that, "For the time being the world wide Communist expansion has apparently been checked. There are indications that the USSR had recognized this situation and has been shifting to less openly aggressive tactics. Since Korea the Soviet bloc has undertaken no new military adventures and it has not increased its aid to Communist insurrectionary movements during the last year. These changes are due in great part to the fact that the principal Western countries have grown politically, economically, and militarily stronger."[11]

President Truman's January 1952 budget message was a public tip-off that the American military buildup would be relaxed. The British and French inevitably followed the American example. The conviction was already widespread in Europe that the military burden could be safely reduced and that "long-haul" policies were appropriate. Even Eisenhower, about to leave SHAPE to run for President, shared this view. He disliked a cutback but believed that war was not now probable, and that defense efforts had to be put on a footing that could be maintained indefinitely.

Contrary to what might be supposed, the British Conservative victory of 1951 was not a boon for rearmament. The Conservative leaders knew their victory was partly due to chafing at the military burden and the Labour government's continuation of wartime controls. Churchill himself thought that war was unlikely in the near future and had long been obsessed with the idea that a new summit meeting could settle everything. On January 11, 1952, Foreign Secretary Eden, the real power in Churchill's last government, expressed confidence that the danger of war had lessened. In February, Churchill warned that rearmament would take longer and cost more than had been expected. Shortly after that, a cutback in expenditures was announced.[12]

The NATO meeting at Lisbon in February 1952 was later supposed to be the high-water mark of the Western military buildup. In fact the tide had ebbed. The meeting agreed on ambitious goals for 1954 that equaled or exceeded those set by the Temporary Council Committee's report. But the most tangible and immediate goals, those set for the end of 1952, were mostly lower than those the Committee had proposed. By the end of 1952, 25 divisions were to be ready on mobilization day, with 461 combat ships and 4,067 planes; within 30 days 51 and ⅔ divisions were to be ready. At the end of 1954, 41 and ⅔ divisions, 504 ships and 9,965 planes should be available at the start of mobilization; the ground forces should reach a total of 89 and ⅔ divisions in a month.

These figures did not include any German units for 1952, but assumed that eight German divisions would be ready at the end of 1954 and increase to 12 after mobilization. Greek and Turkish forces—those countries were formally admitted to NATO at Lisbon—were not counted. But their poorly equipped armies, far out on NATO's southern flank, could add little to the defense of Western Europe. The most immediate problem at Lisbon, resolved in private meetings rather than at the formal sessions, was how to fund the French contribution. Although France raised its own military expenditures and was promised considerable American aid, it cut its projected NATO contribution from 14 to 12 divisions because of the needs of the Indochina War. The Lisbon Conference agreed on a major reorganization of NATO. All civilian functions were consolidated in an international secretariat under a Secretary-General.

But underneath the public triumph of the alliance many European leaders were already sure that the goals were unattainable. They privately warned Acheson and Lovett that their economies were not equal to the planned effort. Within little more than a month, NATO's Standing Group concluded that the goals for 1953 could not be met and had to be reduced by 25 percent. The French government failed to gain support for the taxes its portion of the buildup needed. Acheson, on May 23, admitted that the Lisbon goals were economically beyond reach, although he later believed that things might have been different had sufficient willpower existed. By the fall of 1952, the Defense Department glumly agreed to a figure for a "mobilization day" in 1955 of 62 and ⅔ divisions that included eight German divisions, whose existence depended on the unratified EDC treaty, and, misleadingly, 23 and ⅓ Greek and Turkish divisions. The Lisbon goals for the end of 1952 were approached, but not met. Though 25 divisions were ready, the figure for mobilization day plus 30 fell 10 percent short of the target. The naval forces were unbalanced and only 3,273 planes—many below the standard earlier envisaged—were available. And there was growing reluctance in NATO to set firm goals for 1953 and resentment of American pressure to continue the buildup, all based on the growing conviction that the worst danger was over. The British, in particular, argued that tactical atomic weapons could make up for the lack of ground troops. But the American Joint Chiefs doubted that enough of those weapons would be ready in the near future to make up the difference.[13]

The goal of a NATO capable of throwing back a Soviet invasion receded rather than came nearer. Ironically, the buildup the Western powers had decided on before Stalin chose war faltered as his preparations advanced at top speed.

16

Panmunjom — Negotiations to Deadlock

The Communists seemed ready to resume the Korean armistice talks by late September, but the UN Command wanted to move them to Panmunjom, right on the front line near Kaesong. The delegations finally met again on October 25, resuming the discussion of Item 2 — the line of demarcation. Meanwhile, American attempts to persuade the Soviets of the desirability of an armistice achieved nothing.

The Communists now dropped their insistence on the line of the 38th Parallel. The UN proposed making the line of contact the line of demarcation for the armistice, with small adjustments. The UN would withdraw on the east coast and in the west in exchange for the Kaesong area. Ridgway regarded the city as psychologically valuable, and an item that would strengthen Seoul's defense and placate the ROK government. For his part, Mao Zedong, apparently still planning to renew the war at an early date, agreed on Kaesong's strategic importance. As he explained to Stalin on November 14, it was an advanced post for taking the ROK capital.

The Communists adamantly rejected giving up Kaesong, but proposed a swap of territory giving the UN an indefensible area on the west coast in return for the high ground the UN had recently taken on the east-central front. The UN naturally refused. A complicating factor was that Communist maps showed the front line as lying eight to twelve miles south of the positions actually held by the UN forces. Ridgway insisted on haggling over Kaesong as Washington became exasperated with him. The UN delegates argued that they would have taken Kaesong had it not been the site of the talks, and that they would be effectively trading the coastal islands off North Korea for it. The Communists were predictably unimpressed and refused even to put Kaesong in the proposed demilitarized zone. On November 6, Washington told Ridgway to give up on Kaesong rather than risk a breakdown of the talks.

Both sides seemed to accept that the actual front line would become the demarcation line although they did not agree where that lay. The UN position was that the line of contact on the day that the armistice came into effect would become the demarcation line. But the Communists made clear on November 6 that the demarcation line must be fixed before proceeding to any other agenda items. Their position meant there would be a de facto cease fire. Ridgway and Joy feared that this would relieve the Communists of any pressure to settle the rest of the terms. The blunder of making the demarcation line the second item in the agenda now became apparent, although it could not be finally and absolutely settled until the last moment.

A further source of confusion was supplied by the Soviets. On November 8, Foreign Minister Vyshinsky had made a speech in the UN urging cessation of the fighting in 10 days, a return to the 38th Parallel and a withdrawal of all foreign forces in three months. This was a return to the position the Communist delegation at Panmunjom had abandoned. The Americans believed the Communists had been badly hurt in the earlier fighting and that both the Communist powers now wanted an early end to the war. They optimistically interpreted Vyshinsky's statement as an attempt to bluff the Western powers into accepting the current Communist position by threatening something worse.

In fact, while Mao indicated to Stalin on November 14 that he would like to conclude an armistice soon (and seemed to think that there was a chance it could be achieved by the end of 1951), he regarded dragging out the war for another six months to a year with equanimity. He evinced no further flexibility on the terms. He was sure that the Americans would give in on the demarcation line (that is, accept the Chinese version of where the front line lay) and also that there would be no trouble in arranging an exchange of all prisoners of war although he appears to have already suspected that the Americans would seek a one-for-one exchange leaving them free to spare anti–Communist prisoners from having to return home. Stalin nevertheless may have felt that too much progress had been made toward an armistice, and wished to force the Chinese into line or throw a monkey wrench into the works.

The Chinese seem to have been a bit puzzled by Vyshinsky's speech. On November 20, Stalin lamely explained that the seeming demand for the 38th Parallel had been designed merely to demonstrate the injustice of the American position and that the Communist side had been making concessions for peace.

There were signs of tension between the Soviets, the North Koreans and the Chinese during November 1951 and the following year. This did not prevent the continued buildup of the Chinese forces and Soviet-Chinese cooperation in the germ war fraud, a nasty political warfare operation that will be described later. But there seem to have been quarrels over Korean affairs and revolutionary strategy in the ex-colonial world. In November 1951, the North Korean Ambassador in Beijing was recalled and not replaced for many months; there were reports that the North Koreans and Chinese quarreled over the Chinese drafting Koreans into the Chinese army. In the same month, Soviet ideologists warned that it was dangerous to view the Chinese revolution as the model for seizing power in Asia.

Washington decided to accept the current line of contact as the permanent demarcation line if the rest of the agenda was completed within a definite time limit. Ridgeway and Joy disliked this and were sure that it would misfire. They had to be ordered to accept it on November 14. At Panmunjom the Communists had remained adamant on the "finalization" of the demarcation line. On November 14, they made clear they expected the de facto cease-fire resulting from agreement on this point to extend to air and sea action as well as the ground front. Although they admitted that the arrangement they wanted would not be legally binding, they maintained that for the UN to insist otherwise would show that it was insincere.

Yet again, they seemed to walk a tightrope between an outright breakdown of the talks and a real end to the war, which their overbearing Soviet ally did not want. A de facto cease-fire of this sort would have suited the Communists perfectly by ending the blockade and bombing of North Korea, and allowing them to push their planes forward onto Korean bases. Even if the Communists never attacked again in Korea, Stalin's purpose of tying down Western forces would be fulfilled at no cost. The Americans would not dare reduce the UN Command until a real armistice was signed, an event that Stalin probably expected would never take place. They might even have to increase their forces in Korea and bully their allies into keeping troops there for what many people would regard as an unnecessary effort.

On November 17, the UN delegation offered to accept the current line of contact as the final demarcation line if the rest of the negotiations were completed in 30 days. It was made clear that military operations would go on until the armistice was fully finished. The Communists chewed this over for several days and decided to agree. On November 27, the dispute over the line of contact was settled. The following 30 days saw a de facto cease-fire on the ground, sometimes called the "Little Armistice." In practice, the front line moved little until the war's end.[1]

But its nature changed. During the "Little Armistice" rival fortification systems often likened to those of the Western front in World War I snaked across the 155 miles between the Yellow Sea and the Sea of Japan. Actually, only the UN line resembled that of the earlier war. Its front, except for the sector held by the Commonwealth Division (whose older officers recalled World War I or had been trained by men who did), was a thin, poorly engineered line of trenches and bunkers. The UN positions were often badly built and sited. By contrast, the Communists did not dig in. They dug down, creating a front of fantastic strength, 14 miles deep (and even deeper in some places), reputedly engineered to withstand even atomic weapons. The defense system resembled those used by the Japanese in the last battles of the Pacific War. They burrowed into the hills, driving tunnels from the reverse slopes of hills to the forward slopes to provide perfectly protected gun positions, or altering natural caves to produce the same result. The hollowed hills were connected by a maze of trenches, and living quarters were also underground. Evidently they did not expect to go anywhere in the near future. Their artillery was so well dug in that it could not be moved. (In the last offensive of the war in 1953, the Communists broke through the ROK positions fairly easily, only to quickly outrun their supporting guns.)[2]

On the same day that Item 2 was completed, negotiations began on Item 3 — arrangements to supervise the cease-fire. The Americans regarded this as the most crucial part of the armistice agenda. They wanted an armistice commission with unlimited access to all of Korea and joint observation teams, plus joint air observation over all of Korea. There would be no increase of forces by either side or rehabilitation of facilities, especially airfields. Rotation — that is, replacement of forces already in Korea — would be allowed. Ridgway himself did not think unlimited inspection either necessary or desirable, but felt that the principle must be maintained as a precedent for future negotiations with the Soviets. Preventing airfield reconstruction followed from the general principle that the armistice should not give the enemy military advantages that it had been unable to gain during the fighting. It was especially desirable as a way to reduce the threat of air attack on Japan if World War III began. Military leaders in Washington doubted that the Communists would agree to inspection and unlike Ridgway, they were unwilling to break off negotiations over it.

At the outset, the Communists proposed an early evacuation of the demilitarized zone, the rear areas and coastal islands of each side, and an armistice commission consisting of equal numbers of representatives from each side. The UN delegation found this acceptable, but insisted it was necessary to prevent a buildup of forces, or building or rebuilding military facilities for offensive purposes. But the Communists rejected "free access" by a supervisory organ as unnecessary and as interference in internal affairs. Instead of restrictions on increases, all foreign troops should leave. Argument continued about this for a week. The Communists strongly opposed UN proposals to allow rotation but not reinforcement of forces in Korea, and opposed a ban on rebuilding airfields. They bluntly indicated they would not accept restrictions on airfields, continued to demand withdrawal of all non–Korean forces and rejected UN attempts to use the northern coastal islands as a bargaining counter.

On December 3, the Communists made a seeming concession. They offered to accept restrictions on introducing new forces and weapons into Korea, and to oversee this suggested that neutral nations form a supervisory organ to inspect ports of entry in the rear of either side. (Mao had indicated to Stalin that he wanted only one or two ports of entry subject to inspection.) The UN was thrown into disarray. No one had expected the neutral nations proposal, while the Communists made clear that the restrictions they envisaged were meant to rule out any rotation of troops, and replenishment of weapons and supplies. If their position was accepted, that meant the UN force would wither away, while the Communists would probably evade any limited inspection arrangements that were agreed on. On December 5, UN inquiry into the concept of a neutral nations organ produced a Communist designation of Czechoslovakia and Poland as neutral. Argument began over the nature of ports of entry and whether the restrictions covered aircraft. Ridgway and Joy were left without adequate instructions while Washington developed a new position. Meanwhile, on December 11, the Communists agreed to the UN's long-standing desire to begin discussing Item 4 — prisoners of war — by exchanging data on the prisoners even while Item 3 was being worked on.

On December 12, the UN Command offered to concede the coastal islands and agreed to neutral observer teams as long as they were under the military armistice commission. In return, it insisted on allowing rotation and replenishment. The Communists countered by offering to allow the rotation of only 5,000 men every month — a ridiculously low figure — and indicated their members on the military armistice commission could veto even that. During late December the Communists continued to insist on the right to rebuild airfields. They hinted that they might be more agreeable on rotation and replenishment if the UN caved in on the airfield issue. They rejected a UN offer to drop demands for air reconnaissance in return for acceptance of the UN position on airfields (which was modified to permit civil aviation). Washington had decided to allow the reconstruction of some military airfields as a last resort, but not ones usable by jets. But it reserved the right to make a final decision on that topic. As the 30-day time limit ran out, the issues of airfields, inspection and rotation were unresolved. It also became clear that the disposal of prisoners of war (which will be discussed later) was a major problem in itself.[3]

Ridgway still wanted to block airfield reconstruction. But Washington again began to bend. The agreement of America's allies to a statement warning the Communists that violation of an armistice in Korea might be met by an extension of hostilities seemed an adequate substitute for an airfield ban. In any case other armistice terms forbidding augmentation of forces — if carried out — should prevent planes from being stationed in North Korea. An actual concession on the airfields was held back for a time, however, as a bargaining counter. Air observation would also be given up if need be.

Although Admiral Joy warned on January 8 that "with each passing day, there is less and less reason to think the Communists really want an armistice," bargaining did proceed, and the two sides seemed to approach each other. The next day the Communists agreed to replenishment of material in return for the UN dropping air inspection. A compromise on rotation and inspection developed from January to March 1952. The Communists finally agreed to allow rotation of 35,000 men a month. They opposed roving teams of inspectors and wanted inspection limited to a few specified ports of entry. On March 15, it was agreed that each side would use five ports of entry in its half of Korea — the largest North Korean ports were not on the list. Meanwhile, Item 5 — recommendations to the governments concerned — had been quickly settled along the lines desired by the Communists on February 17.

Yet, while this and much of Item 3 had been settled, new issues had arisen so that Ridgway admitted to the Joint Chiefs of Staff on March 11 that he did not know if the enemy really wanted an armistice or not. Apart from the issues posed by the prisoners of war, a dispute raged over the composition of the neutral nations supervisory organ and inspection teams. The Americans were rather incredibly willing to swallow the Communists' designation of Poland and Czechoslovakia as suitable "neutrals," but choked when the Communists insisted on the ultimate absurdity of designating the Soviet Union as a neutral on February 16. The Americans offered to drop their designation of Norway if the Communists dropped the USSR, but the Communists stood fast. By mid–March there still seemed to be a complete deadlock on the issue of the Soviet Union, the airfields and the whole of Item 4 — repatriating prisoners of war.[4]

The prisoner issue was a complex one. It was not even clear to which side many Korean prisoners properly belonged. In 1950, the North Koreans had incorporated many ROK prisoners into their forces. Later, many of these men had surrendered to or been captured by the UN forces. While occupying South Korea, they had also drafted many southern civilians into their army, while some southern civilians had been mistaken for enemy soldiers and sent to prisoner of war camps. (Men from the latter groups, who numbered 40,000, but not ROK soldiers who had been put into the North Korean army were later reclassified as "civilian internees" rather than prisoners of war.) It was also clear that many North Korean and Chinese prisoners — many of the latter were ex–Nationalists — did not want to return to Communist control.

In July 1951, General McClure, the head of the U.S. Army's psychological warfare branch, had warned of the problem. He suggested that the ex–Nationalists be sent to Taiwan and that the UN Command follow a policy of only voluntary repatriation. The Joint Chiefs and many others found the idea appealing, and not only on humanitarian grounds. They believed that for many Communist prisoners to reject repatriation would be a great propaganda victory for the West and make the Communist leaders nervous about the reliability of their forces, with a desirable restraining effect. And many in Washington remembered the horrible results of the forcible repatriation of Soviet prisoners in 1945–1946 in "Operation Keelhaul." However, it was hard to reconcile voluntary repatriation with the letter of the Geneva Convention of 1949. That clearly envisaged repatriation of all prisoners, although international lawyers were to argue that it did not actually forbid voluntary repatriation which was consistent with the spirit of the convention as a means to protect the rights of prisoners.

Debate over the subject continued for months. Opinions swung back and forth. It was apparent that the enemy would oppose voluntary repatriation and that it risked prolonging the war. General Ridgway, who had originally shown some interest in the idea, turned against it. He feared that it would set a precedent that could be turned against the West in a future war with Communist states. In the future, the Communists might hold a preponderance of the prisoners and might block neutral visits to prisoner of war camps, leaving the West no recourse if they insisted that the prisoners did not want to return home. Admiral Joy felt that delaying an armistice for the sake of voluntary repatriation was fundamentally wrong. The duty of the UN Command was to get back its own men; it was immoral to let them languish in Communist camps in order to protect captured enemies.

16. Panmunjom—Negotiations to Deadlock

This view seems to have been common among professional military men at all levels. The United States had not, however, finally settled on its policy when discussion of prisoners began at Panmunjom in December 1951.

When the sub-delegations detailed to discuss Item 4 met, the UN pressed for a swap of sick and wounded captives, an exchange of information on the rest and for Red Cross visits to the prison camps. The UN delegates tried to avoid discussing the terms of the final prisoner exchange, but the Communists made clear they wanted "all for all" repatriation. On December 18, they agreed just to exchange prisoner lists.

The results were a shock. Although the Communists had earlier claimed taking over 65,000 prisoners, they now claimed to hold just 11,559, most of them ROKs. The Americans alone had 11,500 missing; it later developed that a large proportion had died in captivity. The UN Command reported that it held 132,000 prisoners of war and 37,000 "civilian internees," most of the latter the South Koreans who had been drafted into the North Korean forces. Both sides were furious. The UN Command insisted that the Communists had not reported all the prisoners they held. The Communists denied this, saying that they had "reeducated" and released many prisoners at the front, some of whom had voluntarily joined the North Korean forces. They complained about the UN prisoner lists, which did contain inaccuracies (among other errors, 2,000 prisoners had been counted twice) and the classification of some prisoners as internees. The UN Command raised the issue of South Korean civilian prisoners held by the Communists. The South Koreans estimated that some 20,000 civilians had been carried off to the North, although some of these people may have been Communist supporters who went voluntarily. The Communists finally agreed that displaced civilians could go to the area of their choice — but never carried this out. The UN also brought up the problem of South Koreans who had been forced into the North Korean army. It insisted that those still serving in the Communist forces be returned to prisoner of war status, and that those who had been retaken by the UN should not be considered prisoners of war.

The Communists naturally took the opposite position. They insisted that a prisoner belonged to the army in which he was serving when he had been taken prisoner and claimed that the ex–ROKs in their ranks had volunteered. The Communists thus admitted, or to be more precise, alleged that they themselves had practiced a sort of "voluntary repatriation."

The UN delegation slyly used this as an entering wedge for a proposal to apply voluntary repatriation to all prisoners. On January 2, 1952, the UN delegates proposed that the Red Cross supervise interviews of prisoners. Prisoners would then be exchanged on a one-for-one basis. All prisoners in excess of the one-for-one exchange would be returned unless they opposed repatriation, but would be paroled and forbidden to fight again as would non-repatriates. The Communists resolutely refused to countenance any of this. They ignored the inconsistency of their position and blandly argued that the UN position was incompatible with the Geneva Convention — whose every other provision they had violated. On January 15, the Joint Chiefs of Staff authorized Ridgway to agree to an all-for-all exchange, but not to forced repatriation. They saw the possibility of eventually trading airfield rehabilitation for agreement on the prisoner issue. The Communists remained adamant. Admiral Joy thought they would never accept voluntary repatriation. They appeared ready to give in on some lesser points, such as forbidding returned prisoners to fight again, but Joy concluded during February that there was no prospect of recovering ex–ROK soldiers still in the North Korean Army. The Communists graciously agreed to forget about the ones the UN had captured or freed.

But opinion in the American government hardened in favor of voluntary repatriation. Most Defense Department officials, save for Secretary of Defense Lovett, were ready to drop it to obtain an armistice. But the State Department wanted to insist on it. President Truman — who inclined toward a hard line throughout the Panmunjom talks — backed the Secretary of State. Churchill also strongly favored it. Other Allied officials were not so enthusiastic, but it was popular with the public. However, many seem to have supposed at this time that the policy would not have much effect in delaying an end to the war. Neither did the Chinese, simply because as Mao indicated in a message to Stalin on January 31, he supposed that the Americans could not hold out on the prisoner issue for long. However, on February 8, American policy was settled. Prisoners would not be returned against their will. Various dodges to save face for the Communists or present them with a fait accompli by releasing prisoners who opposed repatriation, were considered but rejected. Ridgway felt that the latter move might cause the Communists to retaliate against captured UN soldiers.

Thus, in mid–March 1952, there was a triple deadlock on airfields, the composition of a "neutral" supervisory organ and prisoner repatriation. Washington advised Ridgway to offer a "package deal," trading airfield reconstruction for Communist concessions on the other issues. Ridgway doubted the Communists would give two concessions for one. He urged a delay while Joy tried to get the Communists to drop the claim that the Soviets were neutral. Washington, against his advice, was ready to accept the alternative of having the Soviets on the supervisory organ if the pretense that it was neutral was dropped.

16. Panmunjom—Negotiations to Deadlock

Meanwhile, attempts were made to secure a trade of sick and wounded along with Red Cross visits to Communist camps. The UN Command tried to determine just how many of its prisoners opposed repatriation. It was reluctant to screen prisoners unilaterally lest the Communists retaliate. It estimated that of 132,000 military prisoners, 28,000 would prefer not to go home but only 16,000 would resist repatriation. Of the 37,000 civilian internees. 30,000 preferred not to return but only 2,000 would strongly resist. On April 1, a UN Command staff officer told a Chinese counterpart that it was estimated that about 116,000 military prisoners would probably be exchanged. The Chinese seemed to tacitly consent to screening the prisoners, evidently still sure that only a few would reject repatriation and that would be acceptable. They issued an amnesty statement that promised their men in UN hands they would not be punished when they got home.

Screening began April 8. Seven of the 17 UN prisoner compounds, holding over 37,000 North Koreans, were tightly controlled by Communists and fiercely resisted screening. After several deaths, they were left alone and *all* prisoners in those compounds were listed as seeking repatriation. Screening of the rest showed that only 70,000 of 170,000 prisoners were willing to return. Over 14,000 Chinese—two-thirds of the Chinese prisoners—did not, it seemed, want repatriation. On April 19, the Communists were informed of this at Panmunjom. They were horrified. Treating the estimates given on April 1 as a promise, they complained of bad faith, and thereafter the Communists totally rejected voluntary repatriation. When the "package deal" was finally presented on April 28 in the form of a draft of the armistice, they showed no interest. The Chinese indicated through the Indian government that they might accept applying voluntary repatriation to the Koreans, but not to their own men. Nam Il told the UN delegation that a minimum of 110,00 men, including all the Chinese, must be returned.[5]

As the UN Command's failure to screen all of the North Koreans showed, it did not securely control its prisoners. Washington had ignored MacArthur's pleas to take them to the United States. They were kept on Koje island off the South Korean coast, guarded by low-grade personnel. Already, in 1951, there had been trouble with the North Koreans. Bloody struggles raged between Communist and anti–Communist prisoners within the compounds; UN personnel dared not enter them at night. The removal of anti–Communist South Koreans when they were reclassified as civilian internees swung the balance to the Communists. Control over the Chinese was not particularly good either, although the UN Command perhaps had less reason to complain about the results. Fanatically anti–Communist, ex–Nationalist non-commissioned officers ran the Chinese compounds. Observers believed that their use of violence and intimidation had swollen the total of nonrepatriates considerably. Chinese-American officers reported to Admiral Joy in mid–April that the screening process was not indicative of real choice. They suggested that removing the current leadership of the compounds would swell repatriates to 85 percent of the total. This did not increase the admiral's enthusiasm for the position he had to defend. It should be noted that had the Chinese prisoners loyal to the Communists seen their future, they might have chosen differently. Those who chose repatriation in 1953 met a reception like that returning Soviet prisoners of war got in 1945: they were put in concentration camps.

The Communist-controlled Korean prisoners were a more serious problem. They were in contact with Pyongyang and directed by Nam Il. A major uprising had been planned at least since January 1952, when General Pak Song Hyon, an important Soviet-Korean, reached Koje, pretending to be a private. Probably originally planned as a move in the general "Hate America" campaign (which will be discussed later), the planned action also served the purpose of discrediting voluntary repatriation. The prisoners were tightly organized and made all sorts of weapons, including spears, knives and Molotov cocktails. On May 7, the Communist prisoners seized General Frank Dodd, the not too bright commandant at Koje, and held him as a hostage, threatening to kill him if force was used. They convened a "people's court" to "try" him for alleged crimes, while American combat units arrived and prepared to break into and break up the compounds. The Communists demanded that the Americans stop their alleged mistreatment of prisoners, which supposedly included using them in tests of germ warfare, poison gas, and nuclear bombs. They also demanded a stop to screening and voluntary repatriation. To save Dodd's life, General Charles Colson, his stand-in, tried to placate the Communists by issuing a statement promising humane treatment. It implied that prisoners had in fact been mistreated and killed. Other phrases implied that screening had been forced on the prisoners. Dodd was freed. He and Colson were demoted for their blunders. The UN forces finally moved into the Communist-run compounds on May 20. With some casualties—mostly to the prisoners—they were disarmed and split into smaller, more manageable groups. The Koje affair was a major embarrassment to a United States not yet inured to national humiliation and damaged international support for voluntary repatriation. A further screening of prisoners showed that just over 83,000 wished to go home. This figure was disclosed to the Communists on July 13. They were not pleased, and again insisted that at least 110,000 men must return. Over the Communists' protests, the UN began releasing the civilian internees it held.[6]

Behind the Front

Admiral Joy's concern with the UN soldiers held in North Korean camps was well founded. One of the few things to be said for the Panmunjom negotiations was that they encouraged the Chinese to improve the treatment of the UN prisoners. It rose to the level of the merely bad.

The North Koreans' treatment of prisoners had been horrible. The Chinese had consistently been more humane, but this was not saying very much. During the winter of 1950–1951, men held by both Communist armies had been driven on long marches with little food. Only in early 1951 did the Chinese, who had captured or taken custody of most of the prisoners, set up permanent camps, mostly in the area along the Yalu. The North Koreans maintained transit and punishment camps around Pyongyang; the most infamous was "Pak's Palace," also known as "Pak's Death House." The vermin-ridden UN prisoners struggled to survive on a 1,200 calories a day diet of cracked corn, comparable to that in Nazi concentration camps. They lacked protein, mineral or vitamins, and received very little medical care. (Chinese officers did give some of their own food to feed American doctors.) Twenty to thirty men died every day of cold, starvation, deficiency diseases, hepatitis, dysentery and worm infestations, sometimes complicated by demoralization that was misleadingly called "giveupitis." The impact of "giveupitis," which indeed did kill some men who although already sick and hungry might have survived, was often exaggerated by ignorant critics after the war who treated it along with the conversion of a few men to Communism as a novel manifestation of American decay. In fact, similar developments had occurred in many groups of prisoners in many times and places. The demoralization of American prisoners in Korea, although sometimes severe, never reached the depths seen among some survivors of Bataan in World War II.

In March 1951, conditions improved somewhat. The Chinese provided more and better food; at the same time they began trying to indoctrinate the prisoners. The latter, they explained, were all "war criminals" guilty of taking part in a war of aggression, but could redeem themselves by conversion to Communism. The Chinese tried to capitalize on the breakdown many men had suffered during the period of starvation. But while many men had been demoralized, few were in a state of mind favorable to their captors. Although the Chinese directed a special effort at winning over American Negroes and Spanish-speakers and turning them against the rest, this too was a complete failure. The techniques of "thought reform" that had served the Chinese Communists with some effectiveness against their fellow countrymen just did not work well against Westerners. (The more intensive form of "brainwashing" applied to some Air Force prisoners in 1952 was something different and will be dealt with later.) Despite much scapegoating of the prisoners by malicious or ignorant commentators, very few were converted. Most were bitterly anti–Communist and became more so. The few collaborating "progressives" did help make life more miserable for the rest, especially the courageous "reactionaries" who openly contested the Chinese line. After mid–1952, an earlier policy of lecturing prisoners en masse having failed, the Chinese left much of the indoctrination task to small study groups led by "progressives," with cigarettes or extra food as inducements for those who professed the right ideology. The general treatment of prisoners had improved once the armistice talks resumed in October 1951. The Chinese if not their allies, evidently thought the war might end or be interrupted fairly soon. The Chinese also took control of the military prisoners and civilian internees who had been held by the North Koreans. Of some 7,190 Americans known to have been captured, 2,730 or 38 percent had died, a worse record even than that compiled by the Japanese in World War II. Almost all had died in the first year, with only 19 dying in the last two years of the war. The British prisoners, who had mostly been captured much later than the Americans in April 1951, fared better. Of 1,060 only 82 died. There is, however, good reason to believe that a large number of men listed as "missing" and later as "presumed dead" were taken to China and never returned. At least some disappeared into the ever-hungry maw of Stalin's slave labor empire. This was especially true of captured F-86 pilots; 15 returned at the end of the war but many more may have been sent to the Soviet Union.[7]

Developments in the year since negotiations had begun were a grim commentary on the hopes of July 1951. There had been bloody battles in the summer and fall. These had subsided but were replaced by a slow steady bleeding of casualties by shelling, patrols and raids. The Communists' ground and air strength had nearly doubled while the UN Command had grown only slightly. Nearly a million men faced 700,000 UN troops in Korea, and the Communists were far better supplied with tanks and artillery than a year before. The enemy had nearly 2,000 planes in Manchuria alone. The Soviets had built the Chinese Air force to 1,830 aircraft, while 5,000 Soviet planes stood ready in East Asia. The Far East Air Force and the few non–American UN air units had only 1,440 planes, along with a few hundred Navy aircraft. The Joint Chiefs of Staff's planners frankly admitted that the Korean War could not be brought to an end with the forces available. As the official historian Walter Hermes noted, the American position in Korea had been reduced "to a gamble that the Chinese did want peace and that the limited military pressure that the Far East Command's forces could apply would secure that peace." Plans were laid to build up the South Korean forces so that eventually the American forces could withdraw even if there was no armistice. In September 1952, the Americans decided to increase the ROK army from 10 to 12 divisions.[8]

For much of 1952 and 1953, the front line was relatively quiet, although the UN forces noted an increase in enemy artillery and mortar fire. The war was largely confined to outpost positions and the no man's land between the two sides. Outpost hills such as East Berlin, Jane Russell Hill, Luke the Gook's Castle, Million Dollar Hill and Pork Chop Hill became well-known. There were occasional limited-objective attacks by the UN and raids to snatch prisoners, but there were widespread doubts about the wisdom of either. Such raids became a particular source of contention between the British and their American corps commander (although the Commonwealth Division's U.S. Marine neighbors thoroughly agreed with the British). Ridgway and General Mark Clark, who replaced Ridgway in May 1952, were increasingly reluctant to authorize even small attacks, and those launched were not favorably regarded at home. The Chinese were more aggressive. They held back for much of 1952, fearing that the Americans planned a major landing, probably on the west coast. When this did not materialize, they decided to attack themselves. (The Americans mounted an elaborate deception effort in mid–October to lead the Communists to think that were about to land at Kojo on the east coast, to draw the Communist forces out into the open and expose them to air attack. But the effort was evidently mounted too late to have any effect.) The Chinese had some initial successes against outposts, which encouraged them to attack on a larger scale in October 1952. This led to major battles especially against the ROK 9th Division and outposts of the U.S. 2nd and 7th Divisions, resulting in the bloodiest fighting since the Heartbreak and Bloody Ridge battles. Diversionary attacks by the U.S. 7th Division did not go very well, but the Communists suffered heavily. Yet their fall offensive cost the UN forces 9,000 killed and wounded.[9]

The UN Command did not expect to do more than hold its own on the ground. The real struggle, from its point of view, was in the air where the Americans tried to apply the only sort of pressure available.

Air Pressure

Although far more men were killed in the stalemated ground fighting, it was in the Korean skies that an attempt was made to reach some sort of strategic decision.

The Americans maintained domination of the air without too much difficulty as the Communists continued rotating air units in and out of Manchuria, withdrawing them as soon as they had some experience. (Against this, however, growing enemy defenses were making it more difficult for the old B-29s, now flying at night, to hit targets deep in Korea and return.) During 1952, reorganization and more supplies from the United States improved the supply situation in the Far East Air Force, and more aviation engineer units arrived to improve the often crowded, low-grade Korean airbases. An additional F-86 squadron and a Thunderjet wing reinforced the FEAF. With plane production increasing, plans were laid for a true air buildup in early 1953. Two fighter-bomber wings and the South African squadron would convert to a fighter-bomber version of the F-86. F-86s and F-84s would completely replace the older F-51 and F-80s. In June 1952, new F-86Fs, with more powerful engines and modified wings providing better performance at high speeds and more fuel capacity, reached the Sabrejet units. Some F-86Es were refitted with the new type of wing. With the F-86F the Americans at last had a fighter that was unmistakably superior to the MIG-15. A fighter direction unit and radar station was established on Cho-do island off northwest Korea, giving the Americans a further advantage.

How to apply airpower was a problem. By early 1952 it was clear that the interdiction campaign was not working; at least, it would not force the enemy to retreat or make peace. The Air Force evolved an "air pressure" strategy (a hybrid of "strategic" and "tactical" air attacks) that was enthusiastically seconded or even anticipated by the Navy, which had never liked interdiction. Attacks on the North Korean railroad system would continue on a smaller scale to keep it in a condition where it could not support a sustained enemy offensive. Most of the air effort would be directed in a flexible offensive against any vulnerable targets of military or economic importance to the enemy, from troop billets to factories. By destroying items of value not just to the enemy war effort inside Korea but to the Communist powers, such attacks might raise the costs of the war to the Soviets and Chinese to the point that they might decide that it was not worth going on.

The most important target system remaining in North Korea was the still untouched hydroelectric power system that supplied much power to

China as well as North Korea, and had remained off limits to attack. The Suiho (Supung) dam alone supported the fourth biggest hydroelectric plant in the world and provided 23 percent of Manchuria's power needs in 1952. The importance of the power plants had long been known, but studies showed that a surprising amount of industry still remained or had been rebuilt in North Korea itself, especially in areas bordering on China and the USSR that had been safe from attack. There were also many valuable mines in the north that shipped much ore to the Soviets and could be knocked out of action by attacks on their above ground installations. Beginning on June 23 with a strike from all four available Navy carriers on Suiho, four days of well-planned, massive attacks wrecked the power plants. The attack on the Yalu dam installations aroused some protest in Western Europe, partly because it seemed like an "expansion" of the war (some of the critics seemed to think that the Americans were attacking targets inside Manchuria), and partly because the Americans had not consulted their allies in advance.

Periodic follow-up attacks over the next year would keep the power plants largely out of action. The Americans then concentrated their attacks on chemical and metals plants, mines and the small munitions plants that supplemented supplies from the Soviet Union. Navy carrier strikes also hit some supply and transportation targets in the far northeast that had been off-limits as too close to the Soviet border. By late 1952 even these categories of targets had largely been flattened. A grimmer accompaniment of the "air pressure" strategy—morally more dubious but curiously less criticized than the Yalu dams strikes—was a series of fire-bomb attacks by B-26 light bombers on 78 small towns and villages along the Communists' main supply routes, which the Communists used to shelter troops and supplies. These strikes were preceded by warning leaflets, and lists of the places to be destroyed were read in advance over the radio. Yet they must have caused considerable harm to civilians. Many fled to new temporary villages tucked away in canyons or that were otherwise safe from attack. A more useful development was the "Cherokee strike," devised by and named after Admiral J.J. Clark. Starting in October 1952, these concentrated on hitting supply dumps and troop concentrations near the front but beyond artillery range, which proved to be relatively exposed and lucrative targets. The air pressure attacks did not end the war, but were less costly in men and planes than interdiction, and made the enemy pay a high price for continuing the war. They certainly made Kim Il Sung desperate to end it, and at least some of the Chinese leaders agreed. The Soviets and Chinese had to bring in more war material while their economies were denied Korean power and products. At least in a small way the air pressure strategy hurt the enemy alliance and hindered Stalin's plans. The Americans would have been well advised to adopt the new strategy a year earlier.[10]

On the advice of George Kennan, now the American Ambassador in Moscow, the air pressure attacks were intensified while Zhou Enlai and a Chinese delegation visited Moscow in late August and September. Zhou evidently wanted both Soviet agreement to an armistice and more aid. He got promises of the latter, but not the former. The transcripts of Zhou's meetings with Stalin make curious reading. The two men circled around the issues, while, as Votjech Mastny put it, they "outdid each other in professions of intransigence." Zhou may have been in a difficult position since Mao appears to have favored a harder line than he did, while he dared not show any weakness or apparent disloyalty toward Stalin. Stalin, for his part, occasionally seemed to sound conciliatory in discussing the Korean armistice issues, only to quickly reverse himself. Evidently he wished to avoid alienating the Chinese. Both men admitted that the North Koreans were desperate to end the war, but Stalin cheerily maintained that they would just have to put up with it. Zhou indicated that China was willing to stick out for two or three more years of war. He did suggest that it might be acceptable if the UN held some prisoners back. Stalin seemed to agree at first, but when Zhou said that Mao wanted the return of all prisoners, Stalin seemed to agree with this too. Zhou reported that Mao maintained that the war was to the advantage of the Communist powers since China was tying down the Americans and helping stave off a world war. Stalin readily agreed with that, as well, and belittled American power, that, he declared depended on air power and the atomic bomb, which alone could not win a war without infantry. The Americans soldiers, he jeered, were few and incompetent. Stalin's "solution" to the prisoner issue was to have the Chinese hold back the same percentage of the captives they held as the UN kept of their men. In his last meeting with Zhou on September 13, he indicated that he was not against transferring the Communist prisoners who refused repatriation to Indian custody, but evidently only on the understanding that they would then be handed over to China. He spoke too of developing a "parallel organization" to replace the enemy dominated UN. The Stalin-Zhou communiqué announced that the Soviets would stay in their Port Arthur base after the originally planned departure date at the end of 1952. This was probably distasteful to the Chinese, but seemed acceptable as a deterrent to a naval blockade of China. Stalin agreed to close relations between China and the Mongolian People's Republic.

Shortly after Zhou left Moscow, a compromise on revolutionary strategy surfaced. The Chinese withdrew the most extreme claims for the originality of Mao's strategy and accepted a softer line toward the "neutralists," while the Soviets reaffirmed the importance of the Chinese revolution. During the summer, the Soviets started the publication of Mao's works in Russian. Stalin evidently moved, grudgingly, toward a more equal relationship with Mao. If he had not decided to do this before, he finally dropped Gao Gang. Presumably he concluded that he could no longer afford the luxury of disposing of Mao before World War III began and decided to leave the solution of the Chinese problem for later — perhaps for World War IV. Or perhaps he hoped that China would be so battered in the coming war that it would be no problem. According to Khrushchev, the new Soviet Ambassador to China, A.S. Panyushkin, who arrived in Beijing on December 9, was ordered to betray Gao Gang to Mao. Out of deference to Stalin, Mao waited until 1954 to finish with Gao, who "committed suicide."[11]

Dealing with Rhee

On the other side of the front, the Americans faced a different sort of intrigue: Syngman Rhee's ambitions to make himself dictator. Rhee was increasingly senile, erratic and power-hungry. His many silly statements had embarrassed the Americans and the UN. On May 24, 1952, Rhee put the temporary capital of Pusan and some other areas under martial law. He had some of his opponents in the National Assembly arrested on trumped up charges of treasonable contacts with the Communists. Rhee hoped to force the dissolution of the Assembly, and to get a new one elected that would amend the constitution to create a second legislative house and provide for popular election of the president, who was currently chosen by the legislature. Rhee could not expect reelection, at least without openly intimidating the Assembly. But he, or the clique currently manipulating him, calculated that elections would favor him or could be rigged. On May 28, General Van Fleet and the ROK Army's Chief of Staff asked Rhee to lift martial law. Van Fleet bluntly told Rhee he saw no justification for it. Rhee did not change course.

The U.S. Embassy in Korea strongly favored blocking Rhee and even getting rid of him entirely. Charge Lightner warned that ending martial law was not enough. Rhee would still be able to intimidate his opponents by using the police and mob violence. He bitterly described Rhee's actions as "thumbing his nose at the United States." General Clark was reluctant to act. He warned that he did not have enough troops to deal at the same time with a Communist offensive, the Koje "prisoners" and intervene at

Pusan. Even Clark, however, described Rhee's actions as "diabolical." Many State Department officials favored a hard line with Rhee, including an ultimatum backed up by a military takeover of Pusan by ROK forces under Clark's control. On June 2, President Truman personally rebuked Rhee. Rhee then dropped the idea of dissolving the Assembly, but declined to back down further. Acheson did not favor a tough line. He disliked military intervention and believed that "Rhee under some controls" would still provide the best ROK leadership. He was willing to see the constitution amended to allow direct election of the president, although martial law must end and the jailed assemblymen had to be freed. Military intervention in the affairs of the government the United States was defending and against the only South Korean well known outside his own country, in the midst of an unpopular war and an election year, was not appealing.

The administration persisted in seeking a "compromise," although Ambassador Muccio warned that Rhee was completely irrational and not an effective leader. On June 13 Assistant Secretary of State Hickerson observed that "if Rhee succeeds the United States will be constantly embarrassed in the future by the character of Rhee's conduct, and the Communists will have a rich source of material for attacking the United States and the free world generally." Rhee had to be forced to back down unconditionally, and, if need be Clark should intervene with ROK forces. Hickerson's warnings were amply justified. Van Fleet had already had to stop Rhee from firing the ROK Chief of Staff for trying to run a non-political army. Other officials thought that there was no good alternative to Rhee, but argued that the principle of maintaining a constitutional regime was more important than that. Moreover, the ROK military was loyal to the constitution and would gladly obey Clark in action against Rhee. But they did not get their way, and Rhee persisted. On July 2, he got the Assembly to amend the constitution as he desired. The jailed assemblymen were freed, and martial law ended on July 28.[12]

The crisis ended in victory for Rhee and a major disaster for the Americans. They were humiliated because Rhee had used them and the UN as a shield for his ambitions. By breaking down the rule of law, he had not eliminated the vast moral difference between the South Korean regime and the Communists, but he had reduced it somewhat. Rhee's rule, while infinitely milder than that of Kim Il Sung, proved a disaster. Much American aid was wasted, and South Korea marked time economically until Rhee was overthrown in 1960. Civilian constitutional government revived only in the 1980s.

The American backdown was not only bad for Korea. It was a horrible example of weakness in dealing with the increasingly common problem of unstable regimes in backward countries. To show irresolution in dealing with dictators or would-be dictators like Rhee set a dangerous precedent. It is true that South Korea lacked many prerequisites for democracy. And the Americans and other Western countries could not very well run around forcing democratic governments on underdeveloped countries, many of which were even worse terrain for free institutions than Korea. But in a country secured by hundreds of thousands of American troops, where thousands of lives were lost, it would have been reasonable to expect something better than passively suffering Rhee's intrigues.

The Armistice Talks Are Recessed

At Panmunjom, the two sides went round and round on the repatriation issue without result. On October 8, the armistice talks recessed for an indefinite period. Shortly after, an attempt was made by India, secretly prompted by the American Ambassador in New Delhi, Chester Bowles, to end the war through the UN General Assembly. The Indian scheme was based on partially separating the problem of the prisoners from the rest of the armistice. It involved having the UN Command turn the prisoners over to a separate repatriation commission composed of UN Command and Communist countries. Those who wished to go home would do so immediately, while a postwar political conference would decide the fate of those who refused to go home. The Commonwealth countries and many other American allies favored the plan. But, despite the fact that the Indians had gone into action at their request, the American leaders disliked it. Acheson in particular regarded the proposal as too vague and opposed leaving the prisoner question unresolved when the armistice was signed. He suspected that in practice prisoners opposed to repatriation would be held until they changed their minds. Perhaps he was overly suspicious— Nehru personally favored voluntary repatriation, though others in his government did not — but after India's behavior over the Japanese peace treaty his distrust was understandable. Under American pressure, the scheme was modified and became somewhat more acceptable, although Acheson still disliked it. The Chinese were shown the draft proposal by the Indians and seemed ready to accept it.

But, as before, the Communist acted to unite people against them. The Indian proposal, introduced in the UN on November 17, was violently denounced by Andrei Vyshinsky on November 24 as incompatible with the Geneva Convention. A few days later the Chinese followed suit. The General Assembly adopted the Indian plan, but the Communists remained inflexible. Vyshinsky's remarks, like those a year earlier, strongly suggested that the Soviets feared the Chinese might seize a face-saving way out and, wanting the war to go on, had intervened to force them into line. That the Soviets wanted the war to continue was something many observers had come to suspect during 1952. The CIA in July did believe it probable that both Communist powers wanted an armistice, but admitted there was no conclusive evidence of their intentions. At the same time, Ambassador Kennan advised the State Department that the current situation probably seemed, on balance, satisfactory to the Soviets. On November 26, John Foster Dulles, soon to become Secretary of State, advised President-elect Eisenhower that the Soviets wanted the war to go on as a diversion to allow them to maintain their position in Manchuria, and divide the United States from its allies.[13]

The armistice negotiations remained recessed until after Stalin's death.

It is noteworthy that while negotiations on the demarcation line had resulted in a UN success, those on arrangements for supervising the ceasefire were a failure. The Communists did accept the UN Command's minimum requirements on rotation and replenishment. But they largely foiled its program for inspection and preserving the military balance at the time of the armistice. It is probably no accident that the negotiation of Item 3 took place in a period when military pressure on the Communists had greatly eased. The exact military situation in Korea may have been of only moderate interest to Stalin — as long as the war went on without drastic reverses and the Americans were tied down, he was reasonably content — but it probably had some influence on the Chinese. It cannot be assumed, however, as many later critics of the Truman administration did, that had the Americans continued to take the offensive on the ground during the armistice talks, which would have been unpopular and politically very difficult, if possible at all, the Chinese would have quickly come to terms. Mao himself seems to have been ambivalent about ending the war. And, given Stalin's apparent wish to have the Korean War go on indefinitely or until it merged into World War III, it is by no means clear that anything the Americans could have done in 1951 and 1952, short of implementing MacArthur's program would have forced an end to the war in Korea. The most that can be said is that cutting short offensive operations in 1951, the long delay in switching to a more effective air strategy and insisting on voluntary repatriation made it easier for Stalin to handle the Chinese and keep them fighting. And, although the Communists finally swallowed the American position on repatriation *after* Stalin's death, it was something less than the unalloyed triumph for human rights often supposed. Apart from the difficulty of determining the real wishes of the UN's prisoners of war who were largely controlled by pro- or anti–Communist fanatics among their number rather than their nominal captors, the publicity given to securing freedom of choice for those in UN hands obscured, then and later, the failure to secure the return of the South Korean civilians carried off to the North and ROK prisoners drafted into the North Korean army. And, although it could not be blamed on the UN negotiating position, it was doubtful if many American prisoners were allowed to exercise any choice at all.

17

Stalin's Last Year

The years 1952 and early 1953 saw no dramatic action, except perhaps in the Korean skies. The war and the armistice talks remained stalemated, and the Soviets and their allies did not launch new, overtly aggressive actions. There was little real diplomatic activity between East and West.

But jockeying for position continued, in what Stalin regarded as a "prewar" period or the first, concealed stage of World War III. Stalin redoubled actions aimed at splitting the Western coalition, albeit without much success. The propaganda campaign against the Western powers, aimed at isolating and discrediting the United States as, the leader of the coalition, reached an unprecedented level of shrillness and hysteria. In fact, some began to suspect what Stalin was planning. Although the West had let its rearmament efforts slow down and the Truman Administration had effectively given up winning the Korean War during 1952, there were ominous signs of American impatience with the war's dragging on. While the new Eisenhower administration was not anxious to "expand" the war and took its time to decide what to do, there was a growing feeling in the United States that things were intolerable. Had the Korean War lasted much longer, this might have led to actions that could have dangerously split the Western alliance or an explosion that might have wrecked Stalin's plans—or both.

In February 1952, the propaganda war against the United States and Britain shifted into high gear. What became known as the "Hate America" campaign started with a speech by Ambassador Malik at the UN on February 2. Malik declared that the "Anglo-American bloc" had already begun a world war "by waging war against the peoples of Africa and Asia, who are striving for independence and freedom."

The principal features of the campaign were present from the beginning.

Implicit in Malik's speech were the claims that a world war was already underway, that Western aggression was directed most immediately against the colonies and ex-colonies whose only possible friends and protectors were the Communist powers already fighting Western imperialism in Korea and Southeast Asia, and the total identification of British and American policies—while partly exonerating France, actually the most "reactionary" Western power in colonial matters. The whole amounted to almost a caricature of Lenin's theory of imperialism. As in other things, in his last years Stalin had exaggerated Lenin's ideas and his own practices to their ultimate absurdity.

With Malik's speech, worldwide propaganda against the United States intensified. The Communists revived on a much greater scale earlier charges that the United States was waging biological warfare against North Korea and China. The immediate origins of the biological warfare campaign are still uncertain. The initiative may have been taken by the Chinese. Their field commanders on January 28 had evidently submitted "genuine" reports that disease outbreaks in North Korea might be the result of American attacks. Mao and the Chinese leaders had soon concluded this was incorrect, but decided the idea might nevertheless be useful. The Soviets first announced the actual germ war campaign that began a few weeks later, and wove it into a much larger and elaborate pattern of attack.

On February 18, a Korean-language broadcast of Radio Moscow denounced the Americans for spreading typhus and smallpox in North Korea. (It also accused them of poisoning wells and sending lepers into North Korea, but these quaint stories were soon forgotten.) On February 22, the North Koreans themselves repeated the charge. Zhou Enlai endorsed it on February 24 and sent a protest the next day to the "World Peace Council" (the nominal executive body of the Soviet-controlled "Peace Movement"). The Americans indignantly denied the charge. On March 8, Zhou announced that China too had been attacked by American planes dropping rats, bugs, shellfish and chicken feathers as disease vectors.

These fables were not a bolt from the blue. They had been foreshadowed by earlier claims, going back a year or more. (The point is important because it has sometimes been suggested that the germ war propaganda, or the "Hate America" campaign in general, was a reaction to the American stand on the prisoner of war issue, or, even more absurd, to a February 1952 report of the American House of Representatives that correctly indicted the Soviets as responsible for the Katyn Forest massacre of Polish prisoners.) In 1949, while trying the Japanese officers responsible for biological warfare experiments in China, the Soviets had charged that the Americans were already preparing to use biological weapons and linked them to the Japanese. They hit a sensitive spot here. The Americans had let men responsible for crimes at the experimental stations captured by the Soviets and who had escaped to Japan avoid prosecution in return for information about what had gone on there. There were still earlier precedents. Stalin had long liked to accuse his enemies of using germs and poisons. Some victims of the Great Purge in the 1930s had been accused of plotting to spread anthrax or poison food supplies. As the Cold War intensified, he drew on these fond memories for inspiration. In June 1950, the Soviets accused the Americans of spreading potato beetles over East Germany, Poland and Czechoslovakia to ruin crops. In the spring of 1951, they claimed that the Americans had dropped tree larvae on Eastern Styria in the Soviet Zone of Austria. In 1951 the first tentative accusations of attacks on humans began. On May 5, *Pravda* and *Izvestiya* reported that the Americans had tested germ weapons on Chinese prisoners of war, while on May 8 Pak Hon-yong, the North Korean Foreign Minister, accused the Americans of spreading smallpox in Korea. But these accusations were soon de-emphasized. Moscow may have decided that it was the wrong season of the year to accuse the Americans of spreading disease, or it may have seemed unwise to simultaneously open armistice talks and launch a particularly nasty propaganda campaign.

At any rate, the attack shifted into low gear for a time, with only an occasional outburst. In August 1951, the "Peace Movement" charged the Americans with waging a campaign of extermination in Korea by wantonly destroying towns and food supplies, while Pravda reprinted North Korean accusations that the Americans had used poison gas.[1] The full-blown germ war campaign of 1952 soon ran into difficulty. On March 11, Acheson asked the International Red Cross to investigate the charges. It accepted immediately, and on March 12 sent an offer to investigate to Beijing and Pyongyang. The Chinese and North Koreans did not even reply. On April 23 they refused the World Health Organization's offer of aid. The Communists launched their own "investigation." A well-known "front organization," the International Association of Democratic Lawyers, sent a commission to North Korea. It merely took its hosts' word for what had happened. But the Soviets and Chinese knew they needed "proof" for their claims and pursued a dual line of endeavor to secure it.

At the end of March, the World Peace Council formed an International Scientific Commission (ISC) including Dr. N.N. Zhukov-Verezhnikov, the Vice President of the Soviet Academy of Medical Sciences, and several Western medical men who were all Communist "fellow-travelers."

17. Stalin's Last Year

Anyone who remained in the latter category by 1952 had a strong stomach and was proof against either scruples or evidence. The ISC visited North Korea and Manchuria in July. Its report, published in September, confirmed official claims that American planes had dropped bugs and clams infected with bubonic plague, cholera, typhus and anthrax. There were indications even in the ISC report that the specimens collected were "plants," and it was noticeable that all had been collected in North Korea and at sites along the Soviet-controlled railroads in Manchuria where Soviet disease-control teams had worked since 1946. The Soviets were better equipped than their allies to fabricate such evidence. Like the fact that the public campaign started in Moscow, this seems to suggest that the whole effort was originally a Soviet rather than a Chinese initiative. The ISC report was paralleled by another effort to develop proof by extracting "confessions" from captured American airmen. (This incidentally, is another piece of evidence that in early 1952 the Communist powers, or at least the Soviets, did not want or expect an early armistice in Korea. The early release of the prisoners involved would have been embarrassing.) The methods used dated back to the Great Purges and duplicated those used in contemporary purges in the European satellites. In late February Kenneth Enoch and John Quinn, who had been shot down in January and initially received routine treatment, were accused by their captors of having dropped germ bombs. The Chinese and North Koreans employed the "conveyer" method perfected under Nikolai Yezhov in the 1930s, torture combined with continual interrogation and sleep deprivation until the victim was exhausted and disoriented. Enoch and Quinn were remarkably stubborn, holding out for two months—far more than could reasonably have been expected—before signing "confessions" prepared with the help of the British and Australian traitors Alan Winnington and Wilfred Burchett. Winnington and Burchett prevented Enoch and Quinn, and other Americans, from inserting "jokers" in their confessions that would prove to Americans at least that the confessions were false. The confessions were broadcast from Pyongyang on May 4. Enoch and Quinn were the first of 107 Americans known to have been accused of participating in germ warfare. Of that number 38 broke down and signed confessions, not all of which were used. Amazingly, 40 resisted to the last and never confessed. The other 29 were never heard of again. The Communists may have planned a mass show trial of those who confessed, but such ideas were dropped after Stalin's death.

The confessions were given enormous publicity throughout the world. At least in the West, the germ war propaganda was a failure, gaining no credence outside Communist ranks. In Asia, however, it may have had limited success. It is arguable that, apart from some clumsiness in execution, its only fault was that it was 15 years too early. In the feverish atmosphere of the late 1960s and afterwards, it might have enjoyed more success. Some elements of the Soviet ruling group evidently thought so. In the 1980s they launched a similar but subtler campaign, spreading rumors that the Americans had created the AIDS (HIV) virus to wipe out the people of Africa.

The germ war propaganda was accompanied by other charges of atrocities against Communist prisoners of war that made use of the events at Koje. The Americans were accused of burning 800 men alive on Koje and using 1,400 prisoners as guinea pigs in nuclear tests. "British imperialism" received a few slaps as the British were accused of using poison gas in Malaya.[2]

Soviet propagandists wove all these accusations into the thesis that the Americans were worse than the Nazis and were engaged in a vast genocidal plot. The germ war accusation and the "confessions" of the Americans bore the same relation to Stalin's overall plans in the early 1950s that the claim of a "Trotskyite-Right Opposition-Nazi" conspiracy and the confessions of Bukharin and others had to the Great Purges and plans for the Nazi-Soviet Pact in the 1930s. On June 4, *Pravda* declared that the American military had "surpassed the Hitler brigands by using in Korea such methods of mass destruction as napalm bombs and chemical and germ weapons." Koje was compared unfavorably with the Nazi extermination camp at Maidenek.

G. Alexandrov's article in *Pravda* on June 7, entitled "Malthusian Doctrine and Koje Island" expounded the full-blown thesis behind the "Hate America" campaign. It cleverly linked Western worries about overpopulation (something that had begun to be widely discussed in the late 1940s), conventional Communist denunciations of "Malthusianism," memories of the Morgenthau Plan and the attempt to win over the former Axis powers. There was no real danger of overpopulation, but a decadent capitalist world far gone in its general crisis could not support even the existing world population. The "death island" of Koje and the germ bombs were just pilot projects for a master plan to reduce the world population by eliminating 700 million people. This effort would include reducing the population of Germany by 30 million and that of Japan by 50 million, as well as the destruction of vast numbers of Chinese, Koreans, Vietnamese and Filipinos.[3] (Even the Americans' allies were not safe.)

The implications of this loony view of the world are obvious. If accepted, it was complete justification for war; it even demanded war. The alleged use of germ bombs against China as well as Korea neatly provided a "legal" justification to invoke the Soviet-Chinese alliance when the Soviets wanted to do so. And if Asians and Germans were convinced that the charges against the Americans were true, they would be forced onto the Soviet side in self-defense, regardless of how anti–Communist they were.

The "Hate America" campaign made strangely little impression on the general public and most Western officials. Even before 1952 the tenor of Communist propaganda had become bizarre. Constant denunciations not only of Wall Street and imperialism, but everything Western from jazz to science fiction, were combined with arrogant and absurd claims that everything had been invented or discovered, if not by Russians, at least on the territory of the Soviet Union. Nevertheless, some observers were perturbed and suspicious. Mark Clark and others wondered if the germ war propaganda was a prelude to Communist use of germs in Korea, or even to a world war. Even the hardened and experienced George Kennan was shaken and worried. He later commented that "my arrival in Moscow coincided with a chorus of vituperation, directed against the United States, which for sheer viciousness and intensity had no parallel, as far as I know, in the history of international relations." He was not pleased that Washington took it with "blasé indifference."

Despite his long-standing inclination to play down the danger of the Soviets deliberately starting a war, he wondered on June 6 if it might be an attempt to overcome morale problems. The Kremlin might be steeling the population for some severe test. In a dispatch of July 30, he estimated that the Soviets probably wanted the Korean War to go on, although they might be interested in an arrangement getting both Americans and Chinese forces out of Korea. He believed they genuinely found voluntary repatriation unacceptable. Only increased pressure — short of anything, such as attacks on Manchuria, likely to provoke all-out war — would force its acceptance. He warned that those presently dominant in Soviet councils had taken the position that they would never again have to deal respectfully with non–Communist regimes. In effect, the Soviets had severed diplomatic relations and were not afraid of war. He thought they would like "at this time to avoid it. But they do not fear it, particularly in (the) sphere of strategic bombing as much as we might think they ought to." He blamed this tendency on Malenkov and Beria. (In fact they reversed the policy when they got in the saddle.) On September 8 he judged that the Soviets considered war "quite possible and perhaps likely" although they were not committed to starting one. They did not want war but would accept it with some confidence, while preferring the "partial war." But he admitted this assessment could be too optimistic. It is striking how close Kennan came to the truth. But in the last resort his preconceptions about

Soviet attitudes to war made him shy away from deducing Stalin's decision for war.[4]

The main Soviet diplomatic move of 1952 was an attempt, foreseen by Acheson, to disrupt the agreements on the European Defense Community and the contractual agreements with West Germany.

On March 10, the Soviets sent identical notes to the Western occupying powers. Their tone was an odd contrast to the fantastic campaign of abuse that had started in February. They were unusually civil, avoiding recriminations over Western policies in Germany. The Soviet proposal was largely a rehash of the older Warsaw and Prague Declarations, suggesting the formation of a united neutral Germany with the frontiers supposedly fixed at Potsdam. All foreign troops would leave within a year. But a new feature seemed an abrupt departure from earlier Soviet policy. Germany would be allowed to have its own army, navy and air force, with their size subject to unspecified limitations.

This shocked many in the West, especially in France. It embarrassed the French Communists who had harped on the evils of German rearmament, a position with which many non–Communists in France and elsewhere had had a good deal of sympathy. Yet, this reversal of the Soviet stance should not have been all that surprising, since in 1951 the Soviets had conceded that Japan, the other major ex-enemy, could rearm to some extent.

The Soviet proposal provided for unrestricted peacetime industrial production, as well as guarantees of "democratic rights," full political rights for ex–Nazis, other than war criminals, and banning organizations "inimical to democracy and the maintenance of peace." Acheson and his British and French counterparts were sure these items were "jokers." In practice, the Soviets could interpret them to exclude democrats and stack the government in favor of the Communists—if the Soviets really expected negotiations to result in an agreement, which they doubted. They believed it was nothing more than a delaying ploy. But the note had much popular appeal, not only in Germany. Although allowing a rearmed Germany was a slap in the face for those who disliked German rearmament, there was nevertheless much support in France for four-power discussions on Germany. The British Labour Party, over its leader's opposition, passed a resolution against ratifying the contractual agreements until a four-power conference had taken place.

After careful consultation, the Western powers rejected obliging a united Germany to be neutral or conceding exclusive control of any German armed forces. They pointed out that the Potsdam conference had not in fact fixed Germany's eastern frontier. The focus of the replies, suggested by Foreign Secretary Eden, dealt with the prerequisites for a peace treaty and the mechanics of creating an all–German government that could sign one, which was something the Soviets had not gone into. A UN commission should assure proper conditions for free all–German elections. A bitter exchange of notes resulted, in which the Soviets exploited German criticism of the Adenauer government's reluctance to take up the offer. They offered to discuss free all–German elections, but rejected the UN commission or reconsidering the Potsdam frontiers (which were still controversial in Germany). In a supporting move, the East Germans warned that if the West Germans rearmed there might be a "civil war" or a "new Korea." Public opinion finally forced a reluctant Chancellor Adenauer to speak in favor of four-power talks, though he rejected a neutral rearmed Germany or delaying the arrangements with the Western powers. The EDC and contractual agreements were signed.

In the final analysis, most people in the West regarded the Soviet offer as a trick to delay Western rearmament. Even if it was not, they feared that a rearmed Germany would play both sides against one another, or would be drawn, even against its will, to one side — probably the Soviets. The latter might be harking back to the policy they had favored in the 1920s and 1930s as a second choice after a Communist Germany: an alliance with a reactionary nationalist Germany against the Western powers. But the alleged "missed opportunity" to unite Germany became a bitter source of recrimination in Germany for many years and even enjoyed some currency elsewhere. There was no missed opportunity. Stalin had meant merely to bring down the Adenauer government and arouse German nationalism against the Western powers. And he had no interest in giving up East Germany. It would have been most unlike him to forfeit his grip on something he already had in exchange for the mere hope of gain. The Soviet notes had been cleverly worded to obscure the fact, but there was no real evidence even in the exchanges that the Soviets were ready to hold free elections or allow the formation of an independent German government. The East Germans were actually launching a drastic new program for "building socialism."[5] As usual in German affairs, the overt Soviet negotiating position on Germany was not congruent with what was going on in the zone under their control, and even less compatible with the oft-repeated thesis that Soviet policy was based on mortal fear of renewed German aggression.

To the end, Stalin had great faith in appealing to German and Japanese nationalism and steering these forces against the West, as the last published work attributed to him, *Economic Problems of Socialism*, made clear. Possibly much of it was written by Mikhail Suslov, the prime ideologist for his successors. It was issued in September 1952, shortly before the Nineteenth Party Congress. Much of this dull and confused work was a tribute to Stalin's own genius and a justification of existing economic policies (all-out priority for heavy industry and Party leaders' control of economic decisions, as opposed to enlarging the role of lower-level economic planners).

In foreign affairs, Stalin reaffirmed the doctrine that the world was split into two camps. But he stressed that the Western camp was weak and badly split under the façade of American domination. The Americans were "tumbling downhill toward economic crisis." The "temporary relative stabilization" of capitalism no longer existed. But the other capitalist countries, which the Americans had put "on rations," would not tolerate American domination and oppression endlessly. This applied with particular force to West Germany and Japan. "The major vanquished countries," Stalin remarked, were "now languishing in misery under the jackboot of American imperialism." But "only yesterday these countries were great imperialist powers and were shaking the foundations of the domination of Britain, the USA and France in Europe and Asia. To think that these countries will not try to get on their feet again, will not try to smash the U.S. regime, and force their way to independent development, is to believe in miracles." The possibility of wars between capitalist countries still existed, and he suggestively recounted Germany's course after World War I: "Of course, when the United States and Britain assisted Germany's recovery they did so with a view to setting a recovered Germany against the Soviet Union, to utilizing her against the land of socialism. But Germany directed her forces in the first place against the Anglo-French-American bloc. And when Hitler's Germany declared war against the Soviet Union, the Anglo-French-American bloc, far from joining with Hitler's Germany, was compelled to enter into a coalition with the USSR against Hitler's Germany. Consequently, the struggle of the capitalist countries to crush their competitors proved in practice to be stronger than the contradictions between the capitalist camp and the socialist camp. What guarantee is there, then, that Germany and Japan will not rise to their feet again, will not attempt to break out of American bondage, and live their own independent lives? I think there is no such guarantee."

Oddly, this essay was often read as merely advocating the general thesis that conflicts and wars between capitalist countries were more likely than war between the Soviet bloc and the West, and even misread for this as a rejection of the old Communist thesis that war was inevitable as long as capitalism existed, which Stalin specifically denied. Stalin's absurd remarks about Germany and Japan have often been overlooked. It is likely that the specific predictions were more important than the general theory.[6]

Stalin was not active at the first Party Congress held since 1939. He left the keynote speech to Malenkov and rarely appeared. No radical change in foreign policy took place before his death. Instead, he apparently embarked on plans that logically should have been incompatible with war preparations, including schemes for a new purge and possibly deporting the Jews to Siberia. But he did not live long enough to carry out such plans.

On the night of March 1–2, Stalin apparently suffered a cerebral hemorrhage. He lingered until March 5. Or, possibly, he was murdered.[7] World War III was called off, at least for the time being, on account of a death. And the Korean War was transformed back from the first phase of World War III to "just" a limited war.

18

The End of the War

The American election campaign of 1952 was perhaps exceptionally bitter, although in retrospect there seems to have been no great difference between the two presidential candidates. For perhaps the last time Americans enjoyed a choice between two honest and able men; in later years they would count themselves lucky to have even one running for President. The new president would prove enormously popular, and, perhaps more important, was universally trusted in a way unlike any of his successors. Even the substantial number of liberal Democrats who regarded Eisenhower as a senile old goof who hardly ever did anything right never doubted he was a man of complete integrity.

Discontent over Korea, worry over the adequacy of American foreign policy and the Communist threat, that for part of the public blurred into a wildly exaggerated issue of internal security, played an important part in Eisenhower's victory. There were many signs during the campaign of American impatience with the situation. Eisenhower cleverly played on this with his famous, if non-committal and empty promise, "I will go to Korea."

Eisenhower's nomination represented a rejection, indeed the final downfall, of the Republican's isolationist wing. But his election was neither an endorsement of the continuation of Truman' policies nor a complete repudiation of them. During the campaign, the Republicans presented themselves as the tougher of the two parties on the Cold War, and talked of "liberating" East-Central Europe. But when analyzed their position reduced to a stronger insistence on European integration, more emphasis on Asia and vague talk of a more "dynamic" policy. "Liberation" — a theme emphasized by incoming Secretary of State Dulles far more than Eisenhower — was to be a "peaceful" process, with support for Tito and similar figures at least an initial stage. In fact, at the edges, "liberation" blurred

18. The End of the War

into the most distinctive, but also most secret aspect of Dulles' policies—a renewed and greater stress on driving a wedge between the Soviets and the Chinese. He did not envision a return to the strategy pursued before the Korean War of trying to persuade the Chinese that the Americans were basically friendlier to them than the Soviets were. Instead, as he had explained in a letter to Chester Bowles in March 1952, he intended to follow the opposite line and split the enemy alliance by bringing maximum pressure to bear on the weaker partner, making China's way as hard as possible as long as it was allied to the Soviets. Tito, he noted, had not broken with Stalin because the United States had been nice to him. Given Mao's mentality, this analysis was even truer for China than it had been for Yugoslavia.

Dulles' policy worked faster than he had expected, although he would not live to see how right he was. In other respects, contrary to what is often supposed, the Eisenhower-Dulles policies were not a major departure from those of the Truman administration. There is little justification for the common idea that there was a greater "militarization" of policy than under Truman or that American commitments were greatly extended under Eisenhower. So far was the new administration from seeking a drastic break with the immediate past that it did not even draw up a new formal policy statement (NSC-162/2,) to replace NSC-135 until the president had been in office for most of a year.[1]

When Eisenhower took office, ending the Korean War remained the most immediate problem for American policy. But he had no fixed plan, merely the intention to conclude peace on "honorable terms" without major fighting if possible. But if the Communists remained refractory, he might have to expand the war.

This was by no means a new idea. The Truman administration, even after the MacArthur hearings, had continued to contemplate proposals to expand the war or at least drop the restrictions accepted in late 1950. (It has already been noted how restrictions were lifted on bombing Rashin and later the hydroelectric plants and other targets near the Soviet Union and China.) Popular support for a stronger course remained considerable. In July 1951, the Joint Chiefs of Staff had recommended lifting some restrictions and bombing and blockading China if the armistice talks failed. There was growing confidence in late 1951 and 1952 in the military and the CIA, although less so in the State Department, that the Soviets would not go to war if China was attacked, as long as Communist rule there was not threatened. Churchill agreed with this view and favored bombing but not blockading China if the armistice talks failed completely. The CIA, unlike Ambassador Kennan, thought that the Soviets did want an armistice. During 1952, there was also growing readiness to use Chinese Nationalist troops in Korea, which the head of the military advisory group on Taiwan thought was now feasible. In May 1952, Mark Clark requested the dispatch of two Nationalist divisions. He also favored expanding the ROK Army. In September, Washington approved building it up to 12 divisions. After taking office, Eisenhower approved a further expansion to 14 divisions.[2]

The Communist powers, for their part, were well aware of American impatience. In late 1952 the Chinese concluded there would be an attack in 1953, mainly amphibious and probably against the west coast of Korea, and built up their defenses there. They doubted, however, that the Americans would employ nuclear weapons, at least on a large scale. Stalin told Mao on December 27 that his anxieties about an attack in the spring were correct, but that it was quite possible that Eisenhower would change these plans, although Mao was right to "count on the worst." He indicated, however, that Mao's latest request for military supplies in 1953 were impossible to fulfill. Only one-fourth of what he asked for could be provided.[3]

In its last months, the Truman administration had already tried bluffing the enemy into agreement. The CIA spread rumors that the Americans planned to carry the war to China if peace was not concluded. The Joint Chiefs had asked Mark Clark to consider plans for future operations with all restrictions removed except for attacks on the USSR, or the use of nuclear or chemical weapons.

Clark personally favored a drive to the Yalu. But he warned that an offensive would require considerable reinforcements, as well as lifting restrictions on operations against China. In October 1952 he produced plans for a drive to the Pyongyang-Wonsan line in three phases lasting 20 days each. Aside from air and naval action against China, this would require reinforcements of three American or other UN divisions, two more ROK divisions, two Chinese Nationalist divisions, 12 artillery and 20 antiaircraft battalions. Clark favored the use of tactical nuclear weapons, but held that this was not essential to his plan. But when Eisenhower visited his command in December, he showed no interest and did not even let Clark give him a detailed briefing. Clark realized that Eisenhower did not intend to win the war if he could help it. During his visit to Korea, Eisenhower avoided association with Rhee. He only agreed to meet the South Korean dictator after it was pointed out that Koreans would regard it as an insult if he did not.

Eisenhower worked up to a threat to expand the war slowly and cautiously. On February 2, 1953, he announced that the "neutralization" of the Taiwan Strait had been ended, leaving the Nationalists free to attack the mainland of China. In fact, the Nationalists had been conducting raids on the coast with American help since 1951, without much apparent result. The so-called "unleashing" of Jiang Jieshi was not followed by increased activity, although Eisenhower's announcement caused much unhappiness in both allied and neutral countries.

The administration considered unilaterally releasing non-repatriate prisoners or alternatively expanding the war. Eisenhower and Dulles were sure that an offensive would require using tactical nuclear weapons, as well as attacks outside Korea. The Secretary of State deplored the fact that nuclear weapons had been put in a special category as particularly bad; he regarded this a success for Soviet propaganda. Unlike Eisenhower, he favored a drive to the waist of Korea although as in 1950 he regarded going all the way to the Yalu as too provocative to the Soviets and Chinese. On March 6, he told Foreign Secretary Eden that, while the United States had not decided on its course of action, he favored an advance to the waist. Eden was surprisingly agreeable as long as the British were consulted in advance.

The military was not particularly enthusiastic about the effect of nuclear weapons in Korea, suspecting the Communists were just too well dug in for them to have a dramatic effect. All intelligence estimates rated the enemy position in Korea as extremely strong, and the CIA believed that blockading and bombing China would not in themselves make the enemy accept a settlement on UN terms.

NSC-147, an analysis issued on April 2 of possible courses of action in Korea, examined alternatives ranging from continuing the present course while trying to replace American units with ROK divisions, to an all-out drive to unite Korea that included attacks on China (NSC-147 excluded the consideration of using nuclear weapons or Chinese Nationalist forces). The study made clear that any effective course required more American forces and building up the ROK Army (a move already planned.) A drive to the waist would involve heavy losses and going to the Yalu would be even bloodier. The maximum effort involved in the last would require five more U.S. divisions or the equivalent, two more bomber groups and four and a third fighter wings, and two more aircraft carriers. An offensive to the waist alone would take nine to twelve months to prepare. Since the UN Command was unlikely to start a major offensive in winter, this meant that decisive action could not begin until the spring of 1954. The American people, it was thought, would probably support any vigorous course of action, but most UN members and even America's allies would be reluctant to support anything stronger than increased pressure in Korea itself. NSC-147 was not fully conclusive since it excluded consideration of some factors that could be favorable to an offensive, but it pointed up the difficulties involved. State Department officials warned that expanding the war beyond Korea would gravely strain the Western alliance. Dulles and his deputy, Walter Bedell Smith, seem to have been alone among top officials in favoring an advance to the waist of Korea. Dulles felt it was necessary to give the Chinese a "licking" to impress Asia. He wanted to reopen discussion of armistice provisions settled earlier, but Eisenhower warned that even Americans would not stand for that. During May, the military warned that none of the courses of action involving operations outside Korea could be carried out without nuclear weapons (pointing to serious limitations in the process that had produced NSC-147) and reaffirmed the conclusion reached as far back as 1950 that there were no good targets for them in Korea itself. On May 19, the Joint Chiefs recommended that, if the war dragged on there should be a drive to the waist, using nuclear weapons and begun with maximum surprise.[4] But by then the issue seemed increasingly academic. The administration's consideration of stronger measures was overtaken by Stalin's death and changes on the enemy side.

The Turn in the Communist World

The Cold War was a gigantic clash between social systems, but the very concentration of power in the leadership of the Communist world meant that the life and death of individual dictators—in 1924, 1953 and 1985—could mean far more than any change in leadership in the West.

With Stalin's demise the triumvirate of Malenkov, Beria and Khrushchev took over the Soviet government. But Khrushchev, the final winner of the succession struggle, soon became General Secretary of the Communist Party. Stalin's plans for war lapsed with his death. There were clear changes in course in foreign policy and much else. Even had the new ruling group been inclined to carry on Stalin's policies, they were too busy fighting among themselves and even feared a popular upheaval. The first and most violent part of the succession struggle did not end until Beria's arrest in July. In true Stalinist style, it was "discovered' that he had been an "imperialist agent" since 1920.

The new leaders did, however, quickly agree to end the Korean War. Zhou Enlai, in Moscow for Stalin's funeral, readily concurred with the idea, which was officially registered in a resolution of the Soviet Council of Ministers on March 19. The verbose declaration admitted that it was necessary to change the line previously followed, but tried to obscure (while making the point), that the Communist side had to cave in on the question of voluntary repatriation.

The Chinese and North Koreans were bluntly informed that it was urgent to start by giving a favorable answer to the UN Command's recent proposal to exchange sick and wounded prisoners. Supporting moves by the Communist governments must follow to indicate that they were now

18. The End of the War

ready to resolve the whole prisoner question. The Panmunjom talks must resume. There were signs of haste, even perhaps panic, in Soviet actions related to Korea in the late winter and spring of 1953, as though Stalin's successors (or killers?) were terrified by how close he had come to launching a disastrous world war. They may have been scared enough by the possibility that the actions the United States was considering might snowball out of control. They began pulling Soviet air units out of Korean combat with what the Chinese might well have considered unseemly haste. During April, they also abruptly ended the germ war campaign. The latter was also entangled with the succession struggle. S.D. Ignatiev, the Minister of State Security who had been Stalin's tool in his plans for purge (but who also happened to be a protégé of Khrushchev), was fired for, among other things, falsely reporting to the Soviet government that the germ war charges were true. The Soviet Ambassador to North Korea was sacked for the same reason. Both men were obviously scapegoats for policies decreed by Stalin and Mao. The particular charges against them remained secret, but it is possible that, had the international situation gotten worse, they might have been sacrificed in a public trial to placate the Western powers.

On March 15, Malenkov made remarks that indicated a desire to reduce tensions. This was shortly followed by an open change in the Communist stand on the prisoner issue in Korea. In quick succession, the "Doctor's Plot" that had formed the background to Stalin's plans for a purge was denounced as a fraud. *Pravda*, without attacking Stalin directly, criticized the "cult of personality" that had surrounded him. A "new course" was set in economic affairs. Some consumer goods prices were cut, and more lenient policies adopted toward the peasants. The new rulers were aware of the crisis in Soviet agriculture and even alluded to it publicly. This was the start of a general liberalization that took clearer shape under Khrushchev. The extremes of one-man tyranny, terror and purges that had marked Stalin's rule ended. Amnesties began reducing the slave labor empire.

Over the next few months, "New Course" policies were extended to the satellites. The East German leaders tergiversations about copying the new Soviet polices led to an uprising on June 17, and there were disturbances in other satellites. The Soviets soon renounced Stalin's territorial claims against Turkey, reestablished relations with Israel (broken in 1952) and let Russian women who had married Westerners leave the USSR.[5] The Soviet rulers avoided further internal upheavals and settled into a stable (perhaps too stable) regime. To be sure, they remained highly aggressive. Khrushchev's policies would sometimes be bolder than Stalin had been, at least before 1951.

The Armistice Talks Resume

On February 22, pursuing a proposal advanced by the International Red Cross, General Clark had written directly to the Communist commanders to propose an exchange of sick and wounded prisoners. On March 28, rather to his surprise, they replied favorably. On March 30, Zhou Enlai said that prisoners of war who did not want repatriation could be handed over to a neutral state. On April 11, liaison officers arranged the exchange of sick and wounded men. The exchange, named "Little Switch," took place between April 20 and May 3. The UN Command thought the number of men handed over by the Communists— 684 — was incredibly small, but 6,670 Chinese and North Koreans were exchanged.

A final settlement took time as the two sides circled about the issues. The Communists wished to save face by obscuring their about-face on repatriation and maximize their chances to persuade their men to return. The Americans were cautious, and naturally suspicious.

The Communists also planned actions at the front to secure the best possible demarcation line. They had expected an amphibious landing behind their lines. Once Mao decided that the UN forces would not attack, he resolved on April 3 to launch a final offensive of his own in June. The Communists began transferring troops from the coasts to the front. Local attacks were undertaken in April. One of these led to the famous battle of Pork Chop Hill. Pork Chop, an outpost just in front of an important part of I Corps defense line near the Iron Triangle, was held by an understrength company of the U.S. 7th Division. On April 16–17, a Chinese assault overran most of the hill. After bitter fighting, including the biggest artillery bombardments of the entire war, the Americans recaptured the hill.

Full sessions of the armistice talks resumed on April 26. The Communists initially wanted all non-repatriates shipped to a neutral state. They would be held there for six months during which efforts could be made to persuade them to accept repatriation. Their final disposition would be settled only by a post-armistice political conference. The Americans considered six months an excessive period, wanted a neutral country to take custody of the non-repatriates in Korea itself, and did not want to leave them hostage to the results, if any, of a political conference.

On May 7, the Communists made more concessions. The prisoners could stay in Korea and the period in which they could be held for persuasion was cut to four months. A Neutral Nations Repatriation Commission would take custody of the prisoners. The negotiations now revolved about a time limit on deciding the non-repatriates' disposition and decision-making procedures for the Commission. The Communists began to dig in their heels when the UN Command argued for an early release of Korean non-repatriates and limiting the period of detention to 60 days. These demands, partly made to placate Rhee, were widely questioned in the West. It seemed that an impasse was again developing.[6]

But the Chinese were under growing pressure. The Soviets were pulling out. After May 8, their airmen withdrew from combat. The less-experienced Chinese MIG pilots were slaughtered. Although with the end of the war approaching the U.S. Air Force loosened the normal standards for evaluating victory claims, there is no doubt that a great many MIGs went down for very small American losses. In one month 77 MIGs were counted destroyed while no American planes were lost. By the end of the war, the Americans had destroyed 345 Soviet MIGs and 224 flown by Chinese pilots (North Korean losses are unknown but probably were not very numerous). Just 103 F-86s had been lost. Although the actual ratio of air losses was not as favorable as the 11 to 1 or even 14 to put forward by optimistic sources after the war, it was still a great achievement for a small air force whose planes did not enjoy a vast advantage in performance, and which was always greatly outnumbered.

On May 13, the Americans after long consideration began attacking the irrigation dams that provided water for the North Korean rice crop. (In September 1952 British carrier planes had already attacked the sluice gates at the mouths of some North Korean rivers, a secondary component of the irrigation system.) There were considerable qualms about the morality of attacking the dams, and the Americans embarked on it on a small scale and with mental reservations. Only those dams whose destruction would flood critical railroad lines were attacked. Fighter-bombers smashed two dams in quick succession, causing tremendous devastation. A third dam was damaged, but saved from destruction by lowering the water level, which meant a smaller rice crop. Had several dams been attacked at the same time, even that inadequate countermeasure would not have prevented a disaster. The air pressure strategy had finally found a decisive target. Had the admittedly brutal measure of blasting the dams been undertaken a year or more earlier, the enemy might have been faced with an insupportable burden of supplying both their armies and the Korean civilian population with food brought from outside Korea.[7]

At the diplomatic level, the Americans began to deploy the threat of an expanded war, which many would wrongly believe was decisive in bringing it to an end. On May 22, Dulles told Nehru that the war would be expanded unless an armistice came soon. Dulles expected Nehru to pass this on to the Chinese. (He denied doing so, which is hard to believe.) Charles Bohlen, now the American Ambassador in Moscow, conveyed a similar hint to Soviet Foreign Minister Molotov on May 28. On June 3, Molotov indicated orally that the Soviets had persuaded the Chinese and North Koreans to accept the American view. The Americans settled on a "final position" that was presented at Panmunjom on May 25. It offered minor concessions to the Communists. They would have more time to persuade non-repatriates to return, and all non-repatriates would go to neutral custody. Over the next two weeks, the Communists accepted the UN position after some slight revisions. On June 8, the armistice was largely settled, except for the final demarcation line. The Communists did not accept a proposal that the line agreed on in November 1951 be used.

If anyone thought the war was going to end without more bloodshed, they were overly optimistic.

Mao had given the final go-ahead for a last offensive during the UN stalemate. Some attacks had been already been made on the American 25th Division in late May, but the UN concession on May 25 led him to shift the target to the ROKs. On June 10, the final offensive began against ROK II Corps on the east-central front. The Chinese pushed down the Pukhan valley where the ROK line formed a shallow salient. The offensive ended on June 16 after capturing some territory, although the ROKs performed better than they had in 1951.

By now, the UN Command was more worried about the ROKs than for them. The South Koreans, and here Rhee really spoke for his people, had bitterly opposed an armistice all along. They wanted an all-out offensive and victory. Rhee threatened to withdraw from the UN Command. Even granting the need for an armistice, he disliked the role given India as chairman of the Neutral Nations Repatriation Commission and objected to turning Korean non-repatriates over to the custodians. He intended to acquiesce only after extracting the maximum political, military and economic price from the Americans. He had long wanted a bilateral defense pact and a vast expansion of his army. (The Americans favored this but considered it prudent to defer forming more ROK divisions until after the armistice.) The Americans feared that Rhee might be crazy enough to carry out his threats to attack independently and laid plans to seize him to prevent this. They were not sure whether he was bluffing or mad, or both. Despite pledges of aid, Rhee continued to threaten to disregard the armistice. On June 7, he demanded limits on the projected political discussions that included barring Indian and Communist representatives from South Korea, expansion of his armed forces and a mutual security pact with the United States. He ordered ROK officers in the United States to return home and refused to visit Washington for high-level talks. There was an element of the ludicrous in the gaga dictator of a weak ally

18. The End of the War

trying to dictate to the United States, but no one at the time thought it was funny. The warnings of those who had forecast endless trouble if Rhee was not dealt with in 1952 were being fully borne out.

On June 18, after Rhee refused to consent to the armistice in return for aid and a mutual security pact, ROK guards let 25,000 North Korean prisoners who opposed repatriation break out of their camps. They melted into the civilian population and could not be recovered. There was an explosion of rage at Rhee throughout the world—curiously far greater than any anger at the Communists for their last-minute offensive—and widespread fear that the armistice arrangements would crumble.

But, after an embarrassing session at Panmunjom at which the Communists asked some pointed questions, it became clear that this would not happen. Indeed, as Charles Bohlen and others noted, Rhee's actions, even if motivated by the desire to cause the war to go on, strongly suggested that the prisoner of war problem could have been solved much earlier simply by opening the gates of the POW camps. Some of the anger at Rhee may even have stemmed from chagrin at seeing the Gordian knot cut by the senile and irascible South Korean ruler.

The unpleasant sessions at Panmunjom were followed by unpleasant sessions with Rhee. He seemed shaken by the reactions to what he had done, and the Americans began to bring pressure to bear. But Rhee still tried to bargain. He finally promised not to obstruct the armistice in return for a mutual security pact, long-term military and economic aid, and an agreement that the Americans and South Koreans would pull out of the postwar political conference within 90 days if nothing was accomplished. He could probably have gained all that without tactics calculated to rouse such hostility.

Moreover, the Communists felt they had a score to settle with him. On June 24, the Chinese renewed the offensive against the ROKs on the east—central front. They had probably been inclined to this all along. Heavy fighting lasted through July 20. The final Chinese effort broke through the ROKs holding the right of the U.S. IX Corps front, wrecking the ROK Capital Division and hurting others. They also hit elements of the American front, and the Americans gave up Pork Chop Hill. A true breakthrough was probably impossible with the Communist artillery immobilized in tunnels, but they had inflicted nearly 53,000 casualties in June and July, mostly on the South Koreans.. The Chinese leaders were pleased they had "straightened out" their front, even at heavy cost to both sides. Nevertheless, the armistice was duly signed on July 27, going into effect 12 hours later. The Communists violated it almost immediately, bringing more weapons, especially aircraft, into North Korea and holding back a number of American prisoners until 1955.[8] The postwar political conference held in 1954 predictably failed to solve the Korean problem. Korea was completely overshadowed by the problem of Indochina. Nevertheless, despite many ugly incidents, the armistice has lasted to the present.

Along with the death of Stalin, the Korean armistice brought the first phase of the Cold War to an end. World War III had been avoided, perhaps by a narrow margin. But whether the world had really been saved or only spared for a worse fate, only the future could tell.

Notes

Chapter 1

1. William Stueck, *The Road to Confrontation* (Chapel Hill: University of North Carolina Press, 1981); Robert Blum, *Drawing the Line* (New York: Norton, 1982); Gordon Chang, *Friends and Enemies* (Stanford: Stanford University Press, 1990), pp. 3–75; Chen Jian, *China's Road to the Korean War* (New York: Columbia University Press, 1994), pp. 45–49; Tang Tsou, *America's Failure in China 1941–1950* (Chicago: University of Chicago Press, 1963). John Lewis Gaddis, *The Long Peace* (New York: Oxford University Press, 1987), pp. 72–95, 149–167. This gives the best brief survey of the wedge strategy.

2. Chen, *China's Road to the Korean War*, pp. 10–12, 19–22, 36–44, 64–68, 71–72; 78–84; Michael Sheng, *Battling Western Imperialism* (Princeton: Princeton University Press, 1997); Vojtech Mastny, *The Cold War and Soviet Insecurity* (New York: Oxford University Press, 1996), pp. 85–90, 93; Vladislav Zubok and Constantine Pleshakov, *Inside the Kremlin's Cold War* (Cambridge: Harvard University Press, 1996), pp. 56–65; Sergei N. Goncharov, John W. Lewis, Xue Litai, *Uncertain Partners* (Stanford: Stanford University Press, 1993), pp. 14, 22, 31, 42–43, 46, 48–49, 87–97; Shu Guang Zhang, *Mao's Military Romanticism: China and the Korean War 1950–1953* (Lawrence: University of Kansas Press, 1995), pp. 10–20, 33, 35, 38–41. Sheng makes the strongest case that Soviet-Chinese Communist differences have been wildly exaggerated, or even invented. Most other historians see at least somewhat more conflict in their relationship, and there are considerable differences among serious scholars in evaluating the Soviet-Chinese relationship in 1949–1950. It is noteworthy that Russian historians seem to take a more cynical view of Stalin's attitude to Mao than Chinese or Chinese-American scholars do.

3. Zubok and Pleshakov, *Inside the Kremlin's Cold War*, 73; Goncharov, Lewis, Xue, *Uncertain Partners*, 109, 212; Kathryn Weathersby, "Soviet Aims in Korea and the Origins of the Korean War," *Cold War International History Project Working Paper Number 8*, pp. 44–45. For perceptive comments on Stalin's mentality in his later years, see George F. Kennan, *Russia and the West Under Lenin and Stalin* (New York: New American Library, 1961), p. 361. Interesting speculations on Stalin's aims in 1950 emphasizing their possible anti-Chinese aspects can be found in Weathersby; a view foreshadowed in Adam Ulam's *The Rivals* (New York: Viking Press, 1971). A more extreme version of the thesis suggested by Weathersby and Ulam can be found in Richard C. Thornton, *Odd Man Out* (Washington: Brassey's 2000), embedded in other, more bizarre conspiracy theories.

Chapter 2

1. *Foreign Relations of the United States 1950, Volume V* (Washington: Government Printing Office, 1978), pp. 509-518. After the first reference, *Foreign Relations* volumes will be abbreviated as FRUS with date and volume number

2. Richard Rhodes, *Dark Sun* (New York: Simon and Schuster, 1995); Richard G. Hewlett and Francis Duncan, *Atomic Shield* (University Park, Pennsylvania: Pennsylvania University Press, 1969) pp. 369-409.

3. *Foreign Relations of the United States 1950, Volume I*, (Washington: Government Printing Office 1977), pp. 142-143, 145-147, 160-167, 234-293, 312-313; *Foreign Relations of the United States 1950* Volume IV, (Washington: Government Printing Office 1980), pp. 1075-1077; 1099-1101, 1150-1154, 1164-1183; John Lewis Gaddis, *Strategies of Containment* (New York: Oxford University Press, 1982), pp. 90-109; Royal Institute for International Affairs, *Documents on International Affairs, 1950*, (London: Oxford University Press, 1951), pp. 96-116; Eric F. Goldman, *The Crucial Decade and After* (New York: Vintage 1960), pp. 134-136; Samuel Stouffer, *Communism, Conformity and Civil Liberties* (Garden City: Doubleday, 1954); Robert Griffith, *The Politics of Fear* (Lexington, Kentucky: University of Kentucky Press, 1970), pp. 123-130, 195-263; Earl Latham, *The Communist Controversy in Washington* (Cambridge: Harvard University Press, 1965), pp. 393, 406-411.

4. Goncharov, Lewis, Xue, *Uncertain Partners*, pp. 9-10; George McCune, *Korea Today* (Cambridge: Harvard University Press, 1950), pp. 46-48; Gregory Henderson, *Korea* (Cambridge: Harvard University Press, 1968), pp. 114-120; Robert A. Scalapino and Chong-sik Lee, *Communism in Korea* (Berkeley: University of California Press, 1972), pp. 231-247. Cf. Dae-sook Suh, *The Korean Communist Movement* (Princeton: Princeton University Press, 1967), pp. xi, 253, 297-299, 301-302. A much different revisionist interpretation of postwar Korea is given in Bruce Cumings, *Origins of the Korean War* (Princeton: Princeton University Press, 1981). This writer finds it difficult to relate Cumings account of events in South Korea to other sources, and impossible to relate his account of North Korea to any other source.

5. James F. Schnabel, *Policy and Direction: The First Year* (Washington: Office of Chief of Military History, 1972), pp. 8-11; John Lewis Gaddis, " Korea in American Politics, Strategy and Diplomacy 1945-1950" in *The Origins of the Cold War in East Asia* edited by Yohosuke Nagai and Akira Iriye (New York: Columbia University Press, 1977), pp. 277-278; Charles Dobbs, *The Unwanted Symbol* (Kent, Ohio: Kent State University Press, 1981), pp. 17-31; Peter Lowe, *The Origins of the Korean War*, second edition (New York: Longman, 1997), pp. 13-20.

6. *Foreign Relations of the United States 1946, Volume VIII* (Washington: Government Printing Office 1969), pp. 616, 640-642; Scalapino and Lee, *Communism in Korea*, pp. 283, 311-320, 323-329, 332-358, 390-391, 921-923, 926; Suh, The *Korean Communist Movement*, pp. 312-314, 316-321; Koon Woon Nam, The *North Korean Communist Leadership* (University of Alabama Press, 1974), pp. 13, 51; Chen, *China's Road to the Korean War*, pp. 107-109; Goncharov, Lewis, Xue, *Uncertain Partners*, pp. 131-134.

7. McCune, *Korea Today*, pp. 46-50, 93, 114, 123-125, 268-270; Henderson, *Korea*, pp. 120-133, 136-151, 153-160; A.Wigfall Green *The Epic of Korea* (Washington: Public Affairs Press, 1950), pp. 51-105; Grant Meade, *American Military Government in Korea* (New York: King's Crown Press, 1951); Scalapino and Lee, *Communism in Korea*, pp. 264, 269-270, 272; Lowe, *The Origins of the Korean War*, pp. 22-36.

8. *Foreign Relations of the United States 1945* Volume II (Washington: Government Printing Office, 1967), pp. 618-619, 627, 641-643, 696-700; Carl Berger, *The Korea Knot* (Philadelphia: University of Pennsylvania Press, 1957), pp. 55-64; Dobbs, *The Unwanted Symbol*, pp. 33-67.

9. *FRUS 1946 Vol. VIII*, pp. 614, 628-632, 640-642, 645-646, 648-652, 658-659; Scalapino and Lee, *Communism in Korea*, pp. 233-235, 237-245, 249-254, 262-265, 268-273, 276-285; Suh, The *Korean Communist Movement*, pp. 300-302, 304; Koon Woon Nam, The *North Korean Communist Leadership*, pp. 72-75; Berger, *The Korea Knot*, p. 66; McCune, *Korea Today*, p. 50; Dobbs, *The Unwanted Symbol*, pp. 52, 71-76.

Notes—Chapter 2

Yo Un-hyong often appears in Western accounts as "Lyuh Woon Hyung."

10. *FRUS 1946, Vol. VIII*, pp. 617–621, 623–630, 641–642, 645–646, 652–654, 657–666, 669–670; Berger, *The Korea Knot*, pp. 62–68.

11. *FRUS 1946 Vol. VIII*, pp. 687–689, 699–703, 720–723, 730–731, 754–756, 766, 768; Scalapino and Lee, *Communism in Korea*, pp. 281–285, 287–288, 290–302; Charles B. McLane, *Soviet Policy and the Chinese Communists* (New York: Columbia University Press, 1958), p. 252; Herbert Feis, *Contest Over Japan* (New York: Norton 1969), pp. 130–131.

12. *FRUS 1946, Vol. VIII*, pp. 687–689, 715–716, 726–729, 743, 770, 772, 774–778, 785–786; *Foreign Relations of the United States 1947, Volume VI* (Washington: Government Printing Office, 1972), pp. 653, 707–709, 711, 747–751, 852; McCune, *Korea Today*, pp. 73–84, 86–95, 244; Dobbs, *The Unwanted Symbol*, pp. 44–46. 86–92.

13. *FRUS 1947, Volume VI*, pp. 632–635, 640–643, 648–651, 655–657, 682–683, 700–707, 743, 757–760; *Foreign Relations of the United States 1948, Volume VI* (Washington: Government Printing Office, 1973), pp. 1164–1170; Dobbs, *The Unwanted Symbol*, pp. 98–152; Stueck, *The Road to Confrontation*, pp. 75–79, 86–87; Berger, *The Korea Knot*, pp. 72–81, 84–99; McCune, *Korea Today*, pp. 68–79, 137–149, 223–270; Scalapino and Lee, *Communism in Korea*, pp. 305–312; Gaddis, " Korea in American Politics, Strategy and Diplomacy 1945–1950," pp. 277–298; Robert K. Sawyer, *KMAG: Military Advisors in Korea* (Washington: Department of the Army, 1962), pp. 13–17, 28–29; Schnabel, *Policy and Direction*, pp. 30–33. Glenn D. Paige, "Korea," in *Communism and Revolution*, edited by Cyril Black and Thomas Thornton (Princeton: Princeton University Press, 1964), pp. 223–227.

14. Stueck, *The Road to Confrontation*, pp. 104–111, 151–159; Berger, *The Korea Knot*, p. 90; Martin Caidin, *The Fork-Tailed Devil* (New York: Ballantine, 1971), p. 174; D. Clayton James, *The Years of MacArthur, Volume III* (Boston: Houghton Mifflin, 1985), pp. 397–401; Schnabel, *Policy and Direction*, pp. 30, 33–35.

15. *FRUS 1947, Volume VI*, pp. 745, 843–846; Scalapino and Lee, *Communism in Korea*, pp. 284, 300–301, 926; *New York Times*, October 25, 1947, p. 6; *North Korea: A Case Study in Communist Takeover* (Washington: Government Printing Office, 1961), pp. 16–17; Kathryn Weathersby, " New Findings on the Korean War," *Cold War International History Project Bulletin* No. 3 (Fall 1993), Kathryn Weathersby, "To Attack or Not to Attack? Stalin, Kim Il Sung, and the Prelude to War," *Cold War International History Project Bulletin No. 5*, Weathersby, *Soviet Aims in Korea and the Origins of the Korean War*; Evgueni Bajanov, "Assessing the Politics of the Korean War, 1949–1951," *Cold War International History Project Bulletin* No. 6–7; Sawyer *KMAG*, p. 105.

16. Chen, *China's Road to the Korean War*, pp. 87–88, 101; Goncharov, Lewis, Xue, *Uncertain Partners*, pp. 99–105, 135–142, 149–154; Shu Guang Zhang, *Mao's Military Romanticism*, pp. 44–45; Zubok and Pleshakov, *Inside the Kremlin's Cold War*, pp. 62–63; Weathersby, "New Findings on the Korean War" pp. 1–10; Weathersby, "To Attack or Not to Attack?" pp. 1–10, 12–13; Weathersby, *Soviet Aims in Korea and the Origins of the Korean War*, pp. 23–37; "New Russian Documents on the Korean War" pp. 2–3, 10–14; Dieter Heinzig, "Stalin, Mao and Cold War Origins," *Cold War International History Project Bulletin, Number 6–7*; Nikita Khrushchev, *Khrushchev Remembers* (Boston: Little, Brown, 1970), pp. 366–373.

17. Kathryn Weathersby ("New Findings on the Korean War") and Goncharov, Lewis and Xue have argued that the Korean War was at least partly, if not mainly, aimed at China, and that Stalin expected, or at least hoped, that the Americans would react to the attack in Korea by protecting Taiwan. Elsewhere, Professor Weathersby has suggested that Stalin may have taken the view that given the attitude of Rhee, as well as his own puppets, war in Korea was inevitable and that it was not unlikely that the balance would turn in favor of the South with its bigger population. Therefore it was advisable for the Communists to strike while they could still win.

It has occasionally been argued that since Kim suggested the attack on South Korea, the war was really a "civil war" not a Soviet initiative in the Cold War. It is difficult to take this idea seriously. Kim may have sold

Stalin on the idea of a war, but he was also well aware that he ran North Korea at Stalin's pleasure. As he himself said when talking to Shtykov, Stalin's word was law. It is difficult to regard a war he had to ask permission to launch as a genuine civil war; and the very existence of his regime was the product of Soviet intervention. Contrary to bizarre theories common in the 1970s and 1980s, the Soviet documents make clear that, whatever he was later, Kim was a Soviet puppet in the period covered by this book.

Richard C. Thornton in *Odd Man Out* propounds—along with the bizarre argument that the U.S. government was well aware in advance of the North Korean attack—the thesis that Stalin planned the North Korean attack to fail. His aim was to draw the United States into outright war with China in Korea as well as get it to deny Taiwan to Mao. It is difficult to reconcile this thesis with well established facts, and it seems that Stalin was in fact badly shaken when the Americans entered the Korean War.

18. Goncharov, Lewis, Xue, *Uncertain Partners*, pp. 109, 212; David Holloway, *Stalin and the Bomb* (New Haven: Yale University Press, 1994), pp. 239-246, 250, 264, 270. Steve Zaloga, *Target America* (Novato, California: Presidio Press, 1993), pp. 77, 79-86.

19. Robert A. Scalapino, *The Japanese Communist Movement* (Berkeley: University of California Press, 1967), pp. 60-67, 79-81, 84; Paul Langer and Rodger Swearingen, *Red Flag in Japan* (Cambridge: Harvard University Press, 1952), pp. 200-215; Toshio Tsukahira, *The Postwar Evolution of Communist Strategy in Japan* (Cambridge: MIT, 1954), pp. 50-72; Peter Calvocoressi, *Survey of International Affairs 1949-1950* (London: Oxford University Press, 1953), p. 44.

20. Bela K. Kiraly, "The Aborted Soviet Military Plans Against Tito's Yugoslavia," in *At the Brink of War and Peace*, edited by Wayne C. Vucinich (New York: Brooklyn College Press, 1982), pp. 273-281; Bela K. Kiraly, "Military Aspects," in *The Hungarian Revolution of 1956 in Retrospect*, edited by Bela K. Kiraly and Paul Jonas (Boulder: East European Quarterly, 1977), pp. 61-62.

21. Roy Appleman, *From the Naktong to the Yalu* (Washington: Department of the Army, 1961), pp. 7-19; Schnabel, *Policy and Direction*, pp. 35-40; Sawyer, *KMAG*, pp. 43-114; Berger, *The Korean Knot*, pp. 93-95, Scalapino and Lee, *Communism in Korea*, pp. 388-390, 393-396; *North Korea: A Case Study in Communist Takeover*, pp. 16-17, 114; Korea Institute for Military History, *Korean War, Volume I*, (Lincoln: University of Nebraska Press, 1997), pp. 43-55, 79-89, 138.

Chapter 3

1. Appleman, *South to the Naktong, North to the Yalu*, pp. 19-35; Sawyer, *KMAG*, pp. 114-134; *Korean War*, I, pp. 156-237; Clay Blair, *The Forgotten War* (New York: Times Books, 1987), pp. 58-61, 75; Bevin Alexander, *Korea: The First War We Lost* (New York: Hippocrene, 1986), pp. 2-4, 25-31; David Rees, *Korea: The Limited War* (Baltimore: Pelican, 1970), pp. 3-5.

2. *Foreign Relations of the United States 1950, Volume VII* (Washington: Government Printing Office, 1976), pp. 109-121; Arthur Radford, *From Pearl Harbor to Vietnam* (Stanford: Hoover Institution Press, 1980), p. 175; *Military Situation in the Far East*, Hearings before the Armed Services Committee and the Foreign Relations Committee, United States Senate, 82nd Congress, 1st Session, 1951, 5 vols. (Washington: Government Printing Office, 1951), Part III, pp. 1991-1992; George F. Kennan, *Memoirs, 1925-1950* (New York: Bantam, 1967), pp. 417-418; Paul Nitze, "The Evolution of National Security Policy," in *The Lessons of Vietnam*, edited by W. Scott Thompson and D.D. Frizzell (New York: Crane, Russak, 1977), pp. 3-5; Blair, *The Forgotten War*, pp. 58, 87; Schnabel, *Policy and Direction*, pp. 61-65; Glenn D. Paige, *The Korean Decision* (New York: Free Press, 1968), p. 75-76; Robert Donovan, *Tumultuous Years* (New York: Norton, 1982), p. 95.

3. *FRUS 1950, Vol. VII*, pp. 125-156; Dean Acheson, *Present at the Creation* (New York: New American Library, 1970), pp. 524-528; Harry Truman, *Years of Trial and Hope* (New York: New American Library, 1965), pp. 377-382; Paige, *The Korean Decision*, pp. 84-124; Donovan *Tumultuous Years*, pp. 187-197, 200, 204-205.

4. *FRUS 1950, Vol. VII*, pp. 157-166, 211, 218-220; Acheson, *Present at the Creation*,

pp. 527–531; Paige, *The Korean Decision*, pp. 12–206, 212–214, 230–232, 234–237; Donovan *Tumultuous Years*, pp. 198–223; Anthony Farrar-Hockley, *The British Part in the Korean War Vol. I* (London: Her Majesty's Stationary Office, 1990), pp. 44, 47,89–91; Lowe, *Origins of the Korean War*, p. 193.

5. *FRUS 1950 Vol. VII*, p. 229; *Khrushchev Remembers*, pp. 369–370; Kiraly, "Military Aspects," p. 62; Glenn D. Paige, *1950 Truman's Decision* (New York: Vintage 1970), pp. 129–134; Paige, *The Korean Decision*, pp. 209–210, 214–216, 247; Goncharov, Lewis, Xue, *Uncertain Partners*, pp. 157–159; John Lewis Gaddis, *We Now Know*, (New York: Oxford University Press, 1997), p. 76; Shu Guang Zhang, *Mao's Military Romanticism*, pp. 55–59, 67, 75–76; Chen, *China's Road to the Korean War*, pp. 126–127, 131, 136–137, 164; Allen S. Whiting, *China Crosses the Yalu* (Stanford: Stanford University Press, 1960), pp. 45–54; Tsou, *America's Failure in China, Vol. II*, pp. 561–563; Adam Ulam, *Expansion and Coexistence* (New York: Praeger, 1968), pp. 521–522; Weathersby, *Soviet Aims in Korea and the Origins of the Korean War*, passim.; Weathersby, " New Russian Documents."

6. *FRUS 1950, Vol. I*, pp. 324–330; *FRUS 1950, Vol. VII*, pp. 227–228, 240–241, 247–254, 258–259, 262–263; Paige, *The Korean Decision*, pp. 221–268; Schnabel, *Policy and Direction*, pp. 75–79; Donovan, *Tumultuous Years*, pp. 210–224; Blair, *The Forgotten War*, pp. 75–84.

Chapter 4

1. Schnabel, *Policy and Direction*, pp. 45–59; Blair, *The Forgotten War*, pp. 27–29, 48–50, 74, 92; James, *The Years of MacArthur, Vol. III*, pp. 326–330, 402–403, 412; Radford, *From Pearl Harbor to Vietnam*, pp. 142, 175; Robert F. Futrell, *The United States Air Force in Korea*, revised edition (Washington: Office of Air Force History, 1983), pp. 55–62, 67–69, 72, 87; Farrar-Hockley, *The British Part in the Korean War Vol. I*, pp. 42, 61–62, 65; Walter Karig, *Battle Report: The Korean War* (New York: Rinehart, 1952), p. 7.

2. Appleman, *South to the Naktong, North to the Yalu*, pp. 50–58, 62–63, 101–108, 117–119; Schnabel, *Policy and Direction*, pp. 106–107, 139–141; Futrell, *The United States Air Force in Korea*, pp. 29–32, 44–51, 58–61, 68, 85–87; Richard Hallion, *The Naval Air War in Korea* (Baltimore: Nautical and Aviation Publishing Co., 1986), pp. 37–40, 45–46; Shtykov to Stalin, 1 July 1950, Shtykov to Stalin, 4 July 1950, Stalin to Shtykov 6 July 1950, Shtykov to Stalin, 8 July 1950, in Weathersby, "New Russian Documents on the Korean War."

3. Appleman, *South to the Naktong, North to the Yalu*, pp. 58–105, 117–119; Schnabel, *Policy and Direction*, pp. 83–97, 141; Blair, *The Forgotten War*, pp. 89–115; Korea Institute, *The Korean War*, pp. 314, 317; Futrell, *The United States Air Force in Korea*, p. 91; Alexander, *Korea: The First War We Lost*, pp. 52–54, 76–107; Sawyer, *KMAG*, p.137, Appleman, *South to the Naktong, North to the Yalu*, pp. 122–181; Blair, *The Forgotten War*, pp. 125, 128–141.

4. Appleman, *South to the Naktong, North to the Yalu*, pp. 101–108, 182–188, 195–197, 210–221; Sawyer, *KMAG*, pp. 141–148; Blair, *The Forgotten War*, pp. 155–156, 163–169; Alexander, *Korea: The First War We Lost*, pp. 108–112; Korea Institute, *The Korean War*, p. 340.

5. Karig, *Battle Report*, pp. 83, 107–112, 130; Conrad Crane, *American Airpower Strategy in Korea, 1950–1953* (Lawrence: University of Kansas 2000) pp. 28, 40; Futrell, *The United States Air Force in Korea*, pp. 103–126, 175, 183–198; Hallion, *The Naval Air War in Korea*, pp. 38–39; Appleman, *South to the Naktong, North to the Yalu*, pp. 251–265, 376–379; Korea Institute, *The Korean War*, pp. 431–449; Eduard Mark, *Aerial Interdiction in Three Wars* (Washington: Center for Air Force History, 1994), pp. 273–285; John Lansdown, *With the Carriers in Korea* (Wilmslow, England: Crecy, 1997), pp. 24, 26; Alexander, *Korea: The First War We Lost*, pp. 122–124. It is worth noting that the horrors experienced by South Korean civilians, all too often at UN hands as well as Communist hands, for a long time went unnoticed until the recent publication of dubious claims about American atrocities at No Gun Ri. It is a curious fact that the oldest books on the Korean War, published during the war itself, were franker about these matters than many works published later. Even some contemporary Hollywood movies

confronted such issues, such as Samuel Fuller's great film, "*The Steel Helmet.*" An otherwise undistinguished 1952 movie, "*One Minute to Zero,*" showed Americans calling artillery fire down on refugees being used as human shields by the Communists.

6. Appleman, *South to the Naktong, North to the Yalu,* pp. 252–254, 266–375; Korea Institute, *The Korean War,* pp. 451–505; Alexander, *Korea: The First War We Lost,* pp. 127–147; Blair, *The Forgotten War,* pp. 190–219; Futrell, *The United States Air Force in Korea,* pp. 138–139; Paik Sun Yup, *From Pusan to Panmunjom* (New York: Brassey's, 1997), pp. 31–32, 40–43; William T. Bowers and William M. Hammond, *Black Soldiers, White Army* (Washington: Center of Military History, 1996).

7. Appleman, *South to the Naktong, North to the Yalu,* pp. 289–486; Blair, *The Forgotten War,* pp. 238–261

8. *FRUS 1950 Vol. VII,* pp. 312–316, 327–330, 359–360, 426–427; Acheson, *Present at the Creation,* pp. 543–544; Whiting, *China Crosses the Yalu,* pp. 59–61, 69–78;

9. Truman, *Years of Trial and Hope,* pp. 404–408; Donovan, *Tumultuous Years,* pp. 255–265; James, *The Years of MacArthur, Vol. III,* pp. 456–460; John Spanier, *The Truman–MacArthur Controversy and the Korean War* (New York: Norton, 1965), pp. 68–77.

Chapter 5

1. Schnabel, *Policy and Direction,* pp. 106, 139–154, 159; James, *The Years of MacArthur, Vol. III,* pp. 465–475; Robert Heinl, *Victory at High Tide* (Baltimore: Nautical and Aviation Publishing Co., 1979), pp. 25–69; Walt Sheldon, *Hell or High Water* (New York: Ballantine, 1973), pp. 5–10, 37, 44–54, 89, 95; 97–98, 100–101, 104–114, 216; Malcolm Cagle and Frank Manson, *The Sea War in Korea* (Annapolis: Naval Institute Press, 1957), pp. 75–87; Shelby Stanton, *America's Tenth Legion* (Novato: Presidio, 1989), pp. 31–98; Appleman, *South to the Naktong, North to the Yalu,* pp. 489–502, 506; Karig, *Battle Report,* pp. 159–191; Blair, *The Forgotten War,* pp. 224–235; Goncharov, Lewis, Xue, *Uncertain Partners,* p.163; Shu Guang Zhang, *Mao's Military Romanticism,* pp. 63, 72–73.

2. Karig, *Battle Report,* pp. 192–242; Sheldon, *Hell or High Water,* pp. 139, 214, 288–310; Heinl, *Victory at High Tide,* p. 79ff. Appleman, *South to the Naktong, North to the Yalu,* pp. 503–541, 596; Shelby Stanton, *America's Tenth Legion,* pp. 66–116; Alexander, *Korea: The First War We Lost,* pp. 197–218; Blair, *The Forgotten War,* pp. 269, 288–294. Alexander, especially on pages 148–149, 217–218, eloquently argues that Inchon was far less risky than was and is usually assumed, and that MacArthur was right in his confidence that the enemy would not and could not mount a dangerous defense there. Given the ease of mining the port, the trouble even a few well-manned artillery pieces could have caused, the cogent advice the Chinese gave the North Koreans and the near revelation of the actual plan, the present author is reluctant to go all the way with this view, although it seems closer to the truth than the other extreme, most strongly expressed by Blair (especially on pages 224, 262, 269–270, 318, 320) that Inchon was a wild gamble. The latter view, however, seems to have been common in the U.S. Navy.

3. Appleman, *South to the Naktong, North to the Yalu,* p. 571; Chen, *China's Road to the Korean War,* pp. 158–159; Alexander Mansourov, "Stalin, Mao, Kim and China's Decision to Enter the Korean War," *Cold War International History Project Bulletin,* 6–7.

4. Appleman, *South to the Naktong, North to the Yalu,* pp. 542–604; Blair, *The Forgotten War,* pp. 278–318; Paik, *From Pusan to Panmunjom,* pp. 50–53; Alexander, *Korea: The First War We Lost,* pp. 222–227; Mansourov, "Stalin, Mao, Kim and China's Decision to Enter the Korean War."

5. Philip Chinnery, *Korean Atrocity* (Annapolis: Naval Institute Press, 2001), pp. 39–58; Appleman, *South to the Naktong, North to the Yalu,* pp. 587–588, 599; James Field *History of United States Naval Operations, Korea* (Washington: US Navy 1962), p. 44; *FRUS 1950 Vol. VII,* pp. 1043–1044, 1420–1421, 1567, 1579–1581, 1586–1587; John W. Riley and Wilbur Schramm, *The Reds Take a City* (New Brunswick: Rutgers University Press, 1951), pp. 31–45, 68–69, 77, 103–127; Burton Kaufman, *The Korean War* (New York: Knopf, 1986), p. 47; Sheldon, *Hell or High Water,* p. 207.

6. *FRUS 1950, Vol. I,* pp. 361–369, 375–

389; *FRUS 1950, Vol. VII*, pp. 386–387, 393, 449–454, 458–461, 469–473, 483–485, 502–510, 528–536, 567–573, 600–603, 607–623, 625, 653–658, 687, 712–714, 753–755; Acheson, *Present at the Creation*, pp. 577–589; Schnabel, *Policy and Direction*, pp. 177–183; Tsou, *America's Failure in China, Vol. II*, pp. 572–574; Farrar-Hockley, *The British Part in the Korean War Vol. I*, pp. 193–196, 203, 209–210, 217–218; Stueck, *The Korean War*, pp. 89–97.

7. *FRUS 1950 Vol. VII*, pp. 949, 951, 959, 990–991, 1007–1010; Schnabel, *Policy and Direction*, pp. 187–192, 195–196, 206–208, 215–230; Rees, *Korea*, pp. 123–129; Blair, *The Forgotten War*, pp. 328–363.

Chapter 6

1. *FRUS 1950 Vol. VII*, pp. 790–793, 797–798, 815–816, 821–827, 851–852, 855, 864–865, 876–880, 897–899, 906–911; Whiting, *China Crosses the Yalu*, pp. 92–115.

2. *FRUS 1950 Vol. VII*, pp. 948–960; Truman, *Years of Trial and Hope*, pp. 415–420; Radford, *From Pearl Harbor to Vietnam*, pp. 241–245; James, *The Years of MacArthur, Vol. III*, pp. 503–546.

3. Shu Guang Zhang, *Mao's Military Romanticism*, pp. 46, 61–67, 74–76; Goncharov, Lewis, Xue, *Uncertain Partners*, pp. 162–166, 173; Chen, *China's Road to the Korean War*, pp. 126–128, 131–132, 137–145, 151–155.

4. *FRUS 1950, Vol. VII*, pp. 1034–1035, 1290–1291; *FRUS 1951, Vol. VII*, (Washington: Government Printing Office 1983) pp. 1446–1447; Mansourov, "Stalin, Mao, Kim and China's Decision to Enter the Korean War"; Chen, *China's Road to the Korean War*, pp. 161–163.

5. Shen Zhihua, "The Discrepancy Between the Russian and Chinese Versions of Mao's 2 October 1950 Message to Stalin," *Cold War International History Project Bulletin*, 8–9; Shu Guang Zhang, *Mao's Military Romanticism*, pp. 77–84; Chen, *China's Road to the Korean War*, pp. 159–160, 172–173, 177, 181–185, 196–204. The above analysis rests mainly on the analysis and interpretations of Mansourov. The reader should be warned that interpreting the Soviet and Chinese positions in this period is difficult and confusing. Earlier interpretations by Shu Guang Zhang, Chen, and Goncharov and his colleagues depended on Chinese accounts that included a false version of the message Mao sent on October 2, which made it appear that Mao had fully assured Stalin at an early date that China would intervene in Korea. It now appears this version of the message was actually a draft that was never sent. Further, it was assumed that Zhou's account of his meeting with Stalin on October 10 was accurate and that Stalin in fact reneged on his promise of support. Soviet records have since made clear that Stalin was entirely consistent on this point. The present writer differs from Mansourov on one point, holding that the available evidence suggests that Mao did in fact decide to intervene on October 2 despite the content of his message to Stalin. Chinese and Chinese–American historians differ on the relative importance of the various Chinese Politburo sessions and Chen Jian regarding the October 2 meeting as decisive, while others attach more importance to the sessions of October 4–5.

6. Chow Ching-wen, *Ten Years of Storm* (New York: Holt, Rinehart and Winston, 1960), pp. 116–117; *FRUS 1950, Vol. VII*, pp. 1290–1291; Goncharov, Lewis, Xue, *Uncertain Partners*, p. 174; Tsou, *America's Failure in China, Vol. II*, pp. 575–576.

7. Yefim Gordon and Vladimir Rigant, *MIG-15* (Osceola, Wisconsin: Motorbooks, 1994), pp. 111, 113; Shu Guang Zhang, *Mao's Military Romanticism*, pp. 84–85; Oleg Sarin and Lev Dvoretsky, *Alien Wars* (Novato: Presidio 1996), p. 70; William T. Y'Blood, *MIG Alley* (Washington: Air Force History and Museums Program, 2000).

8. Robert B. Rigg, *Red China's Fighting Hordes* (Harrisburg, Pennsylvania: Military Service Publishing Company, 1951), pp. 124, 178–206, 214; Shu Guang Zhang, *Mao's Military Romanticism*, pp. 62, 65–66, 93–94; Appleman, *South to the Naktong, North to the Yalu*, p. 716; S. L. A. Marshall, *The River and the Gauntlet* (New York: Time, 1962), pp. 13–14; Roy Appleman, *Disaster in Korea* (College Station, Texas: Texas A & M University Press, 1989) p. 17; Alexander L. George, *The Chinese Communist Army in Action* (New York: Columbia University Press, 1967), pp. 3–5, 32, 121, 157–158, 161, 175.

9. Appleman, *South to the Naktong, North to the Yalu*, pp. 622–669; Alexander, *Korea:*

The First War We Lost, pp. 249–254; Blair, *The Forgotten War*, pp. 339–368; Farrar-Hockley, *The British Part in the Korean War*, Vol. I, pp. 239–260.

10. Appleman, *South to the Naktong, North to the Yalu*, pp. 672–708; Alexander, *Korea: The First War We Lost*, pp. 254–288; Blair, *The Forgotten War*, pp. 370–385; Shu Guang Zhang, *Mao's Military Romanticism*, pp. 95–97; Stanton, *America's Tenth Legion*, pp. 161–163, 173–179.

11. Schnabel, *Policy and Direction*, pp 241–245; Futrell, *The United States Air Force in Korea*, pp. 219–230, 244, 246; Hallion, *The Naval Air War in Korea*, pp. 73–77; Cagle and Frank Manson, *The Sea War in Korea*, pp 224–229; Crane, American *Airpower Strategy in Korea, 1950–1953*, pp. 46–50; Blair, *The Forgotten War*, pp. 375–379, 390–391. There are considerable discrepancies in the sources about which bridges were considered "major" crossings, were actually picked as targets, and how many were actually destroyed and damaged. Until recently it was thought that the first MIG destroyed in Korea was shot down by a USAF pilot on November 8; Soviet sources did not confirm it.

12. *FRUS 1950, Vol. VII*, pp. 1023–1027, 1038–1041, 1078–1081, 1097–1093, 1101–1106, 1116–1122, 1128–1129, 1143–1153, 1168–1170, 1178–1183, 1188–1190, 1193–1196, 1204–1208, 1220–1225, 1231; Schnabel, *Policy and Direction*, pp 237–256, 267–271; Acheson, *Present at the Creation*, pp. 598–605; Karl Lott Rankin, *China Assignment* (Seattle: University of Washington Press, 1964), pp. 65–66, 82; Blair, *The Forgotten War*, pp. 375–379, 390–391, 393–403, 423–426; Rees, *Korea*, pp. 131–137, 143–146; Marshall, *The River and the Gauntlet*, pp. 4–5, 8, 13–14; George, *The Chinese Communist Army in Action*, pp 287–288, 293; Stueck, *The Korean War*, pp. 111–118; Farrar-Hockley, *The British Part in the Korean War*, Vol. I, pp. 292–293, 297–307; Patrick Roe, *The Dragon Strikes* (Novato: Presidio, 2000), pp. 170–180, 191–235; Appleman, *South to the Naktong, North to the Yalu*, pp. 751–752, 755, 769–770.

Much confusion about the nature of policy in November 1950 has been caused by the alibis offered by Washington officials for the defeats in November and December, MacArthur's false claims to have foreseen the magnitude of the Chinese threat and that the defeat was the fault of everyone but himself, and the biases of liberal historians. MacArthur's apologists and others have suggested the defeat was partly caused by the British traitors Burgess and MacLean who supposedly assured the Soviets and Chinese that the Americans would not retaliate against China itself if China intervened in Korea. This, and the general tendency of later writers (e.g. Blair, op. cit.), to suggest that no one but a madman (i.e. MacArthur) ever contemplated "widening the war" to China and that the idea never entered the heads of responsible officials in Washington is contrary to the facts. From NSC 81/1 onwards, the American leaders assumed they would strike China if a major intervention developed. Burgess and MacLean could hardly have assured the enemy on this point and the Chinese continued to fear retaliation. Despite his obstinate insistence on advancing right to the frontier of China, MacArthur was not quite the fire-breathing dragon often portrayed. He did not recommend bombing China until after the defeat in November. The common mistake of all involved was that they just did not realize that a major campaign was underway.

Chapter 7

1. *FRUS 1950, Vol. I*, pp. 331–338, 344–346; *FRUS 1950, Vol. IV*, pp. 1220–1221, 1224–1229; *Documents on International Affairs 1949–1950*, p. 654; Peter Calvocoressi, *Survey of International Affairs, 1952* (London: Oxford University Press, 1955), p. 2; Calvocoressi, *Survey of International Affairs, 1949–1950*, p. 243; D.M. Condit, *The Test of War* (Washington: Office of the Secretary of Defense, 1988), pp. 224–250.

2. Donovan, *Tumultuous Years*, pp. 241–247; Oscar T. Barck, *History of the United States Since 1945*, pp. 180–185; Alan Milward, *The Reconstruction of Western Europe* (London Methuen, 1984), pp. 429, 488–489.

3. Marshall B. Shulman, *Stalin's Foreign Policy Reappraised* (Cambridge: Harvard University Press, 1963), pp. 147, 298 n. 14; William B. Bader, *Austria Between East and West* (Stanford: Stanford University Press, 1966), pp. 157–181; William Stearman, *The*

Soviet Union and the Occupation of Austria (Bad Goesberg:Verlag fur Zeitarchiv, 1960), pp. 118–127.

4. *Foreign Relations of the United States 1950, Volume III* (Washington: Government Printing Office, 1977), pp. 167–172, 180–182, 194–195, 207–208, 210–219, 261–262, 264–266, 273–275, 291–302, 309–312, 341–342, 347–348, 406–411, 426–430, 517–521, 604–605, 1278–1279; *FRUS 1950, Vol. IV*, pp. 691–698, 707–709, 717–721, 723–724, 867–887; Acheson, *Present at the Creation*, pp. 565–577, 593–594; Konrad Adenauer, *Memoirs* (Chicago: Regnery, 1966), pp. 267–268, 271–293; Calvocoressi, *Survey of International Affairs, 1949–1950*, pp. 7–8, 145–167; Condit, *The Test of War*, pp. 312–334.

5. *FRUS 1950, Vol. IV*, pp. 1254–1258; *FRUS 1950 Vol. VI*, pp. 1230–1237, 1305–1306, 1332–1336, *Foreign Relations of the United States 1951, Volume VI* (Washington: Government Printing Office, 1977), pp. 808–811, 888–895; 1432–1436; Acheson, *Present at the Creation*, pp. 557– 565; Walter Hermes, *Truce Tent and Fighting Front* (Washington: Department of the Army, 1966), pp. 220–222, 361–362; James, *The Years of MacArthur, Vol. III*, pp. 241–242, 344–348; Martin Weinstein, *Japan's Postwar Defense Policy* (New York: Columbia University Press, 1968), pp. 2, 51, 107.

6. *FRUS 1950, Vol. IV*, pp. 666, 668–670, 902–904, 906; Acheson, *Present at the Creation*, 624, 628–630; Adenauer, *Memoirs*, pp294, 304–306; *Documents on International Affairs 1949–1950*, pp. 167–168, 170–173, 615–618; Shulman, *Stalin's Foreign Policy Reappraised*, pp. 148–150, 153–154.

Chapter 8

1. Appleman, *Disaster in Korea*; Marshall, *The River and the Gauntlet;* William B. Hopkins, *One Bugle, No Drums* (New York: Avon, 1988), pp. 233–265; Billy Mossman, *Ebb and Flow* (Washington: Center for Military History, 1990), pp. 43–83, 103–156; Blair, *The Forgotten War*, pp. 429–455, 473–502; Roe, *The Dragon Strikes*, pp. 134, 236, 240–241, 244–252, 404–405; Shu Guang Zhang, *Mao's Military Romanticism*, pp. 107–116; Farrar-Hockley, *The British Part in the Korean War, Vol. I*, pp. 332–335. As might be expected, there are discrepancies in sources for the Chongchon battle. This is especially noticeable in discussions of the British battalion on November 29–30. The above discussion is largely based on Appleman.

2. Roy Appleman, *Escaping the Trap*, (College Station, Texas Texas A & M University Press, 1990); Roy Appleman, *East of Chosin* (College Station, Texas: Texas A & M University Press, 1987); Hopkins, *One Bugle, No Drums*, pp. 86 ff; Mossman, *Ebb and Flow*, pp. 84–104, 129–142, 172–175; Martin Russ, *Breakout* (New York: Penguin, 2000); Shu Guang Zhang, *Mao's Revolutionary Romanticism*, pp. 116–117; Stanton, *America's Tenth Legion*, pp. 169–232; Hallion, *The Naval Air War in Korea*, p. 83; S.L.A. Marshall, *Battle at Best* (New York: Morrow, 1963), pp. 107–139; Roe, *The Dragon Strikes*, pp. 264–267, 295, 313, 327–328, 334, 379j; 394. The normally sensible Roe inexplicably suggests that Hungnam was evacuated unnecessarily and prematurely; it would seem rather that X Corps was moved just in time to reach South Korea, where it was badly needed.

3. Marshall, *Battle at Best*, pp. 103–104.

4. Appleman, *Disaster in Korea*, pp. 294–362, 381–386; Mossman, *Ebb and Flow*, pp. 157–169; Blair, *The Forgotten War*, pp. 501–502, with typical grandiose certitude, flatly says that Pyongyang could have been held.

Chapter 9

1. *FRUS 1950 Vol. VII*, pp. 1237, 1242–1249; Schnabel, *Policy and Direction*, p. 286; Truman, *Years of Trial and Hope*, pp. 437–442.

2. *FRUS 1950 Vol. VII*, pp. 1253, 1259–1260, 1265–1267, 1270–1273, 1276–1281, 1320–1322, 1605–1610; *FRUS 1950, Vol. VI*, pp. 590–596; Schnabel, *Policy and Direction*, pp. 279–282, 286–287, 291, 295; Acheson, *Present at the Creation*, pp. 616–620; Truman, *Years of Trial and Hope*, pp. 437–450; Rankin, *China Assignment*, pp. 90–91; Donovan. *Tumultuous Years*, pp. 305–312; Richard Stebbins, *The United States in World Affairs 1950* (New York: Harper, 1951), pp. 23–27, 396–399, 426; Crane, *American Airpower Strategy in Korea*, p. 57.

3. *FRUS 1950, Vol. I*, pp. 478–481; *FRUS 1950, Vol. IV*, pp. 1276–1281; *FRUS 1950, Vol. VII*, pp. 1291–1296, 1309–1310, 1444–1449, 1570–1576; *Foreign Relations of the United States 1951, Volume I* (Washington: Government Printing Office, 1979), pp. 4–7; Rosemary Foot, *The Wrong War* (Ithaca: Cornell University Press, 1985), pp. 91–92, 102–103.

4. *FRUS 1950, Vol. VII*, pp. 1323–1340, 1345; Acheson, *Present at the Creation*, pp. 614–617; George F. Kennan, *Memoirs 1950–1963* (Boston: Little, Brown, 1972) pp. 26–32.

5. *FRUS 1950, Vol. VII*, pp. 1361–1374, 1382, 1393–1408, 1435–1442, 1449–1461, 1468–1479; Acheson, *Present at the Creation*, pp. 620–624; Stueck, *The Korean War*, pp. 135–137; Farrar-Hockley, *The British Part in the Korean War, Vol. I*, pp 353–355, 360–369; Farrar-Hockley, *The British Part in the Korean War, Vol. II* (London: Her Majesty's Stationary Office 1995), pp. 17, 19–21.

6. *FRUS 1950, Vol. VII*, pp. 1570–1576; Schnabel, *Policy and Direction*, pp. 281–285, 294–295, 298–301; Mossman, *Ebb and Flow*, pp. 157–161. Blair, *The Forgotten War*, pp. 527, 530–534, follows J. Lawton Collins' memoirs and gives a misleading impression that Collins' and the JCS' assessments in December were more optimistic than they were. In a rare error, Schnabel suggests that the Joint Chiefs never pondered withdrawal from Korea to save Japan. This is hard to reconcile with the records.

7. *FRUS 1950, Vol. I*, pp. 462. 468, 475; Schnabel, *Policy and Direction*, pp. 298–299; Donovan, *Tumultuous Years*, pp. 319–320; Rees, *Korea*, pp. 172–173.

8. *FRUS 1950 Vol. IV*, pp. 919–921; *FRUS 1950 Vol. VI*, p. 1389; *Documents on International Affairs 1949–1950*, pp. 176–182, 618–622.

9. *FRUS 1950, Vol. VII*, pp. 1249, 1387–1389, 1488–1490, 1518–1519, 1522–1523, 1529–1531, 1538, 1540–1541, 1595–1598; Acheson, *Present at the Creation*, pp. 611, 613, 661; Kaufman, *The Korean War*, pp 114–115; Shu Guang Zhang, *Mao's Military Romanticism*, pp. 117–125; Stueck, *The Korean War*, pp. 139–145; Soviet Politburo to Vyshinsky and Roshchin, 5 December 1950, Roshchin to Soviet Government, 7 December 1950 in Weathersby, "New Russian Documents."

10. Acheson, *Present at the Creation*, pp. 631–640; Kaufman, *The Korean War*, pp. 117, 122–132; Spanier, *The Truman-MacArthur Controversy and the Korean War*, pp. 156–162; Justus Doenecke, *Not to the Swift* (Lewisburg, Pennsylvania: Bucknell University Press, 1979), p. 196; John Mueller, *War, Presidents and Public Opinion* (New York: Wiley, 1973), pp. 48, 52, 58–61, 102–105.

Chapter 10

1. Shu Guang Zhang, *Mao's Military Romanticism*, pp. 116–117, 123–125; Mossman, *Ebb and Flow*, p. 164; Appleman, *Disaster in Korea*, pp. 363–364; Futrell, *The United States Air Force in Korea*, pp. 262–263.

2. Y' Blood, *MIG Alley*, pp. 14–16; Futrell, *The United States Air Force in Korea*, pp. 248–253, 261, 281; Rigant and Gordon, *MIG-15*, pp. 140–143; Thomas Hone "Korea" in *Case Studies in the Achievement of Air Superiority* edited by B. Franklin Cooling (Washington: Center for Air Force History, 1994), pp. 467–468; Frank Everest, *The Fastest Man Alive* (New York: Berkley 1986), p. 162.

3. Appleman, *Disaster in Korea*, pp. 323–325, 355–359, 365, 371, 390–395, 397; Roy Appleman, *Ridgway Duels for Korea* (College Station, Texas: Texas A & M University Press, 1990), pp. 3–4, 12, 16, 25, 30, 38, 98; Mossman, *Ebb and Flow*, pp. 176–178, 182, 199; Matthew B; Ridgway, *The Korean War* (New York: Popular Library, 1968) pp. 89–92; Blair, *The Forgotten War*, pp. 548, 550–555, 566–585; Schnabel, *Policy and Direction*, 297, 303–307; Futrell, *The United States Air Force in Korea*, pp. 248–253, 261–262.

4. *FRUS 1950, Vol. VII*, pp. 1625, 1630–1633; *FRUS 1951, Vol. VII*, pp. 41–43, 55–56, 71–72, 77–79; Schnabel, *Policy and Direction*, pp. 309–315, 320–325, 328–329; *The Journals of David Lilienthal, Volume III* (New York: Harper and Row 1966), pp. 117–121; Richard Rovere and Arthur Schlesinger, *The MacArthur Controversy and American Foreign Policy* (New York: Farrar, Straus and Giroux, 1965), p. 219.

5. Appleman, *Ridgway Duels for Korea*, pp. 13–92; Mossman, *Ebb and Flow*, pp. 180–206; Blair, *The Forgotten War*, pp. 592–606; Shu Guang Zhang, *Mao's Military Romanticism*, pp. 127–133; Mao to Stalin, 8 January 1951, in Weathersby, "New Russian Documents."

6. Appleman, *Ridgway Duels for Korea*, pp. 28–30, 96–138; Mossman, *Ebb and Flow*, pp. 184–185, 196–197, 199, 210, 216–227; J.D. Coleman, *Wonju* (Washington: Brassey's 2001) pp. 50–68.

7. Appleman, *Ridgway Duels for Korea*, pp. 148–197; Mossman, *Ebb and Flow*, pp. 228, 237–247; Blair, *The Forgotten War*, pp. 654–658, 673–681; Schnabel, *Policy and Direction*, pp. 333–339; Marshall, *Battle at Best*, 70, 77–100; Shu Guang Zhang, *Mao's Military Romanticism*, pp. 134–139; Ridgway, *The Korean War*, p. 114. MacArthur's insistence on the importance of taking Seoul may have been the only instance in which he seriously influenced the development of the campaign in Korea after December 1950.

8. Coleman, *Wonju*, pp. 68 ff.; Appleman, *Ridgway Duels for Korea*, pp. 178, 198–303; Mossman, *Ebb and Flow*, pp. 249–300; Shu Guang Zhang, *Mao's Military Romanticism*, pp. 138, 141–144.

9. *FRUS 1951, Vol. I*, pp. 19, 33–40, 60–82; *FRUS 1951, Vol. VII*, pp. 102–105; Schnabel, *Policy and Direction*, pp. 325–326, 329–330, 342–344; Mao to Stalin, 27 January 1951 in Weathersby, "New Russian Documents."

10. *FRUS 1951, Vol. VII*, pp. 4–7, 9–12, 15–18, 27–33, 37–40, 64, 91–92, 117–118; Acheson, *Present at the Creation*, pp. 661–662; Kaufman, *The Korean War*, pp. 130–131; Rees, *Korea*, pp. 202–204; Stueck, *The Korean War*, pp. 151–54; Farrar-Hockley, *The British Part in the Korean War, Vol. II*, pp. 19–21, 25–28.

Chapter 11

1. Karel Kaplan, *Dans les Archives du Comite Central* (Paris: Albin Michel, 1978), pp. 162–169. Western historians have been curiously reluctant to deal with the issues raised by this disclosure. Few English-speaking accounts even mention it. Stueck, *The Korean War*, pp. 161–162, seemingly finds it simply incredible that Stalin could have decided on war. Mastny, *Cold War and Soviet Insecurity*, pp. 113–115, makes some characteristically interesting, but uncharacteristically uncertain comments on the issue.

2. *Report of the Royal Commission on Espionage, 22nd August 1955* (Sydney, 1955), pp. 59–60, 63–65, 68–74, 85, 163, 252–253, 330–335; Vladimir and Evdokia Petrov, *Empire of Fear* (New York: Praeger, 1956), pp. 237, 264–265, 293; Holloway, *Stalin and the Bomb*, p. 292.

3. Helmut Koenig, "Der Konflikt Zwischen Stalin and Togliatti um die Jahreswende 1950/51" *Osteuropa* (October 1970), pp. 669–706; Kennan, *Memoirs 1950–1963*, p. 94.

4. Naum Jasny, *Soviet Industrialization* (Chicago: University of Chicago Press, 1961), pp. 252 n.20, 427; Thomas Wolf, *Soviet Power and Europe* (Ithaca: Cornell University Press, 1970); Arnulf Baring, *The Uprising in East Germany* (Ithaca: Cornell University Press, 1972), pp. 17–19.

5. Boris Nicolaevsky, *Power and the Soviet Elite* (New York: Praeger, 1965), pp. 170–171; Robert Conquest, *Power and Policy in the USSR* (New York: St. Martin's Press, 1967), pp. 129–191; Georges Bortoli, *The Death of Stalin* (New York: Praeger, 1975), p. 32; Holloway, *Stalin and the Bomb*, pp. 240–244, 284–287, 292, 295–303; Steve Zaloga, *Target America* (Novato: Presidio 1993), pp. 79–86.

6. Jasny, *Soviet Industrialization*, pp. 236–238, 241, 308–312, 322–325, 359, 426–429; Roy Medvedev, *Let History Judge* (New York: Vintage, 1973), pp. 485–488; Conquest, *Power and Policy*, pp. 126–127.

7. *FRUS 1950, Vol. VII*, pp. 487–488; *FRUS 1950, Vol. VI*, pp. 371–373; Goncharov, Lewis and Xue, *Uncertain Partners*, pp. 109, 212, along with Holloway, op cit., suggest that as far back as late 1949 or early 1950 Stalin may have begun pondering a much earlier world war than earlier envisioned.

8. *Khrushchev Remembers*, p. 392.

9. E.G. Shulman, *Stalin's Foreign Policy Reappraised*, p. 26; Kennan, *Memoirs 1950–1963*, pp. 91, 340–341. It should be noted that these authors referred merely to a trend of intensification of the Cold War — neither believed that Stalin actually planned to start a war.

10. Royal Institute of International Affairs, *Documents on International Affairs 1951* (London: Oxford University Press, 1953), p. 290.

11. *FRUS 1951, Vol. VII, Part 2*, p. 1491.

12. Mao to Stalin, 13 August 1951, Mao

to Stalin, 14 November 1951, in Weathersby, "New Russian Documents."

13. *FRUS 1950, Vol. VI*, pp. 289–293, 296–306; *FRUS 1951, Vol. VII, Part 2*, pp. 1476–1503, 1519–1535, 1542–1548, 1550–1552, 1557–1562, 1583–1584, 1588–1589, 1716; Stueck, *The Korean War*, pp. 157–159

Chapter 12

1. Coleman, *Wonju*, pp. 242–257; Appleman, *Ridgway Duels for Korea*, pp. 307–315, 318–385; Mossman, *Ebb and Flow*, pp. 301–344; Schnabel, *Policy and Direction*, pp. Ridgway, *The Korean War*, 115–122; Farrar-Hockley, *The British Part in the Korean War, Vol. II*, pp. 69–70, 76;

2. *FRUS 1951, Volume VII*, pp. 165, 174–177, 189–194, 203–206, 232–233, 246–247, 253–254, 470–472; Schnabel, *Policy and Direction*, pp. 335–336, 338–339, 345–364; Ridgway, *The Korean War*, pp. 122–129; Foot, *The Wrong War*, p. 131; Farrar-Hockley, *The British Part in the Korean War, Vol. II*, pp. 58, 103; Appleman, *Ridgway Duels for Korea*, pp. 409–410; Mossman, *Ebb and Flow*, p. 344.

3. Appleman, *Ridgway Duels for Korea*, pp. 393–429, 438–448; Mossman, *Ebb and Flow*, pp. 348–369.

4. Cagle and Manson, *Sea War in Korea*, pp. 398–439; Mao to Stalin, 27 January 1951, in Weathersby, "New Russian Documents"; Shu Guang Zhang, *Mao's Military Romanticism*, pp. 145–147; Appleman, *Ridgway Duels for Korea*, 316–317, 347, 416; Mossman, *Ebb and Flow*, pp. 255–256, 313; Schnabel, *Policy and Direction*, p. 336.

5. Futrell, *The United States Air Force in Korea*, pp. 287–289, 313, 317–324, 331–337; Cagle and Manson, *Sea War in Korea*, pp. 231–239, 267–272; Shu Guang Zhang, *Mao's Military Romanticism*, pp. 169–170, 174–176; Lansdown, *With the Carriers in Korea*, pp. 90, 101, 110–111, 125–126, 130, 458; Hallion, *The Naval Air War in Korea*, pp. 90–95; Y'Blood, *MIG Alley*, pp. 14, 19–21; Rigant, *MIG-15*, pp. 121, 125, 131–132, 134, 137; Crane, *American Airpower Strategy in Korea*, pp. 82–83; Mark, *Aerial Interdiction in Three Wars*, pp. 290–298.

6. *FRUS 1951 Vol. VII, Part 2*, pp. 1579–1581; Stueck, *The Korean War*, pp. 178–185; Farrar-Hockley, *The British Part in the Korean War, Vol. II*, pp. 80–85; Truman, *Years of Trial and Hope*, pp. 497–510; William Sebald, *With MacArthur in Japan* (New York: Norton, 1965), pp. 221–230; Schnabel, *Policy and Direction*, pp. 357–361, 365–377; Joseph Goulden, *Korea: the Untold Story of the War* (New York: Times Books, 1982), pp. 476–478; Blair, *The Forgotten War*, pp. 719–720, 742–743, 758–760, 767–770, 783–789, 794–797; Pogue, *George C. Marshall: Statesman*, pp. 482–483; James, *The Years of MacArthur Vol. III*, pp. 578–594; Rovere and Schlesinger, *The Truman-MacArthur Controversy and American Foreign Policy* originally published as *The General and the President*, is an excellent contemporary account. It is a comment on the level of the literature regarding the Truman-MacArthur conflict that, although the product of liberal partisans in 1951, it is actually fairer to the general and often more careful than academic studies of much later vintage.

7. *FRUS 1951, Vol. VII*, pp. 313, 355–356, 365–366; Farrar-Hockley, *The British Part in the Korean War, Vol. II*, p. 164; Ridgway, *The Korean War*, pp. 127–128; Blair, *The Forgotten War*, pp. 755–756; Crane, *American Airpower Strategy in Korea*, pp. 70–73; Stueck, *The Korean War*, p. 180–181; Richard Stebbins, *The United States in World Affairs, 1951* (New York: Harper, 1952), p. 98; *New York Times*, March 26, 1951, p. 12, April 5, 1951, p. 1.

8. *FRUS 1951, Vol. VII, Part 1*, p. 158, Part 2, pp. 1497, 1561–1566, 1616–1619, 1623; Cagle and Manson, *The Sea War in Korea*, p. 236; Field, *History of United States Naval Operations Korea*, pp. 343–344.

9. Appleman, *Ridgway Duels for Korea*, pp. 378–380, 410, 447–562; Mossman, *Ebb and Flow*, pp. 367–502, 551–552, 556–568; Blair, *The Forgotten War*, pp. 793–905, 930; Lynn Montross, *US Marine Operations in Korea Vol. IV* (Quantico, Virginia: US Marine Corps, 1962); pp. 99–128, 132, 151–152; Shu Guang Zhang, *Mao's Military Romanticism*, pp. 138, 145–152; Schnabel, *Policy and Direction*, pp. 387–392, 398, 400; Farrar-Hockley, *The British Part in the Korean War, Vol. II*, p. 112; Futrell, *The United States Air Force in Korea*, pp. 308, 317, 363–368, 390; George, *The Chinese Communist Army in Action*, pp. 9–12, 138, 157–158, 167; Mikhail Kapitsa, *KNR* (Moscow: Politizdat, 1969), p.

37; *New York Times,* June 2, 1951, p. 2; *FRUS 1951, Vol. VII, Part 1,* pp. 394–398, 439–442, 487–492.

Chapter 13

1. *Military Situation in the Far East,* pp. 6–9, 23–24, 42–49, 57–58, 67–69, 78, 80, 130–131, 135–137, 167–168, 171, 177, 196–198, 207, 215–216, 219, 249–265, 273–276, 298.
2. Ibid., pp. 351–352, 354–355, 365–366, 370, 397–398, 402, 432, 482–484, 500, 515, 632, 669, 731–733, 741–742, 891, 895–897, 993, 1055–1057, 1133, 1218–1219, 1538, 1587, 1718–1720, 1730, 1764, 1878.
3. Ibid., pp. 23–24, 57, 107, 197, 268, 333, 337, 368–369, 482–484, 647–648, 674, 743, 751, 882, 886, 963–965, 1003, 1011, 1013, 1188–1189, 1220, 1262, 1379, 1385, 1388, 1393, 1398–1399, 1402–1403, 1410–1411, 1456, 1491, 1503, 1584, 1588, 1620, 1733, 1763, *FRUS 1951, Vol.VII,* p. 426; Foot, *The Wrong War,* pp. 135–142.
4. *FRUS 1951, Vol. I,* p. 90; Elmo Roper, *You and Your Leaders* (New York: William Morrow, 1957), pp. 163–164; John Norman, "MacArthur's Blockade Proposals Against Red China," *Pacific Historical Review* (May 1957), pp. 161–174; Mueller, *War, Presidents and Public Opinion,* pp. 103–104; Foot, *The Wrong War,* p. 156.
5. Frank Dorn, *Walkout* (New York: Pyramid, 1973), pp. 125–127; Foot, *The Wrong War,* p. 140; *Department of State Bulletin,* May 28, 1951, p. 842–843.
6. *Military Situation in the Far East,* pp. 3555, 397–398, 891, 1133, 1418, 1512–1518, 1773; *FRUS 1951, Vol.VII,* pp. 291, 1391; Foot, *The Wrong War,* p. 148; Schnabel, *Policy and Direction,* p. 328. Even some official historians uncritically accept the "mutual sanctuary" thesis; such as the usually able Hermes in *Truce Tent and Fighting Front,* p. 503.
7. *FRUS 1951, Vol.VII,* pp. 667–668, 881–882, 1106–1109; Foot, *The Wrong War,* pp. 148–153, 176; Hermes, *Truce Tent and Fighting Front,* pp. 56, 107; Pogue, *George C. Marshall: Statesman,* p. 488.
8. *FRUS 1951, Vol.VII, Part 2,* pp. 1503–1506, 1510–1514, 1598–1605, 1673–1682. These documents have been curiously overlooked by later historians. The whole issue of the vulnerability of China to MacArthur's proposed actions has gone unexamined or been treated dishonestly by many authors. Nationalist military capabilities to be sure were quite low in 1951, a fact that Jiang did not hide. He said on May 16 that an invasion of the mainland would need six months of preparation after he received adequate equipment and supplies, an estimate similar to that privately given by Nationalist leaders for whom the Americans had more respect. Joseph Ballantine, *Formosa* (Washington: Brookings Institution, 1952), pp. 201–202 n. 7; Rankin, *China Assignment,* pp. 90–91, 200–201; Schnabel, *Policy and Direction,* p. 319–320. Why Jiang publicly assured the Communists they had little to worry about for the time being is an interesting question.

Chapter 14

1. Stalin to Mao, 5 June 1951; Mao to Stalin, 5 June, 1951; Stalin to Mao, 13 June 1951; Mao to Stalin, 14 June 1951; Mao to Stalin, 13 August 1951; Mao to Stalin, 14 November 1951; in Weathersby, "New Russian Documents"; Bajanov, "Assessing the Politics of the Korean War," pp. 16–17; Farrar-Hockley, *The British Part in the Korean War, Vol. II,* pp. 184–185; Stueck, The Korean War, pp. 216, 220–221; Shu Guang Zhang, *Mao's Military Romanticism,* pp. 153, 155–156, 158.
2. *FRUS 1951, Vol.VII,* 285–288, 315, 447–454, 460–462, 473–476, 483–486, 507–511, 536–538, 541, 551–552; Acheson, *Present at the Creation,* pp. 684–686; Stueck, *The Korean War,* pp. 204–206, 212; Simmons, *The Strained Alliance,* pp. 198–200.
3. *FRUS 1951, Vol.VII,* pp. 577–578, 609–612, 637–638; Hermes, *Truce Tent and Fighting Front,* pp. 16–20; Mao to Stalin, 30 June 1951, Stalin to Mao, 30 June 1951; Mao to Stalin, 3 July 1951, in Weathersby, "New Russian Documents"; Shu Guang Zhang, *Mao's Military Romanticism,* pp. 153, 155–156. Cf. Alexander, Korea: *The First War We Lost,* pp. 427–433; Blair, *The Forgotten War,* pp. 927–939, for views critical of Ridgway and the American stand, which seem to be based on a misapprehension of Communist intentions.
4. *FRUS 1951, Vol.VII,* pp. 649–656, 660–663, 684–698, 704–706, 724–730, 735–737; *Negotiating While Fighting: The Diary of*

Admiral C. Turner Joy at the Korean Armistice Conference edited by Allan E. Goodman (Stanford: Hoover Institution Press, 1978), pp. xi, 3, 16–22; William H. Vatcher, *Panmunjom* (New York: Praeger, 1958), pp. 24–43; Hermes, *Truce Tent and Fighting Front*, pp. 20–35; Farrar-Hockley, *The British Part in the Korean War, Vol. II*, p. 233; Paik, *From Pusan to Panmunjom*, pp. 165–166, 175; Stueck, *The Korean War*, p. 224.

5. *FRUS 1951, Vol. VII*, pp. 739–745, 747–762, 764–766, 769–770, 777–783, 785–788, 794, 797–798, 801–810, 819–821, 828–829, 842–846, 848–854; Vatcher, *Panmunjom*, pp. 44–73; Hermes, *Truce Tent and Fighting Front*, pp. 36–46; Mao to Stalin, 13 August 1951 in Weathersby, "New Russian Documents."

6. *FRUS 1951, Vol. VII*, pp. 610, 667–668, 771–774, 838–842; Hermes, *Truce Tent and Fighting Front*, p. 19; Futrell, *The United States Air Force in Korea*, pp. 403, 408, 447.

7. Hermes, *Truce Tent and Fighting Front*, pp. 80–83, 181; Montross, *US Marine Operations in Korea, Vol. IV*, pp. 180–192, 239, 261; Blair, *The Forgotten War*, pp. 448–450; Farrar-Hockley, *The British Part in the Korean War, Vol. II*, pp. 218–231; Paik, *From Pusan to Panmunjom*, pp. 176–178; Shu Guang Zhang, *Mao's Military Romanticism*, pp. 158–163.

8. Hermes, *Truce Tent and Fighting Front*, pp. 58–66, 104–105, 202, 207–214; Sawyer, *KMAG*, pp. 178–183; Futrell, *The United States Air Force in Korea*, p. 402; Paik, *From Pusan to Panmunjom*, pp. 162, 174; Farrar-Hockley, *The British Part in the Korean War, Vol. II*, pp. 59, 61, 207.

9. Futrell, *The United States Air Force in Korea*, pp. 403–427; Y'Blood, *MIG Alley*, pp. 23–30; Hone, "Korea," pp. 467–481, 488–490; Farrar-Hockley, *The British Part in the Korean War, Vol. II*, p. 318; Shu Guang Zhang, *Mao's Military Romanticism*, p. 179; Rigant, *MIG-15*, pp. 121–133; Crane, *American Airpower Strategy in Korea*, pp. 85–86, 91. An interesting memoir is Douglas Evans *Sabre Jets Over Korea* (Summit, Pennsylvania: Tab Books, 1984).

10. Shu Guang Zhang, *Mao's Military Romanticism*, pp. 159–163, 166–176; Mark, *Aerial Interdiction in Three Wars*, pp. 299–319; Lansdown, *With the Carriers in Korea*, pp. 126, 130, 178; Farrar-Hockley, *The British Part in the Korean War, Vol. II*, pp. 317–318; Futrell, *The United States Air Force in Korea*, pp. 324–340, 434, 437–471; Cagle and Manson, *Sea War in Korea*, pp. 239, 241–279; Hallion, *Naval Air War in Korea*, pp. 102–105; Crane, *American Airpower Strategy in Korea*, pp. 83–86.

Chapter 15

1. Scalapino, *The Japanese Communist Movement*, pp. 81–93; Tsukahira, *The Postwar Evolution of Communist Strategy in Japan*, pp. 73–88; Langer and Swearingen, *Red Flag in Japan*, pp. 213–215, 241, 243–248.

2. *FRUS 1951, Vol. VI*, pp. 810–811, 833–835, 1119–1133; Roger Buckley, *Occupation Diplomacy* (Cambridge: Cambridge University Press, 1982), pp. 181–191; Weinstein, *Japan's Postwar Defense Policy*, pp. 59–63, 107; Michael M. Yoshitsu, *Japan and the San Francisco Peace Settlement* (New York: Columbia University Press, 1983), pp. 54–65, 67–83; Frederick Dunn, *Peace-Making and the Settlement with Japan* (Princeton: Princeton University Press, 1963), pp. 109–158.

3. *Documents on International Affairs 1951* pp. 579–603, 607–608; *FRUS 1951, Vol. VI*, pp. 1270–1271; Acheson, *Present at the Creation*, pp. 696–706; Dunn, *Peace-Making and the Settlement with Japan*, pp. 175–186; E. J. Lewe Van Aduard, *Japan From Surrender to Peace* (New York: Praeger,1952), pp. 209–226.

4. *FRUS 1951, Vol. III*, pp. 1086–1102; Calvocoressi, *Survey of International Affairs, 1951*, pp. 140–141; Acheson, *Present at the Creation*, pp. 710–713; Shulman, *Stalin's Foreign Policy Reappraised*, pp. 170–171.

5. *FRUS 1951, Vol. III*, pp. 415–416, 450–455, 731; *The Eisenhower Diaries*, edited by Robert H. Ferrell (New York: Norton, 1981), pp. 180, 191–193; Drew Middleton, *The Defense of Western Europe* (New York: Appleton-Century Crofts, 1952), p. 111; Condit, *The Test of War*, pp. 340–341, 373.

6. Condit, *The Test of War*, pp. 354–361; Calvocoressi, *Survey of International Affairs, 1951*, pp. 33–39.

7. *FRUS 1951, Vol. III*, pp. 755–757, 774–778, 789–798, 801–805, 840–841, 849–852, 885–891, 903, 909, 970–1047; *Foreign Relations*

of the United States 1952–1954, Volume V (Washington: Government Printing Office 1984), pp. 7–11, 51, 76, 83, 87–95; Acheson, Present at the Creation, pp. 707–708, 713–717, 746–751, 776–778, 781, 785–787, 818–825; Condit, The Test of War, pp. 384–389; Calvocoressi, Survey of International Affairs, 1951, pp. 106–110; Peter Calvocoressi, Survey of International Affairs 1952 (London: Oxford University Press, 1955), pp. 7, 55, 58–112.

8. FRUS 1951, Vol. I, pp. 31, 76–82, 100–106, 112–116, 127–157; Acheson, Present at the Creation, pp. 717–719; Condit, The Test of War, pp. 254–264.

9. Acheson, Present at the Creation, pp. 729–731; Condit, The Test of War, pp. 370–377.

10. FRUS 1951, Vol. I, pp. 182–207, 224–239; Foreign Relations of the United States 1952–1954, Volume II (Washington: Government Printing Office 1984), pp. 2–4, 9–17; Condit, The Test of War, pp. 265–283; Hermes, Truce Tent and Fighting Front, pp. 130–133.

11. FRUS 1952–1954, Vol. II, pp. 11–17, 21–45, 58–73, 89–113, 117–123, 144–156, 166, 202–205, 231–234.

12. The Eisenhower Diaries, pp. 212–213; Calvocoressi, Survey of International Affairs 1952, pp. 29, 41–43.

13. FRUS 1952–1954, Vol. V, pp. 107–173, 177–179, 198–218, 315; Acheson, Present at the Creation, pp. 327–329, 794–802; Condit, The Test of War, pp. 344, 376–384.

Chapter 16

1. FRUS 1951, Vol.VII, pp. 952–962, 1001–1004, 1009, 1031, 1041–1047, 1066–1067, 1072–1073, 1079–1081, 1087–1093, 1117, 1120–1123, 1125–1134, 1136, 1139–1143, 1159–1161, 1171; Mao to Stalin 14 November 1951, Stalin to Roshchin, November 20, 1951, in Weathersby, "New Russian Documents"; Shu Guang Zhang, Mao's Military Romanticism, p. 222; Negotiating While Fighting, pp; 51, 63–65, 67–92; Hermes, Truce Tent and Fighting Front, pp. 112–121, 176–177; Vatcher, Panmunjom, pp. 69–85; Simmons, The Strained Alliance, pp. 211–213; Donald Zagoria, "Some Comparisons Between the Russian and Chinese Models," in Communist Strategies in Asia, edited by A. Doak Barnett (New York: Praeger, 1963), pp. 15–18.

2. Hermes, Truce Tent and Fighting Front, pp. 180–181, 351; Rees, Korea, pp. 301–302; S.L.A. Marshall, Pork Chop Hill (New York: Jove, 1986), pp. 5–11; Shu Guang Zhang, Mao's Military Romanticism, pp. 162, 216, 225; Farrar-Hockley, The British Part in the Korean War, Vol. II, pp. 354–355.

3. FRUS 1951, Vol.VII, pp. 1177, 1206–1208, 1212–1237, 1239, 1250–1252, 1321–1331, 1345, 1366, 1377–1382, 1401–1402, 1420–1421, 1427–1428; Negotiating While Fighting, pp. 83–143; Hermes, Truce Tent and Fighting Front, pp. 121–130, 152–153; Vatcher, Panmunjom, pp. 88–89.

4. Foreign Relations of the United States 1952–1954, Volume XV (Washington: Government Printing Office 1984), pp. 4–7, 13, 17–18, 70–72, 80–81, 90–91, 117–119, 125–128; Hermes, Truce Tent and Fighting Front, pp. 152–166; Vatcher, Panmunjom, pp. 99–113; Farrar-Hockley, The British Part in the Korean War, Vol. II, pp. 252–254.

5. FRUS 1951, Vol.VII, pp. 791–794, 857–859: FRUS 1952–1954, Vol. XV, pp. 32–34, 40–44, 56–59, 66–67, 72, 76–81, 90–91, 98–99, 125–128, 135–138, 142–153, 184–185, 247–249, 395–398; Negotiating While Fighting, pp. 144–145, 147–148, 152, 154–160, 172, 174, 178–179, 188, 191–194, 214–217, 349–350, 367, 375, 381; Hermes, Truce Tent and Fighting Front, pp. 135–153, 163, 167–174, 240–243; Vatcher, Panmunjom, pp. 116–141; Rosemary Foot, Substitute for Victory (Ithaca: Cornell University Press, 1990), pp. 87–101, 109–119, 124–126, 129–130; Farrar-Hockley, The British Part in the Korean War, Vol. II, pp. 262–266, 282–285; Mao to Stalin, 31 January 1952, in Weathersby, "New Russian Documents"; Stueck, The Korean War, pp. 250–261.

6. Negotiating While Fighting, pp. 354–356; Hermes, Truce Tent and Fighting Front, pp. 236–262; William L. White, The Captives of Korea (New York: Scribners, 1957); Foot, Substitute for Victory, pp. 109–120, 124–126, 129–131; Farrar-Hockley, The British Part in the Korean War, Vol. II, pp. 282–289.

7. Rees, Korea, pp. 328–346; Farrar-Hockley, The British Part in the Korean War, Vol. II, pp. 266–278, 409–413; Albert Biderman, The March to Calumny (New York: MacMillan, 1963); Chinnery, Korean Atrocity!, pp. 88–258.

8. *FRUS 1952–1954, Vol. XV*, pp. 180–183, 430–446; Hermes, *Truce Tent and Fighting Front*, pp. 199–201, 283–284, 293, 331–332, 340–342.

9. Hermes, *Truce Tent and Fighting Front*, pp. 283–285, 303–310; Shu Guang Zhang, *Mao's Military Romanticism*, pp. 225–231; Farrar-Hockley, *The British Part in the Korean War, Vol. II*, pp. 354–361.

10. Futrell, *The United States Air Force in Korea*, pp. 475–536, 612–619, 635–639; Y'Blood, MIG Alley, pp 31–38; Crane, *American Airpower Strategy in Korea*, pp. 113–129; Cagle and Manson, *The Sea War in Korea*, pp. 347, 440–468, 474; Hallion, *Naval Air War in Korea*, pp. 132–139.

11. *FRUS 1952–1954, Vol. XV*, pp. 430–435; Shu Guang Zhang, *Mao's Military Romanticism*, p. 222; Mastny, *Cold War and Soviet Insecurity*, p. 147; *Khrushchev Remembers: The Last Testament*, pp. 277–279; *Pravda*, August 24, 1952, pp. 3–4; Futrell, *The United States Air Force in Korea*, pp. 522–529; Mao to Zhou Enlai, 16 September 1952, in Weathersby, "New Russian Documents"; "Talks With Mao Zedong and Zhou Enlai, 1949–1953," in *Cold War International History Project Bulletin*, 6–7; Zagoria, "Some Comparisons Between the Russian and Chinese Models," pp. 18–19.

12. *FRUS 1952–1954, Vol. XV*, pp. 252–256, 264–269, 274–276, 279–286, 290–295, 301–308, 324–338, 349–351, 376, 402–404; Hermes, *Truce Tent and Fighting Front*, pp. 345–347.

13. *FRUS 1952–1954, Vol. XV*, pp. 430–435, 441–445, 554–557, 623–625, 637–645, 692–693; Chester Bowles, *An Ambassador's Report* (New York: Harper, 1954), pp. 242–243; Acheson, *Present at the Creation*, pp. 886–898; Hermes, *Truce Tent and Fighting Front*, pp. 265–281, 403–404; Mastny, *Cold War and Soviet Insecurity*, pp. 148, 161; Stueck, *The Korean War*, pp. 278–283, 286–289, 300–305; Foot, *Substitute for Victory*, pp. 131–133, 152–156; Farrar-Hockley, *The British Part in the Korean War, Vol. II*, pp. 331–335, 340–350.

Chapter 17

1. Milton Leitenberg, "New Russian Evidence on the Korean War Biological Warfare Allegations," in *Cold War International History Project Bulletin 11*; Kathryn Weathersby, "Deceiving the Deceivers," in *Cold War International History Project Bulletin 11*; Shu Guang Zhang, *Mao's Military Romanticism*, pp. 181–186; John Clews, *The Communists' New Weapon—Germ Warfare* (London: Lincolns Praeger, 1953), pp. 26–28; Rees, *Korea*, pp. 352–353; Stebbins, *United States in World Affairs 1952*, pp 25; *Current Digest of the Soviet Press, Vol. III, No. 8* (April 7, 1951), p. 20; *Current Digest of the Soviet Press Vol. III, No. 18* (June 16, 1951), p. 19; *Current Digest of the Soviet Press Vol. III, No. 33* (September 29, 1951), p. 4.

2. Clews, *The Communists' New Weapon—Germ Warfare*, pp. 7–25, 29 ff.; Robert Conquest, *The Great Terror* (New York: Collier, 1973), pp. 194–202; Calvocoressi, *Survey of International Affairs 1952*, pp 187–188; Biderman, *The March to Calumny*, pp. 77–79; White, *The Captives of Korea*, pp. 147–151, 166–167, 174–175, 259. *Current Digest of the Soviet Press Vol. IV, No. 8* (April 5, 1952), pp. 4–5; *Current Digest of the Soviet Press Vol. IV, No. 9*, (April 12, 1952), pp. 12–13; *Current Digest of the Soviet Press Vol. IV, No. 10* (April 19, 1952), pp 31–32; *Current Digest of the Soviet Press Vol. IV, No. 18* (June 14, 1952), pp. 13–14.

3. *Current Digest of the Soviet Press Vol. IV, No. 33* (July 19, 1952), pp. 3–5.

4. *FRUS 1952–1954, Vol. XV*, pp. 430–435; Kennan, *Memoirs 1950–1963*, pp. 123–134, 327–351.

5. Royal Institute of International Affairs, *Documents on International Affairs, 1952* (London: Oxford University Press, 1953), pp. 86–105, 186–190; Mastny, *Cold War and Soviet Insecurity*, pp. 134–137; Acheson, *Present at the Creation*, pp. 803–806; Calvocoressi, *Survey of International Affairs 1952*, pp. 88–90, 109–128; Stebbins, *United States in World Affairs 1952*, pp. 138–149; Shulman, *Stalin's Foreign Policy Reappraised*, pp. 191–194; Wolfe, *Soviet Power in Europe*, pp. 27–31.

6. Mastny, *Cold War and Soviet Insecurity*, pp. 147–149; "Economic Problems of Socialism," in *The Essential Stalin* edited by H. Bruce Franklin (New York: Anchor, 1972), pp. 471–473.

7. Mastny, *Cold War and Soviet Insecurity*, pp. 153–168; Conquest, *Power and Policy in the USSR*, pp. 129–195.

Chapter 18

1. *FRUS 1952–1954, Vol. II*, pp. 264–281, 323–326, 360–366, 379–385, 394–434, 576–597, 833–836; Calvocoressi, *Survey of International Affairs 1952*, pp. 11–17; Louis L. Gerson, *John Foster Dulles* (New York: Cooper Square 1967), p. 331n. 16; Gaddis, *The Long Peace*, pp 174–189; Kennan, *Memoirs 1950–1963*, pp. 175–183; Rees, *Korea*, pp. 388–401.

2. Hermes, *Truce Tent and Fighting Front*, pp. 56, 332, 340, 357–358, 366–368; Stueck, *The Korean War*, pp. 283–285; Foot, *Substitute for Victory*, pp. 148–150, 155–156, 164–168, 172, 176, 184, 196; *FRUS 1952–1954, Vol. XV*, pp. 527–528, 548–550; Rees, *Korea*, pp. 402–405; Crane, *American Airpower Strategy in Korea*, pp. 155–159.

3. Stalin to Mao, 27 December 1952, in Weathersby, "New Russian Documents"; Shu Guang Zhang, *Mao's Military Romanticism*, p. 232.

4. *FRUS 1952–1954, Vol. XV*, pp. 769–777, 805–812, 817–818, 825–827, 838–857, 865–877, 880–882, 886–895, 1012–1017, 1059–1068; Hermes, *Truce Tent and Fighting Front*, pp. 332, 366, 408–409; Vatcher, *Panmunjom*, pp. 179–202; Rees, *Korea*, pp. 418–420; Crane, *American Airpower Strategy in Korea*, pp. 155–159; Foot, *The Wrong War*, pp. 184, 204–226; Frank Holober, *Raiders of the China Coast* (Annapolis: Naval Institute Press, 1999).

5. Mastny, *Cold War and Soviet Insecurity*, pp. 168–183; "Resolution of the USSR Council of Ministers, 19 March 1953," in Weathersby, "New Russian Documents"; Seweryn Bialer, *Stalin's Successors* (New York: Cambridge University Press, 1980); Conquest, *Power and Policy in the USSR*, p. 195–260.

6. *FRUS 1952–1954, Vol. XV*, pp. 788–790, 824–825, 829–831, 877–879, 902; Foot, *Substitute for Victory*, pp. 167–169; Hermes, *Truce Tent and Fighting Front*, pp. 409–425; Shu Guang Zhang, *Mao's Military Romanticism*, p. 242; Marshall, *Pork Chop Hill*; Stueck, *The Korean War*, pp. 313ff.

7. Futrell, *The United States Air Force in Korea*, pp. 652–657, 667–672, 681; Lansdown, *With the Carriers in Korea*, pp. 289–290, 299–301; Y'Blood, *MIG Alley*, p. 40; Crane, *American Airpower Strategy in Korea*, pp. 160–163, 167.

8. *FRUS 1952–1954, Vol. XV*, pp. 910–915, 940–943, 1046–1048, 1068–1069; Hermes, *Truce Tent and Fighting Front*, pp. 425–497; Foot, *Substitute for Victory*, pp. 169–193; Charles Bohlen, *Witness to History* (New York: Norton, 1973), pp. 349–352 ; Rees, *Korea*, pp. 416–434; Stueck, *The Korean War*, pp. 323–336.

Bibliography

"(OH)" denotes an official history

Acheson, Dean. *Present at the Creation*. New York: New American Library, 1970.
Adenauer, Konrad. *Memoirs*. Chicago: Regnery, 1966.
Alexander, Bevin. *Korea: The First War We Lost*. New York: Hippocrene, 1986.
Appleman, Roy. *Disaster in Korea*. College Station: Texas A & M University Press, 1989.
_____. *East of Chosin*. College Station: Texas A & M University Press, 1987.
_____. *Escaping the Trap*. College Station: Texas A & M University Press, 1990.
_____. *From the Naktong to the Yalu*. Washington: Department of the Army, 1961. (OH)
_____. *Ridgway Duels for Korea*. College Station: Texas A & M University Press, 1990.
Bader, William B. *Austria Between East and West*. Stanford: Stanford University Press, 1966.
Bajanov, Evgueni. "Assessing the Politics of the Korean War, 1949–1951." *Cold War International History Project Bulletin*, no. 6–7.
Ballantine, Joseph. *Formosa*. Washington: Brookings Institution, 1952.
Barck, Oscar T. *History of the United States Since 1945*. New York: Dell, 1965.
Baring, Arnulf. *The Uprising in East Germany*. Ithaca: Cornell University Press, 1972.
Berger, Carl. *The Korea Knot*. Philadelphia: University of Pennsylvania Press, 1957.
Bialer, Seweryn. *Stalin's Successors*. New York: Cambridge University Press, 1980.
Biderman, Albert. *The March to Calumny*. New York: Macmillan, 1963.
Blair, Clay. *The Forgotten War*. New York: Times Books, 1987.
Blum, Robert. *Drawing the Line*. New York: Norton, 1982.
Bohlen, Charles. *Witness to History*. New York: Norton, 1973.
Bortoli, Georges. *The Death of Stalin*. New York: Praeger, 1975.
Bowers, William T., and Hammond, William M. *Black Soldiers, White Army*. Washington: Center of Military History, 1996. (OH)
Bowles, Chester. *An Ambassador's Report*. New York: Harper, 1954.
Buckley, Roger. *Occupation Diplomacy*. Cambridge: Cambridge University Press, 1982.
Cagle, Malcolm, and Manson, Frank. *The Sea War in Korea*. Annapolis: Naval Institute Press, 1957. (OH)
Caidin, Martin. *The Fork-Tailed Devil*. New York: Ballantine, 1971.
Calvocoressi, Peter. *Survey of International Affairs 1949–1950*. London: Oxford University Press, 1953.
_____. *Survey of International Affairs, 1952*. London: Oxford University Press, 1955.
Chang, Gordon. *Friends and Enemies*. Stanford: Stanford University Press, 1990.

Chen, Jian. *China's Road to the Korean War*. New York: Columbia University Press, 1994.
Chinnery, Philip. *Korean Atrocity*. Annapolis: Naval Institute Press, 2001.
Chow, Ching-wen. *Ten Years of Storm*. New York: Holt, Rinehart and Winston, 1960.
Clews, John. *The Communists' New Weapon – Germ Warfare*. London: Lincolns Praeger, 1953.
Coleman, J.D. *Wonju*. Washington: Brassey's, 2001.
Condit, D.M. *The Test of War*. Washington: Office of the Secretary of Defense, 1988. (OH)
Conquest, Robert. *The Great Terror*. New York: Collier, 1973.
_____. *Power and Policy in the USSR*. New York: St. Martin's Press, 1967.
Crane, Conrad. *American Airpower Strategy in Korea, 1950–1953*. Lawrence: University of Kansas, 2000.
Cumings, Bruce. *Origins of the Korean War*. Princeton: Princeton University Press, 1981.
Current Digest of the Soviet Press.
Department of State Bulletin, May 28, 1951, pp. 842–843.
Dobbs, Charles. *The Unwanted Symbol*. Kent, Ohio: Kent State University Press, 1981.
Donovan, Robert. *Tumultuous Years*. New York: Norton, 1982.
Doenecke, Justus. *Not to the Swift*. Lewisburg, Pennsylvania: Bucknell University Press, 1979.
Dorn, Frank *Walkout*. New York: Pyramid, 1973.
Dunn, Frederick. *Peace-Making and the Settlement with Japan*. Princeton: Princeton University Press, 1963.
The Eisenhower Diaries. Ed. by Robert H. Ferrell. New York: Norton, 1981.
Evans, Douglas. *Sabre Jets Over Korea*. Blue Ridge Summit, Pennsylvania: Tab, 1984.
Everest, Frank. *The Fastest Man Alive*. New York: Berkley, 1986.
Farrar-Hockley, Anthony. *The British Part in the Korean War*. Volume I. London: Her Majesty's Stationery Office, 1990. (OH)
_____. *The British Part in the Korean War*. Volume II. (London: Her Majesty's Stationery Office, 1997. (OH)
Feis, Herbert. *Contest Over Japan*. New York: Norton, 1969.
Field, James. *History of United States Naval Operations, Korea*. Washington: US Navy, 1962. (OH)
Foot, Rosemary. *Substitute for Victory*. Ithaca: Cornell University Press, 1990.
_____. *The Wrong War*. Ithaca: Cornell University Press, 1985.
Foreign Relations of the United States 1945. Volume II. Washington: Government Printing Office, 1967.
Foreign Relations of the United States 1946. Volume VIII. Washington: Government Printing Office, 1969.
Foreign Relations of the United States 1947. Volume VI. Washington: Government Printing Office, 1972.
Foreign Relations of the United States 1948. Volume VI. Washington: Government Printing Office, 1973.
Foreign Relations of the United States 1950. Volume I. Washington: Government Printing Office, 1977.
Foreign Relations of the United States 1950. Volume IV. Washington: Government Printing Office, 1980.
Foreign Relations of the United States 1950. Volume V. Washington: Government Printing Office, 1978.
Foreign Relations of the United States 1950. Volume VI. Washington: Government Printing Office, 1980.
Foreign Relations of the United States 1950. Volume III. Washington: Government Printing Office, 1977.

Foreign Relations of the United States 1950. Volume VII. Washington: Government Printing Office, 1976
Foreign Relations of the United States 1951. Volume I. Washington: Government Printing Office, 1979.
Foreign Relations of the United States 1951. Volume III. Washington: Government Printing Office, 1979.
Foreign Relations of the United States 1951. Volume VI. Washington: Government Printing Office, 1977.
Foreign Relations of the United States 1951. Vol. VII. Washington: Government Printing Office, 1983.
Foreign Relations of the United States 1952–1954. Volume II. Washington: Government Printing Office, 1984.
Foreign Relations of the United States 1952–1954. Volume XV. Washington: Government Printing Office, 1984.
Futrell, Robert F. *The United States Air Force in Korea*, revised edition. Washington: Office of Air Force History, 1983. (OH)
Gaddis, John Lewis. *The Long Peace.* New York: Oxford University Press, 1987.
———. *Strategies of Containment.* New York: Oxford University Press, 1982.
———. "Korea in American Politics, Strategy and Diplomacy 1945–1950." In *The Origins of the Cold War in East Asia*, edited by Yohosuke Nagai and Akira Iriye. New York: Columbia University Press, 1977.
———. *We Now Know.* New York: Oxford University Press, 1997.
George, Alexander L. *The Chinese Communist Army in Action.* New York: Columbia University Press, 1967.
Gerson, Louis L. *John Foster Dulles.* New York: Cooper Square, 1967.
Goldman, Eric F. *The Crucial Decade and After.* New York: Vintage, 1960.
Goncharov, Sergei N.; Lewis, John W.; and Xue, Litai. *Uncertain Partners.* Stanford: Stanford University Press, 1993.
Gordon, Yefim, and Rigant, Vladimir. *MIG-15.* Osceola, Wisconsin: Motorbooks, 1994.
Goulden, Joseph. *Korea: The Untold Story of the War.* New York: Times Books, 1982.
Green, A.Wigfall. *The Epic of Korea.* Washington: Public Affairs Press, 1950.
Griffith, Robert. *The Politics of Fear.* Lexington, Kentucky: University of Kentucky Press, 1970.
Hallion, Richard. *The Naval Air War in Korea.* Baltimore: Nautical and Aviation Publishing Co., 1986.
Heinzig, Dieter. "Stalin, Mao and Cold War Origins." *Cold War International History Project Bulletin*, no. 6–7.
Heinl, Robert. *Victory at High Tide.* Baltimore: Nautical and Aviation Publishing Co., 1979.
Henderson, Gregory. *Korea.* Cambridge: Harvard University Press, 1968.
Hermes, Walter. *Truce Tent and Fighting Front.* Washington: Department of the Army, 1966. (OH)
Hewlett, Richard G., and Duncan, Francis. *Atomic Shield.* University Park, Pennsylvania: Pennsylvania University Press, 1969. (OH)
Holloway, David. *Stalin and the Bomb.* New Haven: Yale University Press, 1994.
Holober, Frank. *Raiders of the China Coast.* Annapolis: Naval Institute Press, 1999.
Hone, Thomas. "Korea." In *Case Studies in the Achievement of Air Superiority*, ed. by B. Franklin Cooling.Washington: Center for Air Force History, 1994. (OH)
Hopkins, William B. *One Bugle, No Drums.* New York: Avon, 1988.
James, D. Clayton. *The Years of MacArthur.* Volume III. Boston: Houghton Mifflin, 1985.
Jasny, Naum. *Soviet Industrialization.* Chicago: University of Chicago Press, 1961.
Kapitsa, Mikhail. *KNR.* Moscow: Politizdat, 1969.

Kaplan, Karel. *Dans les Archives du Comité Central*. Paris: Albin Michel, 1978.
Karig, Walter. *Battle Report: The Korean War*. New York: Rinehart, 1952.
Kaufman, Burton. *The Korean War*. New York: Knopf, 1986.
Kennan, George. *Memoirs 1925–1950*. New York: Bantam, 1967.
———. *Memoirs 1950–1963*. Boston: Little, Brown, 1972.
———. *Russia and the West Under Lenin and Stalin*. New York: New American Library, 1961.
Kiraly, Bela K. "The Aborted Soviet Military Plans Against Tito's Yugoslavia." In *At the Brink of War and Peace*, edited by Wayne C. Vucinich. New York: Brooklyn College Press, 1982.
———. "Military Aspects." In *The Hungarian Revolution of 1956 in Retrospect*, edited by Bela K. Kiraly and Paul Jonas. (Boulder: East European Quarterly, 1977.
Koon Woon Nam. *The North Korean Communist Leadership*. Birmingham University of Alabama Press, 1974.
Khrushchev, Nikita. *Khrushchev Remembers*. Boston: Little, Brown, 1970.
Koenig, Helmut. "Der Konflikt Zwischen Stalin and Togliatti um die Jahreswende 1950/51." *Osteuropa*, October 1970, pp. 669–706.
Korea Institute for Military History. *Korean War*. Volume I, Lincoln: University of Nebraska Press, 1997.
Langer, Paul, and Swearingen, Rodger. *Red Flag in Japan*. Cambridge: Harvard University Press, 1952.
Lansdown, John. *With the Carriers in Korea*. Wilmslow, England: Crecy, 1997.
Latham, Earl. *The Communist Controversy in Washington*. Cambridge: Harvard University Press, 1965.
Leckie, Robert. *Conflict*. New York: Avon, 1964.
Leitenberg, Milton. "New Russian Evidence on the Korean War Biological Warfare Allegations." *Cold War International History Project Bulletin*, No. 11.
The Journals of David Lilienthal Volume III. New York: Harper and Row, 1966.
Loeffler, Melvyn. *A Preponderance of Power*. Stanford: Stanford University Press, 1992.
Lowe, Peter. *The Origins of the Korean War*. 2nd edition. New York: Longman, 1997.
Mansourov, Alexander. "Stalin, Mao, Kim and China's Decision to Enter the Korean War." *Cold War International History Project Bulletin*, no. 6–7.
Mark, Eduard. *Aerial Interdiction in Three Wars*. Washington: Center for Air Force History, 1994. (OH)
Marshall, S.L.A. *Battle at Best*. New York: Morrow, 1963.
———. *The River and the Gauntlet*. New York: Time, 1962.
Mastny, Vojtech. *The Cold War and Soviet Insecurity*. New York: Oxford University Press, 1996.
McCune, George. *Korea Today*. Cambridge: Harvard University Press, 1950.
McLane, Charles B. *Soviet Policy and the Chinese Communists*. New York: Columbia University Press, 1958.
Meade, Grant. *American Military Government in Korea*. New York: King's Crown Press, 1951.
Medvedev, Roy. *Let History Judge*. New York: Vintage, 1973.
Middleton, Drew. *The Defense of Western Europe*. New York: Appleton-Century Crofts, 1952.
Military Situation in the Far East. Hearings before the Armed Services Committee and the Foreign Relations Committee, United States Senate, 82nd Congress, 1st Session, 1951, 5 vols. Washington: Government Printing Office, 1951.
Milward, Alan. *The Reconstruction of Western Europe*. London: Methuen, 1984.
Montross, Lynn. *U.S. Marine Operations in Korea*. Volume IV. Quantico, Virginia: U.S. Marine Corps, 1962. (OH)

Mossman, Billy. *Ebb and Flow*. Washington: Center for Military History, 1990. (OH)
Mueller, John. *War, Presidents and Public Opinion*. New York: Wiley, 1973.
Negotiating While Fighting: The Diary of Admiral C. Turner Joy at the Korean Armistice Conference, Edited by Allan E. Goodman. Stanford: Hoover Institution Press, 1978.
Nicolaevsky, Boris. *Power and the Soviet Elite*. New York: Praeger, 1965.
Nitze, Paul. "The Evolution of National Security Policy." In *The Lessons of Vietnam*. Edited by W. Scott Thompson and D.D. Frizzell. New York: Crane, Russak, 1977.
Norman, John. "MacArthur's Blockade Proposals Against Red China." *Pacific Historical Review*, May 1957.
North Korea: A Case Study in Communist Takeover. Washington: Government Printing Office, 1961.
Paige, Glenn D. "Korea." In *Communism and Revolution*, Edited by Cyril Black and Thomas Thornton. Princeton: Princeton University Press, 1964.
_____. *The Korean Decision*. New York: Free Press, 1968.
_____. *1950 Truman's Decision*. New York: Vintage, 1970.
Paik Sun Yup, *From Pusan to Panmunjom*. New York: Brassey's, 1997.
Petrov, Vladimir, and Petrov, Evdokia. *Empire of Fear*. New York: Praeger, 1956.
Radford, Arthur. *From Pearl Harbor to Vietnam*. Stanford: Hoover Institution Press, 1980.
Rankin, Karl Lott. *China Assignment*. Seattle: University of Washington Press, 1964.
Rees, David. *Korea: The Limited War*. Baltimore: Pelican, 1970.
Report of the Royal Commission on Espionage, 22nd August 1955. Sydney, 1955.
Ridgway, Matthew B. *The Korean War*. New York: Popular Library, 1968.
Rigg, Robert B. *Red China's Fighting Hordes*. Harrisburg, Pennsylvania: Military Service Publishing Company, 1951.
Riley, John W., and Schramm, Wilbur. *The Reds Take a City*. New Brunswick: Rutgers University Press, 1951.
Roe, Patrick. *The Dragon Strikes*. Novato, California: Presidio, 2000.
Roper, Elmo. *You and Your Leaders*. New York: William Morrow, 1957.
Rovere, Richard, and Schlesinger, Arthur. *The MacArthur Controversy and American Foreign Policy*. New York: Farrar, Straus and Giroux, 1965.
Royal Institute for International Affairs. *Documents on International Affairs 1949–1950*. London: Oxford University Press, 1951.
_____. *Documents on International Affairs, 1951*. London: Oxford University Press, 1953.
_____. *Documents on International Affairs 1952*. London: Oxford University Press, 1953.
Rhodes, Richard. *Dark Sun*. New York: Simon and Schuster, 1995.
Russ, Martin. *Breakout*. New York: Penguin, 2000.
Sarin, Oleg, and Dvoretsky, Lev. *Alien Wars*. Novato, California: Presidio, 1996.
Sawyer, Robert K. *KMAG: Military Advisors in Korea*. Washington: Department of the Army, 1962. (OH)
Scalapino, Robert A. *The Japanese Communist Movement*. Berkeley: University of California Press, 1967.
_____, and Lee, Chong-sik. *Communism in Korea*. Berkeley: University of California Press, 1972.
Schnabel, James F. *Policy and Direction: The First Year*. Washington: Office of Chief of Military History, 1972. (OH)
Sebald, William. *With MacArthur in Japan*. New York: Norton, 1965.
Sheldon, Walt. *Hell or High Water*. New York: Ballantine, 1973.
Shen Zhihua. "The Discrepancy Between the Russian and Chinese Versions of Mao's 2 October 1950 Message to Stalin." *Cold War International History Project Bulletin*, no. 8–9.
Sheng, Michael. *Battling Western Imperialism*. Princeton: Princeton University Press, 1997.

Shu Guang Zhang, *Mao's Military Romanticism: China and the Korean War 1950–1953*. Lawrence: University of Kansas Press, 1995.
Shulman, Marshall B. *Stalin's Foreign Policy Reappraised*. Cambridge: Harvard University Press, 1963.
Spanier, John. *The Truman-MacArthur Controversy and the Korean War*. New York: Norton, 1965.
Stalin, Josef. "Economic Problems of Socialism." In *The Essential Stalin*, edited by H. Bruce Franklin. New York: Anchor, 1972.
Stanton, Shelby. *America's Tenth Legion*. Novato, Calofornia: Presidio, 1987.
Stearman, William. *The Soviet Union and the Occupation of Austria*. Bad Goesberg: Verlag fur Zeitarchiv, 1960.
Stebbins, Richard. *The United States in World Affairs, 1950*. New York: Harper, 1951.
_____. *The United States in World Affairs, 1951*. New York: Harper, 1952.
Stouffer, Samuel *Communism, Conformity and Civil Liberties*. Garden City: Doubleday, 1954.
Stueck, William. *The Road to Confrontation*. Chapel Hill: University of North Carolina Press, 1981.
Suh, Dae-sook. *The Korean Communist Movement*. Princeton: Princeton University Press, 1967.
"Talks with Mao Zedong and Zhou Enlai, 1949–1953." *Cold War International History Project Bulletin*. no. 6–7.
Tang Tsou. *America's Failure in China 1941–1950*. Chicago: University of Chicago Press, 1963.
Truman, Harry. *Years of Trial and Hope*. New York: New American Library, 1965.
Tsukahira, Toshio. *The Postwar Evolution of Communist Strategy in Japan*. Cambridge: MIT Press, 1954.
Ulam, Adam. *Expansion and Coexistence*. New York: Praeger, 1968.
_____. *The Rivals*. New York: Viking Press, 1971.
Van Aduard, E. J. Lewe. *Japan from Surrender to Peace*. New York: Praeger, 1952.
Vatcher, William H. *Panmunjom*. New York: Praeger, 1958.
Weathersby, Kathryn. "Deceiving the Deceivers." *Cold War International History Project Bulletin*, no. 11.
_____. " New Findings on the Korean War." *Cold War International History Project Bulletin*, no. 3.
_____. *Soviet Aims in Korea and the Origins of the Korean War*. Cold War International History Project Working Paper Number 8.
_____. "To Attack or Not to Attack? Stalin, Kim Il Sung, and the Prelude to War." *Cold War International History Project Bulletin*, no. 5.
Weinstein, Martin. *Japan's Postwar Defense Policy*. New York: Columbia University Press, 1968.
White, William L. *The Captives of Korea*. New York: Scribners, 1957.
Whiting, Allen S. *China Crosses the Yalu*. Stanford: Stanford University Press, 1960.
Wolfe, Thomas. *Soviet Power and Europe*. Ithaca: Cornell University Press, 1970.
Y'Blood, William T. *MIG Alley*. Washington: Air Force History and Museums Program, 2000. (OH)
Yoshitsu, Michael M. *Japan and the San Francisco Peace Settlement*. New York: Columbia University Press, 1983.
Zagoria, Donald. "Some Comparisons Between the Russian and Chinese Models." *Communist Strategies in Asia*, edited by A. Doak Barnett. New York: Praeger, 1963.
Zaloga, Steve. *Target America*. Novato, California: Presidio, 1993.
Zubok, Vladislav, and Pleshakov, Constantine. *Inside the Kremlin's Cold War*. Cambridge: Harvard University Press, 1996.

Index

Abakumov, Viktor 172
Acheson, Secretary of State Dean 26, 38, 51, 52, 54, 57, 58, 77, 78, 91, 113, 118, 119–120, 122, 123, 139, 140, 142, 143, 144, 147, 148, 149, 180, 186, 205, 207, 215, 217, 229, 235, 236, 243, 262, 263, 268, 272
Adenauer, Chancellor Konrad 118, 268
Air operations 64, 66, 68, 69, 70–71, 72, 74, 85, 108–110, 128, 134, 152–154, 160–161, 164, 166, 188–192, 199, 201, 203, 222–226, 258–260, 283
"air pressure" 258–260, 283
Air War College 79
Airborne operations 105, 186
Aircraft carrier operations 60–61, 63, 71, 85, 109–111, 154, 189, 225 226, 259, 283
Aircraft types: Avenger 134; B-26 Invader 128, 189, 225, 259; B-29 Superfortress 71, 74, 109, 141, 189, 191, 192, 222–224, 225, 258; C-47, 130; Corsair 61, 71, 72, 134, 135, 225; F3D Skynight 224; F9F Panther 109; F-51 Mustang 64, 68, 74, 258; F-80 Shooting Star 63, 192, 222, 258; F-82 Twin Mustang 63, 64; F-84 Thunderjet 110, 152–153, 192, 222, 258; F-86 Sabrejet 60, 110, 153–154, 160, 192, 203, 222, 223, 224, 258, 283; F-94 Starfire 224; Meteor 8 222; MIG-15, 60, 108, 109, 153–154, 192, 203, 222–223, 226, 258, 283; Mya-4 (Bison) 173; P-38 Lightning 37; RB-29 109; RB-45 223; RF-80 111; Skyraider 61, 71, 199, 225; Stormovik 43, 199; Tupolev-85 172; Tupolev-95 (Bear) 173; Yak fighters 43, 108, 199
Albania 8, 16
Allison, John 91
Almond, Gen. Edward 80, 81, 82–83, 86, 94, 112, 124, 125, 129, 131–132, 133, 136, 138, 146, 161, 162, 164, 165, 166, 200, 201, 202, 203
American Federation of Labor 36
Amphibious operations 63, 66, 68, 77, 80–87, 155, 160, 163, 184, 188, 202, 220, 257, 278
Amtracs 85, 86
Anderson, Gen. Orvil 79
Andong (China) 45, 192
Andong (Korea) 184
Arab-Asian bloc 148
Armistice negotiations 5, 178, 212–219, 231, 239, 240–241, 244–255, 256, 263–265, 282–285; airfields 247–250, 252; demarcation line and demilitarized zone 216, 218–219, 244–245, 264; first recess 219; inspection and supervision 216, 247–250, 252, 264; "package deal" 252–253; prisoners of war 216, 250–255, 260, 263–265, 282–285; removal of non-Korean forces 216–217; rotation 248–249, 264; second recess 263
Artillery 36, 43–44, 61, 65, 83, 88, 100,

311

104, 125–126, 131, 159, 166, 167, 199, 200, 212, 220, 247, 282
Atomic weapons 9, 10, 11, 52, 99, 141, 142, 171, 172, 173, 174, 196, 278, 279
Atrocities 74, 89–90, 154, 255–256
Attlee, Prime Minister Clement 11, 145
Australia and Australians 63, 105, 222, 228, 229
Austria 117, 268

Badger, Adm. Oscar 49
Bajpai, Sir Girja 175
Barr, Gen. David 129
Belgian Battalion 198
Belgium 16, 142
Bereitschaften 41, 118, 119, 122
Beria, Lavrenty 172, 271, 280
Berlin 7, 16, 23, 25, 118
Berlin Blockade 16, 23, 174
Bevin, Foreign Secretary Ernest 118
Blockade 58, 143, 146, 156–158, 204, 205, 207, 209, 215, 219, 260
Bloody Ridge 220, 257
Bohlen, Charles 91, 92, 140, 143, 283, 285
Bolte, Gen. Charles 240
Bonin islands 122, 123, 229, 236
Bowles, Chester 263, 277
Bowling Alley 74, 76
Bradley, Gen. Omar 48, 51, 52, 79, 112, 139, 144, 146, 205, 207, 208
Brainwashing 256
Britain 6, 7, 8, 9, 12, 15, 24, 53–54, 58, 63, 77, 93, 113, 116, 118, 120, 142, 145, 150, 196, 228, 229–230, 232, 234–235, 237, 239, 242–243
British Army units: 27th British (later Commonwealth) Brigade 75, 88, 90, 105, 106, 107, 127–128, 138, 159, 166, 184, 197, 199; 29th Brigade 159, 160, 197; Gloucester Battalion 198–199
British Commonwealth 58, 263
British Commonwealth Division 221, 247, 257
Bulganin, Nikolai 23
Bulgaria 8, 9, 11, 49
Burchett, Wilfred 269
Burma 16, 24, 50, 169, 178, 179, 231
Byrnes, Secretary of State James 12, 15, 31

Cairo Declaration 182

Canadians 134
Carlson's Canyon 190
Carpet bombing 74
Central Intelligence Agency 48, 49, 91, 97, 111, 113, 142, 145, 196, 208–209, 242, 264, 277
Cepicka, Alexej 170, 171
Chae, Gen. Byong Duk 47
Chen Yi, Gen. 181–183
Cherokee strikes 259
China 17–22, 24, 92–93; armistice negotiations 212–219, 244–253, 282–285; and decision for Korean War 39, 40–41; decision to intervene in war 4–5, 20, 98–104, 293n.5; and Inchon landing 84; initial reaction to war 56; policy toward UN in late 1950–1951 148–150, 168; relations with the Soviets 9, 10, 21–23, 39–41, 98–104, 175, 178–179, 212–213, 245–246, 259–262, 280; secret negotiations with Americans 181–183; vulnerability to MacArthur's proposed actions 208–209; see also Taiwan
China Aid Act 19
China bloc 19, 20, 63, 158, 207
Chinaman's Hat 126
Chinese Air Force 104, 154, 222, 256
Chinese Army ("People's Liberation Army"): characteristics and armament 104–105; defenses in Korea 247; logistics 152, 189–191; tactics 104–105, 126, 198, 247; units: (Northeast Border Defense Army) 56, 99, 101; (3rd Army Group) 197, 198, 200; (3rd Field Army) 108; (4th Field Army) 56; (9th Army Group) 108, 124, 131, 136, 152, 185, 197, 198, 200; (12th Army) 201; (13th Army Group) 56, 84, 99, 104, 108, 124, 125, 197; (15th Army) 201; (19th Army Group) 197, 198; (26th Army) 131; (38th Army) 106, 126, 163; (39th Army) 106, 110, 165; (40th Army) 106, 165; (42nd Army) 106, 108, 124, 126, 129, 164, 165, 188; (50th Army) 108, 124, 163; (58th Division) 131, 136; (59th Division) 131; (60th Army) 185; (60th Division) 131; (63rd Army) 108, 124, 165; (66th Army) 108, 124, 165; (79th Division) 131; (80th Division) 131, 133, 136; (113th Divi-

Index

sion) 128; (115th Division) 111; (124th Division) 108; (125th Division) 164; (180th Division) 202
Chinese Civil War 17–19, 20, 38
Chinese Nationalists 17–19, 22, 53, 57, 92, 139–140, 141, 142, 144, 146, 149, 156, 158, 193, 194, 204, 206, 207, 209, 277, 278, 299n.8
Chinese Titoism 17, 20, 21, 24
Chinhung-ni 130, 134, 135
Chinju Pass 72
Chinnampo 81, 84, 111, 188
Chipyong-ni 163–164, 165–167
Cho-do island 258
Cho Man-sik 29
Chongchon 106, 107, 189; battle of 125–129
Chorwon 45, 220
Chosin Reservoir 124, 133, campaign 129–137
Chumunjin 81
Chunchon 46, 48, 155, 185, 202, 203
Church, Gen. John 48
Churchill, Winston 12, 13, 118, 141, 145, 242, 252
Clark, Lt. Eugene 84
Clark, Adm. J.J. 222, 259
Clark, Gen. Mark 257, 261–262, 271, 277–278
Cloverleaf 73, 76
Clubb, O. Edmund 113, 140, 143, 175
Cold revolution 8
Cold War: before Korean War 1, 3–4, 6, 7–24; outside Korea 115–123, 227–243, 280–281
Collins, Gen. J. Lawton 81, 82, 91, 146, 152, 167, 184
Containment 13
Coulson, Gen. Charles 254
Coulter, Gen. John 89, 127, 128
Council of Economic Advisers 239
Crombez, Col. Marcel 166
Czechoslovakia 12, 16, 248, 249, 268

Dairen 28
Dam attacks 283
Dandong 45, 56, 108
Davidson Line 69
Davies, John Paton 113, 168, 181
Dean, Gen. William 65–68
Decolonization 23–24

Defense Department 25, 50, 79, 92, 119, 122, 143, 234, 252
Desegregation 61, 72, 221
Dewey, Thomas 150
Dodd, Gen. Frank 254
Douglas, Sen. Paul 206
Doyle, Adm. James 82
Drysdale, Lt. Col. Douglas 132
DUKWs 185
Dulles, Secretary of State John Foster 57, 91, 122, 150, 229–230, 264, 276–277, 279–280, 283
Dutch Battalion 59, 154, 165, 167, 200

East Berlin 257
East-Central Europe 8, 9, 11, 13, 14, 27, 171, 172, 276
East German uprising 22, 171, 268, 281
East Germany 22, 27, 30, 41, 273
Economic Cooperation Administration 15
Economic Problems of Socialism 22, 178, 273–275
Eden, Foreign Secretary Anthony 242, 273, 279
Egypt 24, 178, 231, 232
Eisenhower, Gen. and Pres. Dwight D. 34, 57, 120, 151, 180, 221, 233–234, 239, 240, 242, 264, 276–280
Enoch, Lt. Kenneth 269
Ethiopian Battalion 155
European Coal and Steel Community 23
European Defense Community 235–237

Faith, Lt. Col. Don 133
France 8, 9, 16, 59, 118, 120–121, 178, 228, 232, 236–237, 239, 267
Franco, Francisco 235
Freeman, Col. Paul 129, 161, 166
French Battalion 59, 154, 164
Funchilin Pass 134–135

Gallup poll 25
Gao Gang 21, 22, 183, 212, 261
Gay, Gen. Hobart 107
Geneva Convention 250, 252
Germ war propaganda 246, 254, 267–271, 281
German rearmament 4, 117–123, 142, 147, 173, 175, 176, 180, 232, 235–237, 272

Germany 8, 9, 11, 12, 14, 15, 16, 22, 27, 30, 35, 50, 123, 147–148, 272–273
Gloucester Hill 198
Great Purges 174, 268, 269, 270
Greece and Greek Civil War 8, 15, 16, 49, 50, 235, 239, 243
Greek Battalion 155
Gromyko, Andrei 117, 231

H-bomb 25, 171, 174
Hagaru-ri 124, 130, 131, 132, 133, 134, 136
Hamhung 106
Han river 45, 47, 57, 64, 71, 81, 86, 154, 160, 162, 163, 185, 187
Harriman, Averell 28, 78
Harsch, Joseph 54
Hate America campaign 254, 266–271
Heartbreak Ridge 220, 257
Hickerson, John 262
Hickey, Gen. Doyle 82
Hiroshima 9, 11
Hodge, Gen. John 31, 32, 33, 34
Hoengsong 161, 164, 165, 184
Hong Kong 39, 40
Hongchon 47, 161, 164, 185
Hoover, Pres. Herbert 150
Hope, Bob 45
"hot pursuit" 110, 219
Huichon 125
Hungary 9, 42
Hungnam 44, 95, 106, 133, 134, 137, 146
Hwachon dam and reservoir 187–188, 198–199, 200, 201, 202, 220
Hydroelectric plants 110, 111, 112, 113, 143, 208, 219, 258–259, 277

Ignatiev, S.D. 281
Imjin 159, 186, 187, 198
Inchon 45, 56, 63, 66, 68, 80–87, 88, 160, 163, 188, 292n.2
India 24, 53, 77, 93, 169, 178, 230–231, 253, 260, 263, 284
Indochina 3, 39, 51, 98, 102, 140, 149, 168, 175, 179, 196–197, 226
Indonesia 16, 24, 50, 52, 178, 179
Inje 201
Intelligence 48–49, 70, 75, 84, 92, 97, 111, 113, 124, 129, 142, 194, 196, 208–209, 238, 277, 278

Interdiction 70, 71, 110–111, 154, 189–191, 222–226
Iran 8, 9, 10, 12, 13, 14, 16, 24–25, 49, 50, 52, 54, 57, 168, 179, 180, 238
Iron Curtain speech 13
Iron Triangle 45, 89, 187, 197, 200, 203, 282
Italy 8, 9, 15, 16
Iwon 95, 106

Jane Russell Hill 257
Japan 9, 10, 12, 20, 22, 23, 24, 26, 33, 40, 41, 42, 51, 52, 60, 62, 63, 147, 150, 156, 168, 196, 206, 221, 227–232; in Stalin's strategy 22, 40, 41–42, 227–228, 274–270
Japan-American Security Treaty 232
Japanese Communist Party 41–42, 84, 227–228
Japanese National Police Reserve 121, 195
Japanese peace treaty 4, 98, 122, 219, 228, 231, 263
Japanese rearmament 121–1222, 123, 229
Jiang Jieshi 12, 17, 19, 57, 78, 92, 182, 186, 207, 278, 299n.8
Johnson, Secretary of Defense Louis 79, 115, 122
Joint Chiefs of Staff 51, 58, 82, 106, 112, 121, 139, 143, 146, 156, 158, 168, 179, 187, 193–195, 205, 206, 207–208, 214, 215, 219, 234, 239–240, 247, 249, 250, 256, 277, 280
Joy, Adm. C. Turner 215–216, 218, 219, 245, 246, 248, 252, 254

Kaesong 45, 46, 214, 215, 219, 245
Kangnung 184
Kangye 106
Kansas Line 187, 199, 203
Kansong 201
Kapyong 199
Ka-san 76
Kasaniev, Vassili 97
KATUSAs 75, 83, 129
Kean, Gen. William 72
Keiser, Gen. Laurence 127–129
Kennan, Ambassador George 13, 25, 33, 57, 91, 140, 143, 144, 158, 208, 213, 271–273, 277
Kennedy, Joseph 150

Kenya 232
Keyserling, Leon 239
Khrushchev, Nikita 22, 55, 173, 176, 280, 281
Kilchu 190
Kim Il-sung 27, 29, 30, 37–39, 40, 55, 64, 75, 84, 88, 99–100, 102, 103, 212, 214, 259, 260, 262
Kim Kiu-sik 34, 35
Kim Koo 35
Kimpo 45, 81, 85, 153, 160, 163, 222
Kiraly, Gen. Bela 42
Kirk, Alan 91, 143
KMAG 36, 43, 44, 49
Knowland, Sen. William 149, 150, 195, 207
Koje-do 253–254, 270
Kojo 257
Korea: division and prewar developments 9, 24, 27, 28–31, 36; geography 44–45; *see also* North Korea; South Korea
Korean Communist Party 27, 29–30
Korean People's Republic 28, 29, 32
Korean War: American and UN intervention 48–55, 58; Chinese and Soviet intervention 96–114; Chinese offensive of spring 1951 184–203; decision for 38–41; defense of South Korea 60–79; final fighting 1953 282–285; ground offensives in 1951–53 219–221, 257; halting of Communists 152–167; impact on world affairs 115–123, 139–151, 170–180, 227–243; importance of 3; initial ROK defeats 46–48; origins 27–42; place in grand strategy 4, 40–41, 170–180; preparations for 38, 42–43; UN defeat in North Korea 138; UN defeat of North Koreans 80–95; war begins 46; *see also* Air operations; Armistice negotiations
Koto-ri 130, 134, 135
Kum river 65, 66, 156, 157
Kumchon pocket 105
Kumhwha 45, 203
Kunsan 81, 82, 85, 89
Kunu-ri 127

Lemay, Gen. Curtis 60
Li Kenong 216

Li Zonggren, Gen. 92
Libya 116
Lie, Secretary General Trygve 51, 55, 213, 217
Lightner, Charge 261
Lilienthal, David 158
Lin Biao 99, 101, 181
"Little Armistice" 247
Liu Shaoqi 181, 183
Lobov, Gen. 109
Lodge, Sen. Henry Cabot 150
Lovett, Secretary of Defense Robert 118, 240, 252
Lowe, Gen. Frank 78
Luce publications 19
Luke the Gook's Castle 257

MacArthur, Gen. Douglas 5, 6, 27, 34, 36, 48, 52, 54, 57, 58, 60, 61, 62–63, 66, 68, 69, 78–79, 80–84, 85, 93, 95, 97, 106, 108–109, 114, 121, 124, 125, 133–134, 136–137, 139, 141, 143, 145–146, 150, 155, 156–158, 163, 167, 186, 187, 193–195, 204–211, 253, 264; character and abilities 62–63; hearings 196, 204–209; proposals to take war to China 156–158; relief 193–195; view of China 62, 158
Malaya 16, 24, 50, 175, 179, 270
Malenkov, Georgi 271, 280, 281
Malik, Jacob 78, 122, 213–214, 266
Malinovsky, Marshal Rodion 55
Malone, Sen. George 54
Manchuria 9, 10, 18, 19, 21, 26, 28, 30, 31, 56, 84, 97, 98, 108, 140, 183, 185, 186, 189, 207, 215
Manpojin 105
Mao Zedong 4, 17, 20, 21–22, 38–39, 40, 84, 98–104, 148, 149, 152, 155, 163, 175, 178, 181–183, 186, 188, 199, 208, 212, 213, 214, 215, 217, 244, 245, 252, 260, 267, 278, 282
Marshall, Charles Burton 181, 213
Marshall, Gen. and Secretary of Defense and Secretary of State George 18–19, 106, 112, 113, 115–116, 120, 122, 139, 144, 146, 148, 149, 151, 167, 180, 187, 205, 207, 208, 210, 237
Marshall mission 9
Marshall Plan 15–16, 23, 116
Martin, Joe 194

MASH 61
Matthews, Secretary of the Navy Francis 79
McCarthy, Sen. Joseph, and McCarthyism 3, 22, 54, 113, 150, 151, 237
McCloy, John 118
McClure, Gen. Robert 250
McMahon, Sen. Brien 205
Meredith Victory 136
MIG Alley 160–161, 189, 191–192, 223–225
Milburn, Gen. Frank 88, 127, 128
Million Dollar Hill 257
Mines 80, 81, 84, 85, 95
Miryang 76
Mobilization 4, 116
Molotov, Vyachaslav 284
Moore, Gen. Byrant 184
Morocco 116
Moscow agreement 9, 31, 33
Mossadegh, Mohammed 179
MPQ radar 201
Muccio, John 52, 112, 262
Munsan-ni 186, 198

Naktong Bulge 73, 75, 76
Naktong river 69, 73
Nam Il 216, 218, 253, 254
Nam river 72, 74
Namsi 222
National Guard 116, 147, 157, 158, 168, 221
National Security Council 26, 34, 48, 56, 57, 92, 115, 118, 139, 203, 237, 240
NATO 16, 116, 117, 150, 151, 175, 180, 205, 232, 233–236, 239, 242–243
Naval operations 47, 64–65, 71, 74, 80–85
Nehru, Prime Minister Jawaharlal 77, 231, 283
Neutrals and neutralism 22, 24
New Zealand 198, 228, 229, 231
Nicolaevsky, Boris 172
Nie Zhongren 96
Nitze, Paul 25, 180, 237, 239, 241
No Gun Ri 291n.5
No Name Line 199
North Korea: creation of 10, 27–30; military buildup 38, 42–43; occupation of South Korea 90
North Korean Air Force 43

North Korean Army units: I Corps 197; II Corps 77, 155, 161, 162; III Corps 155, 165, 198; V Corps 155, 161, 163, 198, 220; 1st Division 46; 2nd Division 46, 47, 67; 3rd Division 46, 66, 67, 73; 4th Division 46, 65, 66, 67, 73; 5th Division 47, 68, 75; 6th Division 46, 68, 72, 75; 7th Division 46, 75; 8th Division 77; 9th Division 86; 10th Division 74, 185; 12th Division 77; 18th Division 86; 25th Brigade 86; 31st Division 86; 44th Tank Regiment 86; 70th Regiment 86; 78th Regiment 86; 83rd Motorized Brigade 72; 87th Regiment 86; 105th Armored Division 45, 87; 107th Security Regiment 86, 226th Marine Regimen 84; 766th Independent Unit 47
Norway 120, 249
NSC-8 34
NSC-48/5 203
NSC-68 26, 115, 144, 237
NSC-81/1 93
NSC-114 238, 239
NSC-135 241–242, 272
NSC-147 279–280
NSC-162/2 277

Obong-ni 73, 76
Office of Defense Mobilization 116, 147
Ohang-ni 73
Okchon 67
Operation Dauntless 188
Operation Insomnia 225
Operation Keelhaul 250
Operation Killer 184–185, 186
Operation Moonlight 225
Operation Piledriver 203
Operation Punch 163
Operation Ripper 185, 186
Operation Roundup 164
Operation Rugged 187
Operation Saturate 225
Operation Strangle 224
Operation Thunderbolt 164
Ostroumov, Gen. Pavel 171

Paik Sun Yup, Gen. 68, 88, 107, 165, 216
Pak Hon-yong 30, 100, 268
Pak Il-yu 100
Pak Song Hyon, Gen. 254

Index

Panikkar, K.M. 96, 97, 100, 196
Panmunjom 178, 244, 245, 244–255, 263–265, 282–283, 285
Paris Conference of 1951 233
PC-701 47
Peng Dehuai, Gen. 101–102, 148, 152, 163, 165, 186, 188, 199, 200, 201, 212, 216, 219
Petrov, Vladimir 171
Philippine Battalion 155, 199
Philippines 16, 20, 24, 36, 51, 116, 150, 229, 231
Pleven Plan 120
Pohang 68, 71, 73, 74, 75
Poland 8, 11, 248, 249, 268
Policy Planning Staff 25, 91, 113, 168, 181, 237
Pork Chop Hill 257, 282, 285
Port Arthur 260
Posung-Myon 82
Potsdam conference and agreements 9, 123, 272
Prague Declaration 123, 148, 272
Prisoners of war 77, 100, 105, 155, 202, 216–217, 250–256, 260, 268–270, 280, 282–285
"privileged sanctuary" 208, 210
Punchbowl 203, 220
Pusan 28, 45, 47, 57, 68, 69, 72, 88, 155, 196, 261–262
Pusan Perimeter 69–77, 80, 81, 82, 84, 88, 97, 146, 157
Pyongchong 185
Pyonggang 45, 203
Pyongtaek 65
Pyongyang 35, 38, 45, 81, 84, 88, 94, 105, 111, 137, 187, 203, 219, 221–223

Quinn, John 269

Radford, Adm. Arthur 63, 98
Railroads 45, 71, 106, 111, 190–192, 224–226, 258
Rakosi, Matthias 29
Rashin 187, 189, 208, 224, 277
Rayburn, Sam 186
Red Cross 216, 251, 253, 268
Refugees 30, 69–70, 135, 136, 291n.5
Republic of Korea (ROK) Army: development before war 43–44; in early fighting 46–48, 64–65; state of and improvement during war 68, 221, 257, 278; units: (I Corps) 66, 94–95, 129, 133, 161, 165, 197, 200, 201; (II Corps) 106–107, 111, 125–127, 137, 284; (III Corps) 159, 160, 161, 162, 164, 187, 197, 199, 200, 201; (Capitol Division) 47, 197, 285; (1st Division) 46, 47, 68, 74, 76–77, 88, 106, 107, 126, 127, 159, 160, 162, 165, 197, 198; (2nd Division) 47, 159, 161; (3rd Division) 75, 165, 167, 185, 197, 199; (5th Division) 47, 159, 161, 164, 165, 167, 197, 200; (6th Division) 46, 48, 106, 127, 159, 160, 166, 184, 197, 198; (7th Division) 46, 47, 126, 159, 161, 197, 200; (8th Division) 47, 48, 106, 159, 161, 164, 165, 200; (9th Division) 161, 257; (11th Division) 197; (Korean Marine Regiment) 129
Rhee, Syngman 32, 34, 35, 36, 44, 91, 95, 216, 261–263, 283, 284–285
Ridgway, Gen. Matthew 83, 155–156, 159, 160, 161, 162, 163, 164, 165, 166, 184, 186, 193, 195, 202, 203, 214, 215, 218, 221, 224, 244, 245, 246, 247, 248, 249, 250, 252, 257
Roberts, Gen. Lynn 44, 49
Roer dams 187
Romania 8, 9, 11
Roosevelt, Pres. Franklin 12, 49, 147,
Roschin, N.V. 56, 101
Route 2 165
Route 20 155, 184
Route 24 164, 201
Route 24A 166
Route 28 155
Route 29 161, 165, 167, 184
Route 33 186, 198
Rusk, Dean 91, 113, 144, 207
Ryukyus 27, 122, 123, 229, 230

Saamchon 222
Sachs, Alexander 49
Saemal 165
Samchok 48
San Francisco Peace Conference 219, 231
Saudi Arabia 116
Second Indochina War 54, 71, 116, 118, 149, 155, 159, 226
Seoul 28, 31, 45, 46, 47, 64, 65, 80,

84–87, 88, 146, 152, 160, 163, 164, 185, 186, 187, 193, 198, 199, 220, 244
Shanghai 193, 209
SHAPE 120, 234, 242
Shepherd, Gen. Lemuel 82, 83
Sherman, Adm. Forrest 51, 52, 82, 113, 144, 146, 158, 187, 207
Shin Sung Mo 112
Shoepac 130
Shoran 222, 223
Shtykov, Terenti 38, 64
Silvercruys, Baron 142
Sinanju 45
Sinuiju 45, 56, 96, 192, 199
Slansky, Rudolf 172
Slim, Field Marshal William 113, 145
Smith, Gen. Oliver P. 82, 86, 124, 129–130, 132, 134, 161, 184, 200
Song Shihlun, Gen. 124, 131
South African fighter squadron 258
South Korea: before the war 24, 28, 30–36; guerrilla warfare 35; Rhee's coup 261–263; U.S. Occupation 27, 30–35
Southeast Asia 7, 16, 20, 24, 25, 49, 50
Soviet Air Force 88, 103–104, 108, 222–223; units: (29th Fighter Regiment) 104; (97th Air Division) 223; (151st Fighter Division) 104, 153, 192; (303rd Fighter Division) 192; (324th Fighter Division) 192, 223
Soviet-Chinese alliance 21–22
Soviet-Koreans 27
Soviet Union: Cold War policies 4–5, 8–17, 18, 77; decision to end war 280–281; decision to intervene in Korea 98–104; policies in Korea 28–33, 35, 37–41, 56; policies toward China 17, 18–22, 245–246, 260–261; weakness in intercontinental strategic weapons 41, 172–173; West German and Japanese rearmament 122–123
Soyang river 201
Spain 235
Stalin, Josef: and armistice negotiations 178, 212–213, 215, 217, 245, 252, 260; and China's entry into Korean War 100–103; contemplates sending Soviet ground forces into Korea 202; decision for Korean War 37–41; decision for World War III 170–180; general 143, 188, 228, 232, 233, 241, 243, 244, 246, 264, 266, 268, 273–275, 278, 280, 281, 289n.17; plans to attack Yugoslavia 42, 55; policies toward Korean War 55–56, 64, 75, 78, 85, 85, 88; postwar policies 4, 8, 9, 11, 12, 16, 17, 21, 22, 28–29
State Department 25, 31, 49, 50, 78, 91–92, 98, 143, 168, 219, 252
State-War-Navy Coordinating Committee 34
Strategic Air Command 60, 196, 206
Strategic bombing 71, 89, 258–260
Stretchout 237, 239–241
Sudong 108
Suiho 259
Sukchon 105
Sunchon 127–128
Suwon 45, 57, 63, 86, 87, 160, 162
Symington, Stuart 237

Tabu-dong 74, 76
Taechon 222
Taegu 45, 64, 65, 68, 73, 74, 77
Taejon 45, 47, 65, 67, 68, 90, 192
Taft, Sen. Robert 54, 58, 150, 151
Taiwan 19, 20–22, 24, 26, 38, 39, 40–41, 49, 51, 52, 53, 54, 56, 77, 78–79, 98, 102, 149, 150, 169, 182, 190, 196, 207, 213, 214, 229, 230, 250
Tanks 42, 61, 64, 65, 66, 67, 71, 74, 75, 86, 87, 86, 198; M-24, 66; Patton 70; Pershing 70; T-34 42, 64, 65, 74, 75, 87, 198
Thai battalion 155
"Third Party" 181–183, 196, 213
Tibet 140
Tito, Josip 16, 182, 277
Togliatti, Palmiro 171
Tokchon 127
Toktong Pass 130, 134
Tongchon 188, 202
Trans-Siberian Railroad 205, 206
Triangulation Hill 73
Triumph 63
Truman, Pres. Harry 5, 12, 14, 15, 25, 28, 50, 51, 52, 53, 54, 57, 58, 62, 78–79, 93, 95, 97–98, 113, 115, 118, 121, 140, 141, 143, 147, 149, 150, 151, 158–159, 193–195, 204, 235, 240, 252, 262, 266, 267

Truman Doctrine 15
Tupolev, Andrei 172–173
Turkey 10, 12, 14, 15, 33, 49, 50, 235, 239, 243
Turkish Brigade 127–128, 137, 154, 159, 197, 198
"twin tunnels" 164, 166

Uijongbu 45, 46, 47, 198
Ulbricht, Walter 12, 29, 117, 123
United Nations 27, 31, 35, 40, 48, 51, 53, 55, 58, 77, 78, 79, 93–94, 97, 142, 145, 147, 148–149, 160, 169, 182, 214, 263, 266
United Nations Commission on Korea 35, 36, 51
United Nations Temporary Commission on Korea 35
United States: confidence that China will not intervene 92–93; considers expansion of war 276–280; decision to intervene in Korean War 50–55, 57–58; decision to liberate North Korea 90–94; decision to limit war 139–140; decision to protect Taiwan 51–53; defense buildup 116, 238; economy 116; fear of World War III 139–141, 196; hopes to end war 257; issue of declaring war 58; negotiations with Chinese 181–183; policies toward China 9, 12, 17–19, 20, 26, 276–277; postwar policies and Cold War 8–16, 24, 25–26; reaction to defeat in North Korea 139–151; rejection of Nationalist Chinese troops 57–58; stretchout of defense buildup 239–241; *see also* Armistice negotiations; Joint Chiefs of Staff; Truman, Pres. Harry
United States Air Force 36, 60, 116, 238, 240, 258; Far East Air Force 63, 85, 258; Fifth Air Force 63, 64; units: (4th Fighter Wing) 153, 192, 222–223; (27th Fighter Escort Wing) 152; (51st Fighter Wing) 223; (116th Fighter-Bomber Wing) 221
United States Army: buildup 116, 238; condition at start of war 61; weaknesses 137; units: (I Corps) 88, 89, 94, 105, 106, 125, 126, 128, 159, 162, 185, 188, 197, 198, 199, 200, 202, 221, 282; (IX Corps) 89, 125, 127, 159, 162, 166, 184, 187, 188, 198, 199, 201, 202, 221; (X Corps) 82–87, 89, 94, 106, 124, 125, 129–141, 144, 146, 154, 161, 162, 184, 187, 199, 200, 202; (1st Cavalry Division) 61, 66, 68, 69, 73–74, 76, 81, 88, 105, 125, 127, 137, 155, 159, 166, 184, 185, 187; (2nd Division), 70, 75, 76, 81, 89, 126–129, 132, 137, 154, 160, 161–162, 164, 185, 197, 200, 201, 220, 221, 257; (3rd Division) 95, 129, 133–135, 161, 162, 197, 198, 199; (5th Artillery Group) 83; (5th Cavalry Regiment) 73, 107; (5th Regimental Combat Team) 72, 88, 107, 199; (7th Cavalry Regiment) 73, 76, 107, 188; (7th Division) 61, 70, 81, 83, 89, 95, 106, 129, 131, 133, 161, 164, 167, 185, 197, 201, 202, 257, 282; (Eighth Army) 61, 62, 68, 94–95, 106, 107, 124–129, 131, 137–138, 141, 154, 155, 157, 187, 197, 201; (8th Cavalry Regiment) 76, 107; (9th Infantry Regiment) 73, 126; (19th Infantry Regiment) 67, 107; (21st Infantry Regiment) 65, 67; (23rd Infantry Regiment) 126, 128, 129, 161, 164, 200, 201; (24th Division) 61, 65, 66, 73, 77, 88, 106, 125, 159, 160, 197, 201, 221; (24th Infantry Regiment) 72; (25th Division) 61, 66, 72, 74, 89, 126, 127, 137, 159, 160, 161, 163, 164, 167, 185, 197, 198, 199; (27th Infantry Regimental Combat Team) 72, 73, 74, 75; (29th Infantry Regiment) 70; (31st Infantry Regiment) 87, 89, 167; (32nd Infantry Regiment) 86; (34th Infantry Regiment) 66, 67, 73; (38th Infantry Regiment) 126, 128, 165, 167; (40th Division) 221; (45th Division) 221; (92nd Division) 83; (187th Airborne Regimental Combat Team) 105, 161, 164, 167, 186, 197, 200, 201; (Support Force 7) 164–165; (Support Force 21) 164–165; (Task Force Baker) 201; (Task Force Bartlett) 163; (Task Force Dog) 135; (Task Force Dolvin) 126, 163; (Task Force Drysdale) 132; (Task Force Faith) 130, 133; (Task Force Gerhardt) 201; (Task Force Growdon) 186; (Task Force Kean) 72; (Task Force Lynch) 89; (Task Force Maclean) 130, 132; (Task Force Smith) 65; (Task Force Wilson) 126

United States Marine Corps 116; units: (1st Marine Brigade) 70, 72, 73, 76, 81; (1st Marine Division) 76, 81, 82, 83, 85–87, 95, 108, 124, 129–135, 161, 184, 197, 199, 200, 202, 220; (1st Marine Regiment) 85, 130, 135; (5th Marine Regiment) 70, 85, 86, 130; (7th Marine Regiment) 86, 108, 130, 135
United States Navy: Seventh Fleet 51, 52, 60–61, 188–189, 224–226; Task Force 77, 85, 189, 190, 197
Unsan 107, 125
Utah Line 188

Valley Forge 63, 71
Vandenberg, Gen. Hoyt 52, 91, 113, 146, 167, 205, 206, 207
Van Fleet, Gen. James 197, 199, 200, 201, 202, 219, 220, 221, 261, 262
Vasiliev, Gen. 39
Veterans of Foreign Wars 78, 98
Vietnam 3, 16, 24, 54; *see also* Second Indochina War
Virginia Victory 136
Voluntary repatriation 179, 250–255, 260, 263–265, 280
Vyshinsky, Foreign Minister Andrei 245, 263

Waegwan 69, 73, 89
Wake island conference 97–98
Walker, Gen. Walton 61, 63, 67, 69, 70, 72–73, 81, 83, 88, 94–95, 107, 111, 124–125, 127, 131, 137–138, 146, 155
Wallace, Henry 55
War scares 139–151; 170, 177, 196–197
Weapons: bazooka 65, 67, 131; Browning automatic rifle 130; carbine 130; Katyusha rocket 104, 107; light machine gun 130; M1 rifle 130; mountain guns 131; napalm bombs 134; quadruple .50-caliber antiaircraft vehicles, twin 40-mm. pom-pom 127; *see also* Aircraft types; Tanks
Wedemeyer, Gen. Albert 34
West Germany 12, 13, 14, 15, 16, 50, 57, 117–123; 272–273
Wherry, Sen. Kenneth 151
Willoughby, Gen. Charles 49, 111
Wilson, Charles E. 147
Winnington, Alan 269
Wolmi 81, 85
Wonju 68, 155, 161–162, 164, 166, 167, 184
Wonsan 3, 45, 71, 84, 94–95, 106, 129, 133, 187, 188–189, 203, 214, 219; oil refinery 36, 45, 71
Wright, Gen. Edwin 83
Wu Ziuquan, Gen. 147, 149
Wyoming Line 188

Xie Fang, Gen. 216

Yalta 8, 11, 12, 16–17, 19, 23, 25
Yalu river 45, 56, 104, 106, 107, 108, 109–110, 114, 124, 137, 153, 189, 191–192, 193, 222, 259, 278–279
Yangyang 187
Yezhov, Nikolai 269
Yo Un-hyong 32, 33, 34
Yongdungpo 64, 86
Yoshida, Shigeru 121, 229
Yudam-ni 130, 131, 134, 136
Yugoslavia 8, 16, 42, 50, 53, 55, 57, 168, 231, 277

Zakharov, Gen. M.V. 88, 89
Zhou Enlai 56, 80, 84, 96, 97, 99, 101–104, 147, 149, 181, 196, 208, 218, 260, 267
Zhukov-Verezhnikov, Dr. N.N. 268

www.ingramcontent.com/pod-product-compliance
Lightning Source LLC
Chambersburg PA
CBHW051208300426
44116CB00006B/482